Date Due			
Apr 5 '61			
Feb 13 '68			
Apr 24 '68			
May 8 '68			
Dec 4 70			
Dec 16 70			
May 18 73			
Mar 27 74			
Sep 26 74			
Apr 12 '76			
May 14 '76			
Jul 6 '77			
Apr 24 '81			
	PRINTED	IN U. S. A.	

THE NATURE AND AUTHORITY OF THE BIBLE

By the same author:

THINGS WHICH ABIDE

PRINCIPLES OF CHRISTIAN WORSHIP

THE NATURE AND AUTHORITY OF THE BIBLE

by

RAYMOND ABBA

M.A.(Cantab. and Sydney), B.D.(Melbourne)

Acting Professor of Old Testament Studies in the University of Durham
Sometime Warden and Professor of Theology
Camden College, Sydney

MUHLENBERG PRESS · PHILADELPHIA

220
Abm

First published 1958
James Clarke & Co. Ltd.
London

40943
Mar.'61

MADE AND PRINTED IN GREAT BRITAIN BY
THE GARDEN CITY PRESS LIMITED
LETCHWORTH, HERTFORDSHIRE

DEDICATED TO
THE COUNCIL, STAFF AND STUDENTS
OF CAMDEN COLLEGE, SYDNEY
1948–1955

CONTENTS

vii

PREFACE

SOME years ago Canon A. E. Baker, M.A., of York, suggested that I should write a book about the Bible which would gather up, for the educated layman, the chief fruits of twentieth-century biblical scholarship. That is what I have tried to do in this volume. It is an attempt—if I may change the metaphor—to survey the field of recent biblical studies from the viewpoint of the biblical theologian.

Recent years have witnessed a complete change of emphasis in biblical studies. The new attitude, while accepting substantially the earlier work of biblical criticism, which is still valued and continued, seeks to transcend it by constructive theological exposition. Critical and historical analysis are seen as *prolegomena* to biblical theology. While recognizing the human element in the Bible, the emphasis is placed upon its significance as the living and abiding Word of God. That is the background of this book. It springs from the conviction that the Bible is authoritative as the primary witness to the events in time in which the Eternal God has visited and redeemed His people; that it is both the record and the instrument of a unique divine revelation, given through the history of Israel, culminating in Jesus Christ, interpreted by the Church, and authenticated in religious experience. The written Word mediates the authority and the saving power of the Word made flesh. The Bible is the Word of God because through it God Himself speaks to each generation of men.

I have endeavoured to avoid, as far as possible, the technical language of theology in the text so that it may be intelligible to the non-theologian who is prepared to give serious thought to the understanding of the Bible. Footnotes and additional notes on linguistic and critical minutiae, however, are provided for ministers and theological students.

The field is, of course, vast, and my obligations are many and obvious. In addition to the acknowledgements made elsewhere, I am indebted to the editors of the *Expository Times*, *Theology*, the *Scottish Journal of Theology*, and the Australian *Reformed Theological Review* for permission to use material from articles which I have contributed to these journals; to the Epworth Press for permission to reproduce paragraphs from my book, *Things Which Abide* (1944), which is now out of print; and to the Australian Student Christian Movement for allowing me to incorporate parts of my chapter, " Christ as King in the Old Testament," in the study booklet, *Christ the King* (1949). If I have inadvertently omitted any other acknowledgements I offer my apologies.

The present work was already in the press when Professor J. K. S. Reid's valuable book, *The Authority of Scripture* (Methuen), 1957, appeared. I have not therefore been able to make use of it in the text but have referred to it in footnotes.

I am particularly indebted to my former teacher, Professor C. H. Dodd, to Professor H. H. Rowley and to Canon A. E. Baker, who have read the book in manuscript and given much valuable help and criticism; to my colleagues on the staff of Camden College, the United Theological Faculty and the University of Sydney, who helped to clarify my thinking on many points during the seven years of my Wardenship of Camden College; to my secretary, Miss Joan Swales, not only for a meticulous typing of the manuscript, but also for a stimulating interest in its contents; to Mr. A. Douglas Millard, of James Clarke & Co. Ltd., for his personal interest and unfailing helpfulness in its publication; to Mr. F. Lamb and Mr. J. M. O. Rees-Williams for assistance in compiling the list of Acknowledgements and Index; and last, but by no means least, to my long-suffering wife, who has pointed out many infelicities of style, challenged many inadequate statements, and endured many hours of loneliness so that this book could be written.

RAYMOND ABBA

Durham,
January 1958.

ACKNOWLEDGEMENTS

Grateful acknowledgement is made to the following publishers and others for permission to use extracts from copyright publications:

George Allen & Unwin Ltd. for extracts from *The Bible and its Background* by C. H. Dodd, and from an essay by C. H. Dodd in *The Kingdom of God and History* (Oxford Conference); Professor Karl Barth and Hodder & Stoughton Ltd. for extracts from *The Word of God and the Word of Man* by K. Barth; Ernest Benn Ltd. for extracts from *What is Christianity?* by A. Harnack; A. & C. Black Ltd. for extracts from *The Prophets of Israel* and *The Religion of the Semites*, both by W. R. Smith, from *The Worship of the English Puritans* by H. Davies, and from *The Shape of the Liturgy* by G. Dix; Basil Blackwell & Mott Ltd. for extracts from an essay by A. M. Farrer in *Studies in the Gospels* edited by D. E. Nineham, from *The People's Faith in the Time of Wyclif* by B. L. Manning, and from *The Study of the Bible in the Middle Ages* by B. Smalley; Geoffrey Bles Ltd. for extracts from *Miracles* by C. S. Lewis, from *The Meaning of History* by N. Berdyaev, and from *The Resurrection of Christ* by A. M. Ramsay; Professor F. F. Bruce and the Paternoster Press for extracts from *Second Thoughts on the Dead Sea Scrolls* by F. F. Bruce; Professor Millar Burrows and the American Schools of Oriental Research for extracts from *What Mean these Stones?* by M. Burrows; the Cambridge University Press for extracts from *The Bible To-day* and *About the Gospels*, both by C. H. Dodd, from *How Came our Faith* by W. A. L. Elmslie, from *The Teaching of Jesus* by T. W. Manson, and from *Christian Doctrine* by J. S. Whale; the Carey Kingsgate Press Ltd. for extracts from *The Missionary Message of the Old Testament* and *The Unity of the Bible*, both by H. H. Rowley; the Clarendon Press, Oxford, for extracts from *Bible and Spade* by S. L. Caiger, from *A Critical and Exegetical Commentary on Daniel* by R. H. Charles, from *The Idea of History* by R. G. Collingwood, from *Sacrifice in the Old Testament* by G. B. Gray, from *A History of Israel* by W. O. E. Oesterley and T. H. Robinson, and from an essay by C. R. North in *The Old Testament and Modern Study* edited by H. H. Rowley; T. & T. Clark for extracts from Hasting's *Dictionary of the Bible* and *Dictionary of Christ and the Gospels*, from the *Encyclopaedia of Religion and Ethics*, from *The Theology of the Old Testament* by A. B. Davidson, and from *The Gospel History and its Transmission* by F. C. Burkitt; James Clarke & Co. Ltd. for extracts from *The Authority of the Biblical Revelation* by H. Cunliffe-Jones, from *The Theology of Martin Luther* by H. H. Kramm, from *The Rediscovery of the Old Testament* and *The Relevance of the Bible*, both by H. H. Rowley, and from articles by H. Cunliffe-Jones and J. Marsh in *The Presbyter;* the Columbia University Press, New York, for extracts from *Gospel and Law* by C. H. Dodd; J. M. Dent & Sons Ltd. for an extract from *Essays and Addresses* by von Hügel; G. Duckworth & Co. Ltd. for extracts from *The Religious Ideas of the Old Testament* by H. W. Robinson, and from *Prophecy and the Prophets in Ancient Israel* by T. H. Robinson; the Epworth

Press for extracts from *The Old Testament Interpretation of History* by C. R. North, from *The Christian Faith* by T. E. Jessop, and from *Hebrew Marriage* by D. R. Mace; Eyre & Spottiswoode Ltd. for extracts from *A History of Europe* by H. A. L. Fisher, from *Science, Christianity and Truth* by A. E. Baker, and from an essay by J. K. Mozley in *The Christian Faith* edited by W. R. Matthews; Faber & Faber Ltd. for extracts from *Abraham: Recent Discoveries and Hebrew Origins* by L. Woolley, from *The Authority of the Old Testament* by A. G. Hebert, and from *The Riddle of the New Testament* by E. Hoskyns and N. Davey; George G. Harrap & Co. Ltd. for extracts from *The History of Hebrew Civilisation* by A. Bertholet, and from *The Bible and Archaeology* by F. Kenyon; Hodder & Stoughton Ltd. for extracts from *Jesus and the Gospel* by J. Denney, from *The Bible and the Greeks* by C. H. Dodd, from *The First Epistle to the Corinthians* by M. Dods, from *Marriage, its Ethic and Religion* by P. T. Forsyth, from *The Moral Teaching of Jesus* by A. D. Lindsay, from *What is the Faith?* by N. Micklem, from *The First Epistle to the Corinthians* by J. Moffatt, from *The Problem of the Old Testament* by J. Orr, from *The Book of Isaiah* by G. A. Smith, from *Studies in the Teaching of Our Lord* by H. B. Swete, from *Facing the Facts* by J. S. Whale, from *Marriage, Divorce and Repentance in the Church of England* by J. H. Cruse and B. Green, from *Commentary on First Corinthians* by T. C. Edwards, and from two articles by T. M. Lindsay in *The Expositor*; the Independent Press Ltd. for extracts from *Positive Preaching and the Modern Mind* by P. T. Forsyth, from *The Dead Sea Scrolls and their Significance* by H. H. Rowley, and from the *Report of the Commission on the Marriage of Divorced Persons*; the Johns Hopkins Press, Baltimore, for extracts from *From the Stone Age to Christianity* by W. F. Albright; Longmans Green & Co. Ltd. for extracts from *Inspiration* (Bampton Lectures) by W. Sanday; the Lutterworth Press for extracts from *The Divine Imperative* and *Dogmatics*, both by E. Brunner, from *The Relevance of Apocalyptic*, *The Servant of the Lord and Other Essays*, and *An Outline of the Teaching of Jesus*, all by H. H. Rowley, and from *Christian Ethics and the Gospel* by D. E. W. Harrison; Macmillan & Co. Ltd. for extracts from *A Commentary on the Holy Bible* edited by J. R. Dummelow, from *Folk-Lore in the Old Testament* by J. G. Frazer, from *The Holy Spirit in the New Testament* by H. B. Swete, from *Jesus and His Sacrifice* by V. Taylor, from *Nature, Man and God* by W. Temple, and from *The Bible in the Church* by B. F. Westcott; Marshall, Morgan & Scott Ltd. for an extract from *The Inspiration and Authority of the Bible* by B. B. Warfield; Methuen & Co. Ltd. for extracts from *The Authority of Scripture* by J. K. S. Reid; A. R. Mowbray & Co. Ltd. for extracts from *The Authority of the Scriptures* by J. W. C. Wand; John Murray Ltd. for extracts from *The Sermon on the Mount* by C. Gore; Thomas Nelson & Sons Ltd. for extracts from *Peake's Commentary on the Bible*; Professor D. E. Nineham, Dr. A. R. Vidler and the Society for Promoting Christian Knowledge for two extracts from an article by D. E. Nineham in *Theology*; James Nisbet & Co. Ltd. for extracts from *The Christian Way* by S. Cave, from *According to the Scriptures*, *History and the Gospel*, *The Authority of the Bible*, and *The Parables of the Kingdom*, all by C. H. Dodd, from *The World and God* by H. H. Farmer, from *Towards a Christian Philosophy* by L. Hodgson, from *The Fulness of Time* by J. Marsh, and from *The Nature and Destiny of Man* by R. Niebuhr; Oliver & Boyd Ltd. for an extract from *Calvin's Doctrine of the Word and Sacrament* by R. S. Wallace; the Oxford University Press, London, for extracts from *Our Knowledge of God* by J. Baillie, from *The Bible from Within* by A. G. Hebert, from *An Outline of Christian Worship* by W. D. Maxwell, from *Israel: Its Life and Culture* by J. Pedersen, from *The Call of Israel* and *The Fulness of Israel*, both by W. J. Phythian-Adams, from *Science, History and Faith* by A. Richardson, from *Religious Development between the Old and New Testaments* (Home University Series) by R. H. Charles, and from *From Joseph to Joshua* (Schweich Lectures published on behalf of the British Academy) by H. H. Rowley; Penguin Books Ltd. for extracts from *The Archaeology of Palestine* by W. F. Albright, from *The Dead Sea Scrolls* by J. M. Allegro, and from *An Introduction to the Bible* by S. A. Cook; Pickering & Inglis Ltd. for extracts from *Expositions of Holy Scripture: Genesis* by A. Maclaren; Marie Rodell & Joan Davies Inc. and The New American Library of World Literature Inc., New York, for extracts from *The Meaning of the Dead Sea Scrolls* by A. P. Davies; Professor H. H. Rowley and the Committee of Overdale College, Selly Oak, Birmingham, for extracts from *The Authority of the Bible* (Joseph Smith Memorial Lecture) by H. H. Rowley; Martin Secker & Warburg Ltd. for extracts from *The Dead Sea Scrolls* by M. Burrows; the Society for Promoting Christian Knowledge for extracts from essays by J. H. Carpenter, R. H. Lightfoot, J. Lowe, T. W. Manson, A. Peel and C. Peplar in *The Interpretation of the Bible* edited by C. W. Dugmore, from *The Fulness of Sacrifice* by F. C. N. Hicks, and from the Commission Report, *Doctrine in the Church of England*; the Student Christian Movement Press Ltd. for extracts from *The Intention of Jesus* by J. W. Bowman, from *Revelation and Reason* by E. Brunner, from *The Faith that Rebels* by D. S. Cairns, from *Christ and Time* by O. Cullmann, from *Design for Life, Introducing the New Testament, The Unity of the New Testament*, and *The Gospel According to St. Mark*, all by A. M. Hunter, from *An Introduction to Christian Ethics* by R. Niebuhr, from *Christian Apologetics, Preface to Bible-Study, The Miracle-Stories of the Gospels*, and *Genesis I–XI*, all by A. Richardson, from *A Theological Word-Book of the Bible* edited by A. Richardson, from *The Old Testament in the New Testament* by R. V. G. Tasker, from *The Old Testament Against its Environment* by G. E. Wright, from essays by C. H. Dodd, G. Florovsky and G. E. Wright in *Biblical Authority for Today*, and from an article by A. G. Hebert in the *Student World*; The Rev. R. Swanton for extracts from articles by J. McIntyre and D. B. Knox in the Australian *Reformed Theological Review*; Dr. L. D. Weatherhead and Hodder & Stoughton Ltd. for two extracts from *Psychology, Religion and Healing* by L. D. Weatherhead; Sir Leonard Woolley and Ernest Benn Ltd. for extracts from *Ur of the Chaldees* by L. Woolley.

CHAPTER I

WHAT IS THE BIBLE?

IN the East Riding of Yorkshire, some eight miles north of Hull, is the old market town of Beverley with its beautiful medieval minster—one of the finest in Europe. Beverley Minster is the product of successive periods of design and craftsmanship. The choir is Early English; most of the nave is Decorated; the west window is Perpendicular. A stone frith-stool dating from the time of Athelstan—much earlier than any of the present building—is housed within its walls, as is also a recent mosaic memorial to the dead of the first world war.

The Bible is like that. It is the literary deposit of successive stages of religious development. The writings of which it is composed are the work of many authors reflecting different phases of religious thought. It incorporates material much older than any of its complete parts, as well as additions by later hands. The first step towards an understanding of the Bible is therefore the recognition that it is not one book but many. Indeed it is a library of writings covering a period of round about a thousand years. The two familiar divisions of Old and New Testaments are, of course, an indication of at least two stages in its growth.

The books of the New Testament cover only about a century and comprise the classic literature of the Christian Church. They are, for the most part, the incidental products of the Church's life rather than studied theological works—the letters of a busy missionary, the sayings of Jesus collected for the instruction of catechumens, the travel diary of a doctor, the visions of an exiled prophet. All these are incorporated with the central record of the birth and ministry, the teaching and healing, the death and resurrection of Jesus of Nazareth.

I

2—AOB

The Old Testament is more diverse in character. Its writings are spread over some eight or nine hundred years and represent the surviving national literature of Israel. A brief comparison with our own national literature may help us to see it in the right perspective. Suppose you could bind together under one cover the chief literature of the English people. You would find in such a volume histories by Trevelyan and Bede, drama by Shakespeare and Bernard Shaw, legends of King Arthur woven into a poem by Tennyson, more poems by Chaucer and Keats, novels by Jane Austen and Sir Walter Scott, essays by Bacon, a diary by Pepys, a parable by John Bunyan, hymns by Montgomery and Isaac Watts, sermons by Wesley and Dale. So in the Old Testament we may expect to find history and folk-lore, drama and legend, poetry and parable, sermons and hymns. And this is precisely what we do find. For the Jew " the Biblical history occupied the place of national history, of ballad poetry, of folk-lore tales, and of all that, in ages before the invention of printing, took the place of our ' children's literature.' "[1]

The Book of Genesis, for instance, opens with a creation poem and contains the folk-lore of the Hebrew people and the beginnings of their national history. Leviticus is a law-book; Joshua, Judges, Samuel, Kings, Chronicles, Ezra and Nehemiah are history; Job is a drama, Esther an historical novel, Ruth a love-story,[2] the Song of Solomon a number of typically oriental love-lyrics, Jonah a parable.[3] Proverbs and Ecclesiastes are " wisdom literature." The psalms form the hymn-book of the nation and the prophetic works preserve the sermons of their great religious leaders. The apocalyptic writings (e.g. Daniel) are " tracts for the times."

Yet although the Old Testament is, as we should expect, so diverse in its contents, it is different from the national literature

[1] G. Farmer, " Boyhood (Jewish)," in Hastings' *Dictionary of Christ and the Gospels*, vol. i, p. 223.

[2] Goethe regarded it as " the loveliest little idyll that tradition has transmitted to us."

[3] " Ruth as a scarcely altered love-tale; Judith and Jonah, allegorical fictions; Esther, especially in its Greek form, a greatly amplified history, are instances of books which we now have in written forms, but which were once the ' fireside stories ' (to use a Western phrase) of many Jewish homes." —G. Farmer, *op. cit.*, p. 223.

of any other people. And the difference lies in the fact that it all centres in God. It is this fact which gives to the Old Testament a real unity and makes it, despite all its diversity, one book. Its unity is not a literary unity, neither is it an historical unity; it is a theological unity. To make this claim for the Old Testament is not to deny that varying degrees of religious and theological perception are to be found between its covers. Such is manifestly the case: unity does not necessarily imply uniformity. But a theological unity, in the real sense of the word, there most certainly is.

In the first place, the subject of the Old Testament is the Living God. Its writers see the glittering pageant of history in terms of man's experience of God and God's dealing with man. In the creation poem of Genesis, for instance, it is God who is the Creator; and that was by no means an axiom in the ancient world. In the folk-lore it is not a river-spirit that wrestles with Jacob, but the God of Israel.[1] " The distinctive thing about the national ' saga ' or ' legend,' as Israel has preserved it in her sacred literature, is that nowhere does it become a mere ' blowing of the national trumpet.' From the earliest reference to the last, it was always God who acted ' at that time.' "[2] The nation's laws are regarded as the expression of God's righteous will. Its history is the record of what God has done. Thus historian and dramatist, preacher and poet all see God at the very centre of the nation's life.

Secondly, the Old Testament tells of the action of God. When its writers speak about God, they do not speculate about His nature, as did the Greek philosophers; they declare what He has done. They know God, not because their minds have probed into His Being, but because they have seen His mighty acts in history. " The early Hebrews did not think about Jehovah; they believed in Him, and experienced the reality of His sovereignty in the great things which He did for His

---

[1] Genesis xxxii, 24–30. There are indications that in the primitive folk-tale this mysterious being was not Jehovah but a local river-god. Hosea refers to him as an " angel " (Hosea xii, 4). In the present narrative, however, the story has been purged of its original crudities and the encounter is clearly with Jehovah Himself (ver. 28–30). See J. Skinner, Genesis (I.C.C.), p. 411.

[2] J. Marsh, The Fulness of Time, pp. 50–1.

people."[1] God is known to them for what He is by what He does. He is the God of the Red Sea who sends a strong east wind to part the waters and so delivers His people from their enemies. He is the God of Jericho and Ai who goes before His people into battle, scattering the corrupt Canaanites and giving to Israel a good land. He is the God of the Exile who preserves His people in a foreign land and raises up a deliverer, Cyrus, through whom they can return again to their country and rebuild their national life. And all these mighty acts, say the prophets, are leading up to some great final Act, when God will in a special way visit and redeem His people.

From what has been said, another aspect of the theological unity of the Old Testament will have become apparent: it is concerned, in the third place, with the People of God. The Old Testament is really a story—the story of Israel. This story " is a unique history, because Israel was the nation which the Lord God chose, that in it and through it He might carry out His saving Purpose for all mankind."[2] It begins with a parabolic account of the beginnings of the Universe, because the Hebrew writers " believed that the history of their own nation which they were going to relate was of importance for all nations and all men everywhere."[3] The story proper starts with the call of Abraham to leave his home in Mesopotamia that he might become the father of a new nation through which God might reveal Himself to the world, and through which in the fulness of time Christ should come.

Fourthly, the Old Testament from first to last is stamped with the purpose of God. Its history is teleological history; its story unfolds a meaning; its drama moves forward to a climax —the coming of the Messiah. We can trace the unfolding of this purpose, beginning in the creation parables of Genesis, through the new start made with Noah, to the call of Abraham and the promises made to him and to his seed. It continues through the slavery in Egypt, the call of Moses, the Exodus, the Deliverance at the Red Sea and the settlement in Canaan. When the high hopes of David's reign are rent with the disruption and decline of his kingdom, it survives in the prophetic

[1] W. Robertson Smith, *The Prophets of Israel*, p. 42.
[2] A. G. Hebert, *The Bible from Within*, p. 3.   [3] *Ibid.*, p. 12.

expectation of " Great David's greater Son." Through Exile and Restoration the way of the Messiah is prepared and the Old Testament ends on a note of anticipation: " The Lord, whom ye seek, shall suddenly come to his temple."[1]

The insights and expectations of the Old Testament are " fulfilled " in the events which form the theme of the New. In the fulness of time the Messiah is born. The Living God whose action has been discerned in the great historic crises of the past brings them to fruition by visiting and redeeming His people. The ancient People of God is reconstituted as the New Israel. The divine purpose becomes incarnate in Christ and His Church: the Word becomes flesh. And the stage is set for the grand Finale when every knee shall bow and every tongue confess that Jesus Christ is Lord.

Viewed thus in the light of Christ, the unity of the Old Testament is seen to be part of a larger unity—the unity of the Bible as a whole. These diverse writings do in fact constitute one book with an organic unity of its own, so that we can speak quite properly not only of the Scriptures but also of the Bible. The derivation of this name, which in itself expresses the unity of the whole, is significant. It was originally a neuter plural *Biblia*—" The Books "—a word used by Greek writers which passed into the vocabulary of the Western Church. Then in the thirteenth century, as Westcott points out, the Greek neuter plural came to be regarded as a Latin feminine singular, and " ' The Books ' became by common consent ' The Book ' (*Biblia*, singular), in which form the word has passed into the languages of modern Europe."[2]

This organic unity of the Bible makes it contrast strikingly with other sacred books. Five other religions, apart from Christianity and Judaism, may be classified as " book religions "— Mohammedanism with its Koran, Zoroastrianism with its Zendavesta, Confucianism with its Classics, Brahmanism with its Vedas, and Buddhism with its own Canon of Sacred Scriptures. But

not to speak of the enormous superiority of the Bible to these other sacred books, even in a literary respect, . . . we would fix attention only on this one point—the contrast in respect of unity. We seek

---

[1] Malachi iii, 1.   [2] B. F. Westcott, *The Bible in the Church*, p. 5.

in vain in these ethnic Scriptures for anything answering to this name. The Koran, for instance, is a miscellany of disjointed pieces, out of which it is impossible to extract any order, progress, or arrangement. The 114 Suras or chapters of which it is composed are arranged chiefly according to length—the longer in general preceding the shorter. It is not otherwise with the Zoroastrian and Buddhist Scriptures. These are equally destitute of beginning, middle, or end. They are, for the most part, collections of heterogeneous materials, loosely placed together. How different everyone must acknowledge it to be with the Bible! From Genesis to Revelation we feel that this book is in a real sense a unity. It is not a collection of fragments, but has, as we say, an organic character. It has one connected story to tell from beginning to end; we see something growing before our eyes; there is plan, purpose, progress. . . . This is a very external way, it may be granted, of looking at the Bible, yet it is a very important one. It puts the Bible before us at the outset as a unique book. There is nothing exactly resembling it, or even approaching it, in all literature.[1]

The Bible is frequently regarded as being essentially the record, the literary deposit, of a great religious movement. This movement, it is said, grew in much the same way as life developed upon the earth. Its beginnings were small, sometimes crude; its most important development took place during a period of about twelve hundred years; and in this period, as in biological evolution, there are several sudden leaps, several fresh starts.

While there is, admittedly, much truth in this view, we need to recognize that there are strict limitations to the application of the metaphor of growth to the study of the Bible. It is valid in so far as it gives an historical perspective to biblical study, but it is misleading when used as an explanation of biblical religion. " On the one hand, it calls attention to the fact that the Bible is primarily a history covering some two thousand years. Consequently, one cannot examine it through the spectacles of a static conception of time. One cannot expect to find the theology of Paul in the Books of Kings or that of Second Isaiah in the Song of Deborah. On the other hand, however, the metaphor of growth has so pervaded our minds that in both theology and comparative religion we have

[1] J. Orr, *The Problem of the Old Testament*, pp. 31–2.

tended to assume that the gradual evolution of rational concepts is the main problem of our enquiry. . . . In the study of
the Bible, therefore, we tend to assume that the earlier our
literary source material, the more primitive should be its
religious teaching."[1]

One of the basic errors of the Liberal Protestant school of
theologians was its application of the idea of development to
the faith of the Old Testament and its consequent attempt to
fit the religion of Israel into an evolutionary mould. The
biblical revelation cannot be reduced without remainder to
evolutionary categories and explained solely in terms of
development without doing violence to its essential nature;
without, in fact, explaining away its distinctive content. " The
living God, says the Bible, breaks into a people's life and by
mighty acts performs his wonders in their behalf. The people
see, hear, understand, obey, rebel. In so doing they discover
ever more clearly the meaning of their election and of the
purpose of God. This ' challenge-and-response ' nature of the
Biblical point of view cannot easily be accommodated to a
single metaphor such as growth."[2] This fact must be borne in
mind as we survey the progress of biblical history. As Wright
warns us, we must beware of evaluating it in terms of an
ascending scale of values.[3]

There are five main turning-points marking the beginning of
five clearly defined periods in the religious life of Israel which
underlies the Bible.

I. THE PREPARATORY PERIOD

The first turning-point is the call of Abraham. The traditional dating of this epoch-making event was at the end of the
third or the beginning of the second millennium B.C. This was
based on the biblical chronology[4] and the identification of

---

[1] G. E. Wright, *The Old Testament Against its Environment*, p. 10.
[2] *Ibid.*, p. 11.   [3] *Ibid.*, p. 11.
[4] According to I Kings vi, 1, the Exodus took place 480 years before the
foundation of Solomon's Temple (*c.* 967 B.C.), i.e. in *c.* 1447 B.C. Exodus
xii, 40 dates the descent into Egypt 430 years before the Exodus, i.e. in
c. 1877 B.C. Genesis xii, 4; xxi, 5; xxv, 26; and xlvii, 9 require a further
215 years to the migration of Abraham, which brings it to *c.* 2092 B.C.

Amraphel of Shinar, mentioned in Genesis xiv, with Hammurabi of Babylon, who was confidently dated at about 2100 B.C.[1] Since 1935, however, new evidence from Mari, the Amorite capital on the Middle Euphrates, has necessitated a re-dating of Hammurabi, Sydney Smith placing him in the years 1792–1750 B.C. and Albright dating him later still in 1728–1686. Also we now know that there were at least three contemporary kings of this name—Hammurabi of Babylon, Hammurabi of Aleppo and Hammurabi of Kurda, " so that if Amraphel is to be identified with any of them, Abraham must have belonged to the eighteenth or seventeenth century B.C."[2]

The question is further complicated by the fact that the identification of Amraphel with Hammurabi has been abandoned by many scholars and attempts made to date Abraham by identifying other kings mentioned in Genesis xiv. As a result Albright has oscillated between the twentieth or nineteenth century and the seventeenth, finally arriving at c. 1650 B.C.[3] Millar Burrows, on the other hand, assigns Abraham to the traditional date at the beginning of the twentieth century on the ground that " the circumstances reflected in the story of Abraham . . . are true to the conditions of the twentieth and perhaps the nineteenth centuries B.C., but from then on they do not fit the archaeological evidence."[4]

There is thus as yet no general agreement among scholars as to the date of the first and greatest of the patriarchs, nor is there likely to be until more evidence is to hand. As H. H. Rowley observes, " It is clear that none of the proposed identifications is conclusive, and we cannot rely with confidence on Genesis xiv to fix the age of Abraham. In so far as the chapter

---

[1] See the *Cambridge Ancient History*, vol. i, 2nd ed., 1924, p. 154, which gives the date of Hammurabi as 2123–2081 B.C.

[2] H. H. Rowley, *From Joseph to Joshua*, p. 61.

[3] See *Bulletin of the American Schools of Oriental Research*, No. 88 (1942), pp. 33–6; *The Archaeology of Palestine*, 1949, p. 83; Historical sketch in *The Jews, their History, Culture and Religion* (ed. L. Finkelstein), 1949, i, p. 4; " The Old Testament and the Archaeology of Palestine " in *The Old Testament and Modern Study* (ed. H. H. Rowley), 1951, p. 7; and *Gnomon*, xxiii, 1951, p. 397.

[4] See *What Mean these Stones?*, pp. 70–1. Cf. Leonard Woolley, who also dates Abraham at c. 2000 B.C. See *Abraham: Recent Discoveries and Hebrew Origins*, pp. 42 ff. and 259 ff.

is relied on it would lead us to a date in the seventeenth century B.C., and an earlier date can only be defended by disregarding Genesis xiv, 1, or by denying the identification of the names with those of known persons."[1]

The call of Abraham marks the beginning of what the Germans call *Heilsgeschichte*—an untranslatable word for the *sui generis* history which the Bible records, the story of the saving power of God manifest in the world through a particular race of men. Here is the emergence of a new historical muta- tion. This particular man is chosen by God for a particular purpose; he is to be the progenitor of a new nation through which God will give a special revelation of Himself, culminat- ing in Jesus Christ, for the benefit of all mankind. This " scandal of particularity," as it has been called—which we shall consider more fully at a later stage—may be offensive to the modern mind, but it is nevertheless central in the biblical- Christian view of history.

As a matter of fact the Israelites were of mixed blood. They were not pure Semitic stock as are the Arabs. The so-called " Jewish nose," for instance, is really a Hittite characteristic; and both the Amorites, who were Semites, and the Philistines, who were not, have left their trace in the make-up of the race. The Aramaean or Syrian contribution, however, was consider- able, and it is to this branch of the nation's ancestry that most of the early Israelite traditions belong. These traditions carry us back to three fathers of the race—Abraham, Isaac and Jacob, the twelve sons of the latter being the heads of twelve families from which the tribes of Israel claimed descent.[2]

There is no good reason for doubting that these names

[1] " Recent Discovery and the Patriarchal Age," in *The Servant of the Lord and Other Essays on the Old Testament*, pp. 285–6. For a full discussion of this question see H. H. Rowley, *From Joseph to Joshua*, pp. 57 ff. and 114 ff.

[2] D. A. Weiser maintains that it is not necessary to suppose that the patriarchs were originally regarded as belonging to the same family or clan. The significant fact, he claims, is that diverse traditions have been fused together and incorporated into the story of Israel by virtue of a theology of history which emerged from Israel's reflection upon the events of the Exodus. " It was this ideology of history that the Old Testament produced out of its own resources so as to adapt alien material to its own purposes." See *Glaube und Geschichte im Alten Testament*, pp. 34–5. Whether such a conclusion is warranted by the Old Testament evidence seems to the present writer highly questionable, to say the least.

refer to real historical persons. This would not have been generally admitted half a century ago. Wellhausen maintained that Abraham, Isaac and Jacob are " ideal prototypes of the true Israelite." Abraham, far from being an historical person, " might with more likelihood be regarded as a free creation of unconscious art."[1] The patriarchal narratives, he held, give us no historical knowledge of the patriarchs, " but only of the time when the stories about them arose in the Israelite people."[2] The more general view, first put forward by Ewald, regarded the patriarchal stories as indicating the movements of tribes: Abraham is " the personification of the National Migration " towards the south-west.[3] Although Ewald himself held to the individual existence of Abraham, Isaac and Jacob as great national leaders,[4] it became fashionable among later scholars to deny this in the interests of a theory which associated these traditions exclusively with the movements of tribes.

Subsequent research, however, has invalidated this view. As H. H. Rowley observes, " Today there are few who would defend these positions, and there is a more general respect for the historical quality of the stories. This is not merely because a more conservative mood has descended upon Old Testament scholars, but because new light has been shed on the patriarchal age from many quarters."[5] With this may be compared the statement of another authority in this field, W. F. Albright: " So many corroborations of details have been discovered in recent years that most competent scholars have given up the old critical theory according to which the stories of the Patriarchs are mostly retrojections from the time of the Dual Monarchy (ninth to eighth centuries B.C.). . . . The figures

---

[1] *Prolegomena to the History of Israel*, Eng. trans. (1885), p. 320.

[2] *Ibid.*, pp. 318–9.

[3] *History of Israel*, Eng. trans. (1869) p. 274; cf. pp. 287 and 310.

[4] *Ibid.*, p. 305: " To go further and say boldly that all the places in Canaan in which the tradition places the three Patriarchs were only borrowed from the history of the Postmosaic period, and that therefore we know nothing of their historic existence and residence in Canaan, would be quite opposed to wisdom and truth; for a rigorous scrutiny discovers after all a solid background of fact to these primitive histories."

[5] H. H. Rowley, " Recent Discovery and the Patriarchal Age," in *The Servant of the Lord and Other Essays on the Old Testament*, p. 271—an admirable survey of this field of Old Testament scholarship.

of Abraham, Isaac, Jacob and Joseph appear before us as real personalities, each one of whom shows traits and qualities which suit his character but would not harmonize with the characters of the others."[1] And he points out in another place that " Abraham, Isaac, and Jacob no longer seem isolated figures, much less reflections of later Israelite history; they now appear as true children of their age, bearing the same names, moving about over the same territory, visiting the same towns (especially Harran and Nahor), practising the same customs as their contemporaries. In other words, the patriarchal narratives have a historical nucleus throughout."[2]

Such statements must not be taken to imply that archaeology has " proved " the existence of the patriarchs, as is sometimes claimed. Millar Burrows gives a salutary warning against " writers fired by zeal without knowledge " who " have rushed into print with inaccurate statements, doubtless intended for the glory of God but none the less misleading and therefore mischievous." And he makes the pertinent comment that " reverence for the Bible cannot be permanently promoted by making claims on its behalf which will later prove untrue."[3] The plain fact is, as G. E. Wright points out, that " thus far no contemporary record of Abraham has been found outside the Bible."[4] But the customs depicted in the biblical stories and their local colouring are so true to the background of the age, as reconstructed from the extra-biblical evidence, that Alan Richardson is fully justified in maintaining: " That there was a real person called Abraham, who had a son Isaac, and concerning whom the traditions contained in [Genesis] chapters 12 ff. have been collected, can hardly be doubted."[5] While it must be admitted, on the evidence of the Old Testament itself, that some of the stories told of the later patriarchs may refer to the movements of tribes or clans,[6] there can be little doubt

[1] W. F. Albright, *From the Stone Age to Christianity*, p. 183.
[2] *The Archaeology of Palestine*, p. 236.   [3] *What Mean these Stones?*, p. 2.
[4] *The Westminster Historical Atlas to the Bible*, p. 25.
[5] *Genesis I-XI* (Torch Comm.), pp. 131-2.
[6] Cf. J. Pedersen, *Israel: Its Life and Culture*, I-II, p. 14: "But when are the patriarchs tribes, and when are they individuals? Thus *we* ask in our eagerness to individualize our material, but this question is not in the spirit of the old legends, which do not acknowledge the sharp distinction between the history of the individual and that of the tribe."

that such men did exist—men of commanding personality, who have left their imprint deep in the memory of the race.

Sir Leonard Woolley's excavations at Ur of the Chaldees in South Mesopotamia have opened out to us the world in which Abraham lived.[1] Woolley has shown that this city of Ur, the capital of the old Sumerian Empire, was the centre of a high and flourishing civilization which was probably at least two thousand years old when Abraham was born. "The contents of the tombs," he says, "illustrate a very highly developed state of society of an urban type, a society in which the architect was familiar with all the basic principles of construction known to us today. The artist, capable at times of a most vivid realism, followed for the most part standards and conventions whose excellence had been approved by many generations working before him; the craftsman in metal possessed a knowledge of metallurgy and a technical skill which few ancient peoples ever rivalled; the merchant carried on a far-flung trade and recorded his transactions in writing; the army was well organized and victorious, agriculture prospered, and great wealth gave scope to luxury. Our tombs date . . . between 3500 and 3200 B.C., and as the nature of the civilization would lead one to expect, and as has been demonstrated by the discoveries in the rubbish below the tombs . . . by 3500 B.C. this civilization was already many centuries old."[2]

At this time Ur had been shorn of much of its old glory. The ancient Sumerian civilization had reached its final phase and was beginning to disintegrate. In 2170 B.C. the Elamites had invaded the plain, and Ur, along with its other cities, had been sacked. The king of Ur was carried away captive by the invaders and the rule of Sumer now passed to the kings of Isin and Larsa, cities which had once been vassal states. But although no longer the capital, Ur retained its old prestige as

---

[1] See *Ur of the Chaldees: A Record of Seven Years of Excavation* (1929, 2nd ed. 1950) and *Abraham: Recent Discoveries and Hebrew Origins* (1936).

[2] *Ur of the Chaldees*, pp. 87-8. In the Foreword to the second edition (1950), Woolley points out that all his dates must now be reduced by two centuries. "In 1929 scholars were prepared to agree to a date about 3100 B.C. as that of the First Dynasty of Ur; this was the fixed basis for my calculations regarding the earlier periods. Today it is generally agreed that the date of the First Dynasty is more like 2900 B.C." See p. 12.

the centre of moon-worship. Its patrons were the moon-god Nannar and his consort Nin-Gal; and the famous *zikkurat* of Ur was their shrine. So that even in the days of Abraham Ur was a great and prosperous city trading in copper from the Anatolian mountains, lapis lazuli—the stone used for jewellery and inlay—from the Pamir mountains brought via Persia, and amazonite beads from the Nilgiri hills of South India. It was also a centre of textile manufacture, which was carried on not merely as a home craft but on a large scale in factories. There was a regular postal service operating within the empire and the trade routes were protected by police patrols. Coinage did not come into use until the time of the Persian Empire in the sixth century B.C., but what we should call a " paper currency " was in use among the merchants of Ur: letters of credit and bills of exchange, written in cuneiform on clay tablets, served the purpose of cheques.

Woolley estimates the population of Ur in the twentieth century B.C. as at least a quarter of a million, and possibly even half a million people,[1] and he says: " We must revise considerably our ideas of the Hebrew patriarch when we learn that his earlier years were spent in such sophisticated surroundings; he was the citizen of a great city and inherited the traditions of an ancient and highly organized civilization. The houses themselves bespoke comfort and even luxury. Apart from the actual fabric there was little left to throw light on the daily life of the inhabitants, but one or two stores of tablets did bear witness to their intellectual interests. We found copies of the hymns which were used in the service of the temples, and with them mathematical tables ranging from plain sums in addition to formulæ for the extraction of square and cube roots, and other texts in which the writers had copied out the old building inscriptions extant in the city and had compiled in this way an abbreviated history of the principal temples."[2]

It is, then, in this city and district of Ur in the south of Mesopotamia that the earliest traditions of Israel's ancestry begin; and they begin by indicating a movement of Abraham and his family, first northwards, and then to the west and south.[3]

---

[1] See *Abraham: Recent Discoveries and Hebrew Origins*, p. 118.
[2] *Ur of the Chaldees*, pp. 168–9.   [3] See Genesis xi, 31–2; xii, 1–10.

For three great religions—Christianity, Judaism and Islam —the call of Abraham to leave his country and his father's house marks the beginning of a new era. It is significant, however, that the Bible gives no hint of how this call was given. It is concerned with the fact of the call and all that it implied, and not with the means through which it was accomplished. It tells of an epoch-making act of God, " the revelation of a personal God actively taking the initiative and revealing Himself in history."[1]

The call of Abraham and God's Covenant with him mark the beginning of what we might call the divine strategy of using the particular to achieve the universal. Abraham is " the symbol of the beginning and ending of Jewish existence."[2] This particular man is called to be the founder of a particular nation, a " chosen people," through whom God might reveal Himself redemptively to the world. The Bible is not afraid of this " scandal of particularity." It regards the history of Israel as unique; it is the vehicle of the redemptive activity of God: Israel's acts are God's mighty acts. And the Christian Church has always regarded itself as the New Israel, the reconstituted People of God in whom the call of Abraham is completed and consummated.

This preparatory period in the history of Israel has left no direct literary remains. Although Woolley holds that " there are good grounds for believing that the fact of Abraham's existence was vouched for by written documents almost if not quite contemporary with him,"[3] the stories of the patriarchs, as we have them in the Old Testament, were not written down in their present form until the ninth or, at the earliest, the tenth century B.C.

II. The Formative Period

The next turning-point, which marks the beginning of a distinctive Hebrew religion, is the Exodus from Egypt. Although this is one of the best-attested facts in the Old Testament, there is as yet no general agreement as to its precise

[1] R. K. Orchard, *The Open Bible*, pp. 38–9.
[2] A. Richardson, " Abraham," in *A Theological Word Book of the Bible*, ed. A. Richardson, p. 12.
[3] *Abraham: Recent Discoveries and Hebrew Origins*, pp. 41–2.

date. Indeed, as Millar Burrows observes, "here we strike one of the most debated questions in all biblical history."[1]

Three likely periods in the history of the ancient world have been suggested. The first, in chronological order, is the sixteenth century B.C. According to this view, the Exodus is to be equated with the expulsion from Egypt of the Hyksos rulers in c. 1580 B.C. by the founder of the Eighteenth Dynasty —an identification made by the Jewish historian Josephus. The Hyksos, or "shepherd kings," were Asiatics of Semitic or Hurrian stock who conquered Egypt in c. 1730 B.C. and had their capital at Avaris in the Delta region. Their rule therefore lasted for a century and a half—a period which, if the Hyksos be identified in any way with the Israelites, would harmonize well with the biblical tradition that the sojourn in Egypt lasted for four generations.[2]

This, however, conflicts with the other biblical tradition that Israel was in Egypt for 430 years.[3] And there are other more formidable difficulties about a sixteenth-century date. The Hyksos, for instance, cannot be identified with the Israelites without doing violence to the Old Testament sources.[4] Again, allowing the biblical span of forty years for the wilderness wanderings, the entry into Canaan must on this reckoning have taken place in the middle of the sixteenth century, c. 1540 B.C. This leaves a gap of 540 years to the establishment of the monarchy (c. 1000 B.C.), a gap far too wide to be bridged by the period of the Judges.[5] Furthermore, a date in the sixteenth century is contrary to all available archaeological evidence. It has therefore been generally abandoned today.

The second period, for which a much stronger case can be

---

[1] *What Mean these Stones?*, p. 72.

[2] Genesis xv, 16.   [3] Exodus xii, 40.

[4] Albright associates the descent of Jacob into Egypt with the Hyksos conquest. See *Bulletin of the American Schools of Oriental Research*, No. 58, April 1935, p. 15; *Journal of the Palestinian Oriental Society*, vol. xv, 1935, p. 227; *From the Stone Age to Christianity*, 2nd ed., 1946, p. 150. But, as Rowley comments, "it is hard to find in the biblical traditions anything at all in common with the story of the Hyksos invasion. For they tell of the entry of suppliants at an already established court, and not of a victorious entry of conquering hosts." *From Joseph to Joshua*, 1950, p. 75.

[5] "The list of Judges, if taken continuously, amounts to 534 years, but no judge ruled over more than a third of the land."—Flinders Petrie, *Palestine and Israel*, 1934, p. 54.

made out, is the middle of the fifteenth century, *c.* 1440 B.C. This is the time indicated by the chronology of I Kings vi, 1, which dates the Exodus 480 years before the foundation of Solomon's Temple (*c.* 967 B.C.). It fits in perfectly with Garstang's dating of the fall of Jericho round about 1400 B.C.,[1] as also with the identification of the Ḥabiru raids, mentioned in the Tel-el-Amarna letters,[2] with the assaults of the Israelites on the promised land.

But on closer examination, what at first appears to be a very attractive view bristles with difficulties. In the first place, the chronology of I Kings vi, 1, is at variance with the genealogy of Ruth iv, 20–2, in which Nahshon, the brother-in-law of Aaron (Exodus vi, 23; cf. Numbers i, 7), is separated from Solomon by only six generations—which cannot, by any amount of ingenuity, be made even to approximate to 480 years. Secondly, " the account of the conquest of Joshua bears no resemblance to that of the Amarna letters."[3] As Rowley points out, the general picture of the latter is " of trouble in the south and north, but with the centre affected only by the action at Shechem; whereas the general picture of the biblical account of Joshua is of a movement that began in the centre and spread north and south from there."[4] Even Garstang, who argues for the fifteenth-century date, maintains that " no historical connexion can be traced between the Ḥabiru revolution and the original invasion of Canaan by the Israelites under Joshua."[5] Thirdly, if the Exodus took place in the Amarna age, it is surprising to find no reference in the Book of Judges to the Palestinian campaigns of Seti I and Rameses II or indeed any recognition of Egyptian suzerainty.[6]

[1] See J. Garstang, *Joshua–Judges*, 1931, p. 147; *The Story of Jericho*, 2nd ed., 1948, pp. 129–30.

[2] These are a number of cuneiform tablets discovered in 1887 at the site of Ikhnaton's capital on the Upper Nile. They mostly comprise diplomatic correspondence of the fourteenth century B.C. in which the governors of Palestinian cities appeal to the Pharaoh for help against the attacks of a people called *Ḥabiru* or *Sagas*, who are successfully invading the land.

[3] H. H. Rowley, *The Re-discovery of the Old Testament*, 1946, p. 45.

[4] From *Joseph to Joshua*, 1950, p. 44.   [5] *Joshua–Judges*, 1931, p. 255.

[6] Garstang maintains that Egypt is " The Hornet " of Joshua xxiv, 12. He credits Egypt with the deliverances attributed to the Israelite Judges, which is completely at variance with the biblical account. See *Joshua–Judges*, pp. 258–60.

These, however, are not the chief difficulties of the fifteenth-century view; two others are more formidable. In the fourth place, it fails to take account of the statement in Exodus i, 11, that the Pharaoh of the Oppression used Israelite forced labour to build two store-cities, Pithom and Raamses. The latter is the old Hyksos capital, Avaris, which was rebuilt by Rameses II, after whom it is named. But Rameses II belongs to the thirteenth century. The final difficulty concerns the detour which the Israelites were compelled to make round the territories of Edom and Moab.[1] Nelson Glueck has shown that there was no settled population in these territories between the time of Abraham and the thirteenth century B.C.[2] "Had the Exodus through southern Transjordan taken place before the thirteenth century B.C., the Israelites would have found neither Edomites nor Moabites who could have given or withheld permission to traverse their territories."[3]

This brings us down to the third suggested period—the thirteenth century. Both Albright and Rowley favour a thirteenth-century date; but while Albright maintains that the Exodus took place at the beginning of the century, c. 1290 B.C.,[4] Rowley argues for a date in its second half, c. 1230 B.C.[5] This period not only meets the last two difficulties raised by the fifteenth-century view, but is also congruous with the Palestinian archaeological evidence[6] and with the much-discussed text of the Merneptah stele in which the name Israel has the determinative of a foreign people as distinct from that of a foreign land which occurs in the rest of the text. The implication, Albright suggests, is that at this time, viz. 1229 B.C., "Israel

[1] See Numbers, xx–xxi.

[2] See *Bulletin of the American Schools of Oriental Research*, No. 55, September 1934, pp. 3–21; No. 86, April 1942, pp. 14–24; No. 90, April 1943, pp. 2–23.

[3] *Bulletin of the American Schools of Oriental Research*, No. 55, September 1934, p. 16.

[4] *See Bulletin of the American Schools of Oriental Research*, No. 58, April 1935, p. 10; No. 89, February 1942, p. 29; *From the Stone Age to Christianity*, p. 195.

[5] See *Bulletin of the John Rylands Library*, 1938, pp. 243–90; *From Joseph to Joshua*, 1950, Lecture III, pp. 109–63.

[6] According to Albright this points to the thirteenth century as the period in which the main wave of destruction fell in Palestine. See *Haverford Symposium*, p. 23.

3—AOB

was already in Western Palestine in force, but had not yet settled down."[1]

The great objection to a thirteenth-century date for the Exodus is Garstang's dating of the fall of Jericho, which, he maintains, cannot have been later than the end of the reign of Amenhotep III, i.e. 1385 B.C.[2] This, however, is by no means certain, as other eminent archaeologists have challenged Garstang's view. Flinders Petrie maintains that there is evidence for a date after 1300 B.C.[3] and Vincent places the fall of the city between 1250 and 1200 B.C.[4] Albright at first agreed with Garstang's dating[5] but later modified his views in favour of a fourteenth-century date. He is now prepared to admit the possibility of a date in the thirteenth century: " At present the evidence points to a date . . . in the latter part of the fourteenth (century) or the early thirteenth for the fall of Jericho; it must, however, be frankly confessed that our evidence against a date somewhat later in the thirteenth century . . . is mainly negative."[6]

None of these possible periods for the date of the Exodus is without its difficulties, therefore. The available evidence, however, would seem to favour a thirteenth-century date. In any case, the uncertainty regarding the date of the fall of Jericho means that its evidence cannot for the present be a determining factor.[7]

There is no valid reason why we should not follow a deeply embedded tradition and associate this formative period, which the Exodus initiates, with the name of Moses. Such a time

[1] *From the Stone Age to Christianity*, p. 194. Albright is following Borchardt's chronology, which places the accession of Merneptah in 1235 B.C. It is usually dated 1225 B.C., in which case the stele (dated in Merneptah's fifth year) would refer to 1219 B.C.—a time, as Rowley shows, which is not incongruous with an Exodus in *c.* 1230 B.C. See *From Joseph to Joshua*, p. 137.   [2] See *The Story of Jericho*, 2nd ed., 1948, pp. 129–30.
[3] *Palestine and Israel*, 1934, pp. 54–5.
[4] *Revue biblique*, vol. xxxix, 1930, pp. 402–33; vol. xli, 1932, pp. 264–71; vol. xliv, 1935, pp. 583–605; vol. xlviii, 1939, p. 580; Quarterly Statement of the Palestine Exploration Fund, 1931, pp. 104 ff.
[5] See *Joshua–Judges*, 1931, p. 146, note 1.
[6] *The Archaeology of Palestine*, 1949, pp. 108–9.
[7] Cf. Hennequin, *Supplément au Dictionnarie de la Bible*, vol. iii, 1936, col. 413: "Il ne saurait être question de faire état des ' résultats ' acquis à Jéricho pour déterminer la date de l'entrée des Israélites en Canaan."

demands some commanding personality to direct the common
life and fuse together its diverse elements into a unified and
ordered society; so that, as Oesterley and Robinson remark,
" if we had no record of Moses, it would have been necessary
to invent him, for such a work as that ascribed to him demands
the genius and inspiration of an individual almost unique."[1]

Before this time the Hebrews were a number of separate
tribes having, it is true, traditions of a common ancestry, but
with little else to bind them together. Moses roused them from
their slavery in Egypt, brought to them a message of hope,
proclaimed that the God of their fathers was about to deliver
them, and so kindled within them the flame of nationalism.
Thus when this nation first came to self-consciousness it was as
a chosen people of their father's God whom Moses had introduced to them by the new name of Yahweh, rendered as
Jehovah in our English Bible.[2]

The events of the Exodus from Egypt, the Deliverance at the
Red Sea and the ratification of the Covenant with Jehovah
at Sinai were both formative and crucial for the religion of
Israel. While it is doubtful whether all the tribes of Israel were
in Egypt, the memory of Egyptian oppression from which they
were delivered in a remarkable way is embedded so deeply in
the memory of the race that we can be certain that at least one
considerable element in Israelite ancestry went down to the
borders of Egypt and settled there. And, as G. E. Wright says,
" The Exodus or deliverance from Egypt, therefore, is the
central or focal point in Israelite history and faith."[3]

In considering the deliverance at the Red Sea—however we
may explain it—we are dealing indubitably with historic
fact. Natural factors clearly enter into the story. Indeed the
earliest biblical tradition attributes the event to a strong wind.[4]
Gressman, who places the scene of the crossing at the head of

---

[1] *Hebrew Religion: Its Origin and Development*, p. 151.

[2] See Exodus iii, 13–15, and vi, 2–3. Sigmund Mowinckel maintains that
this is not a name hitherto unknown to Moses and the Israelites: " Yahwe
is not *telling* his name to one who does not know it. . . . The whole conversation presupposes that the Israelites know this name already." See *The
Two Sources of the Predeuteronomic Primeval History (J.E.) in Gen. i–xi*, Oslo,
1937, p. 55.   [3] *The Old Testament Against its Environment*, pp. 49–50.

[4] Exodus xiv, 21.

the Gulf of Akaba, suggests that volcanic action may also
have played a part,[1] while Major Jarvis, who locates the crossing near the Bardawil Lake, describes phenomena which he
himself has observed in this district and which would, he
maintains, account for both the receding of the sea and the
pillar of cloud.[2] To admit, however, that we may discern here
certain natural phenomena is not to deny that the event is
what both the Hebrew and the Christian Church have always
maintained, namely, a great delivering act of God. In the
words of H. H. Rowley, " Israel was saved by a signal act of
deliverance in which no human hand played a part. The critical
examination of the narrative may show that the miracle has
been heightened in the tradition, and the numbers of the
Israelites concerned greatly swollen. But no critical examination
can discredit the story that Israel had an amazing deliverance,
a deliverance that could never be forgotten in all her history, a
deliverance that never ceased to call forth wonder and thanksgiving."[3] It was Jehovah who had visited them in Egypt;
He had brought them forth with a high hand and dried up
the Red Sea before them; at the sacred mountain of Sinai
He had bound Himself in a Covenant with them.

These Hebrews left Egypt as a number of tribes; they entered
Canaan as a people. The significance, therefore, of their
wilderness wanderings is that in them these tribes were welded
together into a nation. The process was not complete, of
course, until the establishment of the monarchy; but the idea
of the nationality of Israel was born when the various tribes
combined to enter into the Covenant with Jehovah at Sinai.
The change was brought about through the instrumentality
of Moses, who laid the foundations of their national life on a
firm basis of law, but its accomplishment was due to one thing—
the unifying influence of a common allegiance to Jehovah
their God. The work of Moses is succinctly summarized by
A. W. Whitehouse when he says that " a people was created

---

[1] *Mose und seine Zeit*, pp. 108–21.
[2] Quoted by Oesterley and Robinson, *A History of Israel*, i, p. 87.
[3] *The Re-discovery of the Old Testament*, p. 62. Cf. W. A. L. Elmslie, *How
Came our Faith*, p. 204: " This tradition is historical; for nothing else properly
explains the note of marvelling triumph that resounds in the memory of the
deliverance."

under his leadership, through the establishment among them of a religion whose characteristic features persisted through all the recorded history."[1]

Here, then, is the beginning of the Hebrew Church; here is the time when the religion of Israel took on its distinctive form. " Israel's knowledge of her election by God," says Wright, " must be traced to a theological reflection on the meaning of the Exodus from Egypt. . . . He had humbled Pharaoh and delivered Israel from slavery, had formed a dispirited people into a nation and given them a law and an ' inheritance ' of land. Israel had been in bondage, but was now freed. No abstract words were needed to describe God's being; it was sufficient to identify Him with a simple historical statement: He was the God who had brought Israel out of the land of Egypt, out of the house of bondage (Exodus xx, 2)."[2] And he concludes: " The religion of Israel suddenly appears in history, breaking radically with the mythopoeic approach to reality. How are we to explain it, except that it is a new creation? For this reason, there can be no doubt that the fundamental elements of this faith were established *early* in Israel's history, which means that we are led to Sinai and to the work of Moses. . . . These distinctive elements are the primary data of the Old Testament, that *something* in early Israel which predisposed and predetermined the course of Biblical history."[3]

This period too, however, although it is of vital importance in biblical religion, has left no direct literary remains. While it is certain that Hebrew law rests upon a Mosaic basis, the laws recorded in the Old Testament belong in their present form to a later time. " The Pentateuch as we now have it is not the immediate record of the institutions of Moses, but the last codification of the divine teaching begun by Moses, and carried on and perfected through many centuries by the discipline of history and the word of the prophets who took up Moses' work."[4] Indeed—if we may anticipate for a moment a later point—it was not until some three or four hundred years

[1] " Moses," in *A Theological Word Book of the Bible*, ed. A. Richardson, p. 155.
[2] *Op. cit.*, pp. 13–14, 20–1. Cf. J. Marsh, *The Fulness of Time*, p. 42: " In the Exodus Israel came by her concept of history."   [3] *Op. cit.*, p. 29.
[4] W. Robertson Smith, *The Prophets of Israel*, p. 35.

after his time that the earliest Old Testament records of Moses were written down.

Nevertheless the Exodus is the crucial " time " in the history of Israel. The building of Solomon's temple is dated by reference to it (I Kings vi, 1)—a tribute " parallel to the ' ab urbe condita ' in Rome, or the ' anno domini ' of the Christian era."[1] It is the ground of the prophets' constant appeal for loyalty and obedience to the God who had brought His people out of the land of Egypt, from the house of bondage. " The fundamental fact about Israel, therefore, in the light of her own recorded history, is not that Abraham was her father, with whom God concluded a covenant and in whom He blessed all the families of the earth; but it is the deliverance that God wrought through Moses for the whole people, and the covenant that God concluded through Moses with the whole people."[2]

In short, Moses stands in the same relationship to the Old Israel as does Christ to the New: he is the Deliverer, the Mediator of a Covenant, the Revealer of God. And the Exodus is for the Old Testament what the Cross and Resurrection are for the New—a great redeeming act of God which does for men what they could never have done for themselves, liberating them from slavery, constituting them into a People of God, laying upon them a perpetual obligation of loyalty and obedience.[3]

III. THE CREATIVE PERIOD

About eight hundred years before the birth of Christ there appeared in Israel a succession of notable preachers, the great Hebrew prophets. Their advent marks the third turning-point in the spiritual history of the race. While it was Moses who led this people to pledge themselves to a common allegiance to Jehovah in the Covenant at Sinai, it was Amos and Hosea, Isaiah and Micah who began a new epoch in their religious life. They themselves and their successors were concerned to recall their contemporaries to the Mosaic faith and to sweep away the corruptions that had crept in from the Canaanite

---

[1] J. Marsh, *The Fulness of Time*, p. 43.   [2] *Ibid.*, p. 52.
[3] For a fuller statement of the significance of the Exodus, see J. K. S. Reid, *The Authority of Scripture*, pp. 246 ff.

fertility rites and the practices of other pagan religions with which Israel had come into contact.[1] Their emphasis, therefore, was on the ethical and spiritual implications of the Covenant with Jehovah, and in a time when religion had come to be associated almost exclusively with rites and ceremonies this prophetic teaching was revolutionary.

Taken together, the prophets of Israel form a fairly good cross-section of society—a peasant, a herdsman, a city-dweller, a priest, a minister of state. Each one bears the stamp of his own peculiar upbringing and reflects the conditions of his time. Moreover, it is these very conditions which prompt him to speak; his message springs directly out of them; his words are addressed to a particular situation which has called them forth. Social injustice and corruption wring from Amos his scathing denunciations. The threat of foreign invasion causes Isaiah to proclaim that " in quietness and in confidence shall be your strength." The fall of Nineveh, the stronghold of Assyrian tyranny and aggression, makes Nahum exult in the just retribution of heaven.

The prophet, however, was no mere child of his time. His function was not merely to reflect but to create. Not only was his message called forth by the particular historical situation with which he was confronted; it exercised a formative influence over that situation. Determined by events of the prophet's time, it shaped the course of things to come. According to Sir Winston Churchill, one of the marks of a great man is so to have handled matters during his life that the course of events is continuously affected by what he did.[2] That is certainly true of the Hebrew prophets. They did not live the life of a recluse, isolated and detached from their fellow men; but neither were they the mere mouthpiece of their age. " On the one hand, they were emotionally part of their People, hurrying itself to its doom. On the other, they were emotionally one with the sorrow of God in His frustrated good purpose, so completely had they

---

[1] " The higher view is never put forth by the prophets as a novelty; they regard it as the very foundation of the religion of Jehovah from the days of Moses downwards, and the people never venture to deny that they are right."—W. Robertson Smith, *The Prophets of Israel*, pp. 73-4.

[2] " Joseph Chamberlain," in *Great Contemporaries*, p. 61.

given themselves to His service."[1] Thus we see in the prophets the interplay of the receptive and the creative. The situation which itself prompts their word is in turn moulded by that word, so that the prophet becomes the determining factor in Hebrew history and religion.

A past generation thought of the prophets almost entirely as " foretellers "—men who could predict the future. Hence their function was regarded as the declaration of what was going to happen and their oracles were looked upon as history written beforehand in an enigmatic and obscure way. This view still persists in some quarters; it is, in fact, the view held by many who call themselves " students of prophecy " today. But the historical method of biblical study has made it increasingly evident that to search the prophetic books for enigmatic references to Hitler or to trace in them clues to the postwar politics of Europe is to misunderstand the nature of this great creative movement in Hebrew religion. Hence the prophet came to be regarded as *par excellence* the teacher of the Hebrew race. From being the " foreteller " he was thought of as essentially the " forthteller "—the one who instructs and expounds. So that Dean Margee was content to define a prophet as " the religious teacher of his age, whose aim was the religious education of those whom he addresses."

But this one-sided emphasis upon the prophet as " forthteller " is as misleading as was the previous exclusive emphasis upon him as " foreteller," because in point of fact he is both. He declared the will of God for his time; he expounded the great spiritual principles of the universe; he denounced injustice and hypocrisy. Yes; but you cannot eliminate the predictive element without doing violence to the historical sources of the prophet's life and work. That " foretelling " as well as "forthtelling" is regarded as an essential part of prophesy is clear from Deuteronomy xviii, 22: " When a prophet speaketh in the name of the Lord, if the thing follow not, nor come to pass, that is the thing which the Lord hath not spoken, but the prophet hath spoken it presumptuously: thou shalt not be afraid of him."[2]

---

[1] W. A. L. Elmslie, *How Came our Faith*, p. 197.
[2] Cf. Jeremiah xxviii, 9, which expresses the same idea that it is the fulfilment of the prophet's prediction which authenticates his word.

The significance of the predictive side of the prophet's utterance is admirably stated by H. H. Rowley:

> The prophet was the man of the open eye. He looked on any given situation and he saw it all. He saw through it to the end. He read the inevitable issue of things, and proclaimed it with no uncertain voice. When he saw his fellows plunging headlong in a course of sin and selfishness, he saw the inevitable disasters to which that course must lead. When others lived in the comforts of the present, he declared the sorrows that were being laid up. He *did* predict, but whether the events he predicted were in the near or distant future, they were related to the conditions of his own day and generation. It was never prediction for its own sake, or to impress succeeding generations with his inspired cleverness, but ever with an immediate and practical object—to persuade men to turn from their follies to God, in the hope that they might avert the evils he saw coming. That is the genius of Hebrew prophecy. The prophet looked through the present to the end towards which it was tending. He was essentially a Seer, a man who penetrated human affairs and human situations, and who laid bare their inevitable issue.[1]

To understand the revolutionary nature of the prophetic teaching, we must remember that the eighth-century prophets lived in a time when religion was very largely divorced from morals. It was a time of material prosperity and social change. Wealth flowed into the land, but it passed into the hands of a few to the detriment of the many. The small peasant farmer, who had been characteristic of Israelite society since the settlement in Canaan, was passing away and his ancestral strip of land becoming merged into large estates, worked by what was to all intents and purposes slave labour. The rich oppressed the poor. Justice was corrupted; a small bribe of, say, a pair of sandals was sufficient to secure the condemnation of an innocent man. Merchants defrauded their customers with false weights and measures. Sexual vice was rampant. Yet side by side with this oppression and dishonesty and vice there was an elaborate religious ritual which was punctiliously observed. Those who lived in luxury by bribery and extortion crowded the Temple courts with their offerings of sheep and bulls. They regarded religion as belonging exclusively to the Sanctuary and as having nothing whatever to do with the market

[1] *The Relevance of the Bible*, p. 64.

and the law court and the street. As long as they paid their tithes and brought in their offerings and observed the sacrificial regulations and came regularly to church they might do as they pleased in the busy work-a-day world.

It was to such people that the prophets spoke. They denounced their corruptions. They exposed their false trust in rites and ceremonies. They declared that the God with whom men have to do is One who is of purer eyes than to behold iniquity; that He cared more about righteousness than about ritual.[1]

Lord Melbourne, Queen Victoria's first Prime Minister, once went to hear an evangelical preacher who severely denounced some of the crying iniquities of the time. After the service the statesman was heard to remark, with some indignation: " Things have come to a pretty pass if religion is going to interfere with private life! " That is precisely what the prophets said—that religion *did* interfere with private life, and with public life as well: " Wherewith shall I come before the Lord, and bow myself before the High God? shall I come before him with burnt offerings, with calves of a year old? Will the Lord be pleased with thousands of rams, or with ten thousands of rivers of oil? shall I give my firstborn for my transgression, the fruit of my body for the sin of my soul? He hath showed thee, O man, what is good; and what doth the Lord require of thee, but to do justly, and to love mercy, and to walk humbly with thy God? "[2]

What was the essence of this revolutionary prophetic teaching? It was a higher conception of God. For the Hebrew of Mosaic times Jehovah was the storm-God of the desert; Sinai was his home; He must not be approached by ordinary people whose lives would be imperilled by His presence.[3] There is, of course, a strong ethical element in the Mosaic faith. Indeed, as Rowley reminds us, " it was Moses who gave Israel that rich moral element which was the distinctive thing about their religion."[4] It is not without significance that later generations regarded him as the first and greatest of the prophets.[5] But this distinctive moral element in Jehovah's demands had been over-

---

[1] See Isaiah i, 10–17.   [2] Micah vi, 6–8.
[3] Cf. Exodus xix, 12–13, 20–23.   [4] *The Relevance of the Bible*, p. 60.
[5] See Deuteronomy xxxiv, 10.

shadowed by the ritual requirements which accompanied it and finally obscured by the syncretism which resulted from the merging of the simple cultus of the desert and the agricultural fertility rites of Canaanite Baal-worship.

For the prophets, however, the ethical nature of Jehovah was paramount: He was first and foremost good. The one God who claimed the worship of men was a righteous God; the principles by which He governed the world were justice and truth; and hence He required justice and truth from all who would serve Him. " It was the great Prophets," says Elmslie, " who saw the supreme principle—that men must measure what is right and wrong by the test of Absolute Goodness."[1] This demand for right conduct came first, and all ritual and ceremonial must take a subordinate place.

But the prophet was no mere social reformer; he was first and foremost a man of God.[2] He was one who spoke with an authority not his own. He came neither to declare his views nor to offer his advice, but to deliver a message. He was essentially a herald, a bearer of tidings; he delivered that which he also had received. This unique position of the prophet is seen in Exodus iv, 14 to 16. Moses, called by God to lead Israel out of Egypt, is making the excuse that he is a poor speaker. To which God replies: " Is not Aaron the Levite thy brother? I know that he can speak well. . . . And thou shalt speak unto him, and put words in his mouth. . . . And he shall be thy spokesman unto the people: and he shall be, even he shall be to thee instead of a mouth, and thou shalt be to him instead of God." The word translated " spokesman " is the Hebrew word for prophet—nābi'. Aaron, it is said, shall be Moses' prophet. And this is explicitly stated in Exodus vii, 1: " And the Lord said unto Moses, See, I have made thee a god to Pharaoh: and Aaron thy brother shall be thy prophet."

[1] W. A. L. Elmslie, *How Came Our Faith*, p. 13.
[2] Cf. W. A. L. Elmslie, *Ibid.*, pp. 12–13: " Shall we entitle them Social Reformers? The notion is comically anaemic. Should we call them men of religious genius? They themselves would have rejected that compliment, telling us that the question whether they were clever or ultra-clever men was neither here nor there, because they were what they were, and believed what they believed, for a reason they could describe only by saying that *God* had ' laid His hand upon them ' and ' put His Word in their mouth '; giving them knowledge of truth."

" From these passages," comments H. H. Rowley, " it would appear that the prophet was regarded as the mouthpiece of God. And whenever Hebrew prophecy was true to its genius, it was the mouthpiece of God. The prophet spoke God's message to the men of his own day and generation."[1]

The message of the prophets was good news; not just good advice. They declared that men were not left unaided in their moral struggle: those who sought to serve God by doing right could always count upon His help. Furthermore, " everything that befell Israel was interpreted by the prophets as a work of Jehovah's hand, displaying His character and will— not an arbitrary character or a changeable will, but a fixed and consistent holy purpose, which has Israel for its object and seeks the true felicity of the nation, but at the same time is absolutely sovereign over Israel, and will not give way to Israel's desires or adapt itself to Israel's convenience."[2] The prophets discerned the significance of the political events of their time in the light of their realization of the goodness and power of God. " They interpreted history as manifesting the mighty works of a living God and they looked to the future to vindicate His purposes."[3]

It is extremely unlikely, as we have seen, that the Old Testament contains any immediate literary product of either the preparatory or the formative period of Hebrew religion. We have, however, direct contact with this period of creative prophetic activity through the prophetic books. These documents, which embody the teaching of the prophets, rise to the highest peaks of religious life and are invaluable to us today, not only for their historic importance but because of their abiding worth as revelation and truth. As W. A. L. Elmslie finely observes, " It has grown more and more evident that to understand these men (and the way they made their Faith convincing) opens the direct road to the deepest apprehension of what Christ taught, of how He taught it, and of what He Himself uniquely was."[4]

[1] H. H. Rowley, *The Relevance of the Bible*, p. 62.
[2] W. Robertson Smith, *The Prophets of Israel*, pp. 70–1.
[3] C. H. Dodd, *The Bible and its Background*, pp. 19–20.
[4] *How Came our Faith*, p. 12.

IV. The Period of Conservation and Consolidation

As the prophets had foreseen, the storm-clouds which had been gathering on the horizon of Israel throughout the early part of the eighth century B.C. quickly burst. The armies, first of Assyria in 721 B.C., and then of Babylon in 586 B.C., swept through the land. The tiny kingdoms of Israel and Judah were overthrown and many of their people deported *en masse* to the conquerors' lands. Towards the end of the sixth century B.C., however, little bands of Judaean exiles began to return from Babylon. The Temple and walls of Jerusalem were rebuilt and soon a new Jewish community was re-established in their old home. This marks the fourth turning-point in Hebrew history and religion. And the period of restoration in the sixth and fifth centuries B.C. was essentially a time of conservation and consolidation.

If we are to understand what was taking place in this period and its tremendous significance in the nation's life, we must first glance at the Babylonian exile which preceded it. Two results which emerged from this latter event must be mentioned.

In the first place, the exile cut loose Hebrew religion from its local moorings. From time immemorial the religion of the Israelites had been associated with sacred places and shrines. Furthermore, monolatry rather than monotheism had held sway in the popular mind. Jehovah, it was believed, was the God of Palestine, just as Chemosh was the God of Moab; but outside Palestine His writ did not run. Hence they assumed that the God of their fathers could be worshipped only on their own native soil,[1] and to leave their homeland meant separation from their God. David, therefore, says of his persecutors: " They have driven me out this day from abiding in the inheritance of the Lord, saying, Go, serve other gods."[2] We can well imagine, then, what a terrible calamity the exile was for the pious Jew; not only was he uprooted from his ancestral home, he was also, so he believed, separated from his father's God. " By the rivers of Babylon, there we sat down, yea, we wept, when we remembered Zion. We

---

[1] Cf. Naaman's request for two mules' burden of earth, II Kings v, 17.
[2] I Samuel xxvi, 19.

hanged our harps upon the willows in the midst thereof. For there they that carried us away captive required of us a song; and they that wasted us required of us mirth, saying, Sing us one of the songs of Zion. How shall we sing Jehovah's song in a strange land? "[1]

But by the rivers of Babylon these hapless captives made a great discovery. They discovered that they were not separated from their God after all; they could experience His presence in their concentration camp as well as in the Temple courts. Now the question arises, How were they led to make this discovery? And the answer is, Through the teaching of the prophets. In their lifetime these inspired preachers of righteousness had been solitary men, living on a plane far above that of their contemporaries. They did not draw the crowds; except for a little band of followers they must needs be voices crying in the wilderness. But in the dark days of the exile their teaching came into its own. They had proclaimed that Jehovah was the God, not merely of Palestine, but of the whole earth. It followed then that He could be worshipped in any place—even in Babylon. And they had also taught that God's first requirement of men was righteousness rather than ritual, so it followed that He could be served, if necessary, without the sacrifices on the altar at Jerusalem. This, then, was the first result of the exile: Hebrew religion was liberated from its bondage to sacred places and shrines.

But the exile resulted also, in the second place, in a period of great literary activity. The one link which the exiles had with their own land was the records of the past. And so the old stories were collected and edited, the old legislation was rewritten and revised and brought up to date. These ancient records were found to be a source of inspiration and strength, and thus their religion became more and more the religion of a book.

We are now in a position to grasp the significance of the restoration of the Jewish community in the sixth century B.C. Those who came back from Babylon had learned the lessons of the exile and were determined to incorporate them into their common life. The restored community " was more a church

---

[1] Psalm cxxxvii, 1–4.

than a nation. Its rulers were priests, not kings. As an insignificant province of an alien empire it could have little effective
part in politics. Its interests and energies were concentrated
upon spiritual affairs."[1]

This concentration of interest upon spiritual rather than
temporal affairs resulted in two dominant desires. Realizing
the great spiritual heritage into which they had come, they
purposed first of all to conserve all that was highest and best in
the nation's past. But realizing too that the discipline of the exile
had taught them much, they also determined to incorporate
what they had learned along with that which they had received.

The practical result of these twin desires was the formation
of that collection of sacred books which we know today as the
Old Testament. We owe it to this restored Jewish community
at Jerusalem. They began, naturally enough, by gathering
together all the writings that remained from earlier times.
There were some ancient codes of law which were known as
the Laws of Moses. Old Testament scholars have distinguished
four such codes: (1) the Book of the Covenant (Exodus xx–
xxiii), (2) The Deuteronomic Code, (3) The Law of Holiness
(Leviticus xvii–xxvi), and (4) the Priestly Code—a new codification, in a narrative setting, made by the Jewish priests in Babylon in the fifth century B.C. but embodying ancient regulations
and practices. This was, in all probability, the law brought from
Babylon and introduced to the restored community at Jerusalem
by Ezra in 397 B.C.[2] No one was concerned about how much,
if any, of these codes of law went back to Moses himself.
They were an expression of the legislation that he had given to
the nation, and that was quite sufficient.

Then, too, there were narratives of the early days—stories of
the fathers of the race, Abraham, Isaac and Jacob, the bondage in Egypt, Moses and the Exodus, the wilderness wanderings. Many of these were already embodied in an account
which had probably been in existence since about 700 B.C.
It is known to scholars as JE and combines two main sources—
a Judaean account (J) belonging probably to the late tenth
or early ninth century B.C. with a strong preference for the

[1] C. H. Dodd, *The Bible and its Background*, pp. 20–1.
[2] Nehemiah viii, 1–8.

divine name Yahweh (Jehovah), the use of which it ascribes
to the earliest times, and an Ephraimitic account (E), probably
dating from the early years of the eighth century B.C. and
knowing God by the more general name of Elohim. This
combined JE account also contained a creation story, some
ancient folk-lore and the story of a great flood. It was edited
along with the law codes.

Furthermore, it was remembered that the prophets had
taught that Jehovah was the Lord of history, that His mighty
acts had been seen in the story of the past. And so the whole
story of the nation's life from the very earliest days was written
up in a continuous form, using as a groundwork the narrative
portion of the Priestly Code. Existing accounts and stories—
oral and written—were incorporated into it, like old stones in a
new wall, and the whole was made into a fitting setting for the
ancient codes of law.[1]

This compilation in its finished form comprises the first five
books of our Bible—Genesis, Exodus, Leviticus, Numbers and
Deuteronomy. It was called by the Hebrew name *tôrāh*,
which is usually translated as " The Law " but which really
has the wider meaning of instruction. It was a series of books
which instructed those who read them in the ways of God and
His requirements for men. Here, then, was the nucleus of a
sacred Canon of Scripture, and it is to these five books of the
tôrāh that the Jews have always ascribed the highest authority.

We have already seen that the teaching of the great prophets
has come down to us in the books which bear their names. It
was not long before these prophetic works were placed alongside the *tôrāh* as sacred books. Before this was actually done,
however, they were carefully studied and re-edited and with
them were placed the historical books of Joshua, Judges, I and
II, Samuel and I and II Kings. These books, which incorporate extracts from many ancient sources, were written for
the purpose of interpreting the history of Israel in the light
of the prophetic teaching and were therefore included with it
in this second section of the Hebrew Bible which was called
" The Prophets." It is here that Hebrew religion reaches its
zenith and comes most close to the teaching of Jesus Himself.

[1] See Additional Note on Recent Pentateuchal Criticism, pp. 44–6.

The rest of the Old Testament, as Dodd points out, was compiled by a community which already possessed the Law and the Prophets. " The Law provided the framework, and the prophets the inspiration for a rich and vigorous religious life which developed for several centuries. It found expression in a literature of great variety—poetry, drama, stories, proverbs, and so forth."[1]

It was only by a gradual selective process that the limits of the Old Testament Canon were defined, and that process was not complete until the end of the first century after Christ.[2] It resulted finally in a third compilation of books called " The Writings " being added to the existing Scriptures of " The Law " and " The Prophets." There was, however, some disagreement regarding what should be included in this third section and what should be left out. The Hebrew-speaking Jews in Palestine limited the number to the books of Psalms, Proverbs, Job, Song of Solomon, Ruth, Lamentations, Ecclesiastes, Esther, Daniel, Ezra, Nehemiah, I and II Chronicles. But the Greek-speaking Jews outside of Palestine included in this section the books which comprise the Apocrypha. That is why the Apocrypha is, as it were, half in and half out of the Bible. The veneration with which it is regarded and the authority which is ascribed to it differ in different sections of the Christian Church. Speaking generally, however, Christians have felt that the books of the Apocrypha are on a lower spiritual level than are those included in the Hebrew Canon, although they form a valuable historical link between the Old Testament and the New.

The last five centuries B.C. witnessed a series of political upheavals in the ancient world. After the collapse of the Persian Empire the power states of the East fell one by one before the growing might of Alexander the Great until the Macedonian conqueror ruled the entire Mediterranean world. Thus Judaea, from being an outpost of Persia, was incorporated into Alexander's empire, and, in the years of confusion which followed

[1] *Op. cit.*, p. 24. This does not imply that *all* the " writings " were *composed* after the canonization of the Law and the Prophets.

[2] The Rabbinic Synod held at Jamnia, *c.* A.D. 90, is generally regarded as marking the close of the Old Testament Canon, although there is no record of any formal decision.

his death, came under the successive rules of the Ptolemys of Egypt and the Seleucid kings of Asia Minor. With the decline of the Great dynasties came the growth of the Roman Empire, inheriting their culture as well as their lands. Jerusalem, after a brief spell of independence under the Hasmonaean princes, was besieged and sacked by Pompey in 63 B.C. and Judaea became a province of Rome.

As we have seen, the Old Testament in its present form resulted from the literary activity of these five hundred years or so before Christ. Yet, surprisingly enough, " of the events of the period the literature has little to say, in comparison with the copious records of the preceding five centuries."[1] The reason, as Dodd observes, is that although Judaea was inevitably caught up in these world-shattering events, " their impact upon the Jewish mind was not such as to raise great spiritual issues, or to provoke new understanding of the ways of God with men."[2]

The Maccabaean revolt in the second century B.C. is the one notable exception to this rule, as Dodd goes on to point out. It alone, of all the events of the period, has left its mark on the literature of both the Old Testament and the Apocrypha, since " at this one point history was felt to disclose once again something of the compelling spiritual significance which it had possessed for the prophets, though at a lower level of intensity."[3]

The accession of the Seleucid king Antiochus Epiphanes in 175 B.C. saw the beginning of a bitter struggle for this little Jewish state, a struggle which has left an abiding literary monument in the Book of Daniel. Antiochus was like Hitler in many ways. He was a dictator who attempted to force his own pagan culture and religion upon all his subject peoples:

And king Antiochus wrote to his whole kingdom, that all should be one people, and that each should forsake his own laws.[4]

Judaea seems to have been the only really serious obstacle to his policy of Hellenization, but it was here that Antiochus received a decided check.

This policy of cultural uniformity, *Gleichschaltung*, has become familiar in recent years. Antiochus began in much the

---

[1] C. H. Dodd, *The Bible To-day*, p. 58.   [2] *Ibid.*, p. 58.
[3] *Ibid.*, p. 59.   [4] I Maccabees, i, 41–2.

same way as did our modern dictators: he deposed the high priest and appointed a puppet successor. The process of Hellenizing Jerusalem was then put into operation by the opening of a Greek gymnasium. This attempt to subjugate the life as well as the land of Judaea assumed menacing proportions when a little later the capital was attacked, Sabbath observance and circumcision declared illegal, worship and sacrifice forbidden, and the sacred writings destroyed. Still the long-suffering Jews possessed their souls in patience. Then came the final stroke— an altar to Zeus was set up in the Temple courts, and, as if to add insult to injury, there were sacrificed upon it swine! This was the last straw. The people rose to arms and after a long and bitter struggle led by Judas Maccabaeus and his brothers the pagan tyranny was overthrown.

It was during this conflict when the restored Jewish community was fighting to the death for its ancestral religion and way of life that the Book of Daniel was written. It was written to encourage men and women to be loyal to their faith, whatever the cost. Its unknown author recalls some stories of the Babylonian exile—stories of men who faced a cruel death rather than deny their God. " It is the appeal of a true patriot to his people to remain firm and unmoved in the faith in spite of suffering and even martyrdom. The comfort and inspiration which it brought to the Jews in their hour of trial secured it an imperishable place in their literature, and it was handed over to Christianity as a priceless legacy."[1]

This literary monument of the Maccabaean revolt is significant, because " with Daniel begins the apocalyptic literature of Judaism."[2] The name " apocalyptic " is applied to a distinctive class of Jewish literature which flourished from the second century B.C. to the end of the first century A.D. Most of it is extra-biblical, but the Bible contains two notable examples—the Book of Daniel in the Old Testament and the Revelation of St. John the Divine in the New Testament. It is sometimes called the literature of despair;[3] a better name

[1] H. T. Andrews, " Daniel," in *Peake's Commentary on the Bible*, p. 523.
[2] Bousset-Gressman, *Die Religion des Judentums*, p. 12.
[3] Cf. H. T. Andrews, " Apocalyptic Literature," in *Peake's Commentary on the Bible*, p. 431.

would be the literature of crisis. It springs out of times of calamity and peril but its keynote is not despair but hope. The apocalyptist's despair of the present situation only serves to throw into relief his confidence in the divine deliverance.

There is a close relationship between apocalyptic and prophecy. The apocalyptist is the successor of the prophet, whose work he continues in the changed conditions of his own day. Apocalyptic, as R. H. Charles points out is only another word for " revelation," and apocalyptist for " revealer."[1] " Essentially, therefore, prophecy and apocalyptic were identical, but accidentally they differed in respect of their acknowledged or pseudonymous authorship, the subjects they dealt with, and the periods in which they flourished."[2] They are, " in the main, concerned with the same objects, . . . they use, in the main, the same methods, but . . . whereas the scope of prophecy was limited, as regards time and space, that of apocalyptic was as wide as the universe and as unlimited as time."[3] Essentially, therefore, apocalyptic is " the re-adaptation of the ideas and aspirations of earlier days to a new situation,"[4] but in such a way as to show their universal significance.

There are, however, important differences between prophecy and apocalyptic. The first is the pseudonymous character of apocalyptic: " whereas prophecy generally bears the genuine name of its author, apocalyptic is generally pseudonymous."[5] The apocalyptic writings carry the names of outstanding men of the past—Enoch, Abraham, Moses, Isaiah. But this fact must not be over-emphasized. As Charles points out, " pseudonymity is no more a universal characteristic of apocalyptic than it is an essential one."[6] And H. H. Rowley reminds us that " the ancient Hebrews were not greatly interested in authorship, and we do not know the name of the author of a single book of the Old Testament. For even the prophetic books, though they undoubtedly contain genuine oracles of the

---

[1] ἀποκαλύψις=an unveiling, uncovering, revelation. Apocalyptic purports to disclose what is hidden from ordinary eyes.

[2] R. H. Charles, *Religious Development between the Old and the New Testaments*, p. 14, Note 1.

[3] *Ibid.*, p. 32.   [4] H. H. Rowley, *The Relevance of Apocalyptic*, p. 13.

[5] R. H. Charles, *op. cit.*, pp. 35–6.   [6] *Ibid.*, p. 46.

prophets whose names they bear, could not have been compiled by these prophets."[1]

It is generally supposed that at a time when the Law was supreme, belief in inspiration dead, and the prophetic canon closed, the apocalyptists had to attach some great name to their works in order to gain a hearing.[2] Rowley maintains, however, that it is not necessary to postulate deliberate deceit on the part of these writers. The stories of the first part of the Book of Daniel, he suggests, were originally circulated anonymously one by one as " tracts for the times." " When the author came to write his visions, therefore, also carrying a message of hope for the same circles, he wrote them under the guise of Daniel, not in order to deceive his readers, but in order to reveal his identity with the author of the Daniel stories." He concludes therefore that " pseudonymity was thus born of a living process, whose purpose was the precise opposite of deceit. It only became artificial when it was woodenly copied by imitators."[3]

The second way in which apocalyptic differs from prophecy is in its attitude to the great powers of the ancient world. Generally speaking, this was diametrically opposed to the attitude of the prophets. " To the prophets the great world empires were the instrument in God's hand to execute His will on His faithless people, controlled by the God whose will all history unfolded. To the apocalyptists the great world empires were the adversaries of God, proudly resisting His will, which could not triumph through them, but only in their annihilation."[4] But, as Rowley warns us, " we must beware of making the contrast too sharp or too absolute, or of forgetting that in the prophets there are passages with a definite apocalyptic flavour in this respect."[5]

A third differentiating characteristic of apocalyptic is its excessive use of symbol and imagery, in which animals are

[1] H. H. Rowley, *The Relevance of Apocalyptic*, pp. 35–6.

[2] See R. H. Charles, *op. cit.*, pp. 36–45. Cf. *Eschatology*, 2nd ed., pp. 196–206, *A Critical History of a Future Life*, 2nd ed., pp. 196 ff., *Commentary on Daniel*, pp. xxi–xxiii. Cf. A. W. F. Blunt, *The Prophets of Israel*, p. 109.

[3] *Op. cit.*, p. 36. Cf. *Zeitschrift für die alttestamentliche Wissenschaft*, N.F., ix, 1932, pp. 266 ff.

[4] H. H. Rowley, *The Relevance of Apocalyptic*, p. 35.   [5] *Ibid.*, p. 35.

prominent. " The symbolic acts of the prophets are replaced by elaborate zoological and mythological figures."[1] This kind of imagery became stereotyped into a conventional apocalyptic tradition. " The same figures and symbols reappear in writer after writer. The Book of Revelation in the New Testament cannot be understood at all apart from the other literature of apocalyptic."[2]

By the use of such figurative language a hated tyrant like Antiochus was pilloried as the fourth beast who was slain (Daniel vii, 11), or the little horn of the beast with " eyes like the eyes of man, and a mouth speaking great things " (ch. vii, 8, 25), or as a king like Nebuchadnezzar or Belshazzar whose sacrilegious pride brought swift retribution (Daniel i, 2, and iv, cf. I Maccabees i, 21 ff.; Daniel iii, cf. I Maccabees i, 41 ff.; Daniel v). This technique for heartening an oppressed people became familiar in Europe during the second world war. H. H. Rowley recalls a report in *The Times* on April 25th, 1941, of a poem published in a newspaper in German-occupied Paris. Read in the ordinary way, it praised Germany and attacked Britain; but the meaning was reversed if the poem was read as two stanzas by dividing it vertically. Similarly, stories about Nebuchadnezzar, Belshazzar and Darius would superficially be innocuous, " but those for whom they were written would easily be given the clue to their understanding." " It would be no harder to whisper the clue in Palestine than in Paris, and probably no harder to get past the friends of Antiochus than to get past the Paris censorship."[3]

Fourthly, apocalyptic universalizes the prophetic interpretation of contemporary history. It looks to the future for a solution of the problems of the past and the present, and attempts to penetrate beneath the surface to the deeper meaning of events and to see their significance as parts of a coherent whole. " In the Book of Daniel, for example, we see the working out of the divine purpose in a series of stages, diversely pictured,

---

[1] H. W. Robinson, *The Old Testament: Its Making and Meaning*, pp. 125–6. Cf. " The Religion of Israel," in *A Companion to the Bible*, ed. T. V. Manson, p. 308.
[2] H. T. Andrews, " Apocalyptic Literature," in *Peake's Commentary on the Bible*, p. 433.
[3] See H. H. Rowley, *The Relevance of Apocalyptic*, p. 45.

yet always culminating in the final victory of God."[1] "It is *God* who brings about the imminent change in human affairs for which the apocalyptists hope."[2] And this change will be catastrophic, not evolutionary: "Speaking generally, the prophets foretold the future that should arise out of the present, while the apocalyptists foretold the future that should break into the present. . . . They looked for a great divine intervention in history in the immediate future."[3]

The apocalyptists emphasize the divine purpose and plan by foreshortening history: past and present are brought together under the shadow of the impending end. But the cosmic drama has a supra-mundane setting. It is in the apocalyptic literature that we find the first expectations of a new heaven and a new earth and the beginnings of the doctrine of life after death.

> Apocalyptic was a Semitic philosophy of religion and concerned itself with the questions of whence? wherefore? whither? It sketched in outline the history of the universe and of the angelic and human worlds, the origin of evil, its course and ultimate overthrow. It was thus apocalyptic and not prophecy that was the first to grasp the great idea that all history, human, cosmological, and spiritual, is a unity—a unity that follows inevitably as a corollary to the unity of God as enforced by the Old Testament prophets. Thus whereas prophecy deals with the present destinies of individuals and nations, and their future destinies as arising organically out of the present *and on the present earth* without reference to the life of the individual after death, apocalyptic dealt with the past, the present, and the future as linked together and forming one whole, and thereby sought to justify the ways of God to man.[4]

V. The Period of Fulfilment

The final turning-point in this long historical process is the coming of Jesus Christ and the emergence of the Christian Church. Because Jesus stands in the direct line of the Hebrew

---

[1] H. W. Robinson, *Inspiration and Relevation in the Old Testament*, p. 131. Cf. Daniel ii, 36 ff., vii 1–14.   [2] *Ibid.*, p. 146.

[3] H. H. Rowley, *op. cit.*, pp. 34–5. Cf. H. T. Andrews, *op. cit.*, p. 432: "Apocalyptic arose out of prophecy by developing and universalizing the conception of the day of the Lord."

[4] R. H. Charles, *Commentary on Daniel*, p. xxv.

prophets, this last period has all the revolutionary characteristics of the third; but because He was nevertheless no mere prophet, because in Him there was given, in the words of Newman's hymn, nothing less than " God's Presence and His very Self," the Christian era is unique. It is these characteristics of continuity and uniqueness which mark the Christian Church. The continuity is seen in the fact that from its very beginning the Church appropriated the Old Testament Scriptures as its own, thus laying claim to the rich spiritual heritage of the past. The uniqueness is manifested in its own sacred books of the New Testament for which it dares to claim an even greater authority and worth.

The New Testament is really Volume Two in the story of salvation which is the theme of the whole Bible. It tells how, when the decisive hour of history struck, God fulfilled the great promises made to the men of the old covenant by visiting and redeeming His People in His Son Jesus who was the Messiah; and how the new People of God, which is the Christian Church, went forth to spread the news of that salvation in the wider world.[1]

It is this missionary activity which underlies the New Testament, and its earliest books are missionary letters of St. Paul to churches that he had founded in Asia Minor. The first chronologically is I Thessalonians, written at Corinth in A.D. 49–50 (II Thessalonians follows shortly after) to deal with a particular stituation which had arisen in the Thessalonian Church. Trouble stirred up by Judaizers who were attempting to discredit St. Paul prompted the Epistle to the Galatians, which was written either from Antioch in A.D. 51–2 before the Third Missionary Journey or from Ephesus c. A.D. 52 in the course of that journey.[2] The Corinthian correspondence belongs to the latter part of the Apostle's three years' ministry in Ephesus, c. A.D. 55, and Romans was written from Corinth in A.D. 56 just before St. Paul's last journey to Jerusalem. Four epistles, known as the Imprisonment Epistles, date from Paul's two years' open confinement in Rome—Colossians, Ephesians

[1] A. M. Hunter, *Introducing the New Testament*, p. 20.
[2] Some scholars regard Galatians as the earliest of St. Paul's epistles, having been written just prior to the Council of Jerusalem in A.D. 48. See J. A. Allan, *Galatians* (S.C.M.), pp. 23–4, 39–41, for a recent discussion of the date of the epistle.

(probably a circular letter), Philemon (a private letter concerning a runaway slave) and Philippians.

St. Paul, of course, had no idea that this correspondence would later be regarded as Christian Scripture. His letters were copied and exchanged, however, and in course of time came to be read, along with the Old Testament lections, in the worship of the Church. All the Pauline epistles were in circulation before the first Gospel was written.

Behind the written Gospels there lies the preaching of the Gospel. Indeed for over thirty years after the death and resurrection of Christ the memory of His words and deeds was preserved solely through the spoken word.[1] There are two reasons why no written record was produced in these early days. In the first place, the Apostles and other eye-witnesses of the ministry of Jesus were still alive and could give a first-hand account of His words and works. And secondly, there was no thought of making provision for future generations, for the simple reason that it was believed there would be none. The first generation of Christians were convinced that they were living in the last days; they looked for, not just a near but an imminent return of their Lord; at any moment He might appear on the clouds of heaven to usher in the consummation of the age.

Why, then, were the Gospels written at all? There were several factors that combined to bring about their production. First, as the years passed and the Lord did not appear, it became increasingly evident that the Second Advent might be delayed for some considerable time. Secondly, as time went on fewer eye-witnesses of Christ's ministry were left to tell the story. Soon, if the Advent were still delayed, there would be none. The need for some written record thus became increasingly apparent. Thirdly, a written account was becoming necessary for the instruction of new converts to the faith. As the result of all this there appeared, shortly after the middle of the first century A.D., two epoch-making documents. One was a collection of the sayings of Jesus known to scholars as Q—the initial letter of the German *Quelle*, meaning source.[2] The

[1] See further below, Chapter VII, pp. 241 ff.

[2] Armitage Robinson claimed that he had invented the symbol Q—used simply as the next letter to P=Petrine source of Mark.

other was a papyrus roll which circulated in Rome not long
after the great fire in Nero's reign and bore the title, " The
Good News of Jesus Christ." The first of these books, Q, has
not survived; we know of it only because it formed a main
source of the first and third Gospels. The second book, however, was our Gospel according to St. Mark, which is based,
according to the testimony of a second-century Church Father
named Papias, on the preaching of St. Peter and can be
dated fairly precisely at A.D. 65.

The authors of Matthew and Luke—after the manner of
ancient historians in pre-copyright days—used St. Mark's
Gospel as a main source for their own work. They also incorporated the teaching material contained in Q. Besides these,
however, each drew on a special source of his own—the author
of Matthew reproducing the tradition of the Jerusalem Church
and Luke the tradition of Caesarea. The first Gospel is really
an anonymous work but is linked with the name of the Apostle
Matthew probably because it incorporates what Papias calls the
Logia compiled in Hebrew, or Aramaic, by Matthew. We
cannot be certain what the *Logia* was—perhaps a collection of
Old Testament " proof-texts," but quite possibly the document
Q. The third Gospel is clearly the work of St. Paul's doctor
friend, Luke, and is the first volume of a History of Christianity;
the second volume is the Book of Acts. St. Luke's Gospel is to
be dated at about A.D. 80 and Matthew possibly some five years
later. The Gospel of John, emanating from Ephesus, belongs
to the closing years of the first century and is intended to
supplement and interpret the other three.[1]

The remaining books of the New Testament, with the possible exception of II and III John, II Peter (of doubtful authenticity) and the Pastoral Epistles (I and II Timothy and Titus),
all belong to the first century. The Pastoral Epistles, while containing genuine Pauline fragments, have been compiled by
another hand and may possibly belong in their present form to
a later time.[2]

---

[1] See Additional Note on Recent Synoptic Criticism, pp. 46–8.
[2] So P. N. Harrison, *The Problem of the Pastoral Epistles*. C. H. Dodd,
however, believes that Ignatius knew them, which would make it unlikely
that they are later than A.D. 100.

It will be seen from what has been said that just as the formative period of Hebrew religion in the time of Moses has left no direct literary remains, so too there is nothing in the New Testament that comes to us directly from the lifetime of Christ Himself. The story of His life and activity, like that of the life and times of Moses, was only written down at a later date. But the interval of time which elapsed between the death of Christ and the account of His ministry in the earliest Gospel, St. Mark, is under forty years,[1] as compared with some three or four hundred years in the case of Moses. There are therefore, as Dodd has indicated, points of analogy between the Gospels, which form the core of the New Testament, and the *tôrāh*, which was the nucleus of the Old. Moreover, Christianity is rooted in history; it is based on concrete historical events in which it sees a unique significance—the birth, life, death and resurrection of Jesus of Nazareth. The Gospels, therefore, in which these unique events are recorded have a unique authority for Christians.

Furthermore, just as there are points of analogy between the Gospels in the New Testament and the *tôrāh* in the Old, so too there are certain similarities between the Epistles of the New Testament and the Prophets of the Old. Both come down to us directly from the people concerned and hence both were written earlier than the central nucleus of their respective Canons. Also, in the words of Dodd, " very early the writings of Paul and of other Christian teachers were added to the Gospels, much as the prophets were added to the Law, and with them went the Acts of the Apostles, much as the historical books of the Old Testament went with the Prophets."[2]

The limits of the New Testament Canon, like that of the Old, were only gradually defined, and there were a number of doubtful books which remained for long on the border-line. Some of these, such as Revelation and II Peter, were eventually included in the Canon; others, like the Shepherd of Hermas and the Epistle of Clement, were shut out. But the process of fixing the limits was much quicker than was the case with the

---

[1] See Chapter VII, pp. 241 ff. for a discussion of the bearing of this " oral period " upon the question of the reliability of the Gospels.

[2] *The Bible and its Background*, p. 26.

Old Testament, and by the end of the second century A.D. it was almost complete. The reason for this is to be found in certain happenings in the second-century world.

G. K. Chesterton in his fascinating *Autobiography* tells of a clergyman who " had a love of nosing out the headquarters of incredible or insane sects; and wrote an amusing record of them called Byways of Belief."[1] It was because there sprang up in the second century a crop of " incredible or insane sects "—the bewildering sects of Gnosticism[2]—which all claimed the name of Christian and attempted to secure for their own literature an equal authority with the writings of St. Mark and St. Paul that the Church was compelled to define the limits of its Scriptures and surround itself with the threefold bulwark of Creed, Canon and Episcopate. Thus the Canon of Holy Scripture arose as a protection from " Byways of Belief."

We may conclude this preliminary enquiry into the nature of the Bible by defining it as being essentially the record and interpretation of a divinely ordered series of events in the history of Israel which finds its climax and consummation in Jesus Christ and His Church. Since, therefore, these historic events constitute the basis of the Christian faith, the Bible which records and interprets them is regarded as authoritative by all sections of the Christian Church. Its authority, however, has been variously interpreted, so it is to the interpretation of the Bible that we now turn.

ADDITIONAL NOTE

RECENT PENTATEUCHAL CRITICISM

The Graf-Wellhausen documentary hypothesis, which was almost universally held by Old Testament scholars in the first two decades of this century, presupposes the existence of four chronologically successive documents, J, E, D (Deuteronomy) and P (the Priestly Code), as the literary sources into which the Pentateuch may be analysed. It has generally been assumed that these

---

[1] *Autobiography*, p. 160.
[2] It must in fairness be admitted that some Gnostic leaders like Valentinus and Basilides were serious thinkers.

documents, arranged in this order, epitomize the history of Old Testament religion from the Exodus to the post-exilic period and thus provide evidence for the evolution of Old Testament ideas and institutions.

Since 1920, however, this theory has been repeatedly attacked from all sides, and in recent years Scandinavian scholars have challenged its entire documentary basis. Ivan Engnell, in particular, maintains that instead of sources and " redactors " we have to reckon with units of oral tradition, complexes of tradition and collections of tradition.[1] He finds in the Pentateuch two main independent collections of tradition material: " The first of these comprises Genesis–Numbers and can, with a certain accommodation to the usual terminology, be called the ' P-work,' not because it contains a ' document ' ' P,' but because it received its final shape and therewith its ideological tendency in *a traditionist-circle* which, with certain modifications, shows many of the features which are ascribed by literary-critical research to the ' document P ' or the ' redactor P.' " This had no connection with " the second great collection, ' *the Deuteronomic history-work*,' comprising Deuteronomy –II Kings, which in its definitive shape was formed in another circle of tradition, which may be called the ' D-circle.' " While conceding the original existence of the strata of tradition represented by J and E, Engnell maintains that " they were already at the stage of oral tradition so woven together that it is now an impossible task to resolve them."[2]

Outside Scandinavia the documentary hypothesis, in some form, still holds the field; but the original Graf-Wellhausen theory is undergoing considerable modification. In the first place, there has been in recent years an increasing recognition of the influence of cultic practices in the formation of the Pentateuch.[3] Secondly, and closely related to this, is the emphasis now placed on the role of oral tradition, not only in the pre-literary stage, but also in its continuing influence upon the written documents.[4] It follows, in

[1] Art. " Gamla Testamentet," § 6, *Svenskt Bibliskt Uppslagsverk*, i, col. 659.

[2] See *Gamla Testamentet. En traditionshistorisk inledning*, i, pp. 209 ff. Quoted by C. R. North, " Pentateuchal Criticism," in *The Old Testament and Modern Study*, ed. H. H. Rowley, pp. 67–8. North's essay, to which I am deeply indebted, is an admirable and comprehensive survey of the period since 1920.

[3] See R. Brinker, *The Influence of Sanctuaries in Early Israel*; J. Pedersen, *Israel: its Life and Culture*, III–IV, pp. 726–8; A. Weiser, *Einleitung in das Alte Testament*, pp. 67 ff.

[4] See Gunkel, *Genesis*; Gressman, *Mose und seine Zeit*; Weiser, *op. cit.*, pp. 67 ff.

the third place, that J and E must be regarded as " collectors " of fragments of oral tradition rather than independent " authors "; although each—and more especially J—has left his own stamp on the distinctive form which he has given to the tradition.[1] Fourthly, there is the recognition, for which we are largely indebted to Pedersen, that both pre-exilic and post-exilic material are to be found in all our sources.[2] And finally, Robertson has drawn attention to the fact that many of the differences between J, E and P may be due to divergent local usage and do not necessarily imply pre-exilic and post-exilic editing.[3]

The present position is well summarized by C. R. North: " As matters now stand, the history of any one of the ' documents ' may well be as complicated as the history of the whole Pentateuch was conceived to be only thirty years ago. We can no longer use the figure of a single date-line, but must think rather of a dimensional area, and plot the ages of ideas and institutions upon it with as much precision as we can."[4]

ADDITIONAL NOTE

Recent Synoptic Criticism

The generally held two-document hypothesis, according to which two written documents—Mark and Q—are the primary synoptic sources, was elaborated by B. H. Streeter into a four-document theory. Streeter maintained that the writers of the first and third Gospels, in addition to using Mark and Q, had each a special *written* source—documents which he named M and L respectively.[5] This view does not now command general assent and the special sources of Matthew and Luke are regarded as cycles of oral tradition upon which the Gospel writers drew.

[1] See P. Volz and W. Rudolph, *Der Elohist als Erzähler: Ein Irrweg der Pentateuchkritik?*, Beihefte zur *Zeitschrift für die alttestamentliche Wissenschaft*, vol. lxiii, p. 22; Cf. R. H. Pfeiffer, *Introduction to the Old Testament*, pp. 142 ff., and C. R. North, *The Old Testament Interpretation of History*, pp. 24 ff.

[2] See J. Pedersen, " Die Auffassung vom Alten Testament," *Zeitschrift für die alttestamentliche Wissenschaft*, vol. xlix pp. 161–81; *Israel: its Life and Culture*, III–IV; Cf. A. Bentzen, *Introduction to the Old Testament*, ii, pp. 62 ff.

[3] See E. Robertson, *The Old Testament Problem with two other Essays*.

[4] " Pentateuchal Criticism," in *The Old Testament and Modern Study*, ed. H. H. Rowley, p. 81.   [5] See B. H. Streeter, *The Four Gospels*.

Form-Criticism has distinguished within the Gospels certain " forms " into which oral tradition crystallized in the period before any written documents appeared.[1] (1) The " Passion Narrative " was the earliest of these to take shape. (2) " Pronouncement-Stories " gave a concise account of incidents leading up to a striking saying or action of Jesus. (3) More free and circumstantial reminiscences circulated as " Tales." (4) Parables, isolated sayings and groups of sayings of Jesus were specially treasured. The crucial question is: On what principle did St. Mark arrange the material that came into his possession? Earlier form-critics like Bultmann and Dibelius maintained that the basis of Mark's order was not historical but theological and topical.

In 1932, however, C. H. Dodd propounded the view that along with these independent formulations of oral tradition (*pericopae*) the Church preserved an outline of the ministry of Jesus. This outline, says Dodd, provided St. Mark with an historical framework, though not a complete one, into which he fitted his *pericopae* and groups of *pericopae* according to their respective indications of time and place. Only where there were no such indications does the evangelist seem to have been guided by topical considerations.[2]

This view, implying as it does the substantial historical accuracy of St. Mark's order, has won general acceptance among English New Testament scholars during the last twenty years and is still widely held. But it is now being subjected to searching criticism by D. E. Nineham[3] and, more especially, by A. M. Farrer, who challenges the assumption that St. Mark sets out to give an historical order of events at all. Mark's order, he is convinced, is governed by typological rather than historical considerations: there is a " master symbolism unifying the narrative basis of the Gospel."[4]

Farrer further maintains that we can dispense with the sayings-document Q; the Q hypothesis is made superfluous by his argument that St. Luke knew and used St. Matthew's Gospel as well as St. Mark's. " The literary history of the Gospels," he predicts, " will turn out to be a simpler matter than we had supposed. St. Matthew will be seen to be an amplified version of St. Mark, based on a

[1] See Vincent Taylor, *The Formation of the Gospel Tradition*; Basil Redlich, *Form Criticism*.

[2] See " The Framework of the Gospel Narrative," in *Expository Times*, June 1932. This article has been republished with other essays in C. H. Dodd's book *New Testament Studies* (Manchester University Press).

[3] " The Order of Events in St. Mark's Gospel—an examination of Dr. Dodd's Hypothesis," in *Studies in the Gospels*, ed. D. E. Nineham (Blackwell).

[4] See *A Study in St. Mark* (1951) and *St. Matthew and St. Mark* (1955).

decade of habitual preaching, and incorporating oral material, but presupposing no other literary source beside St. Mark himself. St. Luke, in turn, will be found to presuppose St. Matthew and St. Mark, and St. John to presuppose the three others."[1]

The importance of this recent work is that it raises once again the vital questions: What is the nature and purpose of a Gospel? What is the relationship of the historical, theological, typological and didactic elements within it? Whether or not Farrer's answers are the right ones is another matter. Along with Dodd, Manson and Vincent Taylor, the writer remains unconvinced.

But even if it should be shown that St. Mark's arrangement is typological rather than historical, his witness to the Jesus of history remains. " If," as Nineham observes, " it could be shown that Jesus Christ was not an historical figure, Councils and their Creeds would avail nothing. And not only must we believe that Jesus Christ was an historical figure, we must be able to believe that his life and ministry were such that what is said of them in the Gospels —and indeed in the rest of the New Testament—is, broadly speaking, ' fair comment ' upon them." But, as he goes on to say, " it is one thing to demand that the life on which our religion is based was a genuinely historical life; it is another thing to demand that we should be able to derive from the Gospels an outline account of that life satisfactory to our modern historical standards, methods and curiosity."[2]

---

[1] " On Dispensing with Q," in *Studies in the Gospels*, ed. D. E. Nineham, p. 85.

[2] " The Gospels and the Life of Jesus," in *Theology*, lix, No. 429, March 1956, p. 101.

CHAPTER II

THE INTERPRETATION OF THE BIBLE[1]

I. THE PROBLEM OF THE OLD TESTAMENT

THE Old Testament was the first Christian Bible. It was not merely a part of the sacred Canon as it is today; it was the only Bible the early Church had. The Scriptures which were read when the first Christians assembled to break bread were the Old Testament Scriptures. The texts from which the apostolic sermons were preached were Old Testament texts. And when in course of time the New Testament Canon took shape, it did not displace or supersede the Old Testament Scriptures but was added as an appendix to them.

The way in which the early Church regarded the Old Testament was determined by the attitude of Christ Himself. Not only did Jesus as a Jew draw His spiritual nourishment from the Old Testament; He conceived His ministry and death in terms of it. He saw Himself as its " fulfilment " in the largest possible sense of that word. As C. H. Dodd observes, " The New Testament itself avers that it was Jesus Christ Himself who first directed the minds of His followers to certain parts of the scriptures as those in which they might find illumination upon the meaning of His mission and destiny."[2]

The earliest Gospel, St. Mark, records His reply to the Temple Guard on the night of His arrest in Gethsemane thus: " Are ye come out, as against a thief, with swords and with

[1] Much of the substance of this chapter appears in the Inaugural Lecture, " Recent Trends in Biblical Studies," which I delivered before the United Faculty of Theology at St. Andrew's College in the University of Sydney in 1949, and which was published in *The Scottish Journal of Theology*, Vol. IV, No. 3, 1951.

See further E. C. Blackman, *Biblical Interpretation* (1957), also G. W. H. Lampe and K. J. Woollcombe, *Essays on Typology* (Studies in Biblical Theology, No: 22, 1957).   [2] *According to the Scriptures*, p. 110.

49

staves to take me? I was daily with you in the temple teaching, and ye took me not: but the scriptures must be fulfilled."[1] St. Matthew's report of the same event contains the words: " Thinkest thou that I cannot now pray to my Father, and he shall presently give me more than twelve legions of angels? But how then shall the scriptures be fulfilled, that thus it must be? "[2] St. Luke gives us a glimpse of Jesus meditating upon His approaching death in terms of Isaiah liii: " For I say unto you, that this that is written must yet be accomplished in me, And he was reckoned among the transgressors: for the things concerning me have an end."[3] And this same Gospel in narrating the walk to Emmaus says of the Risen Christ: " And beginning at Moses and all the prophets, he expounded unto them in all the scriptures the things concerning himself. . . . And he said unto them, These are the words which I spake unto you, while I was yet with you, that all things must be fulfilled, which were written in the law of Moses, and in the prophets, and in the psalms, concerning me."[4] All this is summed up in the Johannine saying: " Search the scriptures; for in them ye think ye have eternal life: and they are they which testify of me."[5]

This was the starting-point of the apostolic preaching. St. Paul at the synagogue of Thessalonica, " as his manner was, went in unto them, and three sabbath days reasoned with them out of the scriptures; opening and alleging that Christ must needs have suffered, and risen again from the dead; and that this Jesus, whom I preach unto you, is Christ [i.e. the Messiah]."[6] Apollos at Ephesus " mightily convinced the Jews . . . showing by the scriptures that Jesus was Christ."[7]

The line of reasoning followed is clearly seen in the account of St. Paul's sermon in the synagogue at Antioch in Pisidia (Acts xiii, 16–41). He begins by citing the mighty acts of God which have been manifest in the history of Israel—the choosing of Abraham, Isaac and Jacob, the deliverance from Egypt, the

---

[1] Mark xiv, 48–9.   [2] Matt. xxvi, 53–4.
[3] Luke xxii, 37; cf. Isaiah liii, 12.   [4] Luke xxiv, 27, 44.
[5] John v, 39. C. H. Dodd argues that ἐραυνᾶτε should be taken, not as imperative, but as indicative: " You search the scriptures, in which you suppose you have life: it is they that testify about me." See *The Interpretation of the Fourth Gospel*, pp. 329-39, Note 1.
[6] Acts xvii, 1–3.   [7] Acts xviii, 28.

settlement in Canaan, the accession of David, their greatest king. And he claims that in the coming of Jesus this long chain of mighty acts is completed and consummated, the promise of the past is fulfilled. It is of David's seed that God, according to His promise, has raised unto Israel a Saviour, Jesus.

But the Apostle also claims that in the ministry and death and resurrection of Jesus of Nazareth the deepest insights of the Hebrew Scriptures were fulfilled. It was because the rulers knew not the voices of the prophets which were read every Sabbath day that they fulfilled them in condemning Him. And only in the triumph of the Risen Christ over death and the grave does the picture given in the Sixteenth Psalm find its fulfilment: " Thou shalt not suffer thine Holy One to see corruption." Similarly, in the conversation of Philip with the Ethiopian eunuch the starting-point is an Old Testament passage, Isaiah liii. And here too it is as the fulfilment of one of the deepest insights of the Old Testament that Christ is presented.[1] In Him alone does the portrait of the Suffering Servant which the prophet draws come to life: beginning at the same scripture, Philip preaches unto him Jesus.

The books of the New Testament, as H. J. Carpenter points out, " were written to confirm and interpret the faith in Jesus Christ which was already held and taught in the Church. They were not, as writings, the primary source of that faith at the time when they were written, or, indeed, for some time after that. The faith was handed on by a living tradition, from teacher to teacher and from teacher to convert. The words of the Lord and the teaching of the Apostles were the final authority, but the earliest Christians believed that they possessed those words and that teaching sufficiently without a written record, so that even after the Christian documents, the Gospels and Epistles, had been written and had begun to be disseminated in the Church, it was not felt necessary to make a direct appeal to their written word in the way in which appeal was certainly made to the Old Testament scriptures."[2] It was not until the second century, when there were

[1] Acts viii, 26–35.
[2] " The Bible in the Early Church," in *The Interpretation of the Bible* (ed. C. W. Dugmore), p. 5.

no longer among them any eye-witnesses of the ministry of Christ and the Church had to meet the challenge of a Graeco-Oriental syncretism in the mystery religions and Gnostic cults, that the Gospels and apostolic writings became the touchstone of the faith, the primary authority for the teaching of Christ and His Apostles to which an appeal could be made.

The main problem of interpretation in the second and third centuries concerned the Old Testament and its relationship to the New.[1] For Jewish Christians there was no difficulty here, but for Gentile converts from the Graeco-Roman world the thought-forms of the Old Testament and its sub-Christian morality were baffling and even repulsive. The first attempt to resolve the difficulty theologically was made in the middle of the second century by the Gnostic heretic Marcion. Marcion, a native of Sinope on the shores of the Black Sea, who taught in Rome about A.D. 140, had an acute critical mind and he was quick to perceive the difference in moral tone between the Old Testament and the New. This he attributed to the fact that the God of the Old Testament was not the God of the New; He was an inferior limited God who was just rather than good. This God, Jehovah, had created the world and was responsible for its imperfections. But the supreme God, who was remote and ineffable, had been moved with compassion by the miserable state of men, so He sent His Son, Christ, to deliver them from the tyranny of Jehovah.[2]

Hence Marcion rejected the Old Testament *in toto*. So close, however, is the relationship between the two Testaments that he soon discovered that his repudiation of the Old necessitated an alteration of the New; and a mutilated Gospel of St. Luke together with ten expurgated Epistles of St. Paul was all that he found he could retain. The second-century Church, however, refused to surrender the unity of the Old and New Testaments and met Marcion's assertion by appealing to the New Testament's own presupposition of the Old Testament teaching and background.

Another answer to the problem of the Old Testament was that given by the allegorical view. This was a serious attempt to face

---

[1] This question is fully discussed in Chapter VI.
[2] See E. C. Blackman, *Marcion and his Influence*.

the difficulty and reach a synthesis, and the method used was that of allegory; the Old Testament was made to yield a hidden meaning which was in true harmony with the New. The animals forbidden for food as unclean, for instance, were symbolic of forbidden vices. By this means the awkward places were surmounted and the reader delivered from bondage to the mere letter.

The outstanding early exponent of this allegorical view was Origen,[1] the great Alexandrian theologian of the third century, who maintained that all Scripture has a threefold meaning: " The simple man," he says, " may be edified by the ' flesh ' as it were of the Scriptures, for so we name the obvious sense; while he who has ascended a certain way may be edified by the ' soul ' as it were; the perfect man . . . may receive edification from the spiritual law, which has a shadow of good things to come. For as man consists of body and soul and spirit, so in the same way does Scripture."[2] In fact, as Williston Walker comments, " this allegorical system enabled Origen to read practically what he wished into the Scriptures."[3]

The allegorical view, however, and the idea of hidden meanings in the Bible persist, as we shall see, into the Middle Ages. " We shall find that medieval scholarship will reflect Origen's method, attitude and limitations."[4]

II. THE PRE-CRITICAL PERIOD

It is frequently asserted that the pre-critical view of the Bible from the second century to the eighteenth was essentially literalist, the Scriptures being regarded as verbally dictated to the writers by the Holy Spirit and therefore inerrant. That, however, is a generalization which needs qualification. In the Middle Ages, as represented by the twelfth and thirteenth centuries, for instance, the emphasis of a preaching friar was on

---

[1] Origen was greatly influenced by the first-century Alexandrian Jew, Philo, who has been called ' the Cicero ' of allegory: " The thoroughgoing use of Philonic allegory implied an equally thorough borrowing of the Philonic rules for allegorical interpretation."—Beryl Smalley, *The Study of the Bible in the Middle Ages* (Second ed. 1952), p. 8.

[2] *De Principiis*, iv, 1, 11.   [3] *A History of the Christian Church*, p. 81.

[4] Beryl Smalley, *op. cit.*, p. 13.

the spiritual and moral meaning of Scripture for the hearers
rather than on any question of the verbal inspiration and inerrancy of the text. And in the fourteenth century, as B. L.
Manning observes, " no rigid theory of verbal inspiration
deterred the medieval narrator from adding many suggestive
details to the bare Bible stories."[1] Indeed the literal meaning
was often almost completely obscured by the current method of
interpretation, based as it was on the idea of a multiple sense
of Scripture.

All Scripture, it was said, had four distinct meanings—first,
the literal or historical; second, the allegorical; third, the
anagogical or mystical; and fourth, the tropological or moral.
Thus, according to Stephen Langton, Jerusalem can mean four
different things. Its literal or historical meaning is, of course, the
city on Mount Zion; but allegorically it stands for the Church
Militant, in an anagogical or mystical sense it means the Church
Triumphant, and its tropological or moral meaning is the faithful soul. As Beryl Smalley aptly remarks, " Langton has perfected the art of making the Scriptures say exactly what he
pleases."[2] The literal interpretation was the least esteemed for
purposes of edification. Having no spiritual nourishment in
itself, it was compared by St. Bernard to the outside crust of
the bread, indigestible and dry. " The Books of Moses," says
Master Rypon of Durham, " are rude when considered
historically, nevertheless within they are full of moral senses and
doctrines, useful alike to the preacher and to his audience."[3]

The whole approach to the Bible was thus theological rather
than literal, although the literal sense was never entirely
neglected. " How do you read Scripture without reading the
letter? " asks Hugh of St. Victor. " If the letter is removed what
is left of Scripture? "[4] And, as Conrad Pepler observes, " a
happy phrase of St. Anselm's may serve as a signpost to the
care and energy expended on the letter of Scripture during
these centuries: ' If a man does not bring his own common
sense to bear upon Scripture, the more subtle, the madder, he

[1] *The People's Faith in the Time of Wyclif*, p. 24.
[2] *The Study of the Bible in the Middle Ages* (Second ed. 1952), p. 260.
[3] See G. R. Owst, *Literature and Pulpit in Medieval England*, pp. 58–60.
[4] *De Scripturis et Scriptoribus Sacris*, c. 5.

is.' Common sense demands that the historical meaning of the word written down in the Bible should be first understood, and for that the original language in which it was written should be consulted." And he goes on to remind us that in the thirteenth century " the zeal for an authoritative text and for its direct meaning is here as intense as at any time in the history of Christianity."[1] Clearly, as Beryl Smalley points out, " the twelfth-century masters were feeling dissatisfied. They do not question the system of the fourfold exposition; but they struggle to reduce it to order, to remove its ambiguities."[2]

It is St. Thomas Aquinas who, " perfecting the tentative efforts of his predecessors,"[3] insists upon the importance of the letter in any interpretation of Scripture: " Thus in Holy Writ no confusion results, for all the senses are founded on one —the literal—from which alone can any argument be drawn, and not from those intended in allegory."[4] As before, however, the emphasis is theological rather than literalistic: " The literal sense of Scripture . . . is what the human author expressed by his words; the spiritual senses are what the divine author expressed by the events which the human author related."[5] The value of the literal sense is therefore its use as a basis for allegorical, mystical and moral interpretation by which the teaching of the Church is presented through the medium of the Bible.

The medieval *schema* of biblical interpretation, to which C. H. Dodd has called attention, is the illustration *par excellence* of this theological emphasis in the study of the Bible. The Old Testament is regarded as being essentially prophecy and the New Testament fulfilment; the " type " is fulfilled in the " antitype." " Not only the words of the prophets, but also the actions that make up Old Testament history, foreshadow the action as well as the thought of the New Testament " and " the central and decisive place is held by that which is central in the New Testament: the proclamation of the coming of Christ —His birth, life, death and resurrection—as the controlling fact

---

[1] " The Faith of the Middle Ages," in *The Interpretation of the Bible* (ed. C. W. Dugmore), pp. 38–9.
[2] *The Study of the Bible in the Middle Ages* (Second ed., 1952), p. 234.
[3] *Ibid.*, p. 368.   [4] *Summa Theologica*, 1a, q. i, art. 10, reply obj. 1.
[5] Beryl Smalley, *op. cit.*, p. 300.

of all history, whether before or after, from which the meaning of it all is to be understood."

This *schema* provided a framework for Christian thought and devotion all through the Middle Ages. It shaped the pattern of the Church's services for the Christian Year, with their lessons from the Old and New Testaments, and their liturgical Gospels and Epistles. It is illustrated in the religious art of the period, notably in the stained glass which once adorned the windows of our parish churches. Where the original arrangement of glass can still be seen complete (as, for example, at Fairford in the Cotswolds), you walk up the nave with prophets on your left, uttering their predictions of things to come, and apostles and evangelists on your right, announcing the fulfilment. You thus approach the east end of the church, where the whole Gospel drama is illustrated scene by scene, from the Annunciation of the birth of Christ to His Ascension. Then you turn about, to be confronted by the great west window, with its flaming picture of Doomsday.[1]

Aquinas' insistence on the importance of the literal sense of Scripture was not always remembered in the allegorical extravagances of the later Middle Ages, but it was re-emphasized by the Reformers of the sixteenth century. Himself a professor of New Testament in the University of Wittenberg, Luther's sole criterion for reformation was Scripture. Refusing to renounce his books until they were proved wrong by arguments from Scripture, it is for the authority of Holy Scripture as against human traditions that he stands. He also opposes the authority of Scripture to the " spirituals " of his time who claim an inner light, an inward illumination of the Holy Spirit apart from the written Word. But Luther held no theory of verbal inspiration; he did not need such to give the Scriptures authority for him; the authority of the Word was self-evident. For him " the greatest argument in favour of the authority of the Bible is the fact that the preaching of biblical truth creates faith in men's hearts. Sinful and fallen man, the enemy of God, recognizes sin and is saved by faith, his mind is set at rest, and he becomes once more God's dear child. This is the stupendous miracle which proves the authority of the Bible."[2]

[1] C. H. Dodd, *The Bible To-day*, pp. 19–20.
[2] H. H. Kramm, *The Theology of Martin Luther*, p. 116.

Along with the other leading Reformers, Luther distinguished between the Word of God and the Scriptures which contained it:[1] the Bible was the crib in which Christ is laid. His whole attitude towards Scripture was therefore critical and discriminating, as witness his preference for the Psalms in the Old Testament and St. John's Gospel, the Pauline Epistles and I Peter in the New. James he dismisses as an epistle of straw.[2] Of the Old Testament prophets he admits that while " they guided the people in their day by the right explanation and understanding of God's Word," they " occasionally proclaimed something concerning kings and worldly princes . . . in which they often erred."[3] Albert Peel, therefore, rightly concludes that Luther's attitude " is far from the conception of all scripture as of equal worth and all infallible," and he points out that " here the leading protestants are all in line with Luther."

> That the Scriptures are all of equal worth, and inerrant, are propositions to which they do not assent; what they constantly assert is that their authority lies in their ability to produce in the believer the conviction that they declare the love of God and His power to save.[4]

For Calvin the final authority was the word of Scripture authenticated in the heart by the *testimonium Spiritus Sancti internum*.[5] But although he treats the Bible as an organic whole, he does not ignore differences due to progress in revelation: " When God speaks to babes," he says, " He babbles." You

---

[1] See further below, Chapter VIII, section iii.

[2] H. H. Kramm points out that Luther only accepted as fully canonical those books of the Bible whose authority was undisputed in the Early Church. See *The Theology of Martin Luther*, pp. 111 ff.

[3] *Weimar Ausgabe*, 17, 11, 39, 27.

[4] " The Bible and the People: Protestant Views of the Authority of the Bible," in *The Interpretation of the Bible* (ed. Dugmore), pp. 68–9. Cf. Dorner, *History of Protestant Theology*, i, p. 231: " It is clear that for Luther the great original certainty which attests all other truths, as it is not the authority of the Church, so also it is not the authority of the canon of the Holy Scripture handed down by the Church. It is rather the subject-matter of the Word of God, which, however different may be its forms of expression, is able to attest itself to the hearts of men as the Word of God by itself and its divine power."

[5] *Institutes*, I, vii, 4 and 5. See J. S. Whale, *The Protestant Tradition*, pp. 129-136.

will find no doctrine of mechanical and literal inspiration in
Calvin. His declaration concerning the Scriptures that " the
full authority which they ought to possess with the faithful is
not recognized, unless they are believed to have come from
heaven, as directly as if God had been heard giving utterance
to them "[1] does not warrant Alan Richardson's assertion that
" Calvin believed that ultimately the authority of the Bible was
based upon the fact that it was dictated *verbatim* by God
Himself to the human writers."[2] Such a conclusion is con-
tradicted by Calvin's own use of Scripture, as witness his
doubts regarding the authenticity of James, II Peter and Jude,
and his candid comment on Matthew xxvii, 9: " How the
name of Jeremiah crept in, I confess that I do not know, nor
do I give myself much trouble to enquire.[3] The passage itself
plainly shows that the name of Jeremiah has been put down by
mistake, instead of Zechariah (xi, 13), for in Jeremiah we find
nothing of this sort, nor anything that even approaches to
it."[4] This, and other similar comments, must be placed alongside passages which seem to indicate a belief in verbal inspiration and inerrancy. " In making our judgment about Calvin's
doctrine of Scripture," says R. S. Wallace, " we must . . . give
full weight to his frequent assertion that, even though there is
much that is divine and heavenly about the book, its form at

---

[1] *Institutes*, I, vii, 1.
[2] *Christian Apologetics*, pp. 211–12. Cf. E. Doumergue, *Jean Calvin*, IV,
p. 73: " Calvin did not teach the theory of dictation . . . in the sense of
an inspiration verbal and literal."   [3] *nec anxie laboro*.
[4] *Commentary on Matthew*, xxvii, 9. Cf. Calvin's comment on Acts vii, 16:
" Stephen saith, that the patriarchs were carried into the land of Canaan
after they were dead. But Moses maketh mention only of the bones of
Joseph (Genesis l, 13). And Joshua xxiv (32) it is reported, that the bones
of Joseph were buried without making any mention of the rest. . . . I can
affirm nothing concerning this matter for a certainty, save only that this is
either a speech wherein is *synecdoche*, or else that Luke rehearseth this not
so much out of Moses, as according to the old fame. . . . And whereas he
saith afterward, they were laid in the sepulchre which Abraham had bought
of the sons of Hemor, it is manifest that there is a fault [mistake] in the
word Abraham. For Abraham had bought a double cave of Ephron the
Hittite (Genesis xxiii, 9) to bury his wife Sarah in; but Joseph was buried
in another place, to wit, in the field which his father Jacob had bought of
the sons of Hemor for an hundred lambs. Wherefore this place must be
amended."

times is of the earth, very earthy." And he concludes, " It seems . . . quite impossible that Calvin, if assailed on this point, would give sanction to any doctrine of inspiration that presupposed a different relation between the divine and human elements than the sacramental relation which is so important a feature in Calvin's theology."[1]

Neither Luther nor Calvin, as C. H. Dodd points out, had any intention of abandoning the ancient framework within which the Bible was to be understood. " They themselves were well-instructed in the traditional *schema*, and it controlled the biblical theology of Calvin, for example, not less than that of medieval theologians."[2] It is with the substance and sense of Scripture, in which the sovereign grace of God is supremely revealed, that Calvin is concerned. Thus, in the words of R. H. Lightfoot, " the leading Reformers had assigned to the Scriptures the supreme place indeed, but as a storehouse of divinely communicated knowledge of doctrine and conduct; they had not regarded the Bible as an infallible authority."[3]

The scholarly and independent attitude of the Reformers, however, was not maintained by their followers and successors, and in the seventeenth and eighteenth centuries there was a hardening of the Protestant view of Scripture. " The Puritan held that the Bible was the revealed Word of God from beginning to end, authoritative not only for doctrine but for every aspect of ecclesiastical and human life, an absolute code in everything that it dealt with. It was the expression of the will of God in matters theological, moral, sartorial, military, economic and judicial. Hence it was necessary not only to look for general laws but for detailed guidance in its pages."[4] The Bible thus came to be viewed as inerrant, a collection of texts to which men could appeal as an infallible guide, and in

---

[1] *Calvin's Doctrine of the Word and Sacrament*, pp. 113-14. See also J. K. S. Reid, *The Authority of Scripture*, pp. 29-55, for a penetrating and lucid enquiry into Calvin's view of Holy Scripture.

[2] *The Bible To-day*, p. 21.

[3] " The Critical Approach to the Bible in the Nineteenth Century," in *The Interpretation of the Bible* (ed. C. W. Dugmore), p. 77.

[4] H. Davies, *The Worship of the English Puritans*, p. 5.

the eighteenth century " the doctrine of unerring literal inspiration was almost everywhere held in its strictest form."[1]

The rise of the historical critical view of the Bible in the latter
part of the eighteenth century meant a revolution in Christian
thinking. It was all bound up with the great expansion of the
frontiers of knowledge which began with the Renaissance. The
discoveries of Copernicus, Galileo and Newton had pushed back
the boundaries of the universe, a reign of law had replaced the
older supernaturalism, and the earth with its inhabitants had
been displaced from its supposed position of centrality as the
hub of the planets. New parts of the world had been discovered
and were being explored. There was an increasing confidence
in the unaided power of human reason. Hence in the eighteenth century a spirit of enquiry was abroad and the principle
of authority was being questioned on all sides. As Alan
Richardson observes, " The age of the Enlightenment questioned all things, including the idea of a divinely dictated
corpus of sacred writings."[2] Why should not the inductive
method, which was of such proved value in the field of natural
science, be used in biblical study? We must note, however,
as Dodd points out, that biblical criticism as such was not new.
It is not to be regarded as " an invention of the ' Age of
Reason,' to be hailed as an example of our superior enlightenment or reprobated as an act of irreverence according to
taste. . . . The foundations of biblical criticism were laid in
the first four centuries of the Christian era."[3]

It is, perhaps, unfortunate that Eichhorn should have
labelled this new approach to the Bible the " higher criticism "
—a term little understood and consequently much abused.
As distinct from the lower or textual criticism—the attempt to
recover as far as possible the authentic text, energetically
pursued, as we have seen, in the medieval Church—higher or
source criticism deals with a particular document higher up
the stream, as it were. It attempts to discover its exact date
and authorship, to trace any older sources which have been
used in its composition, to study it in relation to its historical
background, and hence to come to a clearer understanding of

---

[1] Abbey and Overton, *The English Church in the Eighteenth Century*, i, p. 560.
[2] *Preface to Bible-Study*, p. 23.   [3] *The Bible To-day*, pp. 15 ff.

its meaning and purpose. As Lightfoot remarks, " If a student reaches the most conservative conclusions on these topics, he is, by the nature of his study, just as much a higher critic as the exponent of novel or negative theories about them."[1]

III. LIBERALISM

The great Liberal scholars of the nineteenth century were the pioneers of this new critical approach to the Bible, and our debt to them is considerable. In these days when the defects of Liberalism have become increasingly apparent, we are in danger of forgetting the lasting contribution of men like Wellhausen and Bousset, Harnack and Wrede, Driver and Kirsopp Lake. The Liberals laid the foundations of modern biblical scholarship with courage and devotion. Some of their conclusions were admittedly extreme and can no longer be held, but the broad results of their labours—such as the recognition of the composite nature of the Pentateuch, the different strata in the Book of Isaiah and the priority of St. Mark's Gospel— have stood the test of time and been confirmed by subsequent research. They have enabled us, for the first time, to arrange the books of the Bible in their correct chronological order, and, by seeing them against the historical background of their period, to understand their content more fully than ever before. By demonstrating the errors of certain traditional assumptions of authorship, they have released us from problems which had long taxed the intelligence—and the ingenuity—of the best minds. Furthermore, not only have the nineteenth-century Liberal scholars placed in our hands the tools that we need for scientific biblical study; in days when men were asking whether the Bible could withstand the impact of modern critical enquiry, they established once for all the unshakable historical basis of the Christian faith.

Nevertheless the Liberal view of Scripture had certain grave defects which cannot be ignored. In its preoccupation with the human factors of date, authorship and composition, it tended to obscure the divine element in the Bible. The history of religion usurped the place of theology. For the objective fact

[1] *Op. cit.*, p. 78.

of revelation there was substituted man's search for God and his increasing apprehension of the divine. Thus the Old Testament became reduced to the record of an important stage in the spiritual pilgrimage of mankind, or an account of the development of Hebrew religion. Moreover, Liberal criticism stopped short of the goal; it did not go far enough. Its brilliant analysis was illuminating, but it failed to give us that complete synthesis that we need. In short, it became so engrossed in the literary and historical *prolegomena* of biblical study that it never got to grips with the constructive theological task of biblical exposition.

T. W. Manson, in his brilliant and penetrating essay, *The Failure of Liberalism to Interpret the Bible as the Word of God*,[1] finds the fundamental defect of the Liberal approach in its presuppositions. In particular, " the working hypotheses of natural science were allowed to become the dogmas of theology."[2] The scientific doctrine of the universal reign of natural law, for example, precluded any interference on the part of God with the order of Nature; hence it was taken for granted that miracles could never happen.[3] " The effect of this," says Manson, " is to establish a thick plate-glass window between God and the world. The eye of faith can see through the window and observe that there is a God and that He appears to be benevolently disposed towards men; but nothing more substantial than signals of paternal affection and filial trust and obedience can get through."[4]

Furthermore, the theory of evolution—so obviously true in the biological realm—was assumed to be equally valid in the study of religion. The Bible, therefore, far from confronting men with the living and abiding Word of God, showed " the successive stages by which the Hebrew people gradually evolved religiously from the crudities of primitive Semitic superstition to the Prophets and the Law, and eventually to the Gospel." But even here there is no finality; Christianity is just " the best that has been achieved up to date."[5] Revelation thus gives place to conviction. " What we are left with in religion is the

---

[1] See *The Interpretation of the Bible* (ed. C. W. Dugmore), Chapter V.
[2] *Ibid.*, p. 101.   [3] See further below, Chapter V.
[4] *Op. cit.*, pp. 93–94.   [5] *Ibid.*, p. 94.

views held by all the more or less gifted people who have reflected on the divine nature and on human duty and destiny. . . . The presuppositions of Liberalism could only allow conviction, and so conviction must do duty for revelation. The plate-glass window set up between heaven and earth is soundproof."[1]

Liberalism with its fundamental dogmas of the " steel-and-concrete order of Nature " and the impossibility of special revelations was thus " predisposed against a God who intervenes in the world, or in history, whether by deed or word; and predisposed in favour of an interpretation of religion which would make it no more than an element in human civilization, the sum of man's deepest and gradually achieved convictions about ultimate Reality and absolute values."[2] It was these dogmatic presuppositions which vitiated Liberal biblical study. " Having taken up its axioms, which were at variance with the fundamental ideas of the Bible," Manson concludes, " there was no way of carrying the business through which did not involve picking and choosing among the biblical material on a scale and with an arbitrariness quite impossible to justify, and then imposing interpretations on what was accepted which were very far indeed from the original intention of the words. . . . The truth, now coming clearly to light, is that Christianity was being gently and gradually transformed into humanism—and humanism when it is full grown brings forth totalitarianism."[3]

IV. FUNDAMENTALISM

Present-day Fundamentalism is very largely a reaction against the Liberal position. It cannot, however, be said simply to represent the pre-critical view since it can claim neither that its emphasis is that of the Middle Ages nor that its conclusions are those of the sixteenth-century Reformers. It represents rather a further hardening of the particular view of seventeenth and eighteenth-century Protestantism as a result of the impact of the Liberal critical approach. The publication of

[1] *Ibid.*, p. 95.   [2] *Ibid.*, p. 95.   [3] See further below, Chapter V.

Essays and Reviews in 1860, for example, roused Dr. Burgon to assert from the university pulpit in Oxford that " the Bible is none other than the voice of Him that sitteth upon the throne. Every book of it, every chapter of it, every verse of it, every word of it, every syllable of it (where are we to stop?), every letter of it, is the direct utterance of the Most High. The Bible is none other than the Word of God, not some part of it more, some part of it less, but all alike the utterance of Him who sitteth upon the throne, faultless, unerring, supreme."[1] Fundamentalism thus does what both the thirteenth-century preaching friars and the sixteenth-century Reformers refused to do—it insists upon reading the Bible in the flat, as it were. It places the whole of the Old Testament, for instance, on the same level as the New and clings tenaciously to the letter of the former even when it is at variance with the fuller revelation given in Christ. Every word is regarded as having been dictated by God; every statement is inerrant; every command is authoritative. And all must be taken literally, at its face value, as the infallible Word of God.[2]

---

[1] Quoted by A. Richardson, *Preface to Bible-Study*, p. 25.

[2] As A. G. Hebert points out, biblical inerrancy as held by present-day Fundamentalism is a new doctrine: " The modern fundamentalist is asserting something that no previous age has understood in anything like the modern sense." See *The Authority of the Old Testament*, p. 98. This point is ably developed by J. K. S. Reid in his recent valuable book, *The Authority of Scripture*. He shows that, whereas the emphasis of the traditional methods of interpretation (like that of the biblical writers) was upon the spiritual and moral meaning of Scripture, the emergence of standards of exact history and science has virtually banished allegorism (good as well as bad) and left only a bare literalism, which is quite alien to the outlook and intention of the biblical writers. " When this bare literalism is in turn allied to the expectation of finding in Scripture the same kind of thing that is so successfully supplied by science, as happens in modern fundamentalism, then there emerges the ' new doctrine ' of infallibility of modern times which has no real precedent in previous ages. It is out of this unhappy alliance that there develops the acute and distressing tension and conflict between science and religion." Reid calls attention to the fact that the traditional view of inspiration had in practice a certain flexibility—an advantage which the modern view of infallibility cannot claim. " Once the principle of ' exact science ' is invoked and its categories applied, rigidity settles down upon biblical interpretation, and we have on our hands immediately the grave embarrassment of trying to reconcile what is said in the Bible with contradictory conclusions which seem to be on other grounds inescapable. In this situation the appeal to scriptural authority does not solve the problem; it only precipitates intellectual chaos." See *op. cit.*, pp. 158–64.

Admittedly, many sincere Christian people who take this position would vigorously deny that by holding it they were in any way negating God's revelation of Himself in Christ. This, however, is its logical implication, although in point of fact few of its adherents are consistent in applying their theory to the facts of the Old Testament, and most of them do not attempt to relate its difficult features to the fact of Christ. They are not concerned to make a logical synthesis but hold the two facts in tension, as it were, in the mind.[1]

Nevertheless Fundamentalism has performed a valuable service to the Christian Church. In days when the distinctive content of the faith was in danger of being dissolved in the acids of Liberalism, it did preserve the great supernatural facts of biblical religion. And for this it has put succeeding generations in its debt.

But when this has been admitted it remains true that Fundamentalism, no less than Liberalism, is vitiated by its own presuppositions. It begins with the assumption—nowhere claimed in the Bible itself—that the Scriptures are inerrant and *verbally* dictated by the Holy Spirit. All evidence to the contrary, therefore, is ruled out from the start. It presupposes that traditional theories of authorship must be right, and proceeds, in a quite arbitrary manner, to select indiscriminately from any likely source whatever evidence supports its claim, and conveniently ignores the rest. It takes for granted that scientific critical method is bound up indissolubly with the Liberal theology, which it rightly repudiates, and therefore assumes that those who use the critical tools must adopt the Liberal view. So the baby is thrown out with the bath-water.

V. The Changing Emphasis

In recent years, however, there has been a complete change of emphasis in biblical studies. The period which has just ended has been one of intense analytical study of the Bible. Its documents have been subjected to a more careful scrutiny

---

[1] Cf. J. S. Whale's observation that even the most rabid defender of the verbal inspiration and literal inerrancy of the Bible does not, in actual fact, find equal value in or give equal weight to every sentence of Scripture. See *The Protestant Tradition*, p. 131.

than have any other ancient writings, with the result that a flood of light has been thrown on Bible times, enabling us to understand much which for our fathers was obscure. Questions of date, authorship and authenticity have been investigated by some of the ablest scholars of the day, and certain broad principles of scientific biblical analysis have been laid down. The *International Critical Commentary* is a monument to the thoroughness of this historical and analytical work.

But this very necessary and salutary period of analysis has now given place to an equally necessary period of synthesis. This in no way implies any going back upon what have come to be known as the assured results of higher criticism. The critical and historical analysis is taken for granted, but the main concern of the biblical scholar is now to expound the positive message of Scripture as the living and abiding Word of God for today. And instead of emphasizing its obvious diversity, stress is now laid on the essential unity of the Bible and of biblical theology. H. H. Rowley has summarized this changing emphasis in biblical studies thus:

> In recent years a new change is coming over biblical study, whose significance is far too little perceived. The newer attitude does not reject the work of the earlier study, but seeks to conserve all that is of worth in the fruits of every approach. Yet it desires to transcend them. It accepts substantially the work of biblical criticism, but beyond the desire to know the date and authorship of the books of the Bible and the meaning they had for their first readers, it seeks the abiding significance of the Bible, and in particular its significance for this generation. It recognizes all the human processes that went into the making of the Bible, without reducing it to the level of a merely human document, and it acknowledges that its scientific study, which is still valued and continued, is not enough. . . . For the Bible is, primarily and fundamentally, God's word to man, and through all its human processes of authorship and transmission there is a divine process. Its recognition is not new, indeed, but it is claiming a more central place in biblical study, and it is this that constitutes the most significant change of recent years.[1]

This new emphasis is significant in that it seeks to achieve a synthesis of all that is of permanent value in both the critical and the Fundamentalist approach. Literal and historical

[1] *The Relevance of the Bible*, pp. 15–16.

criticism have come to stay; of that there can be no doubt. They are of proved value in biblical research and provide the only sure foundation for accurate exegesis. Critical enquiry, freed from Liberal presuppositions, needs to be relentlessly pursued with all the resources at our disposal. Nevertheless criticism by itself is not sufficient. It is essentially *prolegomena* and as such needs to be completed by theological interpretation; and, as Father Hebert has pointed out, it is about theological interpretation that Fundamentalists really care.[1] So often confronted by barren analytical logomachies and anxious about the logical conclusions of the Liberal position, they tremble for the Ark of God. What they are quite rightly concerned about is the faith, but they wrongly associate the integrity of the faith with a mechanical view of inspiration which is inconsistent with the facts of the Bible itself.

There is need today for Liberals and Fundamentalists to recognize that they have much to learn from each other, for it is in a synthesis of critical method and theological interpretation that the way forward in biblical studies lies. " It is not a matter of discarding wholesale the critical approach in which we were trained and which arrived at much that is true and valuable, but we feel that the method as practised was associated too often with underlying assumptions that need purging and that it tended to stop short of the goal. We *want* something more theological, and to that extent there has been a recovery of a sounder outlook."[2]

VI. The Word of God

There are three main aspects of this new emphasis. The first, which springs from the Barthian theology of the Word of God, is a fresh recognition of the objectivity and authority of the biblical revelation. " The newer attitude," says Rowley, " still recognizes the clear marks of progress in the biblical revelation, yet it does not reduce revelation to discovery. It does not cease to be interested in the development of religion, but its centre of interest is not in man, but in God. It does not find the story

[1] *The Throne of David*, p. 32.
[2] J. Lowe, " The Recovery of the Theological Interpretation of the Bible," in *The Interpretation of the Bible* (ed. C. W. Dugmore), p. 119.

of man's growth in the understanding of God of such absorbing interest that it becomes an end in itself, but rather seeks to perceive in every stage of the process that which is enduringly true of God."[1]

In other words, we are being reminded that in a very real sense God is the Author of the Bible. That is not to deny, of course, the part that men have had in the making of it. As C. H. Dodd remarks, " For a religious book it is often curiously secular, for a divine book, astonishingly human."[2] Neither does the assertion that God is the Author of Scripture commit us to any theory of verbal inspiration or inerrance. The Word of God is given through fallible, sinful men; we have this treasure in earthen vessels. But what is given in the Bible is the Word of God and nothing less. These Christian Scriptures are not merely human accounts of man's search for God; they are the divinely ordered record of God's revelation of Himself, in judgment and in mercy, to man. The books of the Bible, since they are historical documents, must be examined historically. The questions of their human authorship and date are, of course, important for our understanding of them. But in our preoccupation with historical and literary detail, in our just concern regarding the human authors, there must be constantly before our mind the fact that the Author of the whole is God. In the words of H. Cunliffe-Jones, " It is a question whether we take the Bible seriously as the indispensable witness to God's revelation of Himself, or whether we cannot see beyond the multitude of human witnesses. So it must be asserted that God is the Author of the Christian Scriptures and that it is His mind we are anxious to know." " The Bible is the written Word of God not because every word is dictated by God, but because we must take the written word seriously if we are to hear the Word of God."[3]

VII. THE UNITY OF THE BIBLE

In the second place, stress is now being laid on the essential unity of the Bible and of biblical theology. It is only fair to

[1] *The Relevance of the Bible*, p. 17.   [2] *The Authority of the Bible*, p. 152.
[3] Article on " The Authority of the Holy Scriptures," in *The Presbyter*, October 1943.

admit that this essential unity of Scripture, far from being denied, has always been recognized even in the analytical period of biblical study which emphasized the diversity within the Bible; so that even in the heyday of Liberalism Wheeler Robinson could speak of " the familiar unity of the whole [Old Testament] as it lies outstretched from Genesis to Malachi."[1] Nevertheless, it was diversity rather than unity which was stressed—a fact to which the theological language and book titles of the period bear witness. The Old Testament was studied from the point of view of its " religious ideas "; prophetic and priestly religion were set in a sharp antithesis. In the New Testament we were taught to contrast Pauline, Petrine and Johannine Christianity.

The complete change of emphasis is indicated by the titles of books published in the last fifteen years: *The Unity of the New Testament* by A. M. Hunter (1943), *The Old Testament in the New Testament* by R. V. G. Tasker (1946), *An Outline of Biblical Theology* by Millar Burrows (1946), *Biblical Theology: Old and New Testaments* by G. Vos (1948), *The Biblical Doctrine of Election* by H. H. Rowley (1950) *According to the Scriptures* and *The Old Testament in the New* by C. H. Dodd (1952), *The Unity of the Bible* by H. H. Rowley (1953) and *The Faith of Israel* also by H. H. Rowley (1956).

A. M. Hunter has taught us to see that " it is one purpose of God which is being fulfilled throughout both Testaments, one People of God, the story of which is being told from Abel to the apostolic age."[2] R. V. G. Tasker reminds us that " the main theme of the Bible is the covenant-relationship between God and man, a relationship which was initiated by God for the reconciliation of sinful man to Himself. First, He entered into a covenant-relationship with the Israelites, whom He called out of Egypt for the special purpose of revealing through them His purpose for mankind; and later, in the person of His Incarnate Son, He inaugurated a new covenant with the new Israel. The membership of this new Israel consisted of all who accepted Jesus both as the Christ, who fulfilled the prophecies

---

[1] *The Religious Ideas of the Old Testament*, p. 2.
[2] *Introducing the New Testament*, p. 44.

made to the old Israel, and as the Saviour, who by His death and resurrection had won salvation for all mankind."[1] C. H. Dodd points out that " even the most original and individual developments of Christology in the New Testament remain rooted in the primitive body of testimonies from the Old Testament "[2] and the treatment of the Old Testament in the New " represents an intellectual achievement of remarkable originality, displaying penetration into the meaning that lies behind the surface of the biblical text, and a power of synthesis which gathers apparently disparate elements into a many-sided whole, not unsuitable to convey some idea of the ' manifold wisdom of God.' "[3]

It is to H. H. Rowley, however, that we owe the first modern systematic treatment of this theme. The unity which he finds in the Bible is not static but dynamic. It leaves room for diversity since " God was revealing Himself to men of limited spiritual capacity and could only reveal to each what he was capable of receiving. . . . Since God chose to reveal Himself not alone to men, but through them, He was limited by the medium that He chose. That is why the full revelation in human personality required the Incarnation."[4] The unity of the Bible results from the unity of the biblical revelation. " If God was revealing Himself, then there should be some unity about the revelation, since it was the same Being Who was being revealed."[5] Thus " the continuing thread that gives unity to the record is the divine element. For in the Bible we do not have a record of the life and thought of Israel, and then of the Christian Church in its beginnings, but a record of Divine revelation. The unity is not the unity of the spirit of Israel and of the Church, but the unity of the Divine revelation given in the context of history and through the medium of human personality."[6]

There are four main factors which underlie this quickened

---

[1] *The Old Testament in the New Testament* (First ed. 1946), p. 9.

[2] *According to the Scriptures*, p. 123.

[3] *The Old Testament in the New*, p. 21. Cf. *The Bible To-day*, p. 2: "With all its variety there is after all a real unity in this literature. It is not readily discovered by ' dipping,' but forces itself upon the serious and persistent reader."   [4] See *The Unity of the Bible*, pp. 7–8.

[5] *Ibid.*, p. 8.   [6] *Ibid.*, pp. 16–17.

interest in the theological unity of the Bible. The first—which has been the stimulus behind the new emphasis as a whole—is the Barthian theology, to which reference has already been made. In the second place, the pendulum has now swung from the exaggerated emphasis on the Hellenistic background of the New Testament, associated with the work of Deissmann, which resulted from the discovery of the non-literary Egyptian papyri, to a fresh appreciation of the significance of the Old Testament background. As early as 1931 Edwyn Hoskyns and Noel Davey showed that the clue to the meaning of cardinal terms in the New Testament was to be found in the Septuagint rather than in the payri.[1] And in the same year T. W. Manson expressed his conviction that the key to the New Testament is the Old Testament conception of the " saving remnant."[2] Thirdly, there has been a new realization of the theological significance of the Old Testament as not merely *Geschichte* but *Heilsgeschichte*. In this connection W. Eichrodt's work is epoch-making,[3] and among English scholars H. H. Rowley,[4] A. G. Hebert[5] and W. J. Phythian-Adams[6] have made valuable contributions. Fourthly, during recent years there has been a growing recognition of the essential theological unity of each of the two Testaments. In New Testament studies the trail was blazed by C. H. Dodd in his book, *The Apostolic Preaching and its Developments*, which appeared in 1936, and more recently A. M. Hunter has opened up this new approach in *The Unity of the New Testament* (1943). H. H. Rowley in his essay, *The Unity of the Old Testament*,[7] finds also an underlying unity within

[1] See *The Riddle of the New Testament*, Chapter I: e.g. ἐκκλησία = *qāhāl*. Cf. J. Marsh, *The Fulness of Time*, p. 76: The definitions of Greek dictionaries (both Classical and Hellenistic) " must be subordinated to those meanings discovered in the Septuagint translation of the Old Testament, which embody the meanings with which the Hebrew words of the Old Testament are charged." In this connection recent work on the Aramaic background of the Gospels is significant. See C. C. Torrey, *The Four Gospels: A New Translation, Our Translated Gospels*, and M. Black, *An Aramaic Approach to the Gospels and Acts*.

[2] *The Teaching of Jesus*, p. ix.   [3] *Theologie des Alten Testaments*.

[4] *The Re-discovery of the Old Testament* and *The Faith of Israel*.

[5] *The Throne of David* and *The Authority of the Old Testament*.

[6] *The Call of Israel, The Fulness of Israel* and *The People and the Presence*.

[7] *Bulletin of the John Rylands Library*, vol. 29, No. 2, February 1946.

the Old Testament studied in and for itself, which then leads on to the New. There has thus become increasingly apparent what Oscar Cullmann calls, " The Continuous Redemptive Line."[1]

VIII. THEOLOGICAL INTERPRETATION

The third aspect of the new emphasis in biblical studies is the acknowledged necessity for a recovery of the theological inter-pretation of the Bible. This latter, as John Lowe is at pains to point out, has never been entirely lost, but—as he rightly insists—biblical criticism, which should prepare the way for theological interpretation, has tended to become an end in itself and the student has become so immersed in it that very often he has not got on to biblical theology at all.[2]

It is easy [says Hebert] for the student of the Bible to find these studies very barren. They help us to see that the books of the Bible are human books, written by real men. But all this can easily be study *about* the Bible rather than *of* the Bible. It is rather as if the student of Shakespeare were to spend his time in investigating the sources from which Shakespeare drew the material for his plays, and the manner in which the plays were presented in an Eliza-bethan theatre. But we are not studying Shakespeare until we study the use he made of his materials, and appreciate for our-selves the greatness of his work. So it is with the Bible. All these questions which the " critical " books raise are in truth only preliminary to the real study of the Bible, namely, the study of what it was that the biblical writers actually said, the study of the Bible " from within."[3]

Karl Barth puts his sensitive finger on the spot when, speak-ing of commentaries, he says: " I have nothing whatever to say against historical criticism. I recognize it, and once more state quite definitely that it is both necessary and justified. My com-plaint is that recent commentators confine themselves to an inter-pretation of the text which seems to me to be no commentary at all, but merely the first step towards a commentary."[4] This, it must be admitted, was not true of some of the giants of the critical period. A. B. Davidson, G. B. Gray and, more

[1] *Christ and Time*, Part 1.
[2] " The Recovery of the Theological Interpretation of the Bible," in *The Interpretation of the Bible* (ed. C. W. Dugmore), pp. 116–17.
[3] A. G. Hebert, *The Bible from Within*, pp. 2–3.
[4] *The Epistle to the Romans*, p. 6.

especially, George Adam Smith did attempt to give a constructive theological interpretation. But even here the promise was
greater than the achievement, and there has been little
attempt to follow up this side of their work until recent years.

The kind of theological interpretation of the Bible which is
urgently required today will be neither obscurantist nor
Liberal. It will not displace or supersede the historical critical
view, but will be complementary to it. Accepting the critical
and historical analysis of a particular part of Scripture, it will
go on to discover what is its abiding significance in the light of
the fact of Christ. What, we must ask, is the Word of God which
is given in this Scripture for us today?

This demands, as Lowe puts it, that " we will go about it with
a certain expectancy, looking everywhere for theological
truth, even in passages hitherto stigmatized and discarded as
' secondary,' trying constantly to relate it to our condition,
making it (to use one of the current catch-words) ' existential.'
On that element we will dwell, devoting less time and attention
than has been customary to the interesting but relatively unimportant mass of ' background ' information. The trouble with
much of our biblical study was precisely that the background
had become the foreground."[1]

Joseph Woods sums up the attitude of modern biblical
scholars succinctly and concretely: " When the books of the
Bible were written, or by whom, or in what style, how often
they were edited and re-edited, are very interesting matters so
long as they do not allow us to be deaf to what the Bible is
saying to us here and now."[2]

---

[1] J. Lowe, " The Recovery of the Theological Interpretation of the
Bible," in *The Interpretation of the Bible* (ed. C. W. Dugmore), p. 121.
[2] *The Old Testament in the Church*, pp. 121–2.

CHAPTER III

REVELATION THROUGH HISTORY

"GOD," says Victor Hugo, "makes visible to men His will in events, an obscure text, written in a mysterious language." Christianity is an historical religion. It claims, not only that it is founded upon concrete, historical events, but that in these particular events God Himself has acted decisively, authoritatively, mercifully, in this world of men. Hence history, for the Christian, is what Archbishop Söderblom has called "the workshop of revelation." Nevertheless, it is, to revert to the former metaphor, "an obscure text, written in a mysterious language"; so much so that the secular historian may fail to find in it any thread of meaning. This is admitted by the late H. A. L. Fisher in a much-quoted passage in his preface to *A History of Europe*. "Men wiser and more learned than I," he remarks, "have discovered in history a plot, a rhythm, a predetermined pattern. These harmonies are concealed from me. I can see only one emergency following upon another as wave follows upon wave, only one great fact with respect to which, since it is unique, there can be no generalizations, only one safe rule for the historian: that he should recognize in the development of human destinies the play of the contingent and the unforeseen."[1]

In this age of disillusionment which has witnessed the collapse of the nineteenth-century dogma of Progress, it is not easy to avoid Fisher's scepticism unless we bring to history a faith in the providence of God. As Niebuhr remarks, "It is, in fact, impossible to interpret history at all without a principle of interpretation which history as such does not yield."[2] The Christian of necessity interprets historic events in terms of his

[1] *A History of Europe*, preface, v.
[2] *The Nature and Destiny of Man*, 1, p. 151.

own experience of God. The principles which he applies are those which he has discerned as implicit in God's dealings with him as a person. These principles, as much as the events which he seeks to interpret, are the data with which he begins. Hence, in one sense, his judgment of the significance of history must remain a judgment of faith; nevertheless his guiding principles themselves are ultimately derived from history, since his own experience from which they are deduced is itself "historic" —it is part of the time process. "If, as Christians," says Farmer, "we are in any measure able to read the signs of the divine providence in the world, it is not so much because such signs shine in their own light, but because we bring to them from elsewhere a light by which to read them, and, even then, our reading of them can never carry us more than the smallest distance towards a full understanding. At the most we have a glimpse of the divine fingers weaving the pattern of events with mercy and judgment, but very little is discerned in detail of the pattern which is being woven."[1]

I. The Nature of History

We must note, at this stage, a certain ambiguity of the word "history." It refers primarily to events—what actually happens; but it is also used, in a secondary sense, of the record of events, which constitutes the evidence for their having happened. Since the record is the medium of our knowledge of the event recorded—we can, in the very nature of the case, have no *unmediated* knowledge of events of a past age—the two uses of the term are, of course, interrelated.

The saying that history repeats itself is misleading and untrue. History, in the primary sense of the term, consists of events, and events are characterized by their unique particularity. They are non-recurrent. Like different leaves on a tree, they are never exactly the same. It is this uniqueness which is the hall-mark of the historical and which divides it sharply from the cyclic, recurrent element in Nature. The former is the presupposition of the historian, just as the latter is of the scientist. Thus Dodd can speak of "the concrete

[1] H. H. Farmer, *The World and God*, p. 233.

actuality of history, consisting of unique, unrepeatable events."[1]

Not every event, however, is an historical event. To be such it must have sufficient significance to be remembered in the community in which it occurs. An historical record, therefore, is not a mere chronicle; it is not a record of every event but a " record of things worthy to be remembered." Hence the events of which it takes note are those which have a bearing upon the life of the group; those which are important not only for the individuals concerned but also for the community as a whole.[2] Thus, as Croce points out, a process of selection underlies the historical record. The historian must select, and in selecting he must evaluate. But his evaluation will be determined by his own viewpoint, by his own interpretation of events. History, then, consists not merely of events but of events plus their meaning for those concerned. It is, says Tillich, " the totality of remembered events, which are determined by free human activity and are important for the life of human groups."[3]

But one proviso is required by Tillich's definition: history is not entirely determined by free human activity; it is rather the resultant of the interaction of man's free choices and the contingency of Nature. This is the truth expressed by the proverb that man proposes but God disposes. It is tacitly recognized by the familiar clause appearing in a bill of lading or an insurance policy which designates unforeseen natural catastrophe as an " act of God." " The character of the religious and historical process," says Nicolas Berdyaev, " presupposes a profound clash and interaction between the Divinity and man, between Providence, divine fatality and necessity on the one hand, and the unfathomable mystery of human freedom on the other."[4] Instances of this clash leap to mind. Pharaoh thwarted at the Red Sea, Sennacherib's army decimated by plague, the destruction of the Spanish Armada, and, although to a lesser degree, the retreat of Napoleon from

[1] *History and the Gospel*, p. 22.

[2] Collingwood, following Croce, defines history as that which can be rethought. See below, pp. 94 ff.

[3] P. Tillich, in *The Kingdom of God and History* (Oxford Conference), ch. V, p. 108.   [4] *The Meaning of History*, pp. 36–7.

Moscow, all witness to necessity frustrating the free choice of man. Thus, as Bevan maintains, " history is made in part by the voluntary choices of men and in part by natural processes in which, except in so far as they are interfered with by human volition, God's will must be perfectly carried out."[1]

II. THE HEBREW CONTRIBUTION

Having clarified our minds regarding the essential nature of history, we pass on to consider the specific Hebrew contribution towards the understanding of history as the medium of revelation. This interpretation, which is associated with the Hebrews as a whole, really belongs to that creative element in Hebrew religion for which the prophets are responsible. It is therefore with the prophetic interpretation of history that we are concerned. That interpretation is often implicit rather than explicit; it is frequently assumed rather than taught. Indeed it is the basic assumption of the whole prophetic movement, the foundation upon which the superstructure of its teaching rests. Moreover, this contribution of the Hebrew prophets is, as we shall see, basic not only in Hebrew religion but also in the Christian faith. Indeed the whole Christian concept of special revelation depends upon it.

Two diverse interpretations of history were current in the ancient world—the Greek and the Hebrew. The root of their differences is to be found in their respective conceptions of God and the value that each assigned to time.

For both Hebrew and Greek—if the religion of the latter be considered in its mature form—God was One. This fact constitutes the least common denominator of two conceptions which in other respects are antithetical; for the Divine Power of Greek thought has little in common with the God of Hebrew experience. Two alternative schemes of ontology were current among the Greeks—Platonic idealism and Stoic materialism. In the former the Absolute, τὸ ὄν, is conceived of as an idea —the idea of the Good—perceptible to the mind (νοητόν) but transcendent and entirely different from matter of any kind.

[1] Edwyn Bevan, in *The Kingdom of God and History* (Oxford Conference), ch. III, p. 41.

In the latter the Deity is the primal all-pervading fire, itself pervaded by an ordering force (λόγος), out of which the universe had condensed and into which it would finally be reabsorbed; the rise and decay of the world being governed by an iron necessity or fate (εἱμαρμένη). In both cases the Divine was impersonal and static and unrelated to the course of history.[1] Platonism attributed a cyclic nature to the time process, and this idea was developed in the Stoic philosophy. Just as the seasons of the year rotate in a certain fixed order— spring being followed by summer, and this in turn by autumn and winter; and then the whole process beginning again— so, they thought, did all events happen, history periodically repeating itself. Thus Aristotle remarks, " For indeed time itself seems to be a sort of circle."[2]

Time was therefore deprived of any real significance and history reduced to an endless series of recurring cycles. A general conflagration marked the end of each, after which the new cycle came to birth. " All is change," says Marcus Aurelius, " yet need we not fear any novelty; all is the wonted round; nay even the apportionments equal. . . . All comes to stench and refuse at last. . . . All things are alike—familiar, fleeting, foul: everything is as it was in the days of the dead and buried. . . . Anon earth will cover us all; then earth in its turn will change; then the resultant of the change; then the resultant of the resultant, and so on *ad infinitum*. . . . How silly and strange to think anything in life wonderful! "[3] Such a philosophy must of necessity regard history as meaningless since it refused to acknowledge the uniqueness of events. Singularly enough this Greek conception is admirably summarized by two verses of a book written in Hebrew by a Hebrew—the Book of Ecclesiastes: " The thing that hath been, it is that which shall be; and that which is done is that which shall be done: and there is no new thing under the sun. Is there anything whereof it may be said, See, this is new? it hath been already of old time, which was before us."[4]

Ecclesiastes, however, belongs to the Greek period (*c.*

---

[1] Such was the God of the philosophers. A more dynamic conception is found in the Greek poets, especially Aeschylus.   [2] *Physics*, 4: 14.
[3] See *Meditations*, viii & ix.   [4] Ecclesiastes i, 9–10.

200 B.C.), and this passage is not representative of classic Hebrew thought which regarded God as Righteous Will—personal, dynamic and transcendent. He was removed from the world process, yet His power was operative within it. He dwelt in the high and lofty place, yet He came into contact with man. Where?—on the highway of history. God is known to the Hebrew for what He is by what He does. As John Macmurray observes, " What is characteristic of the Hebrew conception of God is that God is primarily a worker."[1] Creation is the beginning of His work; His mighty acts in history attest His sovereignty in spite of all evil powers; He will eventually show Himself as supreme. The Hebrew prophets discerned the significance of what befell their people and behind all the movements of men and nations they saw the directing hand of God. C. H. Dodd summarizes their interpretation thus: " The prophetic writers of the Old Testament, then, declare that a series of events in the history of their people exhibits 'the mighty works of the Lord'; the call of Abraham, the Exodus and the giving of the Law, the conquest of Canaan, the kingdom of David, the Captivity and the Return. Whatever human or natural factors may enter in, the ultimate ground of this series of events is the purpose of God, who freely chose Israel to be His people, and who uses alien peoples to fulfil His designs. But it is to be observed that this purpose is never conceived to be *completely* revealed in the history of Israel: the complete revelation waits for the end of the historical process—an end which most prophets conceive to be close at hand."[2]

The prophets thus view these mighty acts of God in the light of a future event, and their full significance will be seen only when the series is complete. Hence another mighty act still in the future is proclaimed, the last act, the ἔσχατον, which alone can give meaning to the whole. This final event is the Day of the Lord.[3] For the early prophetic writers it is an event within history when Jehovah will vindicate his cause. Associated with it are the purifying and exaltation of Israel and the subjection

---

[1] *The Clue to History*, p. 33.   [2] *History and the Gospel*, pp. 32–3.
[3] See Amos v, 18–20; Isaiah ii, 12, xiii, 6; Jeremiah xlvi, 10; Ezekiel xxx, 3; Joel i, 15, ii, 1, iii, 14; Zechariah xiv, 1; Zephaniah i, 7; Obadiah 15.

of the heathen world. But for the later apocalyptists the transcendent element replaces the historical: the Day of the Lord means a new heaven and a new earth; the dead are raised and the living transformed.[1] " The meaning of history, therefore," says Dodd, " is determined by that which lies beyond history. The events in which the divine action is recognized are interpreted as *interventions* of God from His throne on high. Consequently the End, even when it is thought of as the last event in history, will have the character of a final irruption of the supra-historical into history. When, therefore, the apocalyptists described it in terms appropriate to no conceivable event in history, they effectively indicate the transcendent character which must belong to it. In reaching its conclusion, history passes beyond itself."[2]

It is to the Hebrews, then, that we must acknowledge the beginnings of a philosophy of history.[3] But furthermore, as we shall now see, it is to their prophetic insight, born of direct communion with God, that we owe the basis of that interpretation of events which is integral to the Christian faith. We may fittingly conclude this section with words of Berdyaev which summarize succinctly all that has been said above: " It was the Jews," he says, "who contributed the concept of 'historical' to world history, thereby discharging, in my opinion, the essence of their specific mission. They were the first to conceive the world as historical fulfilment in contradistinction to the cyclic process of the Greeks. . . . For the Jews the idea of history turns upon the expectation of some future event which will bring with it a solution of history."[4]

III. HISTORY THE WORKSHOP OF REVELATION

We shall now attempt to relate this prophetic interpretation of history to the fact of revelation. What do we mean when we

---

[1] See Daniel xii, 1–3, cf. vii, 9–27.

[2] *The Kingdom of God and History* (Oxford Conference), ch. II, p. 20.

[3] " The Hebrew prophets are the first philosophers of history because they apprehend events as a significant whole, determined and fashioned by the eternal creative principle, which, while transcending them, is ever active within them."—H. Knight, *The Hebrew Prophetic Consciousness*, p. 162.

[4] *The Meaning of History*, p. 28.

speak of history as being " the workshop of revelation," to use Archbishop Söderblom's phrase?

All true religion must begin and end in revelation, in a dynamic self-disclosure on the part of God. As Brunner remarks, " There is no religion worth the name which does not claim to be ' revealed religion.' "[1] But as soon as we admit this fact, we are faced by the perennial problem which accompanies it, the problem made urgent today by the teaching of Karl Barth—namely, What is the place of human reason in this self-disclosure of God? How, if at all, are revelation and reason to be related? Are we to concur in the place assigned to natural theology by Roman Catholicism? Or are we to deny any place to it, with Karl Barth? Do we believe in the conception of a natural created link between man and God—even if it be but man's " addressability " (*Ansprechbarkeit*), to use Brunner's term—as the necessary presupposition of revelation? Or do we say with Barth: " There is no human precondition "? In a word, the inescapable problem of revelation is, How is contact made between God and man?

The Hebraic attitude to this problem is that revelation is given in history; that in the events of the time process the mighty acts of God are seen. For the Hebrew the Ultimate Reality is personal; He is Righteous Will as opposed to the neuter and static τὸ ὄν of the Greeks; He is a transcendent God, One who is " other " than the created order, nevertheless He is dynamically near. The Hebrew God is one whose being throbs with the pulse of life, who not only thinks and feels and wills, but who may be known for what He is by what He does. He is the Living God who reveals His power in the world by His breath or Spirit, and His activity is seen, not only in creation, but also in His mighty acts in history. He is not merely interested but also operative in human affairs: Assyria is the rod of His anger and Cyrus His anointed one who shall perform His will.[2] In short, to the Greek life was always a symbol; to the Hebrew it was an instrument of the eternal.

Such a conception of an historical revelation is not, of course, without its difficulties. It must mean that the revelation is temporarily conditioned; that eternal values are not present

---

[1] *The Mediator*, p. 21.   [2] See Isaiah x, 5–15, xlv, 1–4.

as such but are represented through temporal equivalents. How then can the relative reveal the absolute? How can the transcendence of God be represented through the immanent? The immanent must be in some sense the transcendent. These are the problems which confront any Christian doctrine of revelation formulated on the data of Jesus Himself. Philosophically the eternal cannot be brought into the temporal by any intellectual scheme which would include both in some larger unit. Nevertheless, the Christian faith does in fact find the eternal in the temporal; yet it excludes both deism and pantheism. In the words of Butterfield, " It asserts that eternity is brought into relation with time, and that the supra-terrestrial realm, the kingdom of the spirit, is not locked away, for it is here and now, and the two planes of existence intersect."[1] Revelation, however, is more than a general reflection of the divine in Nature; it means nothing less than that direct and purposive activity of God which brings Him to man for man's good—God seeks man.

As Wheeler Robinson rightly insists, Christianity—along with Judaism and Islam—in maintaining that God is active in history, asserts that somehow human nature is capable of receiving the revelation of God. " This can be true only if there is a certain kinship between God and man, so that what is true for man at his highest is also true for God."[2] Now for the Hebrew God can be known by man because of this likeness, this kinship which is suggested by the divine " breath " by which man is animated.[3] And mediation between the divine and the human is seen predominantly in the prophetic consciousness. " Thus saith the Lord " involves that the prophetic consciousness is itself a channel of mediation: the human is taken up in the divine and the divine finds expression in the acts of the human. But the personality of the prophet is never in abeyance; free will and control are left unreconciled. From

[1] H. Butterfield, *Christianity and History*, pp. 120–1.
[2] *Redemption and Revelation*, pp. 164–5. Cf. Barth, *The Doctrine of the Word of God* (Eng. trans.), p. 273. Wheeler Robinson, however, comes perilously near, at times, to equating conviction and revelation. See *op. cit.*, p. 166: " Thus at the ' Land's End ' of human experience we have the intuition that man's conviction *is* God's revelation." Compare what has been said above in Chapter II, pp. 62–3.   [3] See Genesis ii, 7.

this follows the Hebrew conception of history as the actualization of revelation. Revelation comes " through real agents, who give actuality to the divine thought ":[1] Israel's acts are God's mighty acts.

God was thus revealing Himself through a series of events in the history of Israel, a series which was to culminate in the supreme Event of all, the coming into the world of Christ. But the revelation was not given in the mere events alone; they did not speak the Word of God *in vacuo*, as it were. It was through the impact of the event upon the intuitive mind of the prophet that God's revelation was given. It was not, for example, the mere *fact* of the crossing of the Red Sea, or the conquest of Canaan, or the Return under Cyrus which was of itself a part of the revelation to Israel. The mind of the prophet dwelt upon the fact, pondered it, lifted it up into that spiritual realm where he held communion with God, saw it from the angle of the divine, and was thus able to declare its significance in the purpose of God. Revelation was therefore the resultant, as it were, of two factors: it was given through two things— the historic event and the prophetic mind. Neither was sufficient of itself, but through the interplay of both God spoke.

This view of revelation is associated with the late Archbishop William Temple, who propounded it in his Gifford Lectures.[2] With Forsyth, Temple rejects the traditional idea that revelation consists of propositions: " *There is no such thing as revealed truth. There are truths of revelation, that is to say, propositions which express the results of correct thinking concerning revelation; but they are not themselves directly revealed.*"[3] With Ritschl, however, he is anxious to safeguard the objectivity of revelation against the view of Schleiermacher which would reduce it to the subjective religious experience. He maintains, therefore, that " Revelation exists or occurs objectively but is subjectively conditioned."[4] It consists " primarily in historical events, and secondarily in the illumination of the minds of prophets to read those events as disclosing the judgment or the purpose of God. What we find

[1] Wheeler Robinson, *op. cit.*, p. 169.
[2] *Nature, Man and God* (1934), Lecture xii. See also Temple's essay in *Revelation* (ed. Baillie and Martin, 1937).
[3] *Nature, Man and God*, p. 317.   [4] *Ibid.*, p. 318.

in the Old Testament Scriptures is not mainly, if at all, authoritative declarations of theological doctrine, but living apprehension of a living process wherein those whose minds are enlightened by divine communion can discern in part the purposive activity of God."[1] The essence of revelation is therefore " intercourse of mind and event."[2] Its principle is " the interaction of the world-process and the minds, both being alike guided by God."[3] "*He guides the process; He guides the minds of men; the interaction of the process and the minds which are alike guided by Him is the essence of revelation.*"[4] Hence there must be " the coincidence of divinely controlled event and minds divinely illumined to read it aright "[5] for revelation to be given.

During recent years Temple's view has been criticized on the ground that its dichotomy of divine event and inspired interpretation is unreal. Thus Alan Richardson charges Temple with over-simplifying the problem by ignoring the double meaning of the term " history," which, as we have noted, is used for both the actual course of events and the remembrance or record of them. " Doubtless," he says, " history in the former sense was the original object of the interpreted revelation, but our knowledge of the event cannot be simply described as objective. We know of what happened only through the written and interpreted (and therefore subjectivized) history of the biblical record. . . . Not only does the significance of the event for us depend upon our (or the prophets') admittedly subjective interpretation of it, but the very nature of the event, or even whether it occurred at all, is bound up (as far as our knowledge of it is concerned) with our (or the prophets') subjective appreciation of it."[6] He maintains, therefore, that " we cannot thus divide the content of revelation into history and interpretation, the objective and the subjective; whatever history in the former sense of the word may be, history in the second sense, written history, is never simply ' objective.' Any account of historical events is conditioned by the principle of interpretation that has been adopted in the presentation of them. If we do not accept the biblical or prophetic principle

[1] *Ibid.*, p. 312.   [2] *Ibid.*, p. 316.   [3] *Ibid.*, p. 314.
[4] *Ibid.*, p. 312.   [5] *Revelation*, p. 107.
[6] *Christian Apologetics*, p. 146.

of interpretation, it is unlikely that we shall accept the biblical record as true or ' objective ' history."[1] Hence Richardson concludes that Temple's view is only a variant of the Ritschlian theory of the distinction between " theoretical judgments " and " value judgments."[2]

Richardson's insistence on the existential nature of biblical revelation cannot, of course, be denied. In the words of A. E. Taylor, " There are not really two water-tight compartments of the historical process, a ' physical ' sphere and a ' mental ' sphere; there is the one concrete given process with its mental and physical elements interrelating and interacting."[3] Thus, as Wheeler Robinson reminds us "there are no 'bare' facts for the historian,"[4] and " we cannot . . . divide our experience sharply between 'subjective' and 'objective' factors."[5] Nevertheless Richardson misses the real point of Temple's argument. When all this has been admitted, the fact remains, as Richardson himself concedes, that " it must be in some way the whole complex of the events together with their interpretation which constitutes the revelation of God in history."[6] Admittedly *our* knowledge of the events is inseparable from the prophetic interpretation of the biblical record; we can, in the very nature of the case, have no unmediated knowledge of them. But this is irrelevant for Temple's argument. He is not concerned with our knowledge of the events as distinguished from their biblical interpretation; his concern is with the initial process through which the biblical revelation was given. And the prophets, unlike ourselves, were contemporary with the events that they interpreted; they had immediate knowledge of them. They themselves were, it is true, involved in the historical situation of their time and are not, as Richardson rightly insists, to be regarded as " detached philosophical minds coolly making rational inferences from or passing ' value-judgments ' upon ' objective ' historical events."[7] Nevertheless they were confronted by (although involved in) an actual historical situation —Moses by the Deliverance at the Red Sea, Isaiah by the

---

[1] *Ibid.*, pp. 146-7.   [2] *Ibid.*, pp. 147–8.
[3] *The Faith of a Moralist*, ii, p. 169.
[4] *The Old Testament: its Making and Meaning*, p. 76.
[5] *Redemption and Revelation*, p. xxxix.   [6] *Op. cit.*, p. 145.
[7] *Ibid.*, pp. 151–2.

Assyrian menace, Jeremiah by the Babylonian Exile, Deutero-Isaiah by the rise of Cyrus—and it was through their inspired interpretation of these events, which they themselves experienced in their unmediated immediacy, that revelation was given. This is tacitly admitted by Richardson when he concedes that " doubtless history in the former sense (i.e. the actual course of events) was the original object of the interpreted revelation,"[1] but he then confuses the issue by denying (quite rightly) that our knowledge of the biblical events can be simply described as objective, which is another matter.

The " Achilles' heel " of Temple's argument is his concession, in a footnote, that " the appreciation need not be contemporaneous with the event. But till it comes, the event, though revelatory in its own character, is not yet fully revelation."[2] If by this he envisages the interpretation by a prophet of an event of which he himself had no immediate experience, but for the knowledge of which he relied on the memory or record of others, then, of course, the situation is totally changed and Richardson's argument is relevant. But it would be difficult to reconcile this with the idea of the coincidence of event and appreciation in reference to which the footnote is given, and it would seem that what Temple has in mind is rather the subsequent interpretation, after reflection, of an event of which the prophet himself had immediate experience.

" The immediate work of the great prophets," says Wheeler Robinson, " was the interpretation of Israel's history. Under the guidance of Israel's God, the prophet found himself brought to a vision of Israel's history . . . which dominated his thought and shaped his message. The course of events visible to all was the handwriting of Yahweh, which it was the prophet's task to explain to his fellow-countrymen."[3] We must not over-emphasize the " objectivity " of events by ignoring the existential nature of the biblical revelation. But to admit this is not necessarily to deny the dichotomy of divine event and inspired interpretation in the process through which that revelation was given.

[1] *Ibid.*, p. 146.   [2] *Nature, Man and God*, p. 315.
[3] *The Religious Ideas of the Old Testament*, p. 119.

God reveals Himself through His acts in history as much as through the words which He places in the mouth of the Prophets. We ought not to emphasize the historical fact at the expense of the word, any more than we ought to emphasize the word at the expense of the historical fact. It is true, certainly, that historical facts, like the passage through the Red Sea, or the storms of judgment of the Assyrian and Babylonian periods, when the Chosen People where in such distress, only became significant as the manifestation of divine mercy or of divine wrath through the word of the Prophet to the people; but the Prophets do not claim that these historical events only acquire their meaning as revelation through their prophetic word. It is not that they give meaning to history by means of their word, but that God gives them insight into the meaning of the event, which it already contains because God is within it.[1]

IV. Christ the Fulfilment of History

A marked characteristic of early Christian preaching is its appeal to Old Testament prophecy. The New Testament as a whole witnesses to this fact, but especially the speeches of St. Peter in the Book of Acts and St. Matthew's Gospel. To the modern mind there may be in some of these appeals a certain naïveté which makes them unconvincing. Nevertheless their main purpose is clear and valid. They testify to the Christian consciousness that in the fact of Christ—His birth, His ministry of teaching and healing, His passion and death, His resurrection and exaltation at God's right hand—the future event to which the prophets looked has happened, God's final mighty act has been accomplished, the ἔσχατον has entered history. This, as far as we can gather from the New Testament records, was the starting-point of the first Christian preaching. The events comprising the life and death and resurrection of Christ were regarded and proclaimed as eschatological events. They were not merely important, or even the most important, events, but happenings whose significance was decisive, crucial, final. In the fact of Christ these first disciples were conscious of the manifestation in history of something which was not in itself merely historical because it belonged to the eternal order. " The Christian consciousness," says Berdyaev, " . . . held that

---

[1] E. Brunner, *Revelation and Reason*, p. 85.

events were immediate, non-recurrent and unique, and it imposed this conception on historical reality. For it was convinced that an event of central importance in history had taken place; an event that had been completed once for all; a non-recurring, indivisible, incomparable and unique event that was both historical and metaphysical, and that revealed the depths of life; in a word, Christ's revelation."[1]

It was in the light of the fact of Christ that the first Christians were able to read and make sense of the history of the past. This was the final event which gave meaning to the whole series of God's mighty acts. The great historic happenings of the past were but a preparation for it. Israel had been chosen, called, and brought into a covenant relationship with God; His law had been revealed to them; they had been delivered from their enemies and made to possess a good land; the Messianic promise of a future intervention of God to establish in forgiveness a kingdom of righteousness and peace had been given through the prophets; for why?—that at the end of a long period of preparation this peculiar people might receive, in trust for the world, God's final Word in Christ. Thus, as Niebuhr observes, " The 'scandal of particularity' [*einmaligkeit*] in the Biblical interpretation is a necessary part of revelation in Biblical faith."[2]

The fact that these preparatory events took place for the most part on a narrow strip of land on the eastern edge of the Mediterranean and were concerned with a people whose political significance was nil, in no way invalidates their meaning or importance. As Dodd points out, " An historical religion attaches itself not to the whole temporal series indifferently, nor yet to any casual event, but to a particular series of events in which a unique intensity of significance resides. This selection of a particular series is not incongruous with the nature of history itself. The particular, even the unique, is a

---

[1] *The Meaning of History*, pp. 33-4.
[2] *Faith and History*, p. 119. Cf. W. Sanday, *Inspiration*, pp. 126-7: " We do not deny a Divine guiding in other races. Not wholly in the dark did men of other nationality grope after an object of worship and of praise. But it is from the Hebrew stock that we have the Bible, and the Bible is by general consent the highest expression, the most perfect document, of Religion."

category entirely appropriate to the understanding of history; and since one particular event exceeds another in significance, there may well be an event which is uniquely significant, and this event may give a unique character to the whole series to which it belongs." And he goes on to say: " This is in fact the assertion which Christianity makes. It takes the series of events recorded or reflected in the Bible, from the call of Abraham to the emergence of the Church, and declares that in this series the ultimate reality of all history, which is the purpose of God, is finally revealed, because the series is itself controlled by the supreme event of all—the life, death and resurrection of Jesus Christ. This valuation of the series is not imposed upon it from without, but is an integral part of the history itself."[1]

But this final, decisive event was to be the ἔσχατον; this conclusive entrance of God into history was to be the end of history. Alongside of the prophetic expectation of it as an historic event there was the apocalyptic emphasis upon its transcendent character by virtue of which history would be wound up. Moreover, Jesus Himself had spoken of this transcendent aspect of His work which would bring the present order to an end: " Ye shall see the Son of man sitting on the right hand of power, and coming in the clouds of heaven."[2] The New Testament relegates this function of Christ to a Second Advent, but it is clear that this is not at first regarded as a further event but as the consummation of that mighty act which had already taken place in the coming of Christ. The years passed, however, and the Lord did not appear. Hence the indivisible unity of the first and second advents became broken and the latter tended more and more to take the form of a second crisis as yet future. God's mighty act in Christ, however, is continued in the life of the Church which is His Body, until it is consummated by His return as Judge, and thus the real unity of the Incarnation and final Consummation is maintained.

The Christian Church is, therefore, today what the Hebrew nation was in the pre-Christian world—" the axis of universal history," to use Berdyaev's phrase.[3] Just as, in the light of the fact of Christ, the early Christians were able to

[1] *History and the Gospel*, pp. 29–30.   [2] Mark xiv, 62.
[3] *The Meaning of History*, p. 92.

discern within pre-Christian history a process of preparation achieved in and through the Hebrew nation, so we may see in the twenty centuries A.D. a process of reception and judgment which is accomplished through the instrumentality of the Church. By the preaching of the Word and the administration of the Sacraments, men and nations have been continually confronted with the fact of Christ and so called to decision concerning Him. Those who respond are received into the Christian community, and those who reject the appeal declare themselves at enmity with God. In this way the Church is what Dodd has called the instrument of a divine intervention in history,[1] until the final Consummation.

Thus the central event in history is the Incarnation. Our very division of time into B.C. and A.D. is a recognition of this. " The historical work of Jesus Christ as Redeemer forms the mid-point of a line which leads from the Old Testament to the return of Christ."[2] " The mighty Christ-event has given a new center to time, and so it roots in the faith that the fulfillment has already taken place, that it is no longer the Parousia but rather the cross and resurrection of Christ that constitute the middle point and meaning of all that occurs. The entire process that develops in time finds in these events its middle point, first of all in a pure time sense, but then also for purpose of orientation, that is, of giving meaning to the whole."[3]

Paul Tillich, although wrongly minimizing the importance of the historical facts of the Incarnation, has attempted to interpret Christ as " the centre of history " in this latter sense. The Incarnation is the event which has the " power of giving meaning to our existence and of overcoming the threat of meaninglessness." The " centre of history " is " the principle [sic] that gives meaning to our historical activities, that makes history a history of salvation for us, that gives us an expectation of an eternal future in which meaninglessness is conquered."[4] Tillich, however, does not explain what exactly he means by this and in what way the Incarnation is to be related to contemporary history so as to give it meaningfulness. His whole

---

[1] History and the Gospel, p. 162.
[2] O. Cullmann, Christ and Time, p. 57.   [3] Ibid., p. 86.
[4] The Interpretation of History, pp. 264–5.

position has been subjected to a trenchant criticism by John McIntyre, who calls attention to the ambiguity of the word "meaning" in this connection and shows further how Tillich's conception of Christ as the centre of history is incompatible with his view of the mere probability of the events of the Incarnation.[1] McIntyre, however, maintains that, given a right view of the nature of history and its knowability, the conception of Christ as the centre of history is valid in more than a merely temporal sense. Accepting Kierkegaard's dictum that all believers are contemporary disciples of Jesus Christ, and employing Croce's standard of the historical as that which meets a present need, he says of Christ:

> Because of His ability to meet the needs of men and women in every age; because the event that took place in Palestine almost two thousand years ago can be immediately related to the needs of Jew and Greek, barbarian and Scythian, bond and free, Australian and Philippine—for these reasons, Christ is justifiably called the centre of history. He is, therefore, the centre, not primarily because He divides linear history into B.C. and A.D., but because, since He can place Himself at the centre of the lives of human beings, He becomes the centre of those activities which constitute history. No other event in history has that function; certain historical situations have lesser centres for a time, but for every period He is the One whose rightful place is at the centre of the lives of those who participate in historical occurrence. In the same way, we might say that Christ is the centre of history, for the will of God there made known to sinful mankind is that God purposes the total redemption of the world, and that men should work out their own salvation in the totality of their existence—social, economic, political and cultural as well as individual. That will of God is normative wherever history takes place ... and that will judges the injustices, the cruelties, the intrigues and the oppressions that make up so much of history. By virtue of the contemporaneity of the Incarnation with all of history's occurrences, it provides both their judgment and their redemption.[2]

V. The Actuality of Biblical History

One final question confronts us: Granted that revelation is given in the stuff of history, how can we be sufficiently sure that

---

[1] See "History and Meaning," in *The Reformed Theological Review*, vol. VI, No. 2, November 1947, and "Christ and History," *Ibid.*, vol. VIII, No. 3, August 1949.   [2] "Christ and History," *Ibid.*, p. 41.

the alleged historical events really did happen? Are the
"facts" of biblical history certain?[1] This question is crucial
in any discussion of an historical revelation, for, as Wheeler
Robinson has reminded us, " only when we have decided on
a probable series of events, and a parallel series of human
reactions to those events, can we usefully begin to ask how far
and in what way they both *in their blended unity* serve to reveal
God."[2] The very essence of the Christian Faith is the belief that
in the life, death and resurrection of a Carpenter of Nazareth,
who was born in the reign of Caesar Augustus and executed *sub
Pontio Pilato*, God Himself has achieved a final and unique
mighty act for the deliverance and transformation of man.
Christianity is thus rooted in history and has no existence
apart from it: it is not just an abstract system of thought. " If,
for example," says Peake, " we reached the conclusion, on
historical grounds, that Jesus of Nazareth never existed, or that
we have no information we can trust respecting His life and
teaching, if we should see ourselves driven to deny His execution, or, acknowledging it, to believe that it was the end of Him,
it is hard to see how Christianity in any tenable sense could
remain our belief."[3]

But, as we have seen, we can have no uninterpreted knowledge
of these events which lie at the heart of the biblical revelation.
Our knowledge of them, as of all historical events, is inevitably
mediated. We can know of what happened at the Red Sea,
or by the rivers of Babylon, or in Galilee and Judaea only
through the written historical record. But recorded history is,
in the very nature of the case, interpreted, and therefore
subjectivized, history. We may examine and criticize the
historical record; we may assess its value by comparing it with
other accounts of the same event; but one thing we can never
do—we cannot get behind the record to the bare, uninterpreted
event. The Liberal search for the objective " Jesus of history "
behind the theologically coloured records of the New Testament provides a *reductio ad absurdum* proof of the fallacy of its
own presuppositions. It rejected the " subjectivized " New

---

[1] See further, Chapter VII.
[2] " The Theology of the Old Testament," in *Record and Revelation*, p. 304.
[3] *The Bible: its Origin, its Significance and its Abiding Worth*, p. 191.

Testament portrait, only to produce its own subjectivized " lives of Jesus " in which each author sketched the Man of Nazareth according to his own conception. In the words of Langmead Casserley, " we must either consent to see Jesus through the eyes and from the standpoint of the early Church or else resign ourselves not to see Him at all."[1]

The Gospels, as the most rigorous application of Form-Criticism has made abundantly clear,[2] were not intended as historical accounts or biographies of Jesus, but as books witnessing to the faith of the Church in Christ the Redeemer. The closing words of John xx could equally well stand at the end of any, or all, of the Synoptic Gospels: " Many other signs truly did Jesus in the presence of his disciples, which are not written in this book: but these are written, that ye might believe that Jesus is the Christ, the Son of God; and that believing ye might have life through his name."[3] This is not to say, however, that the historic events of the Incarnation are irrelevant for faith, as Barth and Tillich seem to imply. On the contrary, as we have seen, it is with historical events—not ideas—that the Christian Gospel is concerned. It is given through a series of events in the time-process which exhibit the mighty acts of the Lord, culminating in the Incarnation, and with the actuality of these events, therefore, it stands or falls. But what is the criterion of their historical truth?

The " correspondence theory " of truth must, of course, be abandoned; since we can have no immediate knowledge of the events in question, it is impossible to compare the record with the event recorded. Nor does the " coherence theory " stand us in any better stead. The coherence of a story does not of itself enable us to classify it as history rather than fiction or myth. Clearly, some new standard of reference is required, but what objective standard can there be? Is there any escape from a thoroughgoing subjectivism?

This question can only be answered by reference to the principles of modern historiography. The historian does not, as is popularly supposed, begin with a number of historical

[1] *The Christian in Philosophy*, p. 231.
[2] See Additional Note, " Recent Synoptic Criticism," pp. 46–8.
[3] John xx, 30–1.

" facts " accepted on the testimony of his " authorities " and
forthwith proceed to arrange and classify these " facts " in the
most coherent way. The " facts " of history are what he is
anxious to determine; they are the object of his enquiry and
hence emerge only at the end of it. His " authorities," so
called, merely supply a certain amount of " data " of varying
value as " evidence." It is the historian himself, however,
who must select his data. And he not only selects; he criticizes
and evaluates it by bringing to bear upon it a trained historical
imagination. In this way he arrives at the historical "facts."
Francis Bacon laid down, as the first principle of scientific
method, that the natural scientist must " put Nature to the
question." That, *mutatis mutandis*, is also the first principle of
historical method. The historian " puts his authorities in the
witness-box, and by cross-questioning extorts from them information which in their original statements they have withheld,
either because they did not wish to give it or because they did
not possess it. Thus, a commander's dispatches may claim a
victory; the historian, reading them in a critical spirit, will
ask: ' If it was a victory, why was it not followed up in this
or that way? ' and may thus convict the writer of concealing the
truth. Or, by using the same method, he may convict of
ignorance a less critical predecessor who has accepted the
version of the battle given him by the same dispatches."[1]

R. G. Collingwood, accepting Croce's principle that the basis
of historical knowledge is " associative imagination,"[2] finds
the essence of historiography in " the re-enactment of past
thought in the historian's own mind."[3] The historian must
penetrate to the " inside " of events that have happened,
detect the thought that they express, and so re-enact the past in
his own mind. " To the historian, the activities whose history
he is studying are not spectacles to be watched, but experiences
to be lived through in his own mind; they are objective, or
known to him, only because they are also subjective, or activities of his own."[4] But " the historian not only re-enacts past

---

[1] R. G. Collingwood, *The Idea of History*, p. 237.
[2] See B. Croce, *History as the Story of Liberty*, pp. 127–8.
[3] R. G. Collingwood, *op. cit.*, p. 215. See also pp. 282 ff.
[4] *Ibid.*, p. 218.

thought, he re-enacts it in the context of his own knowledge and therefore, in re-enacting it, criticizes it, forms his own judgment of its value, corrects whatever errors he can discern in it."[1] Furthermore, he must reconstruct what happened in periods for which there is no recorded evidence by " interpolating, between the statements borrowed from our authorities, other statements implied by them."[2]

Here what Collingwood calls " *a priori* imagination " comes into play. This is the free, but not arbitrary, imagination of the artist: " Characters and incidents are all alike imaginary; yet the whole aim of the novelist is to show the characters acting and the incidents developing in a manner determined by a necessity internal to themselves. The story, if it is a good story, cannot develop otherwise than it does; the novelist in imagining it cannot imagine it developing except as it does develop." It is also the perceptual imagination " supplementing and consolidating the data of perception in the way so well analysed by Kant, by presenting to us objects of possible perception which are not actually perceived: the under side of this table, the inside of an unopened egg, the back of the moon. Here again the imagination is *a priori*: we cannot but imagine what cannot but be there." Collingwood maintains that " the historical imagination differs from these not in being *a priori*, but in having as its special task to imagine the past: not an object of possible perception, since it does not now exist, but able through this activity to become an object of our thought. . . . There is nothing other than historical thought itself, by appeal to which its conclusions may be verified. The hero of a detective novel is thinking exactly like an historian when, from indications of the most varied kinds, he constructs an imaginary picture of how a crime was committed, and by whom."[3] According to Collingwood, that which makes the historical imagination *a priori* is an innate idea of the past which both controls imaginative historical thinking and is given detailed content by it.[4]

But the function of *a priori* imagination is not confined to filling in the gaps of the historical record; it is " the touchstone

[1] *Ibid.*, p. 215.   [2] *Ibid.*, p. 240.   [3] *Ibid.*, pp. 242-3.
[4] *Ibid.*, pp. 247-9.

by which we decide whether alleged facts are genuine. Suetonius tells me that Nero at one time intended to evacuate Britain. I reject his statement, not because any better authority flatly contradicts it, for of course none does; but because my reconstruction of Nero's policy based on Tacitus will not allow me to think that Suetonius is right. . . . I find myself able to incorporate what Tacitus tells me into a coherent and continuous picture of my own, and cannot do this for Suetonius."[1] Thus, " the *a priori* imagination which does the work of historical construction supplies the means of historical criticism as well."[2]

Collingwood's argument has been stated at some length, and, as far as possible, in his own words, because his conclusion is startling and appears, at first sight, to reduce all historical knowledge to pure subjectivism: "Freed from its dependence on fixed points supplied from without, the historian's picture of the past is thus in every detail an imaginary picture, and its necessity is at every point the necessity of the *a priori* imagination. Whatever goes into it, goes into it not because his imagination passively accepts it, but because it actively demands it."[3]

Are we then at the mercy of the historian's dreams and fancies? Is there no solid ground of objectivity on which to stand? Was Kierkegaard right in maintaining that subjectivity is truth?[4] If so, what becomes of all our talk about revelation through history? What guarantee have we that the imposing structure of the Christian faith is not an illusion, if the supposedly solid stuff of history on which it claims to be built is a mirage?

But is it? There are several observations that we may make regarding Collingwood's assertion:

1. Collingwood himself denies that his epistemology of history is *merely* subjective. Historical thought, he maintains, is not just thought but reflection; it is thought about thought. " So far as this thought is mere thought, the past is merely re-enacted; so far as it is thought about thought, the past is thought of as being re-enacted. . . . Historical knowledge is that special case of memory where the object of present thought

---

[1] *Ibid.*, pp. 244–5.   [2] *Ibid.*, p. 245.   [3] *Ibid.*, p. 245.
[4] See *Unscientific Postscript*.

is past thought, the gap between present and past being bridged not only by the power of present thought to think of the past, but also by the power of past thought to reawaken itself in the present."[1]

Historical thinking is thus objective as well as subjective; there is present in it not only the act of thinking but something that can be thought about. But it is never merely objective. History, since it can only be known through the re-enactment of past thought, " cannot be set before the thinking mind as a ready-made object, discovered as something independent of that mind and studied as it is in itself, in that independence. It can never be studied ' objectively,' in the sense in which ' objectively ' excludes ' subjectively.' It has to be studied as it actually exists, that is to say, as an act. And because this act is subjectivity (though not mere subjectivity) or experience, it can be studied only in its own subjective being, that is, by the thinker whose activity or experience it is. . . . Thus the act of thought in becoming subjective does not cease to be objective; it is . . . the critical study of one's own thought, not the mere awareness of that thought as one's own."[2]

2. According to Collingwood's view, the historian, far from spinning the web of historiography from his own entrails, is in fact apprehending the objective past in the only way in which it can be apprehended. Accepting Croce's dictum that " history is about the past which is present,"[3] Collingwood maintains that all true history is contemporary history in the sense that it can be re-lived by the historian. McIntyre has called attention to the similarity of this view to John Baillie's conception of " mediated immediacy."[4] " The so-called evidence of history," comments McIntyre, " is the medium through which we become immediately aware of the historical events. Whitehead had been content to say that values are eternal objects of thought—but Collingwood goes the whole way and affirms that historical events are equally eternally objects, because they can be apprehended by historical thought at any time."[5]

[1] *Op. cit.*, pp. 293-4.   [2] *Ibid.*, p. 292.
[3] *History as the Story of Liberty*, p. 274.
[4] See J. Baillie, *Our Knowledge of God*, pp. 178 ff.
[5] " Christ and History," *op. cit.*, p. 32.

3. Although, as we have seen (p. 93), the coherence of a story does not of itself guarantee its historicity, the " coherence theory " of truth is relevant if we apply it over a sufficiently large field. The historical imagination is not unrestricted; the picture of the particular bit of the past which it produces at any given time must be congruous with the larger picture of the whole past of which it is a part. As Collingwood remarks, " All history must be consistent with itself. Purely imaginary worlds cannot clash and need not agree; each is a world to itself. But there is only one historical world, and everything in it must stand in some relation to everything else."[1]

There is also a sense in which coherence, or rationality, can be a criterion of objectivity even within the confines of a particular historical field. In the words of Alan Richardson, " a true history will be one which gives us the most coherently rational account of the facts (i.e. data), and it will do this because of the soundness of its principle of interpretation. . . . It is the principle of interpretation which illuminates the past and makes sense of it; and of this our reason will judge by the test of coherence. We may therefore . . . speak of the objectivity of the principle of interpretation in history, since it is this which gives objectivity to our knowledge of the events that have occurred in the past." Applying this to the events of the biblical revelation, Richardson says: " Christians claim that the biblical principle of interpretation, as developed by the prophets and apostles, gives to us, when we accept it, the guarantee that the facts recorded in the Bible are broadly historical. It enables us to explain them coherently and rationally, without having to explain them away, and judged by the test of coherence it is more successful than any other interpretation."[2]

4. There is something else, besides the need for consistency and coherence, or rationality, which conditions the working of the historian's *a priori* imagination; it must be related, all along the line, to the evidence—the data with which he begins. " When a man thinks historically," says Collingwood, " he has before him certain documents or relics of the past. His business is to discover what the past was which has left

[1] *The Idea of History*, p. 246.   [2] *Christian Apologetics*, p. 147.

these relics behind it. For example, the relics are certain written words; and in that case he has to discover what the person who wrote those words meant by them. This means discovering the thought (in the widest sense of that word . . .) which he expressed by them."[1] Here is the crucial test of the objective actuality of any picture of the past which the historian draws. And in spite of his emphasis on the subjectivity of historiography, Collingwood has to admit that " the only way in which the historian or any one else can judge, even tentatively, of its truth is by considering this relation; and, in practice, what we mean by asking whether an historical statement is true is whether it can be justified by an appeal to the evidence."[2]

The evidence, of course, may take many different forms—written record, oral tradition, ethnic customs, philological findings, archaeological remains. In every case, however, it is something objective, something perceptible, something of which the historian has immediate knowledge and which he can therefore " put to the question." Moreover, as his historical knowledge grows, so does his field of evidence. He finds increasingly that facts which he has hitherto regarded as irrelevant for his particular problems can be used as evidence for them by asking the right questions.

Historical evidence thus serves a dual purpose. It is the data with which the historian begins and it is the touchstone to which he continually returns. Its first function is not only to guide the historical imagination but to make possible the historian's re-enactment of past thought by revealing what was in the minds of those whose actions he records. But the historian must continually check the accuracy of his picture; he must be certain that in thinking the thoughts of other men after them, it really is their thought that he re-enacts. This he does

[1] *The Idea of History*, p. 282.
[2] *Ibid.*, p. 246. Alan Richardson observes that, although Collingwood's book is particularly valuable as a critique of naturalistic philosophy or historical positivism (i.e. the assumption that the methodology of the natural sciences is to be taken as the pattern of historical thinking), he does not reach a clear understanding of the true nature of history. In this connection Richardson calls attention to Collingwood's complete failure to appreciate the biblical and Christian understanding of history. As a result, " he never quite frees himself from the naturalistic assumptions which he finds so repugnant." See *Christian Apologetics*, p. 96 f., Note 2.

by continually testing what he creates by the evidence of past thought which is in his hands and by continually checking and rechecking his own evaluation and interpretation of that evidence by reference to the coherence and rationality of the picture that he paints. The datum, which becomes evidence in his hands, does not change—although he may have to alter his evaluation of it in the light of his growing knowledge of the past, of new questions which he may put to the evidence, and of the changed perspective which may result from the discovery of fresh data. But the datum itself, whatever his interpretation of it, is always to hand as an objective criterion of truth.

Never has this criterion been applied more rigorously than in the case of biblical history. For over a century some of the ablest scholars, well trained and disciplined in textual criticism and historical method, have subjected the biblical records to a most searching scrutiny in the light of all the available data, both biblical and extra-biblical. No other ancient documents have undergone such a rigorous examination. And the result is that the substantial accuracy of the biblical narrative has been established beyond reasonable dispute. This, of course, does not imply the acceptance of every detail of the biblical story or the ignoring of its obvious discrepancies. The varied historical data of the Bible must be continually criticized and evaluated historically as is all other historical evidence. But the general outline of biblical history, its great crises—the Exodus; the conquest of Canaan and the establishment of the Monarchy; the Exile and Restoration; the life and ministry of Jesus of Nazareth; the rise and growth of the Christian Church—no competent historian would now dispute. It is at least as well attested as are the Peloponnesian Wars and Julius Caesar's invasion of Britain.

The fact that there are discrepancies in the biblical documents regarding details of the events which they record and that legend and history are sometimes interwoven is of no ultimate consequence for an historical revelation.[1] " If revelation consists, not in the bare events, but in the events as

---

[1] The relationship of myth, legend and history in the Bible is discussed in Chapter IV.

interpreted by the religious consciousness, we can be content even though many of the details are obscure. . . . What concerns us . . . is not the literal accuracy of this or that happening, but whether the interpretation as a whole is valid for the events in their broad totality."[1]

Since, therefore, we cannot legitimately separate event from interpretation in the biblical record, it follows that the criteria of evidence and coherence must be applied together in assessing the actuality of biblical history. As we have seen, a searching examination of the evidence attests its substantial accuracy. Does, then, the Christian interpretation enable us to give the most coherently rational account of the events to which the evidence points? Can we make sense of the data without it?

> The question is no longer whether every detail of the biblical history is literally and minutely true—whether Shem was a hundred years old when he begat Arpachshad and lived five hundred years more after that, whether Joshua made the sun stand still, or whether Herod Agrippa I was smitten in Caesarea by an angel of the Lord and was eaten by worms. Our question now is whether the modern scientific study of the facts of biblical history justifies the Church's view that the only satisfactory interpretation of those events is that they happened according to the will and through the power and guidance of a divine Being, whose character and purpose is revealed to us in them. Can the events of the Exodus from Egypt, or those of the extended period of crisis which culminated in the Exile in Babylon and the Return, or, above all, the events associated with the life and death and resurrection of Jesus Christ be so accounted for by the modern historian that he has no need of that hypothesis?[2]

The truth is surely, as Sanday concludes, that " there is a multitude of phenomena which points towards the positive reality of Revelation, and which are far better explained on that hypothesis than upon any other."[3]

It must be remembered, however, that revelation through history is only apprehended " existentially "; the biblical revelation can be seen for what it is only in the perspective of biblical faith. Without this the *deus revelatus* becomes a *deus absconditus*. The principle of medieval theology, inherited from

[1] C. R. North, *The Old Testament Interpretation of History*, p. xiii.
[2] Alan Richardson, *Christian Apologetics*, p. 91.
[3] W. Sanday, *Inspiration*, p. 430.

St. Augustine, still stands—*crede ut intellegas*. "In the under-standing of history, as in other matters, faith precedes under-standing; and those who bring no faith to history will find no faith-principle in it."[1] Reinhold Niebuhr points out that " the various principles of interpretation current in modern culture, such as the idea of progress or the Marxist concept of an his-torical dialectic, are all principles of historical interpretation introduced by faith. They claim to be conclusions about the nature of history at which men arrive after a ' scientific ' analysis of the course of events; but there can be no such analysis of the course of events which does not make use of some presupposition of faith, as the principle of analysis and interpretation." And of the Bible he says: " While the course of historical events does not inevitably yield the prophetic inter-pretation of events, it is significant that history does justify such an interpretation, once faith in the God of the prophets is assumed.[2]

VI. THE INSPIRATION OF THE BIBLE

The correlative of revelation is inspiration: " Whenever God revealed Himself, He inspired men to receive and to communi-cate the revelation."[3] Inspiration, therefore, is something attributed primarily to men rather than to a book. " What made the inspiration of the book? " asks P. T. Forsyth; and he replies: " It was the prior inspiration of the people and of the men by the revelation."[4] As we have seen, revelation is the resultant, as it were, of the interaction of two things—historic

---

[1] Alan Richardson, *op. cit.*, p. 99.

[2] *The Nature and Destiny of Man*, i, p. 151.

[3] J. Strahan, " Inspiration," in *Encyclopaedia of Religion and Ethics*, vii, p. 347.

[4] *Positive Preaching and the Modern Mind*, p. 16. Cf. W. Sanday, *Inspiration*, p. 127: " Just as one particular branch of one particular stock was chosen to be in a general sense the recipient of a clearer revelation than was vouchsafed to others, so within that branch certain individuals were chosen to have their hearts and minds moved in a manner more penetrating and more effective than their fellows, with the result that their written words convey to us truths about the nature of God and His dealings with man which other writings do not convey with equal fulness, power, and purity. We say that this special moving is due to the action upon those hearts and minds of the Holy Spirit. And we call that action Inspiration."

event and prophetic mind. And since both are divinely guided, the Bible may be spoken of as an inspired record of inspired events. " We cannot hold," says J. K. Mozley, " that the revelation is God's and leave no place for an activity of God in the record which answers to the revelation."[1]

When we speak of the inspiration of the Bible, therefore, we mean that intrinsic divine character of the Book which makes it the vehicle of the historic self-communication of God through Israel and supremely in Christ. The God whose mighty acts it relates speaks to *me* through its pages. " It is through an experience of the spiritual power of the Bible that the term [inspiration] first comes to have a real meaning. . . . It is the testimony of one generation after another that through the Scriptures God finds the soul and the soul finds God."[2] And, as Coleridge observes, " whatever *finds* me, bears witness for itself that it has proceeded from a Holy Spirit."[3]

The inspiration of the Bible is thus related rather to its *content* than to the process by which the biblical writings came into being.[4] Preoccupation with the process has frequently resulted in a view of inspiration which is formal and intellectual and obscures its deep religious significance—a view indeed which is fundamentally Greek and classical rather than Hebraic and biblical.

For Plato inspiration meant ecstatic possession, a condition in which human powers and faculties were suspended and man became a passive instrument in the hand of God. " No man,"

---

[1] " The Bible: Its Unity, Inspiration, and Authority," in *The Christian Faith*, ed. W. R. Matthews, p. 63.   [2] J. Strahan, *op. cit.*, p. 347.

[3] *Letters on the Inspiration of the Scriptures*, Letter i. Cf. A. S. Peake, *The Bible: Its Origin, its Significance, and its Abiding Worth*, p. 384: " It is much more important for us to feel the inspiration of the Bible than to construct an adequate dogma about it."

[4] See W. Sanday, *op. cit.*, pp. 139–40: " There has been a special Divine influence at work. . . . And if we are asked to define the measure of this special influence, we can see it reflected in that wide margin which remains when the common elements of the Biblical religion and other religions have been subtracted and that which is peculiar to the Bible is left." Cf. Karl Barth, *Kirchliche Dogmatik*, I/2, 578: The inspiration of the Bible is not " comparable with any other alleged or real inspiration. For it rests on the relationship of the biblical witnesses to the very definite content of their witness."

he says, " when in his wits, attains prophetic truth and inspiration; but when he receives the inspired word, either his intelligence is enthralled in sleep, or he is demented by some distemper or possession."[1]

> God takes away the minds of the poets and uses them as his ministers, and he also uses diviners and holy prophets, in order that we who hear them may know that they speak not of themselves who utter these priceless words in a state of unconsciousness, but that God is the speaker, and that through them He is conversing with us.[2]

This essentially pagan conception of inspiration was mediated to Jewish and Christian thought through Philo, who maintains that " a prophet gives forth nothing at all of his own, but acts as interpreter at the prompting of another in all his utterances, and as long as he is under inspiration he is in ignorance, his reason departing from its place and yielding up the citadel of the soul, when the Divine Spirit enters into it and dwells in it and strikes at the mechanism of his voice, sounding through it to the clear declaration of that which he prophesieth."[3] Thus we find the second-century apologist, Athenagoras, speaking of the Spirit using the prophets as a flute-player uses a flute[4] and the fourth-century Bishop of Salamis, Epiphanius, likening them to the plectrum which is used to strike the lyre.[5]

Such a view can claim no biblical support, however. In the Old Testament the inspiration of the prophet is admittedly linked with his ecstatic experience. " Any psychological phenomenon which the East does not understand is explained as being due to a ' breathing.' That is to say, some being, usually divine, has ' breathed ' into the person concerned and taken complete control over him. A ' breath ' or ' spirit ' has ' rushed ' upon him, and manifests itself in abnormal behaviour."[6] In the early stages of the prophetic movement the technical phrase used to describe the onset of ecstasy is significant—" the breath (or spirit) of God rushed upon him."[7] And there is good evidence that ecstatic experience continued to play some part in the

---

[1] *Timaeus*, 71.   [2] *Ion* (Jowett's translation).
[3] *De Specialibus Legibus*, iv, 8 (*Philonis Judaei Opera*, ed. Mangey, ii, p. 343).   [4] *Apology*, ix.   [5] *Haereses*, xlviii, 4.
[6] T. H. Robinson, *Prophecy and the Prophets*, p. 20.
[7] See I. Samuel xi, 6.

ministries of the great canonical prophets. But the prophet's own personality is never submerged, his faculties are never held in abeyance; the element of reflection is also present. Hence, as T. H. Robinson points out, " the fact that the prophet's message was thus given through an ecstatic experience does not deprive him of a personal share in its delivery " and " we have no reason to doubt that a prophet's ecstatic utterances were the expression of his own real opinions."[1]

Similarly, in the New Testament St. Paul claims his message is something which he has received from God,[2] he speaks as one possessing the Spirit of God;[3] yet that message is cast in the mould of his own personality and we see him wrestling with all the resources of language to express it. As H. H. Rowley observes, " The truth would seem to be that Paul was charged with a divinely given message, but that for the form in which it was delivered he was himself responsible. He was the ambassador, not the postman."[4]

In the case of the biblical writers, therefore, inspiration comes " not by the suspension of personality, but through the organ of personality."[5] In the words of Wand, " Inspiration does not put man's common faculties to sleep while God is left alone to speak, but it quickens these faculties beyond the point of genius."[6] There is no evidence that God ever violates human personality by withdrawing from man, even temporarily, the freedom with which He has endowed him or over-riding his mental powers and limitations. This is admitted by even so conservative a scholar as James Orr. " There is not," he says, " nor could be in Divine inspiration any suppression of human genius, faculty, or individuality. Limitations in the instrument condition receptivity for the message."[7] Thus, as Swete observes, " the human element in the written word coexists with the Divine after a manner inscrutable to our comprehension."[8]

It is often assumed that the New Testament writers, while

---

[1] *Op. cit.*, p. 44.   [2] Galatians i, 11–12, 15–16.
[3] I Corinthians vii, 40.   [4] *The Relevance of the Bible*, p. 47.
[5] H. H. Rowley, *ibid.*, p. 42.
[6] J. W. C. Wand, *The Authority of the Scriptures*, p. 62.
[7] *The Faith of a Modern Christian*, p. 16.
[8] H. B. Swete, *The Holy Spirit in the New Testament*, p. 339.

having no thought of themselves contributing to a corpus of
inspired literature, regarded the Old Testament Scriptures as
verbally inspired. And such a view of the Old Testament is
attributed to Christ Himself. This assertion, however, takes no
account of the freedom with which the writers of the New Testament cite the Old. Far from being bound by the *ipsissima verba*
of the Hebrew text, they use not only the Greek Septuagint but
also on occasions a free translation which sometimes gives the
impression that they are quoting imperfectly from memory.
And while Jesus appeals to the Old Testament as possessing
divine authority, He does not hesitate to supplant what has
been said by them of old time by " But I say unto you . . ."
or to sweep aside by one pronouncement the Levitical distinction between clean and unclean meats: " This he said, making
all meats clean " (Mark vii, 19, R.V.).

When we remember the extent to which first-century Jews
like Philo and Josephus were influenced by the Greek conception of inspiration, the truly remarkable thing is that the New
Testament writers are bound so little by the letter of the Old,
especially in view of the fact that " it was the accepted belief
in the later Old Testament period that the Spirit was the
source of all revelation, and the belief had been crystallized in
a formal doctrine of inspiration."[1] Indeed, there are only two
New Testament passages—and these are of doubtful authenticity—in which inspiration is directly attributed to the process
by which the Old Testament writings came into being—viz.
II Timothy iii, 16, and II Peter, i, 21. And neither of these,
rightly understood, implies a doctrine of *verbal* inspiration.

The first is rendered in the Authorized Version: "All scripture
is given by inspiration of God, and is profitable for doctrine,
for reproof, for correction, for instruction in righteousness ";
and in the Revised Version: " Every scripture inspired of
God is also profitable for teaching, for reproof, for correction,
for instruction which is in righteousness." Both are possible
translations of the Greek πᾶσα γραφὴ θεόπνευστος, but recent
translators seem to favour the sense of the Authorized Version.
In either case, however, the writer's purpose, as Swete points
out, is to teach not the inspiration of the Old Testament

[1] E. F. Scott, *The Spirit in the New Testament*, p. 165.

Scriptures but their use. " In what sense they are inspired, and whether their inspiration is such as to protect them from error, we are not taught, but only for what ends they were given."[1]

The text of the second passage (II Peter i, 21) is uncertain. In some ancient manuscripts the second clause reads: " Holy men of God spake as they were moved by the Holy Ghost " (as in the A.V.); in others it reads: " Men spake from God, being moved by the Holy Ghost " (as in the R.V.). Among modern translators Moffatt prefers the former reading and the compilers of the Revised Standard Version choose the latter. There seems to have been some confusion between the Greek words ΑΠΟ and ΑΓΙΟΙ, but in either case the sense is the same. And here again the writer is not primarily concerned with the inspiration of Scripture, but rather with its interpretation. This is quite clear when the passage is read in its context: " As prophecy was not given by the will of man, so neither can it be explained by the will of man. God gives both the vision and the interpretation thereof."[2] The word translated " moved," φερόμενοι, conveys the idea of men being carried along by the Holy Ghost as a ship is borne along by the wind. While this is reminiscent of metaphors used of inspiration by pagan writers it does not necessarily imply the Greek view (the idea of the Spirit as the divine " breath " or " wind " is thoroughly Hebraic); neither does it necessitate a doctrine of *verbal* inspiration and inerrancy. Swete, indeed, maintains that " the idea conveyed is not so much inspiration as rapture; the Wind of God carries men before it so that they go where they are driven."[3]

That the Scriptures are inspired, the Church has always believed; but, however much it has been influenced by the Greek view, it has never made belief in *verbal* inspiration a part of its creed. As Swete observes, " Inspiration is not defined in Scripture, and the Church has shewn a wise self-restraint in refusing to enter upon this ground."[4] Calvin's insistence that Scripture " came to us, by the instrumentality of men, from the

[1] *The Holy Spirit in the New Testament*, p. 330.
[2] C. Bigg, *St. Peter and St. Jude* (I.C.C.), p. 270.
[3] *Op. cit.*, p. 329.   [4] *Ibid.*, p. 339.

very mouth of God "[1] does not warrant Warfield's assertion
that " the Spirit's superintendence extends to the choice of the
words by the human authors (verbal inspiration), and preserves
its product from everything inconsistent with a divine authorship—thus securing, among other things, that entire truthfulness
which is everywhere presupposed in and asserted for Scripture by the biblical writers (inerrancy)."[2]   Inerrancy is neither
asserted nor presupposed by the biblical writers as Warfield
claims. And even if it were, as McIntyre observes, " before we
could accept what the Scripture writers had to say about plenary inspiration, we should require to have accepted plenary
inspiration—a patent *petitio principii.*"[3]   Whatever Warfield
may say, his position is not in fact that of classic Reformed
Theology. T. M. Lindsay is quite right when he maintains
that " Calvin does not require a theory of Divine superintendence which has for its object to produce an errorless record.
He asks in the *Institutes* how we can get at the complete credibility and authority of Scripture, and answers that we can only
do so when we learn that God is the Author."[4]   " Formal
inerrancy is not required to make Scripture the pure and
authentic Word of God."[5]   In the Reformers, " the universal
line of thought is that Scripture is inspired because it conveys
the authoritative and infallible Word of God; it is not infallible and authoritative because it is inspired."[6]

This brings us back to our main contention that the inspiration of the Bible has to do with its content rather than with
its evolution.[7]   Its real significance is not merely formal but
religious. " The form of the Bible is human; we can never be
free from the limitations of human records and recorders. But

[1] *Institutes*, I, vii, 5.

[2] B. B. Warfield, *The Inspiration and Authority of the Bible*, p. 173. Cf.
Samuel Chadwick's dictum to his students at Cliff College: " God never
held a dictation class—not even for prophets! "

[3] Review of Warfield, in *The Reformed Theological Review*, vol. ix, No. 2,
p. 20.

[4] " The Doctrine of Scripture," in *The Expositor*, v, 1, p. 289.

[5] *Ibid.*, p. 291.   [6] *Ibid.*, p. 288.

[7] Cf. *Doctrine in The Church of England*, p. 27: " Belief that the Bible is the
inspired record of God's self-revelation to man and of man's response to that
revelation is not for us a dogma imposed as a result of some theory of the
mode of the composition of the books, but a conclusion drawn from the
character of their contents and the spiritual insight displayed in them."

the substance of the whole Biblical material is not a human message but a divine one, the Gospel."[1] " The deeper tone of the one divine voice is heard through the many changing tones of the human voices."[2] Or, to use Eric Fenn's metaphor, " the light which reaches us through the written word is the light of God, but it is refracted in the medium of human experience and human history."[3] Inspiration is essentially dynamic, not static. It is not to be limited to the initial recording of God's mighty revelatory acts; it inheres within the record itself, making it an effectual mode of the Divine Word so that " the effect of the teaching as a whole is as of a communication from another world " and " the total impression conveyed by the Bible is that of a breath from heaven."[4]

VII. THE UNIQUENESS OF THE BIBLE

The Christian claim that the Bible is unique among all literature is not based upon any theory of *verbal* inspiration but follows logically from the Christian belief that God has revealed himself uniquely in the history of the Hebrew people. " Christianity with Judaism, of which it is the child, sees a unique significance in certain events in history. Hence the Bible, which records and interprets these events, is deemed to be unique literature."[5]

The question is sometimes asked, Is not other great literature inspired equally with the Bible? Why, then, should only the Bible be read in Church? Why not also read Shakespeare or Keats? The answer is that while portions of, say, the *Phaedo* of Plato, or Milton's *Paradise Lost*, or Keats' *Ode to a Nightingale* are certainly inspired in the sense that they embody an apprehension of that beauty and truth which belong to the eternal realm and which is given, we are constrained to believe, by the " in-breathing " of God, their inspiration is nevertheless of a different order, a different kind, from that of the Bible.[6]

[1] J. K. Mozley, " The Bible: Its Unity, Inspiration and Authority," in *The Christian Faith*, ed. W. R. Matthews, p. 64.   [2] *Ibid.*, p. 55.
[3] " The Word of God and the Written Word," in *The Student World*, No. 2, 1949.   [4] J. W. C. Wand, *The Authority of the Scriptures*, p. 55.
[5] N. Micklem, *What is the Faith?*, p. 83.
[6] See J. W. C. Wand, *op. cit.*, pp. 52–3.

Someone has suggested that we might, with certain reservations, call it " secular " inspiration as opposed to the " religious " inspiration of the Bible. The difference is ultimately a difference of content.[1] The plain fact is that other great literature, although it may bring us face to face with the eternal values of beauty, truth and goodness, does not lead us to that unique revelation of God in the history of Israel.

The Bible is not a miscellaneous collection of " inspired " literature. It is the record and interpretation of a particular process in the history of a particular nation, through which God was giving a unique revelation of Himself which culminated in Jesus Christ, in whom the divine Word, given in the great crises of Israel's history and uttered by the mouth of the prophets, becomes incarnate in a human personality: " The Word became flesh."

Goethe's Time Spirit in *Faust* sums up the matter in a classic line:

> Thus on the roaring loom of time I ply,
> And weave for God the garment thou seest Him by.

---

[1] Cf. H. H. Rowley, *The Authority of the Bible*, p. 6: " In so far as the Bible is concerned, its inspiration is to be recognized only in so far as it embodies the revelation of God's character and will, and its authority rests on its divine origin, as evidenced by its inspiration."

CHAPTER IV

MYTH, LEGEND AND HISTORY

I. BIBLICAL " MYTHS "

MODERN theologians frequently use the term "myth" to describe those parts of the Bible which are concerned with supra-historical realities—the creation of the world and the final winding up of history. The term is unfortunate because it is liable to give the impression that scholars regard these parts of the Bible as mere fairy-tales. It is not to be wondered at, therefore, that many people, who have long discerned their deep religious significance, should be both suprised and shocked to think that the early stories of Genesis and the New Testament teaching about the Second Coming of Christ and the Last Judgment were being classed with Greek mythology or Aesop's Fables.

But that is to misunderstand the theological use of the term. The Greek word μῦθος means a story—anything delivered by word of mouth. It is used by Homer in this wide sense. From the time of Pindar, however, μῦθος is reserved for the poetic, as distinct from the historic, story (λόγος). Thus in Attic prose it is used to describe a tradition of early times before the dawn of history. The term, therefore, has come technically to mean a story which expresses supra-historical truth in a symbolic form. As C. H. Dodd has put it, a myth tells the story of something that never *happened*, but continually *happens*. Demeter never *lost* or *found* Persephone, but she *loses* and *finds* her every year.

The myth, as expressing a living reality in symbolic form, draws its imagery from that deep substratum of the human mind which the psychologist calls the " collective unconscious." This accounts for the similarity of myth symbolism in widely separated parts of the world between which primitive cultural contact has been impossible,[1] and also for its recurrence in the imagery of our dreams. There is, moreover, as Arnold Toynbee points out,[2] one dominant motif which we find constantly recurring in the myth proper of all peoples—the encounter between two superhuman personalities; Jehovah and the Serpent in the Genesis story, Ahura Mazdah and Angra Mainyu in the Zoroastrian myth, Gods and Demons in the Scandinavian *Voluspa*, Artemis and Aphrodite in Euripides' *Hippolytus*, the Lord and Mephistopheles in Goethe's *Faust*. Toynbee thus finds in mythology a deep insight into the nature of the principle of challenge-and-response which is the basis of his monumental work on the growth and decline of civilizations. The language of mythology is therefore the corrective of the " Apathetic Fallacy " of applying to historical thought a scientific method applicable only to inanimate Nature.[3]

Some of the greatest religious truths can only be expressed in this way. They are outside the scope of scientific analysis and description. They defy the rules of logic. The only adequate vehicle of their expression is a story in the setting of this world but pointing beyond it—what is technically called a " myth." Thus, as Reinhold Niebuhr observes, " mythical thought is not only pre-scientific; it is also supra-scientific. It deals with vertical aspects of reality which transcend the horizontal relationships which science analyses, charts and records. . . . In this sense the myth alone is capable of picturing the world as a realm of coherence and meaning without defying the facts of incoherence. Its world is coherent because all facts in it are related to some central source of meaning; but it is not rationally coherent because the myth is not under the abortive necessity of relating all things to each other in terms of immediate rational unity."[4]

The Word of God given to us in the Bible is, therefore, sometimes expressed in mythical form: it is " truth embodied in a tale." But, as Alan Richardson points out, this does not mean that the early stories of Genesis, for instance, are to be classed with *Cinderella* or Grimms' *Fairy Tales*. " The difference is that

---

[1] See J. G. Frazer, *Folk-Lore in the Old Testament*, part 1.
[2] *A Study of History*, i, pp. 271 ff.   [3] *Ibid.*, i, pp. 7–8, 271.
[4] *An Interpretation of Christian Ethics*, p. 36.

the religious myth corresponds to something which is true in reality, but which cannot be expressed in the language of science or prose, because it concerns ultimates which cannot be measured. . . . When the Nicene Creed says, ' He came down from Heaven,' or when the Apostles' Creed speaks of the Descent into Hell or the Ascension into Heaven, or when it speaks of Christ sitting at the right hand of the Father, these statements are true, but they are true in the sense of myth or poetry, and their religious depth is missed if they are merely taken literally. The express in the language of time and space truths which transcend the temporal and spatial altogether."[1]

We must be careful, however, not to confuse this technical use of the term " myth," as applied to parts of the Bible, with mythology. Even such a conservative scholar as James Orr admits that " we may, if we please, speak of a tradition like that of Eden as ' mythical.' " But he insists, quite rightly, that " ' myth ' in this case must be distinguished from mythology proper, i.e. such weaving of stories about the gods in their relations to each other and to the world as are found in other religions, and have generally their origin in nature-phenomena (e.g. sun-myths, dawn-myths, myths of growth and reproduction, etc.)." And he goes on to assert that " from this element . . . the Biblical religion seems entirely free."[2] Orr wrote these words in 1906. It is noteworthy, therefore, nearly half a century later, to find a modern scholar like G. E. Wright calling attention to " the remarkable fact that the God of Israel has no mythology. Since history rather than nature was the *primary* sphere of his revelation, Israel's effort was to tell the story of her past in terms of God's activity. There was no necessity for nature myths. Yahweh, for example, was no dying-rising God like Baal of Canaan. He was *the living God*."[3]

The Bible encloses human history in a " mythical " framework which begins with Creation and the Fall and ends with the Second Coming of Christ and the Last Judgment. " Both

---

[1] *Preface to Bible-Study*, pp. 77–8.
[2] *The Problem of the Old Testament*, p. 486.
[3] *The Old Testament Against its Environment*, p. 26. We do find in the Old Testament vestiges of old myths, e.g. the victorious fight of the Creator against the dragon of darkness (see p. 116); but they are no longer taken seriously.

myths," says Richardson, " speak of a truth which transcends
time, although they use time-symbols. The idea of the end of
time is as inconceivable as that of its beginning. But whereas
the one myth affirms: ' In the beginning God,' so the other
declares: ' At the end Christ.' "[1] It is against this background,
therefore, that we must see the Genesis Creation narratives.
We miss the whole point of them if we insist upon regarding
them as historic accounts of the first days, or as a scientific
description of the making and peopling of the world. They are
not merely pre-historic and pre-scientific, but supra-historic and
supra-scientific. " When we call the story of the Garden of
Eden a myth," says S. H. Hooke, " we do not thereby deny its
truth; we imply rather that its truth lies deeper than the super-
ficial layer of truth which rests on dates and documentary
evidence."[2]

The Book of Genesis opens with two distinct Creation stories
which diverge considerably in their content and do, in fact,
come down to us from widely separated periods of Hebrew
history. The first, which begins at verse 1 of Chapter i and ends
with verse 4a of Chapter ii, belongs to the latest stratum of the
Pentateuch—the Priestly Code—and was written therefore in
either exilic or early post-exilic times, that is the last half of
the sixth century or the first half of the fifth century B.C. The
second, which is given in Chapter ii from verse 4b to verse 25,
is very much earlier. It belongs to the " J " stratum and hence
is to be dated in the early monarchy, probably the ninth,
or even perhaps the tenth, century B.C.

These two stories are characterized by marked differences of
style. The Priestly one is rather cold and formal and reads
something like a lawyer's document. The earlier one is vivid
and graphic, and the writer " was interested in the kind of
question which one would nowadays address to the Brains
Trust: Why the serpent crawls on its belly, why people wear
clothes, and so on."[3] God, in the Priestly account, is remote
and abstract. He speaks and it is done: " And God said, Let
there be light: and there was light."[4] But in the earlier

---

[1] *Preface to Bible-Study*, p. 77.
[2] *In the Beginning* (Clarendon Bible, O.T., vi), p. 16.
[3] A. Richardson, *op. cit.*, p. 76.   [4] Genesis, i, 3.

document He is presented almost as a man: He forms Adam out of the dust and walks in the garden in the cool of the day. Furthermore, the order of creation is different in each account. According to the Priestly writer, fishes and birds appear on the fifth day, and the animals, and finally man, are created on the sixth day. Moreover both sexes of the human species are formed at the same time: " So God created man in his own image, in the image of God created he him; male and female created he them."[1] In the earlier " J " account, however, man—male only—is created first. Then the lower animals are made and named by man. And finally woman, as a sort of afterthought, is formed out of Adam's rib. As James Frazer puts it: " To relieve the loneliness of man, who wandered without a living companion in the beautiful garden which had been created for him, God fashioned all the birds and beasts and brought them to man, apparently to amuse him and keep him company. Man looked at them and gave to them all their names; but still he was not content with these playmates, so at last, as if in despair, God created woman out of an insignificant portion of the masculine frame, and introduced her to man to be his wife."[2]

It is interesting to compare these Hebrew stories with the Babylonian account given in the Seven Tablets of Creation, sometimes known as the Gilgamesh Epic from the name of its semi-divine hero, Gilgamesh. According to this account the creation of the world is the result of a battle between the god Marduk and the monster Tiamat, who is usually represented as a dragon. The result of the battle is that Marduk slays the monster and cuts her body into two pieces. With one half he makes the earth and with the other half the " firmament " of heaven to hold back the waters of Chaos from the world. In the words of the Epic:

Marduk cleft Tiamat in two like a fish:
The half of her he raised up, and made a covering for the heavens.
He pushed a bolt before, placed watchers here,
Commanded them not to let the waters out.
So the heavens he created.

[1] Genesis i, 27.   [2] *Folk-Lore in the Old Testament* (abridged ed.), p. 2.

With this we may compare Genesis i, 6–7 (" P "): " And God said, Let there be a firmament in the midst of the waters, and let it divide the waters from the waters. And God made the firmament, and divided the waters which were under the firmament from the waters which were above the firmament: and it was so." Incidentally, the Hebrew word for " deep " in Genesis i, 2 (" P "): " And the earth was without form, and void; and darkness was upon the face of the deep," is *t*ʰ*ôm*, which is at least reminiscent of the monster Tiamat in the Babylonian myth. We may also note striking parallels in Isaiah li, 9: " Art thou not it that cut Rahab in pieces, that pierced the dragon? " and in Psalm lxxiv, 13–14: " Thou didst divide the sea by thy strength: thou brakest the heads of the dragons in the waters. Thou brakest the heads of leviathan in pieces."

The Babylonian epic, like the biblical poem, goes on to tell of the creation of sun, moon and stars:

> He prepared stations for the great gods,
> As stars like to them he placed the constellations.
> He lit up the moon to rule the night,
> He ordained it as a night body to mark the days:
> Monthly for ever to go forth giving light to the land.
> At the beginning of the month beaming forth with horns,
> To determine six days:
> On the seventh day the disk shall be half.

And the seventh day is to be set aside for special observance:

> Seventh Day, *Nubattum*, an Evil Day:
> Cooked flesh he shall not eat: he shall not change his coat:
> He shall not put on clean clothes:
> He shall pour no libation:
> No oracle shall speak.
> The physician shall not heal the sick.
> On this day all business is forbidden.

" If," comments S. L. Caiger, " this unlucky day was indeed the forerunner of the Sabbath, it certainly furnishes, as Jastrow observes, 'another illustration of how it came about that the Babylonian and the Hebrew, starting out with so much in common, should have ended by having so little in common.' "[1]

[1] *Bible and Spade*, p. 17.

Finally the Babylonian account tells thus of the creation of man:

> Marduk said,
> Blood will I take, and bone will I build,
> Creating mankind.

With this we may compare Genesis ii, 23 (" J "), where Adam says of the woman, " This is now bone of my bones, and flesh of my flesh." And in the same connection we may note the account given in the Sumerian Hymn to Aruru:

> In accordance with the incantation
> Design a form that man may bear:
> The man like Ninib in form,
> The woman like Nintud in form shall be.

Which at least resembles Genesis i, 26-7 (" P "): " And God said, Let us make man in our image, after our likeness. . . . So God created man in his own image, in the image of God created he him; male and female created he them."

Such striking parallels do not necessarily indicate a dependence of the Hebrew upon the Babylonian account. But they do clearly point to a widespread tradition in the ancient world which was the common ancestor of both. The most significant fact, however, is the infinitely higher level of the Hebrew myth, which needs no pointing out.

Having looked at the chief characteristics of these Genesis Creation stories against the background of religious myths in general and compared them with the similar Babylonian accounts, we are now in a position to enquire into their meaning. A true understanding of them will obviously depend upon a recognition of their real nature. As Richardson says, " Treat the story of the Creation as a literal description of what happened ' in the beginning ' and you are landed in every form of absurdity; regard it, on the other hand, as an attempt to express in temporal pictures a truth about something beyond time, and it is at once filled with religious meaning."[1] What, then, is the truth which it expresses?

It affirms that God alone is the Creator of all things, the *fons et origo* of all being. That was by no means axiomatic in

[1] *Preface to Bible-Study*, p. 76.

the ancient world. Indeed at no point does the particular Hebrew conception of God diverge more from the current Greek conception than in the relation which it posits between God and the world. The Greek deity was not necessarily the creator. Plato doubts whether all things were created by God, while Aristotle maintains that the world came into being, not by a divine act of will, but as a kind of by-product of the process of eternal self-contemplation. The Gnostic sects of the second century A.D. went further and affirmed that the material world was the work of an inferior Demiurge and regarded it as the prison-house of the soul: σῶμα-σῆμα.[1] But for the Hebrews, God as Righteous Will manifested Himself in action; their Object of worship was the Living God who was known by what He did. God revealed His power in the world through His Spirit—the divine breath or wind—and His activity was seen first and foremost in creation. The God of Hebrew thought is not an object of intellectual excogitation but the living Source of all things.

This world is not eternal; there was a time when it did not exist. Scientists can calculate its age; they can discover what happened on it millions of years before man appeared; they can trace the development of life from the cell of protoplasm to man; but they cannot tell us why this happened or how it all began. But a Hebrew poet was once gazing at the world around him and the sky above him when he suddenly realized, in a flash of prophetic insight, that all this was the handiwork of God. " In the beginning," he wrote, " God created the heavens and the earth." We have learnt much since those words were first written, but nothing that we have learnt can take us beyond them. The theory of organic evolution, for instance, in no way conflicts with the Christian doctrine of man as created in the image of God, since it deals only with the process by which he came into being, not with what he essentially is. It merely explains the method by which life developed on the earth; it can tell us nothing of either its origin or its purpose. This biblical myth, therefore, enshrines a truth which is basic in the Christian faith—the assertion of the Epistle to the Hebrews

[1] σῶμα-σῆμα is of course much older than Gnosticism—probably Orphic.

that, " He that built all things is God."[1] " Belief in the creation," says J. S. Whale, " means a way, *the* way, of understanding the present world. It is an act of faith (Hebrews
xi, 3). Creation out of nothing is not to be understood as an
historical event but as a description of existence." This doctrine " is not a cosmological theory, but an expression of our
adoring sense of the transcendent majesty of God and of our
utter dependence upon Him."[2]

A significant feature of the later Creation story in Genesis i
is its introduction of a new and immensely fruitful idea—the
idea of the Creative Word.[3] In place of the crude anthropo-
morphism of the earlier account of Genesis ii, 4 ff, the transcendent God speaks and it is done. " His *Word*, the utterance
of a thinking Mind and a deliberate Will, illuminates the dark
abyss of nothingness, and calls into being things that are not."[4]
The relationship of God to man, Creator to creature, is thus
lifted on to a higher plane. As Dodd observes, the idea of the
creative Word " holds a commanding position in the history of
thought, and, in its developed form, it has become central to the
philosophy of the Christian religion."[5] Genesis i must be read
in the light of John i, which epitomizes the whole story of the
biblical revelation;

> In the beginning was the Word; and the Word was with God;
> and the Word was God. The same was in the beginning with
> God. Through Him all things came into existence; and without
> Him nothing came into existence. . . . He was in the world; and the
> world was made through Him; and the world did not recognize
> Him. He came to His own place, and those who were His own did
> not receive Him. . . . And the Word became flesh, and dwelt among
> us; and we beheld His glory—glory as of the Father's only Son—
> full of grace and truth. (C. H. Dodd's translation.)

Following the Creation stories is the myth of the Garden and
the Fall. Archaeologists have unearthed several examples of
what has come to be called the Adam and Eve Seal. It shows
a fruit tree at each side of which sit two clothed figures, while a

---

[1] Hebrews iii, 4.   [2] *Christian Doctrine*, p. 32.
[3] See C. H. Dodd, *The Bible To-day*, pp. 30–2, 107–9. As John Marsh
points out, this idea derives from the Hebrew conception of history. See
The Fulness of Time, pp. 65–70.   [4] C. H. Dodd, *op. cit.*, p. 31.
[5] *Ibid.*, p. 32.

little way off, standing on the tip of its tail, is a serpent. Until
the discovery of *The Sumerian Epic of the Creation and Paradise* by
Langdon in 1915, these Adam and Eve Seals appeared to be the
only evidence of any parallel story of the Garden of Eden in
Babylonian mythology. They are now, however, generally
regarded as representing a quite different scene in the Gilgamesh
Epic, where a serpent assists Utnapishtim and his wife in
guarding the tree of life.

Langdon's Sumerian Epic, however, does provide us with a
parallel to the Genesis story, but with one important difference
—the Flood comes in between the age of innocence and the
eating of the fruit of the forbidden tree. Here are some extracts,
the first depicting the Age of Innocence:

> In Dilmun, the Garden of the gods,
> Where Enki with his consort lay,
> That place was pure, that place was clean,
> The lion slew not,
> The wolf plundered not the lambs,
> The dog harried not the kids in repose,
> The birds forsook not their young,
> The doves were not put to flight.
> There was no disease nor pain,
> No lack of wisdom among princes,
> No deceit or guile.

Then, for some rather vague reason, there comes the Flood,
after which its sole survivor, Tag-Tug, is back again in the
Garden. Like Adam and Eve, he may eat of the fruit of the
trees of the Garden:

> My king, as to the fruit-bearing plants
> He shall pluck, he shall eat.

But the fruit of one tree is forbidden, and a curse follows his
disobedience in eating of it:

> My king the cassia plant approached:
> He plucked, he ate.
> Then Ninharsag in the name of Enki
> Uttered a curse:
> The face of Life, until he dies,
> Shall he not see.

And so evil and death enter into Paradise:

My brother, what of thee is ill?
My pastures are distressed,
My flocks are distressed,
My mouth is distressed,
My health is ill.

" Such," comments Caiger, " is the tragic end of the Legend of Dilmun. It is the story of a Paradise on earth, of a forbidden tree, of a Happiness that was lost. But when we look for anything corresponding to the strong moral element underlying the Biblical narrative, we look in vain."[1]

The Genesis story is a continuation of the older Creation narrative, the " J " account which begins at Chapter ii, verse 4b, and goes on through Chapter iii. It is perhaps the profoundest " myth " of the Bible, embodying as it does penetrating insights into the basic contradiction of human life—the contradiction between man's essential nature and his empirical state; between man as God intended him to be and man as he actually is. What is described here is neither a discoverable place nor a datable event, but a fact of human experience which is true for every man and woman in every age. " Eden is on no map, and Adam's fall fits no historical calendar. Moses is not nearer to the Fall than we are, because he lived three thousand years before our time. The Fall refers not to some datable aboriginal calamity in the historic past of humanity, but to a dimension of human experience which is always present—namely, that we who have been created for fellowship with God repudiate it continually; and that the whole of mankind does this along with us. Everyman is his own ' Adam,' and all men are solidarily ' Adam.' Thus, Paradise before the Fall, the *status perfectionis*, is not a period of history, but our ' memory ' of a divinely intentioned quality of life, given to us along with our consciousness of guilt. . . . Man's tragic apostasy from God is not something which happened once for all a long time ago. It is true in every moment of existence. If you believe in the Creation, you must go on to believe in the Fall. The symbolism of the one is a necessary complement to the symbolism of the other."[2]

The picture of man which is given to us in this story of the

[1] *Bible and Spade*, p. 20.   [2] J. S. Whale, *Christian Doctrine*, p. 52.

Garden and the Fall is one which repudiates three modern conceptions:

1. The first is the conception of Naturalism. According to this, man is, in the words of a distinguished scientist, " a rather long-lived animal with great powers of enjoyment." Such a conception virtually reduces man to a very complex piece of biological mechanism: he is but a highly developed beast. Not only his actions but his thoughts are determined by physico-chemical processes in his brain cells, by inherited tendencies, and by the action of endocrine glands.

There is, of course, some truth in such an assertion. The biological evidence seems to point to the fact that man is linked by his body to the animal world: he has evolved or developed out of it. But when a Greek philosopher defined man as a two-legged animal without feathers, Diogenes showed the absurdity of his definition by throwing a plucked cockerel onto the table. Human personality is a fact which must be reckoned with. Man may be only a reed, but, as Pascal said, he is a thinking reed: " If the whole universe combined to crush him he would still be the greater, for he alone is capable of knowing that he is crushed." The fact of personality defies any attempt to reduce it without remainder to any mere function of the brain and glands.

This theory goes wrong because it confuses values with origins. Because thought is accompanied by certain processes in the brain, it identifies it with those processes: because man has developed from brute stock, it equates him with the brute. But, as T. E. Jessop remarks, " the only creature that can prove anything cannot prove its own insignificance without depriving the proof of any proof-value. Any radical depreciation of man involves an equally radical depreciation of the scientific thinking which supplies the supposed evidence."[1] In other words, if you reduce man to a beast, if the brain secretes thought as the liver secretes bile, then all his theories—including this one— are worthless.

It is this fact of the uniqueness of human personality which is central in the Genesis " myth." *In imagine Dei factus est.* Man

---

[1] " The Scientific Account of Man," in *The Christian Understanding of Man* (Oxford Conference), p. 37.

is no beast; he is the crown of creation; he is made in the image of God. " The individuality and activity of selfhood emerge in human personality just because it belongs to a higher plane than that of organic evolution."[1]

, 2. The second modern conception of man which this Genesis story repudiates is poles apart from the first: it is the conception of Humanism. Instead of depreciating man to the level of the beasts, it exalts him as lord of the universe: it makes him a god. With Shakespeare in *Hamlet* it says: " What a piece of work is man! How noble in reason! How infinite in faculty! In form and moving how express and admirable! In action how like an angel! In apprehension how like a god! " Its anthem is:

> Glory to man in the highest,
> For man is the master of things.

Its prophet is H. G. Wells.

Swinburne's words have a terrible irony today, and Wells' *Homo sapiens* is the cry of a disillusioned man. But the Victorians really believed that man was the master of his fate, the captain of his soul. They believed that humanity was capable of building for itself Utopia. At the Great Exhibition of 1851 the Prince Consort was quite confident that we were on the eve of the state when

> . . . the war-drums throbbed no longer and the battle-flags were
>   furled
> In the Parliament of Man, the Federation of the World.

But it is not without significance that in this same poem[2] Tennyson

> Heard the heavens fill with shouting and there rained a ghastly
>   dew
> From the nations' airy navies, grappling in the central blue.

Events of the last twenty years supply their own tragic comment.

If the Genesis " myth " asserts that man is not beast, it affirms also that neither is he God. His knowledge may be power, but power to do what? Destroy himself? It points to man's self-sufficiency as the root of his tragic predicament. If

[1] H. W. Robinson, *The Christian Doctrine of Man*, p. 277.
[2] *Locksley Hall.*

he is made in the image of God, he is nevertheless a creature who is dependent upon God. And it is the repudiation of his creatureliness which is, to use Dorothy Sayers' phrase, " man's eldest sin." " We have turned every one to his own way." The Satanic promise, " Ye shall be as gods," is the perennial temptation before which man falls.

3. The third modern conception which is repudiated by the Genesis story is that of Totalitarianism. For nearly three hundred million people man, during the last twenty years, has existed solely for the State. Totalitarianism means that " nationalism is the chief end of Man. The parade ground is its symbol; the ant-heap its working model. The ultimate sanction for what is right lies in the State. It controls and drills the individual from the cradle to the grave, prescribing with pagan ruthlessness not only what he is to do but what he is to believe."[1] In other words, not only does man become a mere robot, a well-oiled cog in the vast totalitarian machine, but it is to the State that his highest allegiance must be given, to the exclusion of everything else.

Against all that, the Genesis " myth " maintains that man was made for God and for Him alone. God seeks his personal fellowship as He walks in the garden in the cool of the day. It is to God alone that his highest allegiance is due. Milton, in his immortal commentary on Creation and the Fall, *Paradise Lost*, pictures the first pair in their early perfection at the close of the day:

> Thus, at their shady lodge arrived, both stood,
> Both turn'd, and under open sky adored
> The God that made both sky, air, earth, and heaven,
> Which they beheld, the moon's resplendent globe,
> And starry pole. . . .

The Shorter Catechism but reiterates the message of this profound Hebrew " myth " when it asserts that man's chief end is to glorify God and enjoy Him for ever.

The best commentary on the Old Testament story of the Fall is the New Testament parable of the Prodigal Son: " I have sinned against heaven, and before thee, and am no more

---

[1] J. S. Whale, *Facing the Facts*, pp. 13–14.

worthy to be called thy son,"[1] and the seventh chapter of the
Epistle to the Romans: " O wretched man that I am! who shall
deliver me from the body of this death? "[2]

Finally, this Genesis " myth " of the Garden and the Fall
depicts the alienation from God which man's sin brings about.
The unhappy pair hide themselves among the trees when God
walks in the garden in the cool of the day, and for their disobedience and rebellion they must leave Paradise:

> In either hand the hastening angel caught
> Our lingering parents, and to the eastern gate
> Led them direct, and down the cliff as fast
> To the subjected plain; then disappear'd.
> They, looking back, all the eastern side beheld
> Of Paradise, so late their happy seat,
> Waved over by that flaming brand, the gate
> With dreadful faces throng'd and fiery arms.
> Some natural tears they drop't, but wiped them soon;
> The world was all before them, where to choose
> Their place of rest, and Providence their guide.
> They, hand in hand, with wandering steps and slow,
> Through Eden took their solitary way.[3]

" The myth closes," says Richardson, " with the picture of
the angel with the flaming sword, excluding sinful man from
Paradise in which stands the tree of life; not by snatching the
fruit of the tree is man to become as God, immortal and all-
knowing; the price of redemption is more costly than that.
But the whole revelation of the Bible completes the myth when
it tells of another tree of life, situated not in a garden but on a
hill outside a city, by which the cost of redemption is borne and
man is admitted to Paradise through Him who became what we
are in order that we might become what He is. 'Behold, the
man is become as one of us.' So in the light of the New Testament are we to understand the insights of the Old."[4]

II. Biblical " Legends "

There are some biblical narratives which belong to a type of
literature that is midway between " myth " and history. They
are classed as " legends." Here again, however, the term is not

---

[1] Luke xv, 18–19.   [2] Romans, vii, 24.
[3] Milton, *Paradise Lost*.   [4] *Preface to Bible-Study*, p. 80.

to be understood in the popular sense of a mere wonder-story or unauthentic fable. The derivation of the modern technical sense of the word is interesting. Coming from the Latin *legenda* —" things to be read," it was originally used to describe written narratives of the medieval Church, and more particularly a chronicle of the lives of saints which was read at mattins or refections. It thus came to refer to any marvellous story of the saints, and thence was used " in the wider significance of the tales of heroes on the borderland between myth and strict history,"[1] so coming to signify any ancient tale. By a curious irony, therefore, the meaning of the term has completely changed. From its primary etymological sense of " something read " it has now come to mean " something told,"[2] the outcome not of earlier documents but of oral tradition, *Sage* as contrasted with *Geschichte*, Folk-lore—" the mass of popular narrative *talk* about the past, which exists in more or less profusion amongst all races in the world."[3]

Both " myth " and " legend " belong properly, therefore, to the pre-literary period of a nation's history, when the memory of events is handed down from generation to generation by oral tradition.[4] They are in fact closely related and not always easy to distinguish. There is, however, one important distinction—the " legend " is based upon historic fact; the " myth " is not. Hence, a " legend " is not necessarily untrustworthy: to skilled investigation it may yield a point of history. " Legend " is therefore to be associated more closely with history than with " myth." The gap between " legend " and " myth " is frequently obscured by the fact that " myths " have a habit of securing an attachment in " legend," although they are really quite independent in origin. Significantly enough " myths " reappear in dreams; " legends " do not. Biblical " legends " embody some of the profound insight of the biblical " myth." It is by virtue of this fact that they become the vehicles of revelation and truth.

[1] A. R. Gordon, *The Early Traditions of Genesis*, p. 78.
[2] " La légende (legenda), c'est ce qui se dit, ce qui doit être raconté." E. Jacob, *La Tradition Historique en Israël*, p. 21.
[3] J. Skinner, *Genesis* (I.C.C.), p. iv.
[4] " Legend is the form which the memory of events assumes in what are called ' heroic ages.' " C. H. Dodd, *The Bible To-day*, p. 54.

The stories of the Flood and the Tower of Babel come into this category of "legend." Based upon the memory of certain events in the ancient world, they are fused with "mythical" notions which convey a deep religious meaning.[1] To these stories we now turn.

When a modern historian makes use of older material, he is careful to indicate his sources by the use of quotation marks and footnotes. No such literary convention, however, was recognized by ancient writers. They freely incorporated existing accounts into their own without being under any obligation to acknowledge their indebtedness. But they used their sources in different ways: where, for instance, they had before them two accounts of the same event, they either incorporated both, side by side, or they wove them together; without, in either case, troubling about any discrepancies. The Creation narratives, as we have seen, furnish us with an example of the first method: two stories of differing dates and divergent contents are placed side by side. The story of the Flood, however, is perhaps the best example of the other use. Here the compiler of the Book of Genesis, using the same two sources—" J " and " P "—has interwoven the two accounts, so that they have to be disentangled before we can piece together each source. But when this has been done, we have two separate accounts each of which forms an almost complete story in itself and possesses all the usual characteristics of the " J " and " P " strands respectively.[2] There are, however, striking differences between these two accounts. For instance, " J " distinguishes between clean and unclean animals, whilst " P," who regards this distinction as being first revealed to Moses, does not of course attribute it to his ancestor, Noah. According to " J " seven of each of the clean animals and two each of the unclean must be brought into the ark, while the directions in " P " are for only two of each kind. " J " attributes the flood entirely

---

[1] C. H. Dodd regards these stories as symbolic " myths," rather than " legends," so placing them in the same category as the stories of Creation and the Fall. See *The Bible To-day*, pp. 112 ff.

[2] The earliest " J " account consists of Chapters vi, 5–8; vii, 1–5, 7–10, 12, 16b, 22–3; viii, 2b–3a, 6–12, 13b, 20–2; while the later " P " narrative is made up of Chapters vi, 9–22; vii, 6, 11, 13–16a, 17a (except " forty days "), 18–21, 24; viii, 1–2a, 3b–5, 13a, 14–19; ix, 1–17.

to rain, whereas for " P " it is caused not only by the opening of the windows of heaven, but also by the breaking up of the fountains of the great deep: the waters of the heavenly ocean and those of the subterranean abyss which had been separated at the Creation are let loose upon the earth. Furthermore, the duration of the flood is different in each account. According to " J " it is forty days before the waters abate, and another three weeks elapse before Noah and his family are able to leave the ark—a total of sixty-one days, nearly nine weeks in all. But " P," with his usual precision, supplies dates for the beginning and the end of the flood, according to which, although the waters began to subside after a hundred and fifty days and the ark grounded on the mountains of Ararat exactly five months after the flood began, the whole inundation lasted for a year—twelve months and ten days.[1] Finally, " J " concludes his story by an account of Noah building an altar and, in gratitude for his deliverance, offering a sacrifice to God. But there is no mention of this in " P," since, according to the Levitical law of his time, Jerusalem was the only place at which an altar should be built, and only a priest must sacrifice.

It is in this story of the Flood that we find the most striking parallels between the Hebrew and the Babylonian traditions. The eleventh tablet of the Gilgamesh Epic tells how Utnapishtim was warned by the god Ea of the coming flood and commanded to build a ship:

> O man of Shurippak, son of Ubara-Tutu, pull down thy house, build a ship, forsake thy possessions, take heed for thy life. Thy gods abandon, save thy life, bring living seed of every kind into the ship. . . . (So Utnapishtim obeyed the god Ea and gathered together the wood and all things needful for the building of the ship, and on the fifth day he laid down the hull. . . .) Also he brought up into the ship all his family and his household, the cattle of the field likewise and the beasts of the field. . . .

[1] Since the Hebrew months were lunar, i.e. twenty-nine days, this makes a total of three hundred and sixty-four days—almost exactly a solar year. Sir James Frazer makes this suggestive comment: " Since the Priestly writer thus assigns to the duration of the flood the approximate length of a solar year, we may safely assume that he lived at a time when the Jews were able to correct the serious error of the lunar calendar by observation of the sun." *Folk-Lore in the Old Testament* (abridged ed.), p. 61.

Then the storm broke, lasting for six days:

> The waters rose above the mountain, like a battle storm they broke loose upon mankind. . . . The gods were fearful of the stormy flood . . . they cowered like a dog. . . .

On the seventh day:

> The sea calmed itself, the storm quieted itself, the storm flood ceased. . . . The land arose, upon the Mount Nizir the ship laid itself. The Mount Nizir held the ship fast, let it not move away. . . . I opened the hatchway, the light fell upon my face, I knelt down, sat me down and wept.

As in the biblical " J " account, birds are sent out from the ship and, like Noah, Utnapishtim offers a sacrifice in recognition of his deliverance:

> I made a libation on the summit of the mountain, twice seven sacrificial vessels set I up. . . . The gods smelled the odour, the gods smelled the fragrance, the gods assembled themselves like flies above the sacrifice.

The result is a divine promise that the catastrophe shall not recur:

> (Ea says) These days by the ornament of my neck I will not forget, I will think upon these days, I will not forget them for ever. The gods may draw nigh to the libation, but Inlil may not go to the libation, because he did not remember, he stirred up the storm flood, and delivered up my mankind to destruction. Thou wise among the gods, hero Bel . . . upon the sinner lay his sins, upon the blasphemer lay his blasphemy, but (all mankind) shall not be exterminated. . . .

Here, then, is a remarkable series of parallels with the Genesis story, but, as Peake observes, " the Hebrew story is immeasurably higher in tone than the Babylonian. In the latter Bel in his anger destroys good and evil alike, and is enraged to discover that any have escaped the Flood. The gods cower under the storm like dogs in a kennel; and when the sacrifice is offered, smell the sweet savour and gather like flies over the sacrificer. In the biblical story the punishment is represented as strictly deserved by all who perish, and the only righteous man and his family are preserved, not by the friendly help of another diety, but by the direct action of Him who sends the Flood."[1]

[1] *Peake's Commentary on the Bible*, p. 143.

10—AOB

Have these flood stories, then, any basis in actual fact? Do they preserve the memory of some unprecedented deluge, by virtue of which they may be classed as " legends," or should they be included along with the Creation narratives in the category of " myth "? Babylonian history has several references to an historic flood, and records have been preserved of the kings, or perhaps dynasties, who reigned before this catastrophe.[1] The most convincing evidence, however, is that provided by the excavations of Sir Leonard Woolley at Ur of the Chaldees, the home of Abraham, in 1929. Underneath the layer of deposits dating from 3000 B.C., Woolley discovered a deep layer of clean, water-laid clay which marked a complete break in the pottery deposits. Below it were other layers of pottery and stone implements, but belonging to a different civilization from those above. Here is Woolley's own description of his discovery:

> The shafts went deeper, and suddenly the character of the soil changed. Instead of the stratified pottery and rubbish we were in perfectly clean clay, uniform throughout, the texture of which showed that it had been laid there by water. . . . The clean clay continued without change . . . until it had attained a thickness of a little over eight feet. Then, as suddenly as it had begun, it stopped, and we were once more in layers of rubbish full of stone implements, flint cores from which the implements had been flaked off, and pottery. . . . The great bed of clay marked, if it did not cause, a break in the continuity of history: above it we had the pure Sumerian civilization slowly developing on its own lines; below it there was a mixed culture. . . .
>
> We had long before this seen the meaning of our discovery. The bed of water-laid clay . . . could only have been the result of a flood; no other agency could possibly account for it. Inundations are of normal occurrence in lower Mesopotamia, but no ordinary rising of the rivers would leave behind it anything approaching the bulk of this clay bank: eight feet of sediment imply a very great depth of water, and the flood which deposited it must have been of a magnitude unparalleled in local history.[2]

Similar flood-deposits of silt and sand were found by Langdon and Watelin at Kish—an ancient city in the North near Babylon which dates back to at least 5000 B.C. and is probably the

---

[1] See Caiger, *Bible and Spade*, pp. 25–6.
[2] *Ur of the Chaldees*, pp. 26–9.

oldest city in the world;[1] by Andrae and Jordan at Warka—
the site of the ancient Erech; and by Andrae, Heinrich and
Schmidt at Fara—probably the city of the flood, Shurippak,
in the Gilgamesh Epic.[2] At Kish, however, there are several
flood-deposits (two of which are separated by nineteen feet of
debris) and at Warka two were found. Only one was noted at
Fara, but it is later than the Ur deposit.

There is as yet no general agreement among archaeologists as
to the interpretation of this evidence. Woolley confidently
asserts, in regard to the evidence at Ur: " There could be no
doubt that the flood of which we had thus found the only possible evidence was the Flood of Sumerian history and legend,
the Flood on which is based the story of Noah."[3] This is
denied, however, by Albright and Burrows. Albright maintains
that " in reality there is no solid basis for this supposed ' evidence.' . . . The inundations shown to have taken place at
Kish belonged to quite different periods from any of those at
Ur. Moreover, none of these inundations, not even the big one
first found at Ur, separate periods; all are found in the middle of
deposits belonging to homogeneous cultures."[4] Millar Burrows,
following Albright, describes Woolley's conclusion as " the
most conspicuous instance of confusing interpretation and
evidence " and claims that " this interpretation is not only
uncertain; it is not even probable."[5] He points out that at
Tell Obeid, only four miles from Ur, Woolley found no silt to
correspond with the Ur flood-deposit, and he claims that " repre-
sentations of Gilgamesh were found at a lower level than the
' deluge ' at Kish, showing that the Babylonian flood-story was
of more ancient origin than this."[6]

Sir Frederic Kenyon, on the other hand, is in substantial
agreement with Woolley's conclusions. He points out that the
evidence as a whole fits in with the Mesopotamian tradition of
the great Deluge.

---

[1] See S. Langdon and M. E. Watelin, *Excavations at Kish* (1929).
[2] See W. Andrae in *Antiquity*, x (1936), pp. 133–45.
[3] *Ur of the Chaldees*, p. 29.
[4] " Recent Discoveries in Bible Lands," in *Young's Analytical Concordance*,
1936.   [5] *What Mean These Stones?*, 1941, pp. 26–7.
[6] *Ibid.*, p. 70. Cf. M. E. Watelin, *Excavations at Kish*, iv, pp. 40 ff. (cited
by Burrows).

Archaeology has given us this tradition, alike in the form in which it is preserved in the earlier Sumerian literature, in that in which it was incorporated in the Gilgamish epic in Assyrian literature, and in the references made to it in the king-lists. The traditional chronology of the country is cut in sunder by a great cleft, a Deluge before which there are legendary dynasties of fabulous durations, and after which there are dynasties which become more and more historical. One cannot doubt that there must be some foundation in fact for a tradition which had fixed itself so deeply in the national consciousness; and here archaeology with its other hand (or rather spade) has revealed physical facts in the site of the ancient city of Ur which furnish material confirmation of the tradition. It is in no way surprising that this tradition was carried by Abraham and his family from Ur, and in Palestine was recorded in the form in which it is familiar to us in the early chapters of Genesis. How far the facts observed on other sites in Babylonia can be equated with those observed at Ur is still uncertain; but the occurrence of a great flood is a fact in Babylonian tradition which cannot be ignored or minimized.[1]

It seems evident, then, that the Hebrew account of Genesis is not a mere copy of a Babylonian myth, as was once supposed; rather, both accounts spring from the diffused memory of an unparalleled catastrophe in the ancient world.[2] For this reason the Genesis story is to be classed, technically speaking, not as a " myth," but as a " legend." It is, nevertheless, a " legend " which is fused with " mythical " notions and its significance in the biblical revelation lies chiefly in the " mythical " insights which it embodies.

The dominant truth contained in this story is the fact that sin inevitably brings destruction. The reason given for the Flood in both the " J " and the " P " accounts is that the one holy God of all the earth could not tolerate the evil of the world. In

[1] *The Bible and Archaeology*, 1940, p. 140.
[2] The story of a great flood is found in the folk-lore of such widely separated people as the Greeks, the Polynesians and the Welsh. Hence C. H. Dodd, while admitting that the biblical story has been coloured by dim memories of a destructive Mesopotamian flood, maintains that it is essentially the Hebrew adaptation of the widespread myth of a supernatural deluge over the whole earth. " The biblical writer has used this old myth to set forth in symbol the idea of God's judgment coming upon man in disaster, but leading up to a new creation." See *The Bible To-day*, p. 114. The widespread existence of such a " myth," however, has still to be accounted for.

the words of Calvin, " It was not overwhelmed with a deluge of waters till it had first been immersed in the pollution of wickedness."[1] The Flood was therefore, he says, " an indisputable and signal judgment of God."[2] But we are not to understand this divine judgment as something capricious. As Alexander Maclaren reminds us, we see here " a very profound truth, not only of the certain divine retribution, but of the indissoluble connection of sin with destruction." He points out that the same word which is translated " corrupt " in Genesis vi, 11 and 12, is used to express " destruction " in verse 13. " This teaches us," he says, " that, in deepest reality, corruption is destruction, that sin is death, that every sinner is a suicide. God's act in punishment corresponds to, and is the inevitable outcome of, our act in transgression. So fatal is all evil, that one word serves to describe both the poison-secreting root and the poisoned fruit. Sin is death in the making; death is sin finished."[3]

In this connection, however, we must be careful to distinguish between two biblical conceptions—the idea of the " wrath " of God and the conception of divine " judgment." The inescapable connection of sin and destruction in personal and social relationships is expressed in the biblical concept of the " wrath " of God. C. H. Dodd has pointed out that in the New Testament this Pauline phrase is used in an almost impersonal way: God is never its subject: it describes, he maintains, the inevitable process of cause and effect in a moral universe— " sin is the cause, disaster the effect "—rather than God venting His anger upon men. It is the observed Nemesis or retribution for sin as exhibited in the facts of the world.[4] Its working out is seen in Romans i, 18–32: when men and women turn their back upon God, personal and social disintegration inevitably result.[5]

This conception of a principle of retribution in the order of the world is not to be confused with the other biblical idea of

[1] *Commentary on Genesis*, p. 247.   [2] *Ibid.*, p. 273.
[3] *Expositions of Holy Scripture, Genesis*, pp. 52–3.
[4] See *Commentary on Romans*, pp. 20–4.
[5] Cf. Proverbs xxix, 18, which might be paraphrased: " Where there is no living revelation, no perceived contact between man and God, there the bonds which hold society together are relaxed and finally broken."

the " judgment " of God, as C. H. Dodd recognizes.[1] " Wrath "
is the inexorable working out of a moral principle in the lives
of individuals and communities; " judgment " is God's personal
action of chastisement within this moral order. The Bible does
not hesitate to say that God raises up a barbarous aggressor
state like Assyria to chastise His own people for their sins.[2]
" It is not suggested that God has *caused* the invader to perpe-
trate his crimes, but merely that, finding the instrument ready
to hand, He uses it for His own end and gives the wicked tyrant
his opportunity."[3] Neither does God condone the barbarity
of the oppressor. " He is not his own master. Though he knows
it not, and his only instinct is that of destruction, he is the rod
in God's hand. And when God shall have used him for the
needed punishment of Judah, then will God visit upon him
his arrogance and brutality."[4]

But the Bible also speaks of God as using the forces of Nature
as the instrument of His chastisement. The armies of Pharaoh
are engulfed in the Red Sea; the host of Sennacherib is decimated by plague; corrupt mankind is destroyed by a flood.
Such retribution is, in the words of Vincent Taylor, " not the
expression of a legal principle, but an ethical and spiritual
manifestation of the Divine activity." It is " the reaction of the
holiness and love of God in a world of moral realities." " Its
final ground is His nature and being, and, in the last analysis,
His love."[5] Both the " wrath " and the " judgment " of God
are indeed aspects of His love. Man's rebellion must be checked
or it will destroy him. " His salvation can be achieved only
by the intervention of God in human affairs by way of judgment
upon man's acts of rebellion; and so it comes about that the
great catastrophes of history, the times of crisis (judgment),

[1] In a private letter Professor Dodd says: " What Vincent Taylor and
other critics have overlooked is that I hold the idea of divine *judgment* to be
valid, while rejecting that of divine ' anger.' Judgment is a rational, moral
form of action; anger is irrational passion. . . . 'Οργή I take to stand for
the principle of retribution in the order of the world; judgment is God's
personal action within that order."   [2] See Isaiah x, 5–19.
    [3] Alan Richardson, *Preface to Bible-Study*, p. 58.
    [4] George Adam Smith, *The Book of Isaiah*, i, p. 171.
    [5] *Jesus and His Sacrifice*, pp. 287–8; cf. A. E. Garvie, *The Christian Doctrine
of the Godhead*, p. 225.

are the seasons of God's ' visitation ' of mankind for the sake of our salvation."[1]

The story of the Flood emphasizes the fact that the judgments of God are accompanied by His mercy. This insight finds expression in both the " J " and the " P " accounts. According to the former, after the sacrifice of Noah when the flood had abated, " the Lord said in his heart, I will not again curse the ground any more for man's sake; for the imagination of man's heart is evil from his youth; neither will I again smite any more every thing living, as I have done. While the earth remaineth, seedtime and harvest, and cold and heat, and summer and winter, and day and night shall not cease."[2] Thus there is expressed the belief that while by the moral law all mankind, except the family of Noah, was wiped out, mankind, though evil, lives in an age of grace under the mercy of a patient God: God goes on giving man a fresh chance. And in the later Priestly account this fact of the mercy of God which always accompanies His judgments is expressed even more forcibly in the covenant which God makes with Noah as representing mankind as a whole: " And I will establish my covenant with you; neither shall all flesh be cut off any more by the waters of a flood; neither shall there any more be a flood to destroy the earth."[3] " God," comments Richardson, " is the God of all nations, not of the Hebrews only, and He has entered into a covenant with man—before He entered into a covenant with Moses—according to which He will maintain the beneficient working of the natural order for man's good, in spite of man's unworthiness: the ' bow in the cloud ' is regarded by the writer of Genesis ix as the recurring sign of God's everlasting mercy."[4] C. H. Dodd sees in the covenant with Noah an implicit extension of the covenant with Israel. This was doubtless the intention of the priestly writer. Through the medium of this old story he set forth the universalism of the prophetic teaching. " The story stands as witness that God's covenant, though historically it was made with Israel, is

---

[1] Alan Richardson, *Preface to Bible-Study*, p. 57.   [2] Genesis viii, 20–2.
[3] Genesis, ix, 9–11. " In the story Noah emerged into a world swept clean by the judgments of the Almighty, and entered into a ' covenant ' with his God."—C. H. Dodd, *The Bible To-day*, p. 114.   [4] *Op. cit.*, p. 78.

applicable to the whole human race, and indeed to all created life—a truth finally established in the universal Gospel of the New Testament."[1]

We turn now to look at the story of the Tower of Babel (Genesis xi, 1–9) which belongs to the " J " strand of Genesis. Mesopotamia abounds in the ruins of tower-temples such as the one here described. Built in the form of a pyramid with seven or eight receding terraces, these *zikkurats*, or *ziggurats*, as they are called by archaeologists, originally rose to some hundred and fifty feet above the plain. Two ruined *zikkurats* in the neighbourhood of Babylon—which is the same name as Babel—have been identified at various times with the Tower of Babel. One, of which little remains, is the temple of Esagila called the Etemenanki or " temple of the foundation-stone of heaven " which is in Babylon itself. The other is Birs Nimrud, or Nimrod's Tower, across the river at Borsippa, eight or nine miles to the south-west, which Caiger described as " a mass of jagged masonry 150 feet above the plain."[2] This is identified by both Jewish and local tradition with the Genesis Tower of Babel, although modern opinion seems to favour the Babylonian Etemenanki. An inscription found at Borsippa says that this Tower of Nimrod was built by an ancient Babylonian king, but left incomplete; its top was not finished. There are the ruins of another *zikkurat* at Ur of the Chaldees. This was built by King Ur-uk, or Urengur, some centuries before the time of Abraham (probably either 2700 or 2300 B.C.). Frazer points out that this tower-temple would be the last object that Abraham would see on the horizon when he took a farewell look backward to his native city. " It is possible that in the minds of his descendants, the conspicuous pile, looming dim and vast through the mists of time and of distance, may have assumed the gigantic proportions of a heaven-reaching tower, from which in days of old the various nations of the earth set out on their wanderings."[3]

There is clearly, however, an aetiological motive in this story. Along with the " myths " of Creation and the Fall and the " legend " of the Flood, it belongs to a well-known class of story which attempts to supply an answer to popular questions.

---

[1] C. H. Dodd, *The Bible To-day*, p. 114.   [2] *Bible and Spade*, p. 28.
[3] J. G. Frazer, *Folk-Lore in the Old Testament* (abridged ed.), p. 146.

Why hasn't the serpent any legs? Why must men work for their bread? Why do women suffer pain in childbirth? Why is there a rainbow? All these are questions which a primitive people would ask, and these early Genesis stories attempt to give an answer. Now we can well imagine how desert nomads, bewildered by the turbulent city life of Babylon, would connect the babel of foreign tongues which they heard in the crowded bazaars with, say, the mysterious unfinished tower which loomed on the horizon at Borsippa across the river eight or nine miles away. That is how the story probably began. It was an attempt to explain two things which people could not understand—why different men should speak different languages, and why a huge *zikkurat* near Babylon should have been left unfinished.

Like the Genesis account of the Flood, the story of the Tower of Babel is a " legend " which embodies the prophetic insights of the Hebrew " myth "; it is a picture of man and his world which is true for all time. In the first place, we see here man attempting to build his own perfect community. Man thinks that by his own efforts he can build up a society, a communal life, in which his highest ideals will be realized. The compiler of the book of Genesis explains the name " Babel " as being derived from the Hebrew verb *bālal*, meaning " to confuse," but the word occurs in ancient inscriptions as *Bab-il*, or *Bab-ilu*, which means " Gate of God." This tower was to reach unto Heaven itself. Men would build and climb until at last they became as gods.

The story of humanity down the ages is the story of the Tower of Babel. Plato, five centuries before Christ, dreams of his ideal Republic.[1] A century later, Alexander the Great conquers the Eastern world and attempts to build a unified and ordered society. Another three centuries pass, and the Roman Empire succeeds it as the kingdom of man upon earth. To come down to recent times, the French Revolution at the end of the eighteenth century is the supreme example of man's

[1] Plato's Republic, it must be admitted, is not quite in the same category as other Towers of Babel. It is conceived as a " pattern laid up in heaven " and is not to be built upon force. Indeed it may be argued that its actualization is dependent, not so much upon human wisdom, as upon what the Hebrews would have called prophecy.

attempt to build his tower apart from God. Democracy was its foundation; liberty, equality and fraternity the chief cornerstones. With these, thinks Voltaire, the whole building fitly framed together will grow into a holy temple—for man! We in our own day have been confronted with two new forms of state absolutism, as powerful as they are ruthless—the totalitarian systems of Fascism and Communism. Each of them is the expression of the same intention, the intention of man to construct his own perfect society, and to do it without God: each attempts to build a city and a tower whose top may reach unto Heaven.

Secondly, we see mirrored in this story the fact that what man actually does build is a monument to his own sin. Later Jewish tradition, which elaborates the details of the " legend," declares emphatically that the whole enterprise was deliberate rebellion against God. It maintains that when the structure had reached a great height, the builders at the top shot arrows towards the sky, and the arrows came back stained with blood. Seeing this, they shouted in triumph, " We have slain all who are in Heaven! "[1] That is precisely what sin is—the attempt to kill God. Man thinks he is the measure of all things; he will direct his own life; he will build his own tower to reach unto Heaven; he will politely bow God out of his universe and himself occupy the throne. When Napoleon pointed out to Laplace, that there was no mention of God in his book, *Mécanique Céleste* the scientist is said to have replied: " Sire, I have no need of that hypothesis." That is the attitude of modern man, toiling feverishly to build his Utopia, respectfully ignoring God. If the chief end of man is to glorify God, as the Shorter Catechism says, then his greatest sin is to live as if God did not exist; to ignore His laws; to act as if he himself were chief arbiter in the universe. Instead of Jerusalem, he builds the " dark satanic mills "—and the atomic bomb! The city and tower of his civilization are an abiding monument to his sin of rebellion against the Most High.

[1] C. H. Dodd regards the story of the Tower of Babel as the Hebrew equivalent of the Greek myth of the rebel Titans " who piled mountain upon mountain to storm the dwelling of the gods." See *The Bible To-day*, p. 115.

Thirdly, although man attempted to build his own community apart from God, although by such an act he rebelled against God, nevertheless, says the story, " the Lord came down to see the city and the tower, which the children of men builded."[1] For a while man is allowed to go his own way, and then God intervenes. But His intervention means judgment; sin results in confusion. The God, however, who comes down to see the city and tower which the children of men build, comes not only in judgment, but in mercy; not only in wrath, but in redemption.

> The Bible affirms that the characteristic failing of man is his *rebelliousness;* he knows, but does not perform, the will of God. His salvation can be achieved only by the intervention of God in human affairs by way of judgment upon man's acts of rebellion. . . . The Bible teaches us to regard the great catastrophes of history (such as that through which we are now living) as something more serious than a mere temporary interruption of mankind's upward and onward march. Rightly interpreted, according to the biblical-prophetic insight, they are the occasions of God's redemptive chastisement, rendered necessary by man's inability to choose and to follow the right way; they are the visitations through which God turns man back from the abyss of destruction towards which he is confidently walking.[2]

Like all Old Testament stories, that of the Tower of Babel needs the Manger of Bethlehem and the Cross of Calvary for its completion. In the fulness of time God Himself came down and took flesh that He might dwell with the children of men. The Christian Gospel is the proclamation that in Jesus of Nazareth God has visited, and redeemed His people. His name is called Emmanuel—God with us. In His Son God has drawn very nigh unto us; He has come to us amid the babel of man's unfinished tower; He has met us amid

> The weariness, the fever, and the fret
> Here, where men sit and hear each other groan.

Not only so; the coming of Emmanuel opens up the real possibility of a united mankind, of which " Babelism " is the parody. The confusion of Babel is reversed by the gift of the

[1] Genesis xi, 5.
[2] Alan Richardson, *Preface to Bible-Study*, pp. 57 and 60.

Holy Spirit at Pentecost when every man heard the Apostles speak in his own tongue.[1]

The position of this story in the Book of Genesis, in relation to what follows, is significant. It was after the builders of the Tower of Babel had been dispersed that God was able to open out a whole range of new possibilities for mankind by the call of Abraham. " Thus the story of Babel makes a transition from the mythical to the historical. It serves to characterize mankind as lying under God's word of judgment at the moment when His creative word came to Abraham, to make a covenant and to found a people."[2] Three questions put by J. W. Welch form a relevant comment: First, " Is it, or is it not true, that every human effort carries within itself the seeds of its own decay, frustration, defeat, and death? " Second, " Is it, or is it not true that human efforts fail because ordinary human nature also carries within itself the seeds of its own decay, frustration, defeat, and death? " And third, " Is it, or is it not true, that once man has escaped from the prison of his own self-sufficiency, the door is open for the inrush of a new power? "[3]

III.   " HEILSGESCHICHTE "

The Bible does not draw any hard-and-fast line between " myth," " legend " and history, since all three are bound together in the " sacred history " which it records. It is with history, and the mighty acts of God in history, that the Bible is primarily concerned. History, therefore, and the prophetic interpretation of history are central in it and " myths " and " legends," as Jacob remarks, " ne se trouvent qu'à l'état de vestiges servant à l'ornementation d'un récit historique ou d'un discours prophétique."[4]

Any modern discussion of the relationship of biblical myth, legend and history must take account of the important work of the Swiss theologian, Professor Oscar Cullmann, of Basle.[5] The Bible, as Cullmann rightly insists, knows nothing of the

[1] See Acts ii, 1–11.   [2] C. H. Dodd, *The Bible To-day*, p. 115.
[3] See " What is the Gospel? " in *Man's Dilemma and God's Answer*, pp. 14–18.   [4] E. Jacob, *La Tradition Historique en Israël*, p. 17.
[5] *Christus und die Zeit* (Christ et le Temps), English translation: *Christ and Time*.

Platonic distinction between time and eternity. History is not a shadowgraph of eternal *forms*. But Cullmann goes farther and maintains that there is no biblical ground for assuming any qualitative difference between time and eternity: time belongs to ultimate reality and eternity is endless time. " In the New Testament field it is not time and eternity that stand opposed, but limited time and unlimited, endless time."[1] Eternity (αἰών) " which is possible only as an attribute of God, is time, or, to put it better, what we call ' time ' is nothing but a part, defined and delimited by God, of this same unending duration of God's time."[2]

Here, however, Cullmann goes too far. In his anxiety to purge Christian thinking of Platonic preconceptions, he loses sight of the distinctively Hebraic conception of the Eternal God. As John Marsh points out, " However right we may be to reject Platonic notions of eternity as a ' nunc stans ' we cannot, consistently with the New Testament, ascribe the limitations of successiveness to God's time; and that means we cannot think of God's ' time ' or his ' eternity ' as endless duration."[3] Marsh puts his finger on the spot when he observes that though Cullmann " has successfully thrown off the Greek habits of thinking about time as cyclical, he has not been successful in getting rid of our modern conceptions of time as chronological "[4]—conceptions unknown in the Old Testament and, though recognized, foreign to the thought of the New. " It is typical of Scripture not to locate an event by defining its place on a chronological scale, but to identify it by its content."[5] The biblical conception is realistic rather than chronological; time is understood as opportunity.[6]

Cullmann's understanding of the biblical terms for eternity, 'ōlām and αἰών, is clearly defective, as Marsh is quick to point out: " While writing a book where the nature of eternity is so

[1] *Christ and Time*, p. 46.   [2] *Ibid.*, p. 62.
[3] *The Fulness of Time*, p. 181.   [4] *Ibid.*, p. 179.
[5] *Ibid.*, pp. 20–1.
[6] See *Ibid.*, p. 21 ff. Cf. J. Marsh, " Time," in *A Theological Word Book of the Bible* (ed. A. Richardson), p. 263: " The biblical conception of time is not that of evolution or progress, or even of chronological succession: it is at bottom one of promise (prophetic and historical) and fulfilment, in which history consists of times bringing opportunities, the basic time and the decisive opportunity being that of the coming of Jesus Christ."

clearly defined, he has not examined the biblical terms for it with anything like the fullness that he has reviewed the New Testament terms for time."[1] Such an examination makes it clear that " even within the bounds of the Old Testament the word 'ôlām came to be used of God in a different way from which it was used of any other object. It becomes plain that the Hebrews were trying to express the qualitatively different nature of the divine ' time,' which is eternity."[2] And the use of the plural αἰῶνες in the New Testament "is to be understood not as an indication that time is endless, but that God's time is other than ours."[3]

Significantly enough, Cullmann himself virtually admits this fact in a footnote, apparently without realizing its implications: " Since eternity in this sense comes into consideration only as an attribute of God, the adjective αἰώνιος has the tendency to lose its time sense and is used in the qualitative sense of divine-immortal."[4]

What has been said in criticism of Cullmann's position in no way detracts from the value of his careful and scholarly work. His book, *Christ and Time*, has made an outstanding contribution to the present-day revival of biblical theology. Even though his conclusions regarding the nature and relationship of time and eternity be wrong and his linear theory of history an over-simplification, he has nevertheless laid a firm exegetical foundation for a theology of *Heilsgeschichte* in which myth, legend and history are comprehended and related. His warning against applying Platonic categories to biblical conceptions is salutary and his insistence upon the interrelationship of time and eternity right.

Eternity is not timelessness; although qualitatively different from time, it is nevertheless related to time and interpenetrates it. The Eternal God is the Lord of all time. History consists of the " times " in which the Eternal visits the temporal in demand and succour, judgment and mercy. In Christ eternal life is offered to mortal man and " the transition to this eternal life can be made in time; but the temporal boundaries of human

[1] J. Marsh, " Time and Eternity? " in *The Presbyter*, Vol. 5, No. 2, p. 9.
[2] *Ibid.*, p. 9.   [3] *The Fulness of Time*, p. 175.
[4] *Christ and Time*, p. 48, note 21.

life do not affect it."[1] Hence the Christian is living in two worlds
—the temporal and the eternal: he is a child of this age, but he
tastes the powers of the age to come: he tabernacles on earth,
but his citizenship is in heaven.

This fact is of profound significance for the understanding of
the " mythical " element in the Bible. The reason why " what
appears frankly as myth and legend in non-biblical literature
appears in the Bible as historical material or as intimately and
inevitably linked up with it "[2] is that in the symbolic imagery of
the Bible " the categories of time are strained with the tensions
of eternity."[3] As Marsh reminds us, " the use of the material is
the significant thing."[4] When the Bible uses the medium of
" myth " to express supra-historical realities, it implies that
these realities are of the same nature as is historical reality, since
" myth," in the words of Niebuhr, " refers to the transcendent
source and end of existence without abstracting it from existence."[5] As Casserley puts it, " The language of mythology
insists that a reality which lies beyond the range of our historical
vision must be more like history, since it is a reality, than like
anything else." And " inherent in this dramatic view of reality
is the intuition or assumption that the realms of pre-history and
metaphysics must be continuous with, and therefore akin to,
life as we know and experience it."[6]

Redemption, moreover, while wrought on the plane of
history, is not concerned exclusively with history; it has to do
with the whole created order; its significance is cosmic in
scope. What Cullmann calls " the continuous redemptive
line," therefore, extends backwards to Creation and the Fall
and forward to the New Heaven and New Earth, and thus
" includes both historically verifiable occurrences and things
beyond the reach of historical testing, such as sagas, which are
set in a historical framework, or myths, which deal with the
processes of creation and nature."[7] Hence " the placing of
history and myth together upon one common line of development *in time* belongs to the essential core of the Primitive

[1] J. Marsh, " Time," in *A Theological Word Book of the Bible* (ed. A.
Richardson), pp. 266–7.   [2] J. Marsh, *The Fulness of Time*, p. 37.
[3] *Ibid.*, p. 27.   [4] *Ibid.*, p. 38.
[5] *An Interpretation of Christian Ethics*, p. 36.
[6] *The Christian in Philosophy*, pp. 244–5.   [7] *Christ and Time*, p. 94.

Christian conception of salvation. The demonstration that a myth is not 'historical' does not imply that the happening whose account it preserves is not 'temporal.'. . . Were the characteristic union of both elements dissolved, however, the line as such would then be destroyed; the history of the primal beginning and of the eschatological drama at the end would then have to be loosed, as being timeless, from that connection with the time development."[1] But in point of fact, " myth " and " legend " derive their significance from their connection with the mighty acts of God in history. " In the New Testament point of view is not the essential thing in the figure of Adam the fact that a second Adam comes *after* him (I Corinthians xv, 46; see also Romans v, 12 ff.)? "[2] Cullmann is right, therefore, when he commends Rudolf Bultmann for at least consistently treating the biblical redemptive process as a whole and refusing to limit the redemptive history to those parts of the process that are open to historical testing, since " in Primitive Christianity the connection of the historical events concerning Jesus of Nazareth with the non historical account of the primal beginning and of the eschatological end is so close that the difference between history and myth is unimportant, not because Primitive Christianity possesses no historical sense, but because there exists here a positive theological outlook which transcends the contrast between history and myth."[3]

Cullmann finds in prophecy the common bond which unites history and " myth " theologically: " We have to do with prophecy not only in the ' mythical ' stories of the beginning and the end, but even in the ' historical ' sections we are dealing not simply with history but with *history viewed from the prophetic point of view.*" Thus, " the redemptive history as a whole is ' prophecy.' Here is the point that transcends the contrast between history and myth. . . . Both are prophecy; but the stories of the beginning and the end are only prophecy, while the middle section, which is open in part to historical testing, is prophecy of a kind that refers to facts that can be historically established, and it makes these facts an object of faith."[4] While

---

[1] *Ibid.,* p. 95.   [2] *Ibid.,* p. 95.
[3] *Ibid.,* p. 96. Cullmann, of course, opposes Bultmann's "mythical" view of the redemptive history. See further below pp. 167–8.   [4] *Ibid.,* p. 97.

admitting, therefore, that " the difference of primal and eschatological history from actual historical occurrence may and indeed should be taken into account," he nevertheless concludes that " the Primitive Christian understanding of the history of salvation is correctly understood only when we see that in it history and myth are thoroughly and essentially bound together, and that they are both to be brought together, on the one side by the common denominator of prophecy and on the other by the common denominator of development in time."[1]

Cullmann has made a most valuable contribution by his use of the category of prophecy to unite both history and myth. This very compressed statement requires some expansion, however, for his point to be clearly seen.

It must be remembered, in the first place, that the historians of the Old Testament were men of the prophetic school. They wrote from the prophetic point of view and interpreted events in the light of the prophetic faith. This faith maintained that God is the Lord of history; that His actions are not prompted by caprice but spring from His character, which is essentially good —they are therefore always consistent; and that His rule extends throughout the whole world.

Hence, acknowledging God to be the Lord of history, the Old Testament writers learnt from the history of their own people the principles of divine action. Since, however, that action was consistent and its sphere was universal, it followed that these principles were of universal application. But this universal application, by its very nature, could only be expressed symbolically, and the appropriate symbolism lay ready to hand in the myths of the ancient world. Thus the symbolism of the early stories of Genesis—as also of the apocalyptic portions of the New Testament—" is drawn largely from myths current among the Hebrews and other ancient peoples; but the meaning attached to the symbols—and this is the important point—is derived from the prophetic and apostolic interpretation of history."[2] The striking similarity of these early biblical stories with the older Babylonian accounts suggests that they

[1] *Ibid.*, p. 106.
[2] C. H. Dodd, *The Bible To-day*, p. 112.

" may be regarded as adaptations of primitive myths by writers who used them as symbols of truths learned in history. Nominally they refer to pre-history. In fact, they apply the principles of divine action revealed in the history of a particular people to mankind at all times and in all places. They universalize the idea of the Word of God, which is both judgment and renewal."[1]

As C. H. Dodd points out, this is also true, *mutatis mutandis*, of the latter part of the " mythical " framework in which " sacred history " is set. The conception of the Last Judgment is a symbolic picture in which the New Testament writers use the imagery of Jewish apocalypses to universalize a truth born of their own experience of Christ. " Behind the symbolism of Doomsday (often fantastic to our minds) this is the truth: that the verdict upon history, and upon all the actors in it, is pronounced simply by confrontation with the Word of God, made flesh in Christ. Those who had stood under His judgment in history, and acknowledged its finality, knew that He must be judge of quick and dead. As the myth of the Creation and the Fall universalizes the experience of Israel in history, so the symbolism of the last Judgment universalizes the experience of those who found themselves judged by Christ."[2]

The mythical framework of sacred history is thus an essential part of the biblical revelation. An historical revelation is of necessity particularized: it centres in particular events in the history of a particular people, each happening at a particular time and in a particular place. But the whole point of the Bible is that those particular events have a universal significance. Hence the necessity of relating the significance seen to reside in events localized in time and place to men and women of all times and in all places. For this the story or drama is a more adequate medium than any mere statement of fact, as the parables of Our Lord so vividly show. Without the symbolic imagery of Genesis and Revelation, the mighty acts of God in

[1] *Ibid.*, p. 115. John Marsh points out that it was as a result of the Exile that " prophetic vision has seen, with irrevocable clarity, that God's purpose in history must span all history and embrace all creation, if the story of Israel beyond her bitter calamity is to have significance again." —*The Fulness of Time*, p. 73.

[2] C. H. Dodd, *The Bible To-day*, pp. 116–17.

the history of Israel, culminating in the coming of the Messiah and the reconstituting of the People of God, would remain anchored in a corner of the ancient world; "its effect is to universalize the meaning of the revelation which was given to particular people at particular times."[1]

Not only is "myth" the most effective medium for such universalization; it has also the power of particularizing and individualizing the truths which it universalizes: it applies and brings them home to individual men and women in all ages and places. Herein lies the religious value of the biblical myth. For example, the relationship of God to Israel as Creator, Redeemer and Judge—a relationship revealed through His mighty acts in their midst—is universalized in the story of Adam—a significant name meaning "man." God is Creator, Redeemer and Judge, not merely of a particular people of the ancient world residing in Palestine, but of Adam—man. Adam has a twofold nature: he is of the earth earthy, formed of the dust of the ground; he has also an endowment superior to that of the beasts—God has breathed into his nostrils the breath of life. But Adam falls from the divine intention by disobedience and rebellion (just as Israel was a stiff-necked and rebellious people) and forfeits his paradise of communion with God. Nevertheless his Creator and Judge is also his Redeemer— seeking him in the garden; clothing his nakedness (once his glory, now his shame); promising, not only toil, frustration and death as the fruit of his sin, but also deliverance through the seed of the woman who shall bruise the serpent's head.

But when I read the story of Adam it makes a personal appeal: it speaks to my condition and my need. I know that *I* am Adam—made in the image of God, yet rebellious and "fallen" from the divine intention. And what God does for Adam, He does for *me*—seeks and finds me, clothes my shame with His righteousness, offers me a share in the victory of the Seed of the Woman who has bruised the serpent's head.

One final question remains—How can we know that it is Reality, and not fancy, which is expressed in the biblical myth? The prophetic linking of myth and history supplies the answer. As we have seen, the biblical myth is not an end in itself; it

[1] *Ibid.*, p. 119.

expresses on a universal scale some truth learned by a particular people. But the truth expressed in the myth is a truth revealed to that people through *history*. It is essentially the same truth which the prophetic mind has apprehended in a particular historical situation, but universalized in its application. The point is that the biblical myth does not stand alone; it is part and parcel of the whole biblical revelation. Its imagery may be that of the primitive mythology of the ancient world, but the meaning attached to its symbolism is rooted in the stuff of history. It stands or falls, therefore, with the validity of the historical revelation which underlies the Bible as a whole.

CHAPTER V

MIRACLES

ONE of Karl Barth's early published addresses has the
arresting title, " The Strange New World Within the Bible."
To the question, What is there within the Bible? he replies:
" Within the Bible there is a strange, new world, the world of
God. . . . We must openly confess that we are reaching far
beyond ourselves. But that is just the point: if we wish to come
to grips with the contents of the Bible, we must dare to reach far
beyond ourselves. The Book admits of nothing less. . . . A new
world projects itself into our old ordinary world. . . . In it the
chief consideration is not the doings of man but the doings of
God." And he maintains that " the paramount question is
whether we have understanding for this different, new world,
or good will enough to meditate and enter upon it inwardly."[1]

That is the background against which the miracles of the
Bible must be seen if we are to get the perspective right. To
begin by discussing the philosophical question of the relationship of miracles in general to the concept of natural law is to
begin at the wrong end. The question must be faced—and
answered. But it can only be profitably discussed in relation to
biblical miracles when the latter are seen for what they really
are. And miracle, in the Bible, " being fundamentally a religious category and not a scientific or philosophic one, the proper
place to begin is within the sphere of living religion itself."[2]

I. THE SIGNIFICANCE OF BIBLICAL MIRACLES

The word " miracle " is derived from the Latin *miraculum*,
which means a wonderful thing, a marvel. Used in connection

[1] See *Das Wort Gottes und die Theologie*, English translation, *The Word of
God and the Word of Man*, pp. 28–40.
[2] H. H. Farmer, *The World and God*, p. 108.

with biblical religion, it is an unfortunate term and indeed misleading because it " brings into prominence the least important aspect of the Christian *sign*, and that which it shares with pretended prodigies and marvels of every kind."[1] Biblical miracles are not marvels, things to be wondered at; they are essentially " signs " of some special operation within history of the beneficent power of God. In this they contrast markedly with the miracles associated with ethnic religions which " merely exalt their worker, and sometimes . . . are of a kind to force belief in him." These non-Christian miracles " largely consist of power over nature and complete control over its processes, and are often of a most grotesque and obviously improbable kind." They " have seldom a beneficent purpose, nor is there any historic evidence for them, even if they were of such a kind as would require it."[2] In biblical religion " *we* are not called on to consider the credibility of miracles wrought for no apparent purpose, but to exhibit the caprice of some superior power."[3] In this respect the miracles of the Bible differ equally from the mere wonder-stories of the " apocryphal " gospels which credit the child Jesus with the most fantastic and purposeless feats.[4]

Three different Greek words are used in the New Testament to describe miracles—σημεῖα, signs; δυνάμεις, acts of power; and τέρατα, wonders.[5] It is significant, however, that the last word, τέρατα is never used alone, but only in conjunction with one or both of the other terms. Miracles are sometimes spoken of as " signs," sometimes as " mighty works," and sometimes as " signs and wonders " ; but never merely as

---

[1] J. C. MacDonnell, " Miracle," in *The Imperial Bible Dictionary*, ii, p. 246.

[2] J. A. MacCulloch, " Miracles," in *Encyclopædia of Religion and Ethics*, viii, pp. 677–8.

[3] J. C. MacDonnell, *op. cit.*, p. 253.

[4] e.g. The Gospel of Thomas: " This child Jesus, when five years old, was playing in the ford of a mountain stream; and He collected the flowing waters into pools, and made them clear immediately, and by a word alone He made them obey Him. And having made some soft clay, He fashioned out of it twelve sparrows. . . . And Jesus clapped His hands and cried out to the sparrows, and said to them: Off you go! And the sparrows flew, and went off crying."

[5] In the LXX σημεῖον and τέρας translate the Hebrew '*ôth* and *môphēth* respectively.

" wonders." And the word θαῦμα, a marvel—frequently
used of miracles in patristic literature—does not occur at
all in the New Testament. As Alan Richardson observes,
" It is as though the New Testament writers were unwilling
to emphasize the miracles as mere *wonders* (as so many
modern critics have supposed that they do), but desire
rather to point to their *meaning*, their significance as signs."[1]
The Hebrew term *môphēth*, wonder, is admittedly used
alone frequently in the Old Testament, but it is used in a wider
sense. And, generally speaking, the miracles of the Old Testament too are significant acts and not just wonder-stories. In
the Bible, therefore, " it is as *signs*, indicating the intervention
of divine power, and the character of each dispensation which
they accompanied, that miracles chiefly concern us."[2]

The Bible presents what William James calls the personal and
romantic view of life. Its whole approach is essentially religious.
Its point of reference is not man but God. Human life is seen
not in terms of evolution and " laws of Nature " but *sub specie
aeternitatis*. All is of God and for God. Man is made in the
image of God; the crown of creation, nevertheless a creature
dependent upon God, made for fellowship with God, whose
chief end is to glorify God and enjoy Him for ever. This biblical,
religious view of life, therefore, " recognizes personality,
individuality, the living relation of God with living human
beings in mercy and in judgment and in Fatherly care."[3]
Thus " man moves on the borderland of the rational and
spiritual worlds. He belongs in part to both. The higher is his
heritage as much as the lower; but of the first he enjoys as yet
but rare glimpses."[4] Moreover, " if the Bible really contains,
as we believe, the record of God's revelation of Himself to men,
we should expect it, while clearly in touch with every-day
human life, to abound in traces of its special origin and purpose.
We should expect it to offer us frequent glimpses of a higher
order of things, beyond the range of our ordinary perception—
to exhibit, in fact, a miraculous element."[5] We see then that

[1] *The Miracle-Stories of the Gospels*, p. 46.
[2] J. C. MacDonnell, *op. cit.*, p. 246.
[3] D. S. Cairns, *The Faith that Rebels*, p. 149.
[4] " Miracle," in *A Commentary on the Holy Bible*, ed. J. R. Dummelow,
p. cxxii.   [5] *Ibid.*, p. cxv.

" one great purpose of the Bible's miraculous record, culminating as it does in that Resurrection miracle without which subsequent history is inexplicable, is to warn us against the spirit which would discredit and reject those priceless glimpses when they are presented, and elect to live always on the lower plane."[1]

Definitions of miracle are almost as numerous as definitions of religion; and when applied to biblical miracles they are for the most part equally unsatisfactory. For example, C. S. Lewis begins a stimulating discussion on miracles by stating that he uses the word to mean " an interference with Nature by supernatural power." He is clearly not altogether happy about such a definition since he admits in a footnote that it is crude and " popular " and explains that he is adopting it for the purpose of coming to grips with questions which " the common reader " associates with miracles.[2] This may be quite justifiable when dealing—as Lewis is in this part of his book—with miracles in general. But it would be quite inadequate for a discussion of biblical miracles. Being confined, as it is, to the philosophical aspect of miracles, it begins at the wrong end. The same criticism applies to H. H. Rowley's broad definition of miracle as " a divine intervention in the course of events,"[3] and to James Orr's description as " any deviation from, or transcendence of, the order of nature due to the interposition of a supernatural cause."[4] Even Alan Richardson, who brings out so clearly the significance of biblical miracles, is content with a similarly inadequate definition: " A miracle in the biblical sense is an event which happens in a manner contrary to the regularly observed processes of nature."[5] Quite true as far as it goes, but it does not go far enough. J. A. MacCulloch is a little nearer the mark when he describes miracle as " an occasional evidence of direct divine power in an action striking and unusual, yet by its beneficence pointing to the goodness of God."[6] But even here the emphasis is too much upon the " wonder " aspect of miracle as something " striking and

---

[1] *Ibid.*, p. cxxii.   [2] See C. S. Lewis, *Miracles*, p. 15.
[3] *The Relevance of the Bible*, p. 103.
[4] *The Faith of a Modern Christian*, p. 65.
[5] " Miracle," in *A Theological Word Book of the Bible*, p. 152.
[6] " Miracles," in *Encyclopaedia of Religion and Ethics*, viii, p. 676.

unusual." A better definition is that given by A. M. Ramsey: " A miracle may be called an event wrought by God which does not fit into the hitherto observable laws of nature. It resembles in one way the actions of the free wills of men which disturb the dispositions of nature; and it resembles in another way the operations of the grace of God in human lives."[1] More adequate still is that of A. R. Vidler: " For religion, miracle is the name given to an event in which God is apprehended as acting providentially for a personal end—i.e. for the welfare of human persons—in a peculiarly intense degree."[2]

The miracles of the Bible are to be understood, not in terms of a supernatural interference with Nature, but in terms of a personal relationship between God and man. They belong to the category of providence rather than power. They are indeed outstanding instances of " special providence " which are to be seen against the background of " general providence " which forms so large a part of Christian experience. In them God's love and care for his children come to a burning focus. " *The more intensely personal and individual the succour of God is felt to be, the more appropriate and inevitable the word miracle becomes on the religious man's lips. . . .* In the category of miracle the experience of God as personal reaches its maximum concentration."[3] This is what Alexander Nairne means when he speaks of a miracle as " the Father's love and the Child's trust perfectly in accord."[4]

Miracle is thus related to a special need on the part of man which calls forth a special exercise of divine power on the part of God. And the link between the two—man's need and God's saving power—is prayer. H. H. Farmer sees in these three things the distinctive characteristics which distinguish a miracle from the awareness of God's general providence in religious experience:

First, there is an awareness of serious crisis or need or threat of disaster in the personal life, and of helplessness to deal with it adequately and victoriously through the exercise of ordinary, unaided human powers. Second, there is a more or less conscious

[1] *The Resurrection of Christ*, p. 35.
[2] Booklet on " Miracle " (Church Literature Association), p. 6.
[3] H. H. Farmer, *The World and God*, p. 118.
[4] *Every Man's Story of the New Testament*, p. 42.

and explicit turning to God for assistance. Third, there is an awareness of an *ad hoc* response of God to the situation and to man's petitioning inadequacy in it, so that the crisis is met, the need satisfied, the danger averted, in an event, or combination of events, which would not have taken place had man not so petitioned and God so acted.[1]

It is a significant fact that the miracles of the Bible are not evenly distributed in the course of the history which it records. They are, for the most part, concentrated in three crucial periods and grouped around three great personalities who are central in those periods and indeed typify them. As C. S. Lewis puts it, " They are precisely those chapters in this great story on which the plot turns."[2] The first is the formative period of biblical religion—the time of the Exodus, the Deliverance at the Red Sea, the giving of the Law and the Covenant at Sinai. This was the time when a People of God was constituted and the religion of Israel took on its distinctive form; and the dominant personality under whose leadership it all happened was Moses. The second is the creative period—the time of the prophets when the religion of Israel was threatened by foreign cults and the Mosaic faith endangered by a syncretism in which its distinctive elements would have been lost. It was in the ensuing conflict that the religious and ethical implications of the Covenant were hammered out. This period begins with the struggle of Elijah against the worship of the Tyrian Baal, and for later generations Elijah was always the typical prophet. The third period is the period of fulfilment—the Christian era, in which the story of the past comes to fruition, the hope of Israel is realized when the sovereign rule of God is made manifest in his Son Jesus Christ, and the old Israel is reconstituted as the Christian Church. It is not without significance that the typical personalities of each of these periods appear together on the Mount of Transfiguration.

Miracle is thus associated with the great revelatory crises of biblical history. Indeed the whole biblical revelation is focused in two historic manifestations of the power of God—the miracle of the Deliverance at the Red Sea and the supreme miracle of the Resurrection of Christ. The miracles of the Bible therefore

---

[1] *The World and God*, pp. 122–3.   [2] *Miracles*, p. 119.

are not to be regarded as the mere credentials of revelation; they are part and parcel of it, what Hunzinger calls the phenomenal form of divine revelation.[1] In the words of Wheeler Robinson, " Nature and history alike serve to reveal Him, for they are equally under His control. . . . Nature and history are simply different aspects of the continued activity of God, and miracles are the representative occasions on which that activity specially impresses human consciousness."[2]

Acceptance of the miraculous nature of the biblical revelation does not commit us to an uncritical acceptance of every miracle recorded in the Bible; neither does it imply that the miracles of the Old Testament are to be placed on the same level as those of the New. Before discussing the criteria by which the miracles of the Bible may be assessed, however, something must be said about the theology which they embody.

The biblical miracles as a whole presuppose two theological convictions. The first is that God is the Source of all power.[3] This is not to be confused with the typical Eastern conception of a deity who is omnipotent but absolutely capricious: he may use his power in any way that he wishes, and how he uses it at any particular moment will be determined entirely by his own whim. For the biblical writers God is self-consistent as well as omnipotent: He acts in accordance with His character which is holy: His power is the expression of His righteous will. But He is essentially the Living God, the God who acts. " Throughout the Bible," says Alan Richardson, " God is conceived of as *Power*, the original and only Source of Power, from Whom all other manifestations of power in the universe are derivative. There are therefore no limitations to God's power, by which the world was made; with God all things are possible, and nothing is too hard for the Lord . . . To those who held such a conception of God as power, the question whether He could work ' miracles '—i.e. acts which involve some degree of intervention in the course of nature or history—could present no difficulty."[4] The natural order itself is conceived as

[1] See W. Hunzinger, *Das Wunder*.
[2] *Inspiration and Revelation in the Old Testament*, p. 39.
[3] Dalman points out that God is spoken of as " The Power " in Jewish literature. See *The Words of Jesus*, pp. 200 ff.
[4] *The Miracle-Stories of the Gospels*, p. 2.

realizing His purposes and dependent upon His will. " Consequently the essence of a miracle is not that it is ' unnatural,'
but that it is a specially clear and striking proof of God's power,
and of the freedom He exercises in furthering His objects."[1]

Without this fundamental biblical conception, the acceptance
of the miracles of the Bible is difficult, if not impossible. The
difficulties encountered by the modern man regarding them
are not so much historical or scientific; they are essentially
theological. As Alan Richardson observes, " Disbelief in the
miracles is usually the result of disbelief in the biblical conception of God as the source of all power or in Christ as the veritable
incarnation of the δύναμις of God."[2] It is the inevitable
outcome of " that weakening of the idea of God which is the
radical spiritual malady of our time."[3]

The second theological conviction presupposed in the biblical
miracles is that the divine order of creation has been disrupted
by evil. " There is a disturbing element in the world . . . a
principle at work absolutely contrary to the principle of Law—
what the Bible calls *sin*. . . . If Miracle seems arbitrary and
violent, may it not be because some forcible method is necessary
to redress the balance already upset by the introduction of evil
into a world originally ' very good ' ? . . . When the physician
. . . restores the body to health, although he forcibly interrupts
a series of physical processes which apart from him must have
worked themselves out, he is really ranged on the side of the
natural and normal. . . . May we not say then that in the sphere
of biblical miracle ' the real intervention is not the intervention
of grace, but that of the sin which required it ' ? "[4]

The biblical writers never accept either moral or physical
evil as normal. They regard them as intruders, foes, that will
one day be vanquished and banished. The subjection of man
to natural ills—storms and floods, pain and hunger, disease
and death—is not the unconditioned will of God for him. Man
brings suffering upon himself and his fellows by his departure
from right ways of living and his failure to realize the ends of

[1] H. Schultz, *Old Testament Theology* (Eng. trans.), ii, pp. 192–3.
[2] " Miracle," in *A Theological Word Book of the Bible*, p. 152.
[3] D. S. Cairns, *The Faith that Rebels*, p. 155.
[4] " Miracle," in *A Commentary on the Holy Bible*, ed. J. R. Dummelow,
p. cxxi.

his creation. But God is his Deliverer who comes to his aid in his distress. The miracles of the Bible " show us that we are to think of the Divine Love in the simplest way as delighting in the dispelling of pain, the restoring of sanity, the satisfying of hunger, the preservation of life, the dispelling of premature death."[1] In the words of Bishop Gore, " Miracle is, from this point of view, God's protest against the monstrous disorder of sin. It is God the Creator recreating what man has defaced."[2]

God's power is thus seen to be directed to the restoring of wholeness in His creation; it is redemptive in its nature and in its operation. In a word, it is the instrument of His love, so that ultimately, as Wheeler Robinson puts it, " it is the goodness of God, rather than His power, which is displayed in the so-called miracle."[3]

II. MIRACLES AND HISTORY

" Miracle and historical study are inconsistent," wrote Zeller in 1860, " and he who aims at history can never admit miracle "[4]—a conclusion logical enough if Renan's premiss that " les miracles sont de ces choses qui n'arrivent jamais "[5] be admitted. It was this kind of rationalist dogma that vitiated nineteenth-century biblical study. Renan himself truculently declares that he does not reject the miracles of the Gospels because of any evidence that their writers are untrustworthy; he writes off the Gospels as legends for no other reason than that they recount miracles.[6]

The biblical documents, however, are not to be so easily disposed of. As historical documents they must be examined historically and critically and their evidence weighed; and, as M. C. D'Arcy remarks, " so far as evidence is concerned, that in favour of miracles is overwhelming." Hence, " If . . . we are to be impartial and to take scientific probity for our standard, we cannot close the case against miracles."[7] Nevertheless the

---

[1] D. S. Cairns, *The Faith that Rebels*, pp. 221–2.
[2] C. Gore, *The Reconstruction of Belief*, p. 239.
[3] *Record and Revelation*, p. 330.   [4] *Historische Zeitschrift*, 4, p. 109.
[5] *Vie de Jésus*, Preface, p. xi.   [6] *Ibid.*, Preface, p. xii.
[7] " Christianity and the Modern Mind," in *God and the Universe* (ed. J. L. May), p. 122.

miracles of the Bible can be neither proved nor disproved by the mere appeal to history; they may not be detached from their theological background and examined " impartially " as " bare " events. They must be seen for what they are, that is, as " signs " of the saving revelation of God's power in history.[1] Disregard of their theological significance, as Alan Richardson warns us, " leads inevitably to the attempt to explain away the power of God as it has been revealed in history,"[2] since " the events can be viewed on the lower level of mere event, where coincidence is ascribed to chance, as well as to the higher level at which an explanation is found in the divine purpose."[3]

Historical evidence, however, although of itself inconclusive, is of great value in assessing the worth and credibility of particular miracle stories. Biblical miracles are of many kinds and are found in narratives which differ in historical value. Each therefore must be examined and its credentials scrutinized in the light of all the available evidence. This will include an assessment of the historical value of the source or sources in which it stands, a comparison of various accounts of the incident where more than one exist, and a judgment of its probability in the light of its own character and of the character of God which it implies.

1. *The Old Testament*

This applies particularly to the miracles recorded in the Old Testament. Cairns' assertion that " there is no comparison between the Old Testament miracles and the New in their vital importance for living faith "[4] is too sweeping a generalization. The miracle of the Deliverance at the Red Sea is for the Old Covenant what the Resurrection of Christ is for the New. And the feeding miracles of the Gospels derive much of their

---

[1] Cf. John Marsh, *The Fulness of Time*, p. 14: " The problem of miracle narratives in both Old and New Testaments is not one simply of the adequacy or inadequacy of historical evidence, nor yet of the philosophical possibility or impossibility of certain events. It is also a problem of how men will experience, understand and report historical events, if it be true that God Himself is active in them."

[2] *The Miracle-Stories of the Gospels*, p. 18.

[3] Wheeler Robinson, *Inspiration and Revelation in the Old Testament*, p. 46.

[4] *The Faith that Rebels*, p. 48.

significance from similar actions recorded of Moses (Deuteronomy xviii, 15 ff.) and Elisha (II Kings iv, 42–4). As Alan Richardson points out, they are to be understood as the acts or " signs " of the Messiah: " It was appropriate that Jesus, Who stood between Moses and Elijah on the Mount of Transfiguration, and Who had come to *fulfil* the Law and the Prophets, should authenticate His mission by means of the signs which they had given."[1] Elisha, as the one upon whom Elijah's mantle had fallen, is regarded as continuing his work.

The miracles of the Old Testament, therefore, are not to be dismissed in any summary way, since, as Ritschl says, the Old Testament is the lexicon of the New. Nevertheless it must be admitted that, by and large, they are not to be put on the same level as those of the Gospels. To quote J. H. Bernard's admirable summary:

It is evident that we cannot speak with the same confidence about these that we can feel when describing the miracles of Him who showed in His own person His superiority to death, of Him who is the Prince of Life. For they are narrated in ancient books, the origin of which in many instances is wrapped in obscurity. We cannot claim to have *contemporary* evidence for the miracles of the Old Testament as we have for those of the New Testament. . . . But for us " Vetus Testamentum in Novo patet." The obscurities of the older revelation find their explanation in the fuller light of the later. And if it be a fact that the law was a παιδαγωγὸς εἰς χριστόν, and that Israel was chosen by the Almighty as His instrument for the teaching of the world, then it ceases to be *a priori* improbable that, at exceptional crises in the history of the Hebrews, special manifestations of Divine power might be vouchsafed, which should enable men to say with boldness, " This is the finger of God."[2]

In approaching the miracles of the Old Testament, four things must be borne in mind. In the first place, due allowance must be made for oriental modes of thought and expression which are unfamiliar to our Western minds. We need to beware of what Wheeler Robinson calls " timidly conservative of fundamentalistic formulations " of biblical history " which ask us to believe more than Hebrews themselves ever believed."[3]

---

[1] *The Miracle-Stories of the Gospels*, p. 95.
[2] " Miracle," in Hastings' *Dictionary of the Bible*, iii, pp. 392–3.
[3] *Inspiration and Revelation in the Old Testament*, p. 46.

For example, the ancient fragment from the book of Jasher about the sun standing still at Gibeon, quoted in Joshua x, 12–13a, is poetry to be classed with the words of the Song of Deborah: " The stars in their courses fought against Sisera." The use which the later compiler of the Book of Joshua makes of it is another matter to which we shall return later. The point here is that it is poetry, not prose, and is to be understood as such. Similarly, the account in Numbers xxii, 22–35, of Balaam's ass speaking may well refer to a dream.

Secondly, as is always the case with ancient documents belonging to a period much later than the events they record, the possibility of the growth of legends must be reckoned with. This applies particularly to the stories of Elijah and Elisha. As A. J. B. Higgins observes, " It is natural for incidents in the lives of such remarkable men, who made a lasting impression on their contemporaries, to be exaggerated in the course of time. This is not to deny that some of the stories in question may rest on a historical basis."[1] Wheeler Robinson asserts quite definitely that this has happened: " In these prophetic stories the accretion of the legendary element is obvious, being such accretion as will always gather round forceful personalities in all generations."[2] This fact must not be exaggerated, however. It must be remembered that these Elijah and Elisha stories, in which the familiar marks of legend so often appear, belong nevertheless to one of the oldest sections of the Book of Kings.

Thirdly, it must be remembered that many Old Testament narratives are composite. Accounts of the same event from two or more sources, coming often from widely separated periods, have been either placed side by side (as in the Creation stories) or interwoven (as in the story of the Flood). When a miracle-story is of this nature, it is necessary to disentangle, as far as is possible by critical method, the sources that have been used by the compiler of the narrative in its present form and compare their respective accounts. In this way the growth of legendary tendencies may be discerned in a heightening of the miraculous element in the later source, and sometimes what MacCulloch calls " a more or less non-miraculous substratum " may be

---

[1] *The Christian Significance of the Old Testament*, p. 28.
[2] *Inspiration and Revelation in the Old Testament*, p. 45.

found. A typical example is the story of the crossing of the
Red Sea (Exodus xiv). In the earlier " JE " account, coming
from the late tenth or early ninth century B.C., the Israelites
take advantage of an exceptionally low tide caused by a strong
east wind (verse 21). But in the Priestly narrative, compiled
some four hundred years later, the waters are miraculously
heaped up like walls on either side of them, as they cross
(verse 22).

Again, in the story of the sun standing still at Gibeon
(Joshua x, 12–14) we have an early poetical fragment (verses
12b–13a) from the Book of Jasher—an ancient collection of
national songs—with a prose introduction (verse 12a) and a
prose comment (verses 13b–14) supplied by the later compiler
of the Book of Joshua. The quotation from the Book of Jasher
is part of a very old poem which, like the Song of Deborah,[1]
may be contemporary with the event that it describes:

> Sun, be silent upon Gibeon;
> And thou, Moon, in the valley of Aijalon.
> And the sun was silent, and the moon stood,
> Until the nation had avenged themselves of their enemies.

As H. H. Rowley points out, we have here a poetical account of
a thoroughly credible event: " As [Joshua] drew near it was
towards the hour of morning. . . . Clearly what he wants is
darkness, under cover of which he can fall upon the unsuspecting
foe. . . . It is not the prolonging of the day, but of the night
that is desired. And the need was answered. A storm was
brewing, as the context shows, and the morning was unusually
dark, giving to Joshua the help he needed. This is wholly
credible, and once more we have the timely help of natural
forces in which Israel could find the hand of God."[2] But the
prose comment of the later compiler, who obviously misunderstood the poem, alters the whole character of the incident.
" It heightens the miracle by making it something quite alien
to nature, and supposes the day was unnaturally prolonged to
double the ordinary length. In such a case it would be gratui-
tous to prefer the later prose account, and its rejection does not
depend on an unwillingness to believe in miracle."[3]

[1] See G. Moore, *Judges* (*I.C.C.*), p. 129.
[2] *The Relevance of the Bible*, p. 107.   [3] *Ibid.*, pp. 107-8.

This leads to our fourth observation: In the miracles of the Old Testament the operation of natural forces may often be seen. We have just noted two examples—the deliverance at the Red Sea due, according to the earlier account, to a strong east wind; and Joshua's victory at Gibeon, facilitated by an unusually dark stormy morning. A further instance is seen in the plagues described in Exodus vii–x, which are natural phenomena in Egypt. Their significance therefore is that they should occur concurrently and just at this particular time.

> None of these plagues, except the last, contains anything strange or abnormal; all are events which may naturally take place at the end of the inundation of the Nile. The stagnant water left as the river goes down often reddens with infusoria, and becomes undrinkable, while fish that have been caught in the pools will, of course, die as the ground dries. Frogs naturally find their way from the water on to dry land, and may easily be so numerous as to be a nuisance. The pools breed quantities of mosquitoes, and these, in turn, produce distressing forms of skin disease. Thunderstorms, accompanied by heavy hail, are rare in Egypt, but they do occur, and are naturally alarming. Sand and dust storms which produce deep gloom may quite well take place to the east of the Delta, while locusts are only too frequent a scourge. In all this there is nothing to awake incredulity; the " miracle " will consist in nothing more than the coincidence of all these events, and their exceptional severity.[1]

It must be emphasized that to admit that we may discern certain natural phenomena in such events does not in any way detract from their miraculous nature or make them any less a great delivering act of God. When, for instance, we have attributed the receding of the sea to a strong east wind, we have still to ask why this particular wind should blow with such particular intensity just at that particular time. And the only answer which accords with both the historical evidence and the data of religious experience is the answer of the Book of Exodus that " *the Lord* caused the sea to go back by a strong east wind all that night, and made the sea dry land " (Exodus xiv, 21).

We are now in a position to deduce certain criteria by which to test the credibility of a miracle-story, and in particular to

---

[1] Oesterley and Robinson, *A History of Israel*, i, p. 85.

assess the respective value of the miracles recorded in the Old Testament. There are two yard-sticks by which they may be measured—one historical, the other theological. " While the moral and religious worth of the Old Testament, as the litera- ture of the Divine revelation completed in Christ, demands a respectful treatment of the narratives of miracles, we are bound to apply two tests: the sufficiency of the evidence, and the con- gruity of the miracle in character with the Divine revelation."[1]

The application of these two tests to the miracle of the Deliverance at the Red Sea establishes its credibility beyond reasonable doubt. As far as evidence is concerned, although the details are obscure, no event in the Old Testament is better attested. Part, at least, of the opening stanzas of the Song of Moses in Exodus xv is probably contemporary with the hap- pening itself to which the ancient sources " J " and " E " and the later source " P " bear unanimous witness. Apart from it, indeed, the history and religion of Israel are inexplicable.[2] But not only is the evidence sufficient; the miracle itself is congruous with the total biblical pattern of God's action. It is fitting that an event of such significance for mankind as was the Exodus should be accompanied by special signs of God's providence and power.

When, however, we apply these tests to the Elijah and Elisha stories, the result is not so conclusive. To begin with, the evidence is not nearly so strong: they are attested by only one source, the Book of Kings, and never again alluded to in the Old Testament. On the other hand, the evidence on closer examination proves to be a good deal stronger than is usually admitted. Although they appear in only one historical source, the chapters in which they are found belong to the oldest section of the Book of Kings. Marks of legend there may be, but, as Bernard reminds us, the fact that miracles are attri- buted to no other prophet " shows that it was not the habit of the Hebrews to surround the figure of every prophetical per- sonage with a halo of miraculous glory."[3] It is significant that

[1] A. E. Garvie, " Miracles," in Hastings' one volume *Dictionary of the Bible*, p. 622.
[2] See further below, Chapter VII, pp. 240–1.
[3] " Miracle," in Hastings' *Dictionary of the Bible*, iii, p. 393.

no miracles are ascribed to the favourite characters of the Old Testament—Abraham, Jacob, David and Solomon. The plain fact is, as Bishop Butler observes, that " the Old Testament affords us the same historical evidence of the miracles of Moses and the prophets, as of the common civil history of Moses and the kings of Israel; or as of the affairs of the Jewish nation."[1] On the other hand—with the exception of the contest on Carmel—the miracles of Elijah and Elisha are not integral to the history of Israel as are those associated with the Deliverance from Egypt.

A more decisive difference emerges, however, when the second test is applied—the test of congruity with the biblical revelation as a whole. In this connection, as Preston and Hanson point out, the right question is: " Is this an occasion where a miracle seems appropriate to what we know of God's character? "[2] Put quite concretely in relation to one of the Elisha miracle-stories this means, Is it likely that God, being what He is and dealing with men as He does, would cause an axe head to float for the benefit of a theological student?[3] Alexander Nairne puts his finger on the spot when he says: " The ultimate difficulty about miracles is not that they lie outside the path of our experience, for our experience is continually expanding; but that it is sometimes hard for us to be satisfied that such or such a miracle is morally worth while."[4] As Strachan points out, such miracles as the iron axe-head made to swim (II Kings, vi, 1–7), the poisoned pot rendered harmless with meal (II Kings iv, 38–41) and the dead man raised by contact with Elisha's bones (II Kings xiii, 20–1) have more affinities with the wonder-stories of the medieval saints than with the " signs " recorded in the Gospels.[5]

On the other hand, the feeding of a hundred men with twenty barley loaves (II Kings iv, 42–4) and the healing of Naaman the leper (II Kings v, 1–14) are, as we have seen, significant anticipations of some of the miracles of Christ, and, generally speaking, the miracles of Elijah and Elisha may be

[1] *Analogy*, part ii, ch. vii.
[2] *Study Outline on The Life of Christ*, p. 23.   [3] See II Kings vi, 1–7.
[4] *The Faith of the Old Testament*, p. 172.
[5] See " Elisha," in Hastings' *Dictionary of the Bible*, i, p. 696. Cf. J. B. Mozley, *Eight Lectures on Miracles*, pp. 118–19.

regarded as their credentials authenticating the word of power spoken by God's prophets. " Prophecy being admitted as possible, and the actual prophecies of the Old Testament seers being certified, the ' wonders and signs ' with which their ministry was accredited are deprived of much of that antecedent improbability which . . . attaches itself to miraculous stories in general."[1] In the age of spiritual upheaval and moral conflict in which these early prophets lived, acts which today seem inappropriate may well have been fitting. Garvie, therefore, is surely right in his warning that we should very cautiously apply our sense of fitness as a test of truth to these ancient narratives.[2]

There is, however, another fact which is sometimes overlooked when dealing with the miracle-stories of the Old Testament. Their " truth " does not necessarily depend upon all the events having happened exactly in the way described, or even upon their having actually happened at all. As we have seen, there is cumulative evidence, which cannot lightly be set aside, that at certain great crises of biblical history events did occur which can only be described as miraculous. But if it can be shown that there are legendary elements in a particular story, or even if there are good reasons for believing the story itself to be a legendary accretion rather than a statement of historic fact, it is not for this reason to be dismissed as worthless. Truth may be embodied in a tale, as in the Gospel parables. The " truth " of the story of the Prodigal Son, for example, is in no way affected by the question whether Jesus was narrating an incident which actually took place or making up a story for His own purpose. Indeed, as we have seen in the previous chapter, " myth " and " legend " provide the only appropriate vehicle for conveying some of the most profound truths. The Old Testament miracle-stories, therefore, have an intrinsic value which is quite independent of their historical worth. As H. H. Rowley observes, " When we have decided whether we will accept the account of this miracle as true, or whether we will reject that as untrustworthy, we have not touched the question of the religious use of the stories."[3]

[1] J. H. Bernard, " Miracle," in Hastings' *Dictionary of the Bible*, iii, p. 393.
" Miracles " in Hastings' one volume *Dictionary of the Bible*, p. 623.
[3] *The Relevance of the Bible*, p. 116.

To put the matter concretely: the teaching of the Old Testament concerning the character and activity of God and the nature of His relationship with man is not deduced from, say, the miracles ascribed to Elijah and Elisha; these miracle-stories illustrate what Israel, from its own collective experience, already knew of God. "Interpretation is inseparable from miracles of the Old Testament pattern. We begin at the wrong end if we try first to rationalize them, and to reduce them to their smallest nucleus of historical event. We should begin rather with the faith of both prophet and people, by which the events of the physical world, normal or abnormal, were interpreted in a particular context of history."[1]

H. H. Rowley gives a telling illustration, from his own experience, of this aspect of the stories of Elijah's being fed by the ravens (I Kings xvii, 1–6) and of the widow's barrel of meal and cruse of oil (I Kings xvii, 9–16). On one occasion, when he was in charge of a church, an old lady living in an almshouse slipped into his hand an envelope containing seven shillings and sixpence in response to an appeal he had made for foreign missions. Knowing her circumstances, he asked her to take it back, saying that God would acknowledge the intention of her heart. But the woman was not to be gainsaid. "With quiet dignity," he says, "she reminded me that she was not offering the money to me . . . and that I had no right to refuse her gift." Some time later Dr. Rowley received a thank-offering of five pounds from a lady who requested that he should use it as he wished in his work. His first thought was of the old lady in the almshouse. He had always hesitated to offer her the small sums that were available from the Poor Fund, but he determined now to attempt to leave with her a pound. In due course he called to see her and before leaving asked if she would accept this small gift. To his astonishment the woman burst into tears. At the very moment when he had knocked at the door, she told him, she was on her knees praying that God would meet her need. She could draw no more money for another three days and she had not a scrap of food in the house. "I left," says Rowley, ". . . with a deeper sense of the truth of the message of these Elijah stories: that they who live for God, who

[1] H. Wheeler Robinson, *Inspiration and Revelation in the Old Testament*, p. 43.

in self-forgetting service yield their all to Him, may count on Him."[1]

Some words of Wheeler Robinson supply a fitting comment: " The true approach is to maintain that the things which really happened to the Hebrews might still happen, or rather, that they do happen. But the faith that can interpret them, as they are interpreted in the Bible, is not of every age."[2]

2. *The New Testament*

We have dealt at some length with the miracles of the Old Testament for two reasons: first, they present, in the nature of the case, more difficulties for the modern reader than do those of the Gospels; and second, they have been either dismissed or very summarily dealt with by most writers on this theme.

When we turn from the Old Testament to the New, questions relating to the historical evidence for miracles are more straightforward. The first thing that strikes us is the extent to which miracles are bound up with the whole apostolic testimony contained in the New Testament. They are by no means confined to its later documents; indeed they occupy about a third of the earliest Gospel, St. Mark, and, as Bethune-Baker remarks, " the narratives of these miracles are a large part not only of the Gospels but of the witness they bear to the character of Jesus. . . . This was the kind of thing people believed about Him."[3]

Rudolf Bultmann, in his attempt to commend Christianity to the modern man by " demythologizing " (*Entmythologisierung*) the New Testament, would eliminate its miracles, or interpret them " existentially " (as he would say) in such a way that they ceased to be miraculous—which comes to the same thing. " It is impossible," he says, " to make use of electric light and the radio, and, in case of illness, to claim the help of modern medical and clinical methods and at the same time to believe in the New Testament's world of spirits and miracles."[4] His objection to the miracle-stories of the Gospels is based, not so much upon what he considers to be their incompatibility with the *Kenosis* doctrine of Philippians ii, 6 ff., as upon his supposition

---

[1] *The Relevance of the Bible*, pp. 117–18. [2] *Op. cit.*, p. 46.
[3] *Early Traditions about Jesus*, p. 79. [4] *Kerygma und Mythos*, p. 18.

that they cannot be fitted into the modern scientific view of the world.

We shall consider the validity of this objection later. What must be noted at this stage is the fact that, as Bultmann fails to see, such a " demythologizing " of miracles would mean not a reinterpretation but a radical alteration of the essential teachings of the Christian faith. " What it believes about creation, providence, prayer and (pace Bultmann) about miracle, imply that God is Lord not only of the individual life but of the material universe. And a strictly demythologized Bible would give no basis for such an implication."[1]

The plain fact is that the miracles of the Gospels are integral to biblical history in a way that those of the prophets are not. They " are not evidential accessories, but essential constituents of Jesus' ministry of grace." So much so that " it is impossible to remove the records of miracles from the Gospels without tearing them to pieces, as these works of Jesus are so wrought into the very texture of His ministry."[2] Ironically enough Bultmann is the first to insist on the historical nature of Christianity. He emphatically repudiates the Liberal attempt to reduce it to a number of timeless religious truths and emphasizes the unique and decisive importance of the events of the Christian story. But Bultmann cannot have it both ways, and the words of A. B. Bruce in his Ely Lectures of 1886 remain true: " The reputation of the Gospels for historicity is fatally damaged when once it is conceded that all that savours of miracle belongs to the region of myth and legend."[3] His statement is underlined by C. S. Lewis sixty years later when he asserts that " the accounts of the 'miracles' in first-century Palestine are either lies, or legends, or history. And if all, or the most important, of them are lies or legends then the claim which Christianity has been making for the last two thousand years is simply false. No doubt it might even so contain noble sentiments and moral truths. So does Greek mythology; so does Norse. But that is quite a different affair."[4]

[1] Ian Henderson, *Myth in the New Testament*, p. 33. For an exhaustive enquiry into the mythological element in New Testament Christology, see G. V. Jones, *Christology and Myth in the New Testament*.

[2] A. E. Garvie, *op. cit.*, p. 621.

[3] *The Miraculous Element in the Gospels*, p. 355. [4] *Miracles*, p. 97.

In dealing with the life and ministry of Jesus, we need to remember that we are entirely dependent for our knowledge of Him upon the apostolic testimony embodied in the documents of the New Testament. This is the only evidence that we have; and while we need to examine it critically we may not deal with it arbitrarily without doing violence to our historical sources. Furthermore, if we are rightly to assess this evidence, we need to be quite clear as to its character—we need to see it for what it really is.

One of the most popular books that has come from the pen of Winston Churchill consists of a number of sketches of outstanding personalities whom he has met.[1] In this volume Churchill does not attempt to write the life stories of Arthur James Balfour and Hindenburg, for example; but he does convey to you very forcibly the impression that each of these Great Contemporaries made upon the men and women of his day.

Now that is precisely what the Gospels do regarding Jesus. They are not lives of Jesus—there are too many gaps in the story for them to be that; but they do sketch a portrait of Him which really conveys to us the impression that He made on fishermen and Pharisees two thousand years ago. But what kind of an impression is it that they convey? It is one which seems strange and remote to many people today. It is the impression of a man—a real man like us; one who was often hungry and tired; one who rested on a well and wept at the grave of a friend. But it is nevertheless the impression of a man who was different from every other man. He was like us; yes, but like which of us? He spake as never man spake; at His touch the blind received their sight, the lame walked, the dead were restored to life; even the wind and the sea obeyed Him. That is the kind of Man the Gospels portray. And however difficult some of their stories may seem to us, however far away from life as we know it today, there is one fact which we cannot escape—this was the kind of impression that Jesus made upon His contemporaries. He was the kind of Man who walked upon the sea and fed a multitude from two small fishes and five barley loaves.

We may discredit His miracles if we will. We may reject the

[1] Winston Churchill, *Great Contemporaries*.

evidence as untrue. We may refuse to accept this picture which the New Testament gives. But we may not alter the Gospel narratives to suit our own preconceived ideas. We may not go behind them and write others to take their place. We may not replace their portrait of Christ with our own. Because, as Alan Richardson points out, " if the Gospels do not give us a reliable picture of the Jesus of history, we can have no genuinely historical knowledge about Him."[1] The only Jesus that we can know anything about is the Jesus which they portray. And this is the kind of Man that He was.

It is in this light that the evidence of the Gospels needs to be seen. And when we come to examine it, it becomes quite clear that the evidence that Jesus worked miracles is quite as strong as any other evidence that we have concerning Him. Indeed, " the one incontestable piece of evidence is that all those contemporaries of Jesus of whom we have any record, friends and foes alike, believed that Jesus worked miracles "[2] of the kind described in the Gospels. As Alan Richardson points out, " There is no historical evidence to show that Jesus did not work miracles."[3] And he rightly maintains, therefore, that " if our judgment were to be decided by strictly historical considerations and by nothing else, we could not avoid the conclusion that Jesus worked miracles," since " the evidence that Jesus worked miracles is just as strong, and is of precisely the same quality and texture, as that He taught that God is Father and that His disciples should forgive one another. We cannot *on historical grounds alone* accept the evidence for the one and reject that for the other."[4]

There are three types of miracles described in the Gospels— miracles of healing, Nature miracles, and the raising of the dead. What has been said concerning evidence applies to each, so that here again we cannot *on historical grounds alone* accept the evidence for one type and reject that for another. The evidence for the Nature miracles is as good as for those of healing; so is that for the raising of the dead. No theories of coma can escape the plain fact that those who witnessed the acts were convinced

---

[1] *Christian Apologetics*, p. 170.
[2] Alan Richardson, *Science, History and Faith*, p. 99.
[3] *Christian Apologetics*, p. 170.   [4] *Ibid.*, p. 170.

that the dead had been raised. And, as J. A. MacCulloch points out, " the instances of this are so few in number as to raise a presumption of their truth, for here is exactly where miracles would probably be exaggerated in a fictitious narrative."[1]

MacCulloch reminds us that there is no non-miraculous stratum even in the earliest Gospel documents and that " the date of the documents is sufficiently near to the events recorded to admit of authenticity, and the evidence is as good as anything short of signed scientific evidence is likely to be. The writers were men who knew themselves to be witnesses, and had regard for truth."[2] We have no reason, therefore, on the ground of historical evidence, to doubt the general credibility of the Gospel miracle-stories. Our estimate of their fitness will depend upon our view of the Person of Christ, and to this we shall return later.

The New Testament miracles, however, are not confined to the Gospels; they are continued in the life of the Apostolic Church. The followers of Christ share in the power of God manifested in His mighty works. The beginning of this is found in the Gospels when Jesus delegates this power to His disciples (Mark vi, 7; cf. Matthew x, 1 and Luke ix, 1–2). The twelve are sent out not only to preach but also to heal the sick and cast out demons. According to the late ending of St. Mark's Gospel, the Risen Christ promises that these " signs " shall continue among believers (Mark xvi, 17–18). And in the Book of Acts the power to work miracles is recognized as being present in the Christian Community. Here again we are confronted with strong contemporary evidence so that " it is impossible to evade the consequence that the ministry of the apostles, according to the only records which we have got, was sustained by powers which are beyond the power of man or of nature as known to us. They fall into their place immediately if Christ was what He claimed to be, and the Church which He founded the minister of His grace; but on any other hypothesis they cannot be explained."[3]

[1] " Miracles," in *Encyclopaedia of Religion and Ethics*, viii, p. 682.
[2] *Ibid.*, p. 679.
[3] J. H. Bernard, " Miracle," in Hastings' *Dictionary of the Bible*, iii, p. 392.

III. Miracles and Natural Law

It is ultimately not history, however, but science which provides the modern man's real objection to miracles. His difficulty is not the question of evidence (of which, as we have seen, there is abundance); it arises from the seeming incompatibility of miracles with the modern scientific view of the world. Since the days of Newton the physical sciences have been dominated by the concept of natural law. The universe, it is argued, has come to be regarded as a vast piece of mechanism whose machinery works with the precision and regularity of a clock. Hence it is contended that belief in miracles belongs to a pre-scientific age and can no longer be held by any thinking man. " Miracle is, from the point of view of the scientist, a form of doctoring, tampering (if you like) cheating. It introduces a new factor into the situation, namely supernatural force, which the scientist had not reckoned on."[1]

This objection is not entirely new. It was first raised in the seventeenth century by Spinoza, who maintained that the laws of Nature, which are fixed and changeless, are the decrees of God. He argued therefore that for God to work miracles, which violate the natural order, would be self-contradictory. Hence miracles could not happen.[2] This was really a revival of Stoicism which held that the law of causality was of universal validity. Hence the Stoics deduced that all events happen according to an iron necessity, everything being inflexibly governed by εἱμαρμένη or fate.[3]

As Leonard Hodgson points out, it was this conception of the physical universe as a vast machine working according to rigid laws which formed the background of eighteenth-century Deism. " The deistic use of the potter and clay analogy produced the notion of God as of a celestial clockmaker who had made the machinery and set it in motion, henceforward only interfering with it from time to time to regulate or repair it by acts called miracles."[4] Such a conception of God as having deprived Himself of the freedom to break into the chain of

---

[1] C. S. Lewis, *Miracles*, pp. 70–1.

[2] See *Tractus Theologico-Politicus*, ch. 6.

[3] See Plutarch, *De Fato*, 11, and Alexander Aphrodisiensis, *De Fato*, 22 and 30.   [4] *Towards a Christian Philosophy*, p. 163.

causation by handing over the world to the rule of natural law virtually " relegates Him to the confines of His universe, and assign(s) Him a lesser place in the world of reality than we occupy ourselves."[1]

It is a far cry from the transcendentalism of the eighteenth-century Deists to the immanentism of the nineteenth-century Liberal Protestants. The rejection of miracle, however, is common to both, but it now takes a more aggressive and uncompromising form. The new Liberal school which sprang up in Germany towards the end of the last century—Gunkel, Bousset, Wrede, Weiss, Harnack, Troeltsch—launched a fresh attack on miracle in an attempt to come to terms with the natural science of their day. Their main premiss was the inviolability of natural law; anything which appeared to conflict with this was promptly surrendered. Harnack's words succinctly summarize this position: " We are firmly convinced that what happens in space and time is subject to the general laws of motion, and that in this sense, as an interruption of the order of Nature, there can be no such things as ' miracles.' "[2]

Harnack attempts, however, to make out a case for such of the biblical miracles as may be comprehended within this steel-and-concrete order of Nature. He therefore exercises a quite arbitrary discrimination which is unrelated to historical evidence, his only criterion being conformity with his *a priori* assumption of the inviolability of natural law:

Although the order of Nature be inviolable, we are not yet by any means acquainted with all the forces working in it and acting reciprocally with other forces. . . . We see that a strong will and a firm faith exert an influence upon the life of the body, and produce phenomena which strike us as marvellous. Has anyone ever yet drawn any sure line between the spheres of the possible and the actual? . . . Miracles, it is true, do not happen. . . . That the earth on its course stood still; that a she-ass spoke; that a storm was quieted by a word, we do not believe, and we shall never again believe; but that the lame walked, the blind saw, and the deaf heard, will not be so summarily dismissed as an illusion.[3]

[1] H. H. Rowley, *The Relevance of the Bible*, p. 104.
[2] *What is Christianity?* 3rd and revised ed. (1904), p. 27.
[3] *Ibid.*, pp. 28–9.

He exhorts his readers therefore not to be deterred by miraculous stories. Anything unintelligible may be put aside, since " the question of miracles is of relative indifference in comparison with everything else which is to be found in the Gospels."[1] But he is curiously illogical; what he has taken away with one hand he attempts to put back with the other. Having taken his stand on the postulate of an inflexible order of Nature and made it his sole criterion of credibility, he goes on to say that, although miracles do not matter, " the question on which everything turns is whether we are helplessly yoked to an inexorable necessity, or whether a God exists who rules and governs, and *whose power to compel Nature we can move by prayer* and make a part of our experience."[2] Precisely! But even Harnack cannot have it both ways. We have here an apt illustration of Wendland's comment that Harnack and Troeltsch, though they reject the metaphysical conception of " miracle," " are involuntarily driven to use expressions corresponding to the conception they have rejected, if they are to do justice to their sense of the living action of God."[3]

T. W. Manson points out that the Liberal position was vitiated by its dogmatic presuppositions " drawn from the vigorous, swiftly moving, and very confident scientific thought of the nineteenth century: in particular, the doctrines of the universal reign of natural law and of biological evolution. The effect of the former doctrine was, of course, to discredit all the miracle stories which involve, or appear to involve, any interference with the sacrosanct order of Nature, any tampering with the endless chain of cause and effect."[4] Thus " any interference on God's part in the settled order of Nature is barred."[5] " God must not meddle in His world either by deed or word."[6] Manson rightly goes on to ask why, in that case, the Fatherhood of God and His providential care need to be brought into the picture at all. " If anyone should allege that we need not postulate the impotent benevolence that we choose to call

---

[1] *Ibid.*, pp. 30–1.
[2] *Ibid.*, p. 31 (italics mine).
[3] J. Wendland, *Miracles and Christianity* (Eng. trans.), p. 13.
[4] " The Failure of Liberalism to Interpret the Bible as the Word of God," in *The Interpretation of the Bible* (ed. C. W. Dugmore), p. 93.
[5] *Ibid.*, p. 97.   [6] *Ibid.*, p. 98.

' Father '; if anyone should say ' Show us the order of Nature and it sufficeth us,' there is no very obvious answer. The Fatherhood of God, like the Kingdom of God, becomes just a special way of interpreting Nature."[1] Ultimately all that is left is that " Natural law reigns supreme, unchallenged and unchallengeable in the world."[2] And so " in order to come to terms with nineteenth-century science, Liberalism had to fall out with historical Christianity."[3] The final result of this Liberal apologetic was to undermine the faith which it sought to commend. They made a desert and called it peace.

The philosophy of miracle accepted by traditional Christian theology was that of St. Augustine, who consistently refused to regard miracles as irrational interferences with the natural order. They may seem contrary to Nature, but " how can that be against Nature which is effected by the will of God, the Lord and Maker of all Nature? "[4] " We do not say that God does something contrary to Nature because He acts in a way that is contrary to our knowledge of Nature."[5] He maintains therefore that " a miracle is not contrary to Nature (*contra naturam*), but contrary to what is known of Nature (*contra quam est nota natura*)."[6] This is an important distinction. It cuts the roots of the difficulties raised by the modern scientific outlook. As Alan Richardson points out, " In the nature of the case ' science ' as such can have no objection to the conception of miracle as it is understood in traditional theology, for miracle is merely that which occurs according to the operation of those laws of Nature which are as yet unknown to us."[7] The Liberals went wrong because they were dazzled by the over-confident scientific thought of the nineteenth century and wrongly assumed that it had said the last word.

There are two false assumptions which underlie much confused thinking on this issue. The first is the quite unwarranted assumption of the Naturalist that Nature is the whole of reality, the sum total of all that exists. A glance at the derivation of the

[1] *Ibid.*, pp. 98–9.   [2] *Ibid.*, p. 100.   [3] *Ibid.*, pp. 101–2.
[4] *De Civitate Dei*, Bk. XXI, ch. viii.
[5] *Contra Faustum Manichaeum*, xxvi, 3.
[6] *De Civitate Dei*, Bk. XXI, ch. viii.   [7] *Christian Apologetics*, p. 155.

term will show the implications of this view. The word "nature" comes from the Latin *natura*, which is derived from the verb "to be born" or "to spring up," as is its Greek equivalent, φύσις, from the verb "to grow." "Nature means what happens 'of itself' or 'of its own accord': what you do not need to labour for; what you will get if you take no measures to stop it." Hence "What the Naturalist believes is that the ultimate Fact, the thing you can't go behind, is a vast process in space and time which is *going on of its own accord*. . . . All the things and events (within it) are so completely interlocked that no one of them can claim the slightest independence from 'the whole show.' "[1] Now a miracle is by definition an event independent of the regularly observed processes of Nature and initiated *ab extra* by a Power beyond Nature. But if Nature be the whole of reality this is a contradiction in terms. On these premisses, therefore, there can be no such thing as a miracle.

This assumption, however, fails to reckon with the fact of rational thought. Naturalism leaves no room for human freedom either of thought or of will: it implies a thoroughgoing Determinism. Mind, being itself the product of this vast interlocking system of Nature, has no power of independent thought: all thought is the result of irrational natural causes. But if this be true, it follows that all theories, including Naturalism, are equally valueless. "If," says Haldane, "my mental processes are determined wholly by the motions of atoms in my brain, I have no reason to suppose that my beliefs are true . . . and hence I have no reason for supposing my brain to be composed of atoms."[2] Naturalism is thus self-destructive; it is discredited by its own logic. By proving that there are no such things as proofs, it surrenders its own claim to truth. Once the independence of rational thought be admitted as self-evident, however, Nature can no longer be regarded as the whole of reality. Here is something over and above Nature by which its actual course may be modified. Man's rationality is thus "the little telltale rift in Nature which shows that there is something beyond

---

[1] C. S. Lewis, *Miracles*, pp. 16–17.
[2] J. B. S. Haldane, *Possible Worlds*, p. 209.

or behind her."[1] If this be admitted, the case for miracles is by no means closed.

The second false assumption which is frequently made is that the so-called " laws of Nature " state what must always necessarily occur. They are regarded as ontological entities which determine the course of Nature on the supposition that " an observed regularity in events is somehow also an observed immutable necessity."[2] Laws of Nature, however, are mental concepts, not ontological entities. They are generalizations made on the basis of the observation of certain regularities in the events which have happened hitherto in the phenomenal world. They describe, therefore, what men have observed to occur, not what must necessarily occur. " An observed regularity is only an observed regularity; the necessity we read into it, and in strict science we have no right to affirm it to be there. . . . From the standpoint of such empirical generalizations *anything* may still happen in the future, however much in practical life we are forced to make our decisions on the assumption that the possibilities lie within the limits indicated by our previous experience. . . . An empirical generalization, as made at any one time, can never claim an absolute validity."[3]

This was demonstrated once for all by Hume in his penetrating enquiry into the foundation of the belief in the order of Nature. After pointing out that belief in causality is based only on experience, he goes on to ask what is the foundation of the conclusions that we draw from experience: " Experience can be allowed to give direct and certain information of those precise objects only, and that precise period of time which fell under its cognizance; but why should this experience be extended to future times and to other objects? . . . All inferences from experience *suppose* as their foundation that the future will resemble the past: it is impossible therefore that any arguments from experience can prove this resemblance. Let the course of things be allowed hitherto ever so regular, that alone,

---

[1] C. S. Lewis, *op. cit.*, p. 38.

[2] H. H. Farmer, *The World and God*, p. 148

[3] H. H. Farmer, *ibid.*, pp. 148-9. Cf. J. B. Mozley, *Eight Lectures on Miracles*, p. 29: " We really look at a blank before us, but the mind full of the scene behind, sees it again in front."

without some new argument or inference, proves not that for the future it will continue so."[1]   Mozley's conclusion that " we know nothing in nature of law in the sense in which it prevents miracles " is therefore justified.[2]

The new conception of matter which has emerged in modern physics and revolutionary discoveries in the realm of atomic energy have made the idea of Nature as a closed system subject to a rigid and inflexible reign of " law " quite untenable today. Recent research in psychosomatic medicine has shown the far-reaching influence of mental states not only in functional but also in organic disorders, as witness the much-quoted statement of the *British Medical Journal* that " no tissue of the human body is wholly removed from the influence of spirit." It is becoming increasingly recognized, therefore, that " the so-called ' laws ' summarize what is observable in the world of Nature under the normal conditions of daily life; but they do not preclude the emergence of unusual phenomena, granted the presence of a sufficient cause which, for all we know to the contrary, may be spiritual."[3]

One cause of unusual phenomena may be what Wendland calls " the convergence of the different causal series " which is, as he points out, in principle inexplicable.[4] Apart altogether from any events which may come into the category of " miracle," however, the ordinary course of the physical world is being continually deflected by non-physical forces. This implies, not the breaking of a natural law, but the temporary suspension of one law through the operation of another. As Mozley observes, " Physical laws are suspended any time an animate being moves any part of its body; the laws of matter are suspended by the laws of life."[5] Archbishop Trench gives a familiar illustration: " When I lift my arm, the law of gravitation is not, as far as my arm is concerned, denied or annihilated; it exists as much as ever, but is held in suspense by the higher law of my will."[6] Science can give no adequate account in

---

[1] See *Enquiry Concerning the Human Understanding*, section iv.
[2] *Eight Lectures on Miracles*, p. 39.
[3] Vincent Taylor, *The Gospel According to St. Mark*, p. 141.
[4] *Miracles and Christianity* (Eng. trans.), note 10, p. 284.
[5] *Op. cit.*, p. 129.   [6] *Notes on the Miracles*, p. 18.

terms of physical causation of such voluntary human action; and that is what Lord Kelvin meant when he said that from the point of view of science every free human action is a miracle. "Man," says St. Augustine, "is a greater miracle than all that he can work."[1]

It follows that the order of Nature is not a rigid "steel-and-concrete" system under the domination of iron laws; it is at least sufficiently flexible to allow for the exercise of free human action within it. I as a person can initiate events by an act of will—events which had I not willed them would not in the ordinary course of things have happened. I can pick up a stone and throw it. Had I not picked it up, the stone would have remained on the ground. The law of gravitation did not cease to operate when I threw it, but there was free scope for my own act of will. Thus, as Farmer comments, "Man's whole life is built up on this awareness that he is related to a system which is permanent enough to be resolved into regularities, and plastic enough to leave at least some room for his own will to shape it to his own ends."[2]

Does not this give us a clue to the place of miracles in relation to the natural order? If it gives scope for the exercise of human personality to such an extent that it may be deflected from its normal courses by the mind and will of man, is it unreasonable or unscientific to believe that it may be influenced to an even greater extent by the Mind and Will of God? Belief in miracle is a corollary—a necessary corollary—of belief in a Personal God. "Fundamentally, it means just that there is a living God . . . To believe in the living God and to believe in miracle are the same thing. It is inconsistent to accept the first and deny the second."[3] The element of knowledge latent in the conception of miracle "is the perception that there is a working of God, immediate and personal, not merely in the life of spirit but in that of sense."[4] Belief in miracle thus rests upon the biblical conviction that the universe is essentially a realm of personal relationships. In the words of Farmer, "It is a clinging to the idea of personality in God, in face of all those theories which would reduce the universe to a system of iron laws and

---

[1] *De Civitate Dei*, Bk. X, ch. xii.   [2] *The World and God*, p. 147.
[3] J. Wendland, *op. cit.*, p. 1.   [4] *Ibid.*, p. 241.

banish personality from the ultimate altogether."[1] If God is a Person and His relationship with us is a personal relationship, is it incredible that in a crisis He should exert His Will to deflect the course of the natural order which He has created and cause to happen events which are outside the normal routine of life? A miracle is God coming to man's assistance, in answer to his cry for help, in a time of need. It is the outward and visible sign of the divine initiative in redemption.

Such a conception of the nature and activity of God implies that the physical world is ultimately dependent on God and plastic in His hands; it is incompatible with any ideas of mechanical causation or the inflexible rule of natural law. " It is certain," says Canon Baker, " that a thorough-going belief in the uniformity of Nature cannot be held along with a serious belief in Divine personality, if only because uniformity, so understood, makes it impossible to give any meaning to the notion of God's freedom. He is imprisoned within His own laws. They come between Him and us."[2] The Bible witnesses to the fact that the natural order is not an end in itself; it exists for man, who is the crown of creation. In the language of devotion, the world is a vale of soul-making. It is the theatre of our moral striving, the arena in which, through struggle and conflict, human personality is developed. Its purpose in the providence of God is the perfecting of finite spirits who shall realize the end of their existence in fellowship with Him. Hence the physical order is " the passive instrument of God's will aiming at the creation of free beings. It can be controlled as they can not, and there would be no irrationality in accepting adequate evidence that it had sometimes deviated from its commonly observed uniform manner of behaviour, if that deviation could be thought of as fulfilling the aim of the whole process—the eliciting of perfect finite freedom. It is not without significance that He whom we believe to have been God incarnate thought of the power over storms and bread and mountains as lying in His hands, but of men as those into whose hands He was to give the power over Himself."[3]

---

[1] *The World and God*, p. 126.
[2] A. E. Baker, *Science, Christianity and Truth*, pp. 31–2.
[3] L. Hodgson, *Towards a Christian Philosophy*, p. 117.

IV. The Key Miracle

" If the universe is dominated by a Spirit," says T. E. Jessop, "miracles are possible; if by a Spirit that is love, probable; and if the Spirit has become incarnate, this miracle would make further ones very probable indeed."[1] The Incarnation is not only the focal point of revelation; it is the key miracle of the Bible. By its truth other biblical miracles stand or fall. " Ultimately the historian's answer to the question about the miracles of Jesus will depend upon his answer to the prior question, what he thinks of Christ."[2] If Jesus were a mere man, it is incredible that He should have stilled a storm, or fed a multitude with a boy's snack lunch, or raised the dead. But if He were the Incarnation of the Supreme Being, none of these things is antecedently impossible; indeed they are quite fitting and proper to His Person. " If Christ was what the apostolic testimony declares him to be," says A. R. Vidler, " we cannot say in advance what he could or could not do."[3] The crucial question, therefore, is that which Jesus put to His disciples at Caesarea Philippi: " Whom say ye that I am? " (Mark viii, 29).

An unprejudiced reading of the Gospels shows quite clearly that Jesus thought of Himself as being different from other men. His references to Himself as " the Son " and to God as in a special sense His Father show that He was conscious of a unique filial relationship to God. This consciousness becomes acutely real at His baptism (Mark i, 11); three disciples share it at the Transfiguration (Mark ix, 7; cf. Matthew xvii, 5; Luke ix, 35; II Peter i, 17). In the Parable of the Vineyard (Mark xii, 1–9), Jesus, convinced that He has been sent by God as a final envoy to Israel, quietly assumes a position superior to the prophets (the servants) and implies that He is conscious of a unique relation of sonship.[4] Moreover, He makes tremendous claims for Himself—claims which are not merely ridiculous but blasphemous on the lips of any mere man. He claims a unique relationship to God (Matthew xi, 25–7, Luke x, 21–22,

[1] T. E. Jessop, *The Christian Faith*, p. 15.
[2] A. Richardson, *Science, History and Faith*, pp. 104–5.
[3] A. R. Vidler, *Christian Belief*, p. 53.
[4] Jesus makes a direct allusion to Himself as the εἷς υἱὸς ἀγαπητός, Mark xii, 6; cf. Mark xiii, 32.

" Q "; cf. John xiv, 9, and x, 30) and an exclusive authority in the world of men (Matthew xi, 28-9; x, 37-9, cf. Luke xiv, 26; Matthew viii, 21-2, Luke ix, 59-60, " Q "; cf. Mark i, 22).[1] He claims the power to forgive sins (Mark ii, 5-12). He claims to be the Judge of men at the last day (Matthew vii, 21-3, cf. Luke xiii, 24-7; Matthew xiii, 41-3; Luke xix, 11 ff., Matthew xxv, 14 ff.; cf. Mark viii, 38, Matthew x, 32-3, Luke ix, 26; cf. Luke xxi, 36). In short, the claims which Jesus makes are claims which only God has any right to make. Only one of three conclusions is open to us, therefore: either He was what He claimed to be—Divine, God manifest in the flesh; or He was the greatest deceiver that has ever lived; or He was mad. We may worship Jesus as God Incarnate or we may dismiss Him as a fraud; what we may not do is to venerate Him as a great teacher or a good man: *aut Deus aut homo non bonus*.

The disciples as Jews were strict monotheists; for them worship of any but Jehovah was the supreme heresy. But as they companied with Him, they became conscious of " God's Presence and His Very Self " in this Man of Nazareth. " Beyond all possibility of question, and seemingly by His own deliberate intention, Jesus, so far as they yielded their faith to Him, was taking the place of God. . . . Within the sphere of their personal lives, He had been growing to have to them the values of God, as the object of their absolute faith, their infallible refuge and informer and protector and guide."[2] There was in His Person that quality of the " numinous " which Otto calls the *mysterium tremendum et fascinans*;[3] the sense of " otherness " characteristic of the Divine. " He taught them as one that had authority, and not as the scribes " (Mark i, 22; cf. Matthew vii, 29). The rough fisherman falls down at His knees saying " Depart from me; for I am a sinful man, O Lord " (Luke v, 8). As Cave says, " They followed Him, in spite of all perplexity, because they felt in Him the presence of the Divine, the strange attraction and repulsion of the Holy made manifest in His human life."[4]

[1] It is enough, when revising the divinely-given law of Sinai, for Jesus to say, " But I say unto you." See Matthew v.
[2] C. Gore, *The Reconstruction of Belief*, pp. 348-9.
[3] See R. Otto, *Das Numinosa*, Eng. trans., *The Idea of the Holy*.
[4] S. Cave, *The Doctrine of the Person of Christ*, p. 29.

The earliest New Testament confession of faith consists of three words: "Jesus is Lord." This is not to be understood in terms of the hero-god (κύριος) of the Hellenistic mystery religions, as Bousset and Kirsopp Lake would have us believe; any such idea would be anathema to a Jew. Its meaning is to be sought in the Septuagint where κύριος translates the Divine Name. To say that "Jesus is Lord," therefore, is to acknowledge that He is Very God Incarnate, and nothing less. And this is the heart of the apostolic testimony concerning Him. " In the Christian story," says C. S. Lewis, " God descends to re-ascend. He comes down; down from the heights of absolute being into time and space, down into humanity; down further still, if embryologists are right, to recapitulate in the womb ancient and pre-human phases of life; down to the very roots and sea-bed of the Nature He had created. But He goes down to come up again and bring the whole ruined world up with Him."[1]

This is the supreme miracle which attests all the rest. " It is the Christology which underlies the miracles."[2] To see them in their right perspective, "we must remember that the whole story is of a Person and a time by themselves."[3] Then the miracles of Jesus " are seen to be the natural results within a Spiritual Universe of the appearance of a unique Personality."[4] As Dummelow says, " In the Incarnate what we ordinarily call Miracle is, as it were, normal; for in Him is God personally revealed to man, personally acting under conditions of human life."[5]

The miracles of Jesus are presented in the Gospels as the power of God working in and through Him (Luke v, 17, xi, 20; cf. Mark vi, 14).[6] They are essentially the works of the Messiah, and as such are " signs " or evidences (for those who have eyes to see) both of who He is and of the dawning of the

---

[1] *Miracles*, p. 135.

[2] Hoskyns and Davey, *The Riddle of the New Testament*, p. 125.

[3] A. Nairne, *Every Man's Story of the New Testament*, p. 42.

[4] D. S. Cairns, *The Faith that Rebels*, p. 124.

[5] " Miracle," in *A Commentary on the Holy Bible*, p. cxx.

[6] Cf. A. N. Rowland, *The Fibres of Faith*, pp. 138–9: " His birth was heralded in the Magnificat in terms of power. . . . We are to read in the life of Christ the culminating evidence of the divine power or dynamic of God."

Messianic Age in which the sovereign rule of God is manifested in the world. " The physical miracles are external signs of the supreme Messianic Miracle, the rescue of man from the grip of the powers of evil—from sin."[1] This is how the New Testament miracles are intended to be understood. They are not " wonder-stories " told to enhance the prestige of Jesus by portraying Him as a wonder-worker; neither are they " faith cures " in the generally accepted sense of the term; nor are they to be regarded as mere examples of the power of mind over matter.[2] " They are signs of the presence of Him Who should come and Who is the Victor in the contest with evil, signs also of the Advent of the Kingdom of God."[3] They " fulfil " the prophetic anticipations of the New Age in which the Old Testament abounds. This Age to Come was to be characterized by a special manifestation of the power of God triumphing over the powers of sin and death and restoring the Divine intention in creation. Jesus not only proclaims the dawning of the New Age; He does the mighty works associated with it: His followers taste of the powers of the Age to Come (Hebrews vi, 5, R.V.). His teaching and His miracles are therefore mutually interdependent. As Pascal observes, " Les miracles discernent la doctrine, et la doctrine discerne les miracles "[4]—the miracles authenticate the message and the message interprets the miracles.

When John the Baptist enquires from Herod's prison whether Jesus is the Coming One, his disciples are told to report to him what they have heard and seen: " The blind receive their sight, the lame walk, the lepers are cleansed, and the deaf hear, the dead are raised up " (Matthew xi, 2–6; cf. Luke vii, 19–23).

[1] Hoskyns and Davey, *The Riddle of the New Testament*, p. 120.

[2] See Leslie D. Weatherhead, *Psychology, Religion and Healing*: " After studying the question for many years . . . I cannot completely fit the healing miracles of Christ into the categories of modern psychotherapeutic practice " (p. 40). " While the mental mechanisms which He used can sometimes be identified through our modern psychological knowledge, the miracles certainly cannot be regarded merely as psychotherapeutic treatments " (p. 78). Cf. Bishop Ryle, " The Neurotic Theory of the Miracles of Healing," in *Hibbert Journal*, April 1907: " The ' neurotic theory ' is quite insufficient to account for them."

For a detailed study of the healing miracles in relation to modern psychotherapy, see E. R. Micklem, *Miracles & the New Psychology*.

[3] Hoskyns and Davey, *op. cit.*, p. 125.   [4] *Pensées* ' Des Miracles.'

All these are " signs " of the Messianic Age foreshadowed in the
Book of Isaiah (Isaiah xxix, 18; xxxv, 4–6; xlii, 7); John must
draw his own conclusion. Edwyn Hoskyns and Noel Davey
maintain that all the miracle-stories in Mark are deliberately
narrated as the fulfilment of Old Testament prophecy and
depend for their understanding upon the detection of the Old
Testament allusions. They call attention, for example, to the
cure of the man who was deaf and had an impediment in his
speech (Mark vii, 31–7) and point out that the word μογιλάλος,
" a stammerer," which occurs nowhere else in the New Testament, is used only once in the Septuagint, and that is in Isaiah
xxxv, 5–6: " Then shall the eyes of the blind be opened, and
the ears of the deaf shall hear. Then shall the lame man leap
as an hart, and the tongue of the stammerer shall speak
plainly."[1] The miracles of healing, therefore, are not to be
regarded merely as acts of compassion; they were " the
opening victories in the great campaign against sin and sorrow
which would end in the total destruction of Satan's kingdom."[2]

A further Christological significance of the miracles of healing is pointed out by Alan Richardson—they imply and symbo-
lize the divine forgiveness; they are, as it were, " symbolic
demonstrations of God's forgiveness in action," since " to all
Jews the power to heal meant the breaking of the power of sin."
They therefore raise the whole question of Christ's person and
authority because the power to forgive sins belongs only to God.
This issue is focused in the story of the Paralytic (Mark ii,
1–12) where " Jesus deliberately implies that His healing work
authenticates His power to forgive sins."[3]

The nature miracles of the Gospels are complementary to the
miracles of healing. They too are presented as " signs " of the
divine power and authority of Christ and of the breaking in of
the powers of the Age to Come through the ministry of the
Messiah. There is no distinction between the two. As Cairns
observes, they " are needed to complete the idea embodied in
the healing miracles. They are meant to embody the ideal
will of God and the ideal destiny of man in the Kingdom of

---

[1] Op. cit., pp. 119–20.
[2] D. S. Cairns, The Faith that Rebels, pp. 15–16.
[3] The Miracle-Stories of the Gospels, pp. 60–6.

Heaven."[1] In the Old Testament God is not only the Creator but also the Lord of Nature; all natural processes are under His control.[2] At His rebuke the sea is dried up (Isaiah l, 2); He rules the raging of the sea (Psalm lxxxix, 9). Hence, " that Jesus shares the power of God as the Lord of the mysteries of creation is the main teaching of the stories of the Stilling of the Storm (Mark iv, 35–41) and the Walking on the Sea (Mark vi, 45–52)."[3]

In the case of the feeding miracles (Mark vi, 30–44; viii, 1–10) and the turning of water into wine (John ii, 1–11), St. Augustine points out that the Lord of Nature here performs by a momentary act what he normally accomplishes yearly by natural processes. " They focus at a particular point either God's actual, or His future, operations on the universe."[4] Bread and wine were the main food and drink in Palestine and Jesus Himself likens the Kingdom of God to a Great Supper or Feast (Matthew xxii, 1–10; Luke xiv, 16–24). It may be that these miracles are to be seen against the background of the mysterious Old Testament figure of Melchizedek, King of Salem, who brought forth for Abraham bread and wine (Genesis xiv, 18).[5] The unknown author of the Epistle to the Hebrews certainly makes this link when, on the basis of Psalms cx, 4, he refers to Christ as a priest after the order of Melchizedek (Hebrews vi, 20–vii, 28). " The Christ is the dispenser of the life of God, the author and giver of eternal life."[6] It is significant that in St. John's Gospel the feeding of the five thousand is followed by a discourse on the Bread of Life. Hence A. M. Hunter suggests that the miracle was an acted parable; Jesus " was signifying by word and act that the new life of the Kingdom was now available for men."[7]

---

[1] *Op. cit.*, p. 169.

[2] Cf. Wheeler Robinson, *Inspiration and Revelation in the Old Testament*, p. 47: " Nature is made to be the arena of history, and becomes its instrument."

[3] Alan Richardson, *The Miracle-Stories of the Gospels*, p. 90.

[4] C. S. Lewis, *Miracles*, p. 162.

[5] Philo sees Melchizedek as a type of the Word, who shall " bring forth wine instead of water." See *Legum Allegoriarum*, III, 82 (*Philonis Judaei Opera*, ed. Mangey, i, pp. 102–3).

[6] E. C. Hoskyns, *The Fourth Gospel*, i, p. 199.

[7] *The Gospel According to St. Mark* (Torch Bible Commentaries), p. 73.

In the turning of water into wine (John ii, 1–11) once again
" the Creator of matter is exercising His lordship over it; ' the
modest water saw its God and blushed.' "[1] As C. S. Lewis,
following Augustine, observes, " This miracle proclaims that
the God of all wine is present. . . . Every year, as part of the
Natural order, God makes wine. . . . He constantly turns water
into wine, for wine, like all drinks, is but water modified. Once,
and in one year only, God, now incarnate, short circuits the
process: makes wine in a moment. . . . The Miracle consists
in the short cut; but the event to which it leads is the usual
one."[2] Seen against the background of the Messianic Feast of
Isaiah xxv, 6, it may be regarded as a " sign " of the Kingdom
of God inaugurated by Christ. The new wine of the Kingdom,
now made available to man, is better than the old wine of
Judaism which has become exhausted.

The raising of the dead constitutes another Messianic " sign "
as St. Luke especially is at pains to show. He prefaces his
account of John the Baptist's enquiry whether Jesus really was
the Coming One (Luke vii, 19–23) by the story of the raising
of the widow's son. This is significant in view of Jesus' reference
to the fact that " the dead are raised " (verse 22) in His listing
of the " signs " which the disciples of John have witnessed
and are to report to the Baptist. As Alan Richardson points
out, " it is a sign which John, as the *Elijah Redivivus*, would
surely recognize, for had not Elijah, and Elisha after him,
raised a widow's only son from the dead? (I Kings xvii, 17–24;
II Kings iv, 21–37)." Richardson also calls attention to other
significant Old Testament parallels in the story: the scene of
the miracle, Nain, " was near the ancient city of Shunem,
where Elisha's miracle had been performed. The words of
Luke vii, 15, καὶ ἔδωκεν αὐτὸν τῇ μητρὶ αὐτοῦ, are identical
with those of I Kings xvii, 23 (LXX)." And he observes
that " the exclamation of the bystanders, ' A great prophet
is arisen among us ' (Luke vii, 16), indicates that they have
correctly perceived the Old Testament parallels, and their
further comment, ' God hath visited His people,' is an acknow-
ledgment of the Messianic implication of the miracle."[3]

---

[1] W. Temple, *Readings in St. John's Gospel*, p. 37.
[2] C. S. Lewis, *op. cit.*, p. 163.   [3] *The Miracle-Stories of the Gospels*, p. 113.

Oscar Cullmann shows how the miracles of healing and the raising of the dead are linked together as manifestations of the operation of the Holy Spirit upon the physical organism, temporarily restraining the power of death. This is a " sign " of the Messianic Age in which death is conquered. Man is still subject to the claims of death, however, although it has suffered a final reverse; but the powers of the Age to Come are at work holding back the still active power of death. Hence " this temporary restraining of death through the resurrection power of the Holy Spirit constitutes the deeper meaning of all the New Testament healings of the sick and raisings of the dead."[1]

It must be emphasized that the Gospel miracles are "signs" only for those who have faith in Christ; they are never used to elicit or compel faith. This is true of both the Synoptic Gospels and John. Jesus consistently refuses to use His divine power to satisfy the curious, or to make a display, or to arouse belief in Himself. The significance of His miracles is discerned only by those who see them for what they are—the acts of the Messiah— because they recognize Him for what He is—the Christ. Thus the miracles, like the parables, served as a touchstone, a test, of the spiritual discernment and responsiveness of those who witnessed them. " Many would look, and wonder, and go their way—they had seen a strange sight, *that* they would allow, but it did not touch their souls: while to a few others it would seem as if they had lighted on what they had been watching for all their lives."[2]

The supreme miracle of the Bible is the Resurrection of Jesus from the dead. It is the final seal of His divine authority, the final authentication of all His mighty acts. No event in the New Testament is better attested; none is more significant. It underlies all our records and is presupposed by every writer. It is not an afterthought added as a kind of postscript to the Christian message to give it a happy ending, as H. G. Wells suggested; it is central in it. Here " we are dealing with a belief which interweaves itself, directly or indirectly, with the whole body of teaching in the New Testament."[3] As J. S. Whale puts it, " No

---

[1] See *Christ and Time*, pp. 236–7.
[2] H. Latham, *Pastor Pastorum*, p. 80.
[3] James Orr, *The Resurrection of Jesus*, p. 36.

early Christian wrote a sentence about Jesus which did not
proceed from the conviction that He had risen from the dead
and was present in their midst as the first-born of a new order
of creation."[1] The Resurrection, therefore, belongs to the very
essence of our holy religion; you cannot take it away from
Christianity without radically altering its character, without in
fact making it something other than the classic Christian faith.
The theme of the apostolic preaching was not just a crucified
Saviour, but a risen Lord; not merely Jesus, but Jesus and the
Resurrection. It was Jesus raised from the dead by the power of
God, glorified, exalted to God's right hand. W. E. Orchard
was quite right when he maintained that " our Gospels, as they
stand, would never have been written unless the Evangelists
had been able to complete them with the story of the Resurrection."[2] Its evidence is not just an empty tomb, but the rise
and progress of the Christian Church, which is inexplicable
without it.

As A. M. Ramsey reminds us, the Resurrection of Christ
from the dead can only be understood by those who will think
biblically about it.[3] That is to say, we must know what the Bible
means by death. It does not mean the mere physical fact of
death, but rather an experience associated with it which only
man knows—the experience of having to die; and no experience
can be merely physical for man. " The sense of melancholy
which the anticipation of death induces in the human spirit
is not known in the animal world."[4] Death has this content
for man because having to die is linked in his consciousness
with the one other irrational fact in his world—the fact of sin.
Here is Death's sting. Man sees in it an emblem of what sin
is and does, and having to die becomes for him a sacramental
experience, " the experience," in the words of James Denney,
" in which the final repulsion of evil by God is decisively
expressed."[5] Hence " it is impossible for sinful man to anticipate his end with equanimity."[6]

Death in the Bible is not just the end of us; that is materialism.

[1] *Facing the Facts*, p. 69.
[2] *Foundations of Faith: II Christological*, p. 99.
[3] A. M. Ramsey, *The Resurrection of Christ*, pp. 20 ff.
[4] Reinhold Niebuhr, *The Nature and Destiny of Man*, ii, p. 1.
[5] *The Death of Christ*, p. 160.   [6] Reinhold Niebuhr, *op. cit.*, i, p. 186.

Neither is it the mere dissolution of the body which the soul survives; that is the essence of spiritualism. It is rather, as John Marsh has put it, " the final spiritual crisis, the last ' day ' of decision, the last opportunity. It is the acutest form of the question whether we will have God or no. . . . The issue of death is not whether we have souls or not; nor yet, having them, whether they merely survive the body or are immortal; it is whether we will live with God, which is heaven, or without Him, which is hell." But, as Marsh points out, " Death's tragedy is that we are not entirely free to choose, but are bound by the whole chain of our decisions throughout our life."[1] Apart then from the mercy of God, death for every man must mean final separation from God, for all have sinned and every son of Adam is bound by the chain of his sin so that in this last great crisis he cannot of himself choose to have God.

This is the background against which the Resurrection of Jesus from the dead must be seen if its full significance is to be grasped. Since death means in the Bible a destiny " specially connected with sin and with separation from God," the Resurrection of Christ means " an act of divine victory over both death and sin as the means of the coming of the reign of God."[2] It means that Christ has conquered death *in this biblical sense of the word*: the eternal Son of God who knew no sin experienced death *as sinful men experience it*—as a final and awful separation from God. When the Apostles' Creed says, " He descended into hell," it means that, as does the cry of dereliction from the Cross: " My God, my God, why hast thou forsaken me? " But the miracle of the Resurrection is seen in the fact that this final state of alienation from God was *not* final for Christ: " The third day He rose again from the dead." The Resurrection was no mere resuscitation of a corpse; nor was it the survival of bodily death by the soul of Jesus. It was nothing less than a cosmic triumph—the triumph of God Himself—over the powers of darkness that enslave the will of man and finally alienate him from the face of God. Death, this final and tragic crisis of the spirit of man, is swallowed up in victory.

[1] Quoted from a circular letter to the members of the Congregational Church-Order Group, Easter, 1943.
[2] A. M. Ramsey, *op. cit.*, pp. 20–1.

There is another fact—a fact of far-reaching significance —which emerges when the Gospel miracles are seen in the light of all that is implied by the key miracle of the Incarnation. Not only are they a breaking in of the δυνάμεις of the Age to Come, a manifestation of the power of God; they are also a revelation of the power of perfected humanity, a foretaste of the possibilities of redeemed man. Ever since the Council of Chalcedon in A.D. 451, the Church has been careful to insist, not only upon the full divinity of Christ, but also upon His full humanity. This is in accordance with the apostolic witness of the New Testament. Apollinarianism was declared a heresy because it emphasized the first at the expense of the second; by denying to Christ a human soul, it limited His manhood by confining it to his physical nature. But whatever else the Jesus of the New Testament was, He was fully and empirically man. What He does for men, He does as their Representative. He is what Luther calls the Proper Man, the Representative Man, man as God intended him to be. As such He is the Founder of a new humanity, the Second Adam who, by His perfect obedience, cancels the results of the disobedience of the first Adam, and so restores the divine intention in creation. " In Christ we see something new to human experience—a new level reached in creation—such as it may be supposed would have occurred in any case, even if sin had never been." In the Incarnation there was constituted " a new thing in nature, a new relation of the Creator Spirit, the Spirit of Life, to matter, a new level in the evolution of life, such as would naturally exhibit new phenomena."[1]

The story of life on the earth is not one of gradual uniform development; it resembles a stairway rather than the straight line of a graph. It is a story not just of evolution but of emergent evolution: in the process new elements suddenly appear: there are several sudden leaps, several fresh starts. There may thus appear what Pringle-Pattison describes as " a new plane or level of existence, qualitatively different and, through that difference, opening up a new range of possibilities."[2] It is of such that we catch a glimpse in the miracles of Jesus. They are what the New Testament calls an ἀρραβών—i.e. a part of a

[1] C. Gore, *The Reconstruction of Belief*, p. 241.   [2] *The Idea of God*, p. 97.

payment which is given in advance as a pledge that the whole amount will be paid in due course. As such they are " revelations of the ideal purpose of God for mankind " and " imply the coming into the order of nature of powers that cannot be explained in terms of mere nature." They " must affect our conceptions of the possibilities of man, and the possibilities and range of prayer."[1]

It is a significant fact that the miracles recorded in the New Testament are not confined to Jesus; His powers are delegated to His disciples and continue to be exercised by the Christian Community. Nor are such miracles confined to New Testament times. As Harnack points out,[2] unction was the normal Christian method of healing until well into the third century. Furthermore, on at least one occasion, according to St. Matthew, a disciple shared momentarily in Christ's power over Nature; St. Peter, at the invitation of Jesus, walked on the water (Matthew xiv, 28–31). In this miracle, matter, for Jesus, becomes completely the instrument of spirit: "We see the relations of spirit and Nature so altered that Nature can be made to do whatever spirit pleases."[3] In the case of St. Peter, however, the power of spirit over matter was incomplete and short-lived owing to his lack of faith. The complete power of spirit over matter is dependent upon complete union with God. It is the clear and unambiguous teaching of Jesus that when, through faith and prayer, this union is complete, the powers of redeemed man over Nature will be virtually unlimited (Mark xi, 23; cf. Matthew xvii, 20 and xxi, 21; Luke x, 19; John xiv, 12. Cf. I Corinthians iii, 22 and II Timothy ii, 12. See also Mark ix, 28–9 [omit the words " and fasting " which are probably a scribe's gloss]). Even bodily death will be conquered. According to the biblical view, man, in the intention of God, is immune from it; it results from the derangement of the divine intention in Creation caused by man's rebellious will by which spirit becomes subservient to matter and is thus the wages of sin.

Hence C. S. Lewis describes the present relationship between

---

[1] D. S. Cairns, *The Faith that Rebels*, p. 93.
[2] See *Medicinisches aus der ältesten kirchengeschichte.*
[3] C. S. Lewis, *Miracles*, p. 179.

spirit and organism as abnormal or pathological. "At present spirit can retain its foothold against the incessant counter-attacks of Nature (both physiological and psychological) only by perpetual vigilance, and physiological Nature always defeats it in the end. Sooner or later it becomes unable to resist the disintegrating processes at work in the body and death ensues." But " where spirit's power over the organism was complete and unresisted, death would never occur."[1]

The complete divine intention for man is realized in the resurrection body of Christ who is described in the New Testament as the " first-fruits " of a new humanity. The Resurrection of Jesus was a *bodily* resurrection, as witnesses the empty tomb. The Risen Christ was no ghost; He could eat fish and invite His disciples to touch Him (Luke xxiv, 39–43; cf. John xx, 27). But His body was what St. Paul calls a " spiritual body "; it was no longer subject to the restrictions of time and space and physical obstacles (Luke xxiv, 31 and 36; John xx, 19 and 26). " His spiritual body was material indeed, but it was one in which matter was wholly subservient to spiritual purpose, and no longer in any way an impediment or a restraint."[2]

CHAPTER VI

THE OLD TESTAMENT AND THE NEW

IF you want to motor from the centre of Sydney to the North Shore, you must use the harbour bridge. Apart from a long detour or the possible recourse to a ferry-boat, this is the only way. Hence, northward roads converge on this point, and, once over the harbour, the track begins to fan out. The bridge is the vital link.

The connection between the Old Testament and the New is like that: it consists of one vital link to which all the roads of the former converge and from which all the tracks of the latter spread out. That link is Christ. "If in the Old Testament," says Griffith-Jones, "we see the lines of revelation gradually converging to a point of expectancy realized afterwards in a Person; in the later books of the New Testament we see the radiation of the power of this life through a community into the world at large."[1] To use a figure which I owe to Professor Dodd, *Heilsgeschichte* is shaped like an hour-glass.

The Old and New Testaments are therefore inseparable parts of one organic whole. They are complementary the one to the other. You cannot understand the Old Testament apart from the events which are described and interpreted in the New; and you cannot grasp the real significance of the New Testament without the background and preparation which the Old Testament provides. In the words of Article VII of the Anglican *Articles of Religion*, "The Old Testament is not contrary to the New: for both in the Old and New Testament everlasting life is offered to Mankind by Christ, who is the only Mediator between God and Man, being both God and Man."

[1] "The Bible: Its Meaning and Aim," in *Peake's Commentary on the Bible*, p. 16.

I. THE WITNESS OF THE OLD TESTAMENT TO CHRIST

But how, precisely, is the Old Testament—containing, as it does, unworthy conceptions of God and sub-Christian standards of morality—related to the New? This question, it must be admitted, raises acute problems for the Christian mind.[1] Both the Marcionite and the Fundamentalist positions, at which we have already looked,[2] attempt to solve the problem in the wrong way. The former holds firmly to the revelation of God in Christ in the New Testament (at least in parts of it), but to the exclusion of the Old Testament; the latter virtually places the whole of the Old Testament on the same level as the New and clings tenaciously to the letter of it even when it is plainly at variance with the fuller revelation given in Christ. "We do wrong to the Old Testament," says St. Augustine, "if we deny that it comes from the same just and good God as the New. On the other hand, we do wrong to the New Testament if we put the Old on a level with it."[3]

What, then, is the exact nature of the relationship between the Old Testament and the New? The answer is twofold. In the first place, the Old Testament shows the historical preparation for the events recorded and interpreted in the New Testament. The coming into the world of Jesus of Nazareth was no isolated event; it was the culmination of an historic process, the climax of an historic movement, the final link in a long chain of historic events. We can understand the significance of what He was and did only as we see His Person and Work against the historical background of the people to whom He came. He was born into a land which had been the scene of special divine activity. He inherited the traditions of a nation which knew itself to be in some sense a chosen people. He himself was conscious, not only of a kinship with the Hebrew prophets, but also of a unique vocation which could be described only in terms which they had used. The Old Testament is the record and interpretation of events in the history of Israel in which the saving power of God has been manifested. It is therefore the first chapter in the story of our

[1] See below, Chapter VII.   [2] Pp. 52 and 63–5.
[3] *De Gestis Pelagii*, v (15).

salvation—a story which finds its climax and consummation in Jesus Christ and which is contemporized in the worship and life of the Christian Church.

That is how the New Testament writers themselves regarded the Old Testament Scriptures. " The Old Testament to St. Paul was true as far as it went, but imperfect. The moral laws of Moses had educated man's moral sense, but left the springs of conduct still impotent; the sacrifices had shown that sin must be atoned for, but had failed to make final atonement; the Tabernacle and the Temple had set forth the truth that without the presence of God men can never fulfil their true and proper destiny, but the Temple had become a symbol of national and religious exclusiveness. So the old dispensation was incomplete; unsatisfactory because unsatisfying. It all pointed to something better to come, when shadows would become reality, and prophecy would vanish away because the hour of fulfilment had come."[1]

Running through the whole Christian view of the Old Testament are two basic convictions: first, that God is the Lord of history whose hand is seen in the events of the past; and second, that the story of the past is both incomplete and unintelligible in itself. Only the fact of Christ—His birth and ministry, His death and resurrection and exaltation at God's right hand—can bring it to completion and reveal the meaning of the whole. The unknown author of the Epistle to the Hebrews summarizes it all in a classic verse: " God, who at sundry times and in divers manners spake in time past unto the fathers by the prophets, hath in these last days spoken unto us by His Son."[2]

But the Old Testament not only shows the historical preparation for the coming of Christ; it also contains prophetic insights into the purpose of God—a purpose which finds its complete and supreme embodiment only in Christ. These ancient Hebrew Scriptures are full of portraits which come to life only in Christ; unidentified portraits which remain unidentified until they find their embodiment in the Carpenter of Nazareth. " The prophets were men who, through the grace of God, saw further into the divine purpose than was given to their

[1] R. V. G. Tasker, *The Old Testament in the New Testament* (First ed. 1946), pp. 95–6.   [2] Hebrews i, 1–2.

contemporaries; their insight into that purpose enabled them to describe aspects of it which were more clearly understood when the purpose itself was, in the fulness of time, embodied in Christ, God's purpose made flesh."[1]

One of these prophetic insights is that God comes to meet man in his sin. The Book of Genesis opens with two Creation parables. The second of these portrays Adam and Eve hiding themselves in shame after disobeying the command of God and eating of the forbidden fruit. But it also pictures God Himself coming down, walking in the garden in the cool of the day, seeking his rebellious children.[2] Man in his pride and self-sufficiency attempts to build a city and a tower whose top may reach unto heaven. He will rear the edifice of his own civilization apart from God. Indeed his Tower of Babel will reach unto heaven itself: he will become as God. But " the Lord came down to see the city and the tower, which the children of men builded."[3] Jacob, the impostor, the cheat, is fleeing from his brother's vengeance. Night overtakes him on a bleak moorland waste and he has to sleep under the open sky with the stones as his pillow. But on that moorland waste God meets this wretched man in all his loneliness and fear and guilt: a ladder is set up from earth to heaven: he has to say, " Surely the Lord is in this place; and I knew it not."[4]

It is only in Jesus Christ, however, that this insight finds its complete embodiment. In Christ God has become man; He has come to meet us in our sin—walking in the garden in the cool of the day, coming to us amid the confusion of man's unfinished tower, confronting us in the desert of our frustration and fear. Jacob saw the glory of God on the rocky hillside of Bethel; we discern that glory more clearly on the green slopes of Calvary. There it shines for ever in the face of Jesus Christ, in whom God has visited and redeemed His people.

Another prophetic insight of the Old Testament is that God's requirement from man is perfect obedience. Abraham is commanded: " Take now thy son, thine only son Isaac, whom thou lovest, and get thee into the land of Moriah; and offer him

---

[1] A. Richardson, *Preface to Bible-Study*, p. 66.   [2] Genesis iii, 1–9.
[3] Genesis xi, 1–5.   [4] Genesis xxviii, 10–16.

there for a burnt offering upon one of the mountains which I will tell thee of."[1] And " by faith Abraham, when he was tried, offered up Isaac: and he that had received the promises offered up his only begotten son."[2]

This perfect obedience is the link which unites Abraham and Christ, Moriah and Calvary. The Eternal Son learned obedience by the things which He suffered. " Being found in fashion as a man, he humbled himself, and became obedient unto death, even the death of the cross " (Philippians ii, 8). " Abraham," says Alexander Maclaren, " was rewarded by being made a faint adumbration, for all time, of the yet more wondrous and awful love of the divine Father, who, for our sakes, has surrendered His only begotten Son, whom He loved. Paul quotes the very words of this chapter when he says: ' He that *spared* not His own *Son*, but delivered Him up for us all.' " And he concludes: " Shall we not recognize this as the crown of Abraham's reward, that his act of surrender of his dearest to God, his Friend, has been glorified by being made the mirror of God's unspeakable gift of His Son, to us, His enemies? "[3]

A third prophetic insight of the Old Testament, which finds its complete embodiment only in Christ, concerns the place of vicarious suffering as an instrument of redemption. The great unknown prophet of the exile whose works are bound up with those of Isaiah draws for us one of the most graphic and moving pictures in the Old Testament, the picture of the Suffering Servant of Jehovah: " He was wounded for our transgressions, he was bruised for our iniquities: the chastisement of our peace was upon him; and with his stripes we are healed " (Isaiah liii, 5). Jesus in the upper room quotes verse 12 of this chapter and explicitly applies it to Himself: " For I say unto you that this that is written must yet be accomplished in me, And he was reckoned among the transgressors: for the things concerning me have an end " (Luke xxii, 37).

Again, there is that profound insight of Jeremiah that reconciliation with God, if it is to be achieved at all, can be achieved only from God's side: " Behold, the days come, saith the Lord, that I will make a new covenant with the house of Israel, and

---

[1] Genesis xxii, 2.   [2] Hebrews xi, 17.
[3] *Expositions of Holy Scripture, Genesis*, p. 160.

with the house of Judah. . . . But this shall be the covenant. . . . After those days, saith the Lord, I will put my law in their inward parts, and write it in their hearts " (Jeremiah xxxi, 31–3). Six hundred years passed before the full significance of the prophet's words were realized. Then " the Lord Jesus the same night in which he was betrayed . . . took the cup, when he had supped, saying, This cup is the new covenant in my blood " (I Corinthians xi, 23–5). Only God Himself, working through the mystery of the Passion and Death of Christ, could break down the barrier of men's sin and write His law in their hearts.

The Old Testament is not merely Hebrew literature but Christian Scripture which must be understood in the light of its " fulfilment "[1] in Christ and His Church: *Novum Testamentum in Vetere latet, Vetus Testamentum in Novo patet.*[2]

II. Links Between the Old Testament and the New

We turn now to consider in more detail some of the characteristic themes of the Old Testament which find their fulfilment, through Christ, in the New.

1. *The Covenant*

The Old and New Testaments are two parts of one story—the story of a covenant-relationship between God and man. This fact is embodied in the name by which both parts of the Bible are known: we speak of the Old and the New *Testament*. The word " testament " is derived from the Latin *testamentum*, which is used in the Vulgate to translate the Greek διαθήκη. In classical Greek διαθήκη usually has the same meaning as *testamentum*; it is used for the disposition of property by will, the " last will and testament." But in the Greek version of the Old Testament, the Septuagint, διαθήκη is used to translate the Hebrew word *bᵉrîth*, which means "covenant." This, therefore, is the general meaning of διαθήκη in the Bible. It is used, says Grimm-Thayer, " to denote the close relationship which

---

[1] See John Marsh, *The Fulness of Time*, pp. 78 ff., for an illuminating discussion of the meaning of " fulfilment " in biblical theology.

[2] Augustine, *Quaestionum in Heptateuchum*, ii, 73.

God entered into, first with Noah (Genesis vi, 18; ix, 9 sqq. [cf. Sir. xliv, 18]), then with Abraham, Isaac and Jacob and their posterity (Leviticus xxvi, 42 [cf. II Maccabees i, 2]), but especially with Abraham (Genesis xv and xvii), and afterwards through Moses with the people of Israel (Exodus xxiv; Deuteronomy v, 2; xxviii, 69 (xxix, 1))."[1]

The word " testament " is therefore misleading when used of the two sections of the Bible; we should use the word " covenant " instead. Strangely enough, the Revised Version, while it corrects this error in the actual text—in I Corinthians xi, 25, for example, it substitutes, " This cup is the new covenant in my blood " for the Authorized Version's rendering, " This cup is the new testament in my blood "—leaves the word " testament " in the titles. A substitution of the word " covenant " would have served to express the central, unifying theme of the whole Bible. As Tasker observes, " Instead . . . of speaking of the Old and New Testaments we should strictly speak of the books of the Old and New Covenants."[2]

The relationship between Israel and Jehovah which the Old Testament portrays is, from the very beginning, of an entirely different kind from that which characterized other religions. The dominant conception in the ancient world was that a people was united to its god by some natural tie such as physical descent. The god was the actual father of the tribe or clan which had descended physically from him; and hence their claim upon him was that of a kinsman. He was bound to come to their assistance in time of need—whether they were in the right or not—because of this blood-relationship between them.

There is, however, no trace in the Old Testament of any such natural tie between Israel and their God. On the contrary, the relationship is that of a covenant, an agreement, by which Jehovah and the nation are, as it were, wedded to one another. Jehovah is essentially a *Bundesgott* and Israel a *Bundesvolk*.[3]

> No other people was like Israel: the bond between her and Yahweh was unique. The choice of this insignificant people was not due to her merits, but to his love. . . . There was a covenant

---

[1] *Greek-English Lexicon of the New Testament*, διαθήκη, p. 136.
[2] *The Old Testament in the New Testament* (First ed. 1946), p. 9.
[3] See W. Eichrodt, *Theologie des Alten Testaments*, vol. 1.

between Yahweh and Israel: I, your God, and ye, my people: it is the keynote of the Bible. . . . Israel may be faithless, but Yahweh is " righteous," i.e. loyal; and in spite of his threats and punishment of her, the covenant is renewed and stands firm. Along with Ezekiel's promise of a new heart and spirit (Ezekiel xi, 19 ff.) a new and direct covenant with individual Israelites is announced by a contemporary prophet (Jeremiah xxxi, 31 ff.); even as a new covenant superseding the old one is inaugurated by the sacrificial death of Jesus who is the mediator between God and man. . . . Israel, as a kingdom of priests, was to be also a covenant-people to establish, as later did Christ, harmony between God and man.[1]

The central concept of biblical religion is therefore " that God bears a special relationship to His people, a relationship appropriately designated by the words ' covenant ' and ' election.' "[2]   Schmidt maintains that the Hebrew word for covenant, b^e*rîth*, is a cognate of the Assyrio-Babylonian *birîtu* (from *barû*, to bind), meaning primarily " a fetter," and hence " an alliance " or " a covenant."   The term, he says, was " extended to every alliance, even where the parties were in a position to decide upon a mutually binding decree."[3] Others have found its derivation in the Arabic *barā*, meaning " to sever," on the ground of the ceremonial of passing between the severed parts of an animal, which frequently marked the pledging of a solemn bond (cf. Genesis xv, 7–21).   The common Hebrew phrase *kārath* b^e*rîth*, literally " to cut a covenant," would seem to give support to this view.

Whatever its derivation, however, b^e*rîth* is used generally in the Old Testament for a pact or alliance between men, as, for example, the pledge of friendship between David and Jonathan; but it has also the special sense of the Covenant as a divine ordinance for Israel.   In this case there is no idea of a mutual pact.   " The primary meaning of the term b^e*rîth* in Hebrew may have been either ' agreement ' or ' command,' but, in any case, we must beware of some of the suggestions of the English word ' covenant,' e.g. that Israel and Yahweh met on equal terms."[4]   In fact, as Pedersen observes, " the covenant rarely contains full equality. . . . When two parties unite in the

---

[1] S. A. Cook, *An Introduction to the Bible*, pp. 85–7.
[2] W. Eichrodt, *Journal of Biblical Literature*, lxv, 1946, p. 215.
[3] N. Schmidt, " Covenant," in *Encyclopaedia Biblica*, i, col. 928 ff.
[4] H. Wheeler Robinson, *The Religious Ideas of the Old Testament*, p. 188.

covenant, the one will generally be a greater giver than the other."[1]   In the case of Israel and Jehovah, however, the Covenant is entirely a Covenant of grace constituted by God and offered to His people as a pledge of their gratitude and loyalty to Him. It was not a bargain or a bilateral agreement; much less a legal instrument. That is why the Septuagint translators chose διαθήκη and not συνθήκη to render the Hebrew *berîth*.[2] συνθήκη—an agreement decided on together (συν = together, and τίθημι = to settle or determine)—implies an equality of the partners, whereas διαθήκη—a will by which a person settles the disposition of his property—is essentially something drawn up by one person who thereby determines beforehand the share of those who participate in it. Hence " God's Covenant is a διαθήκη, and not a συνθήκη; that is to say, God fixes the terms of the Covenant and offers it to man that he may accept it: the acceptance is also essential."[3]

The Covenant " was based on the fact of what God had already achieved, and not on His conditional performances."[4] It was " the response of gratitude."[5] As Rowley rightly insists, the whole conception is misunderstood if it is regarded as " an agreement on God's part that so long as Israel was loyal to His worship He would protect her interests, and on Israel's part that so long as God stood by them they would continue to honour Him. . . . Yahweh had saved Israel. Her salvation was an undeniable fact of history. It was already achieved, and that not as a part of any bargain. And now Israel in her gratitude pledged herself to Yahweh with a pledge as absolute as had been her deliverance. The meaning of the Covenant was not that if God would look after Israel Israel would serve Him, but that because He had manifested His grace to her Israel would give Him her loyalty."[6]

The first mention of the Covenant in the Old Testament,

---

[1] J. Pedersen, *Israel*, I–II, p. 294.

[2] Cf. N. Schmidt, *op. cit.*, col. 929: " The deliberate choice of διαθήκη by the Alexandrian translators can scarcely have been due to anything else than a consciousness of the fundamental meaning of *berîth*."

[3] C. H. Dodd, *Études Théologiques et Religieuses*, xxiii, 1948, Nos. 2–3, pp. 11 ff.   [4] H. H. Rowley, *The Biblical Doctrine of Election*, p. 46.

[5] *Ibid.*, p. 48.   [6] *The Re-discovery of the Old Testament*, p. 84.

in this sense of a divine ordinance, is in connection with the story of Noah. He is portrayed after the flood as the second father of the human race, and it is as such that God makes a Covenant with him.[1] He represents mankind as a whole. Hence God's first Covenant is not with any one people but with mankind. It is a Covenant with the whole human race, in which He promises to maintain, for man's benefit, the working of the natural order.

It is after this Covenant with mankind as a whole, represented by Noah, that God selects a particular man, Abraham, as the progenitor of a special race, the Hebrews, who are to be in a unique way His Covenant People.[2] Although it is said that Abraham shall be the father of many nations, it is clearly stated that the Covenant is with the line of Isaac.[3] This Abrahamic Covenant is ratified with the descendants of Abraham at Mount Sinai, and it is by the Covenant relationship established there with the people as a whole that Moses binds together these Hebrew tribes which he has brought out of Egypt into a common allegiance to Jehovah. Hence the Covenant lay at the very basis of Israel's national life. The ceremony by which the bond was sealed at Mount Sinai is vividly described in Exodus xxiv. The people and Jehovah meet together at the sacred mountain. The terms of the Covenant are read out to the assembled tribes, who reply: " All that the Lord hath said will we do, and be obedient." Then the blood of a sacrificed animal is sprinkled on both the altar and the people, symbolizing the uniting of Jehovah and the nation in a common life (ver. 3–8).

This Covenant, it must be emphasized, was a Covenant of grace. Although Israel was repeatedly unfaithful to her Covenant vows, Jehovah never forsook His people; so that they had to say: " He hath not dealt with us after our sins; nor rewarded us according to our iniquities." One great attempt was made, however, to renew the Old Covenant, namely Josiah's Reform in 621 B.C. The Book of Deuteronomy which had been found during the renovation of the Temple and upon which the Reform was based, is referred to as the Book of the Covenant, and the Reform itself was clearly an attempt by Josiah to renew

---

[1] See Genesis viii, 20–2 (" J ") and ix, 9–11 (" P ").
[2] See Genesis xv, 18, and xvii, 4, 7–9.   [3] Genesis xvii, 19–21.

this Covenant relationship with Jehovah which had been so wantonly broken in his father's and grandfather's reigns.[1]

It is against the background of the failure of Josiah's Reform effectively to renew the Old Covenant that Jeremiah's prophecy of the New Covenant is to be seen.[2] Here is perhaps the greatest utterance of the Old Testament. It was, so it seems, out of Jeremiah's disappointment with the result of Josiah's Reform that this oracle sprang. We have reason to believe that the reform movement was at first eagerly welcomed by the young prophet, who looked to it to bring about a national conversion. But the years that followed belied his hopes. " Josiah's reform," says Wilson Cash, " taught him how easy it was to initiate a reformation without necessarily taking one step towards a change in human nature."[3] And so he came to realize that the Old Covenant, whether written on tables of stone, as at Sinai, or in a book like Deuteronomy, was inadequate as the basis of a permanent relationship between God and man. He came to see that the seat of that relationship was the human heart, which is deceitful above all things and desperately sick (Jeremiah xvii, 9). He looked forward, therefore, to the time when God would restore *there* the broken relationship with man:

> Behold, the days come, saith the Lord, that I will make a new covenant with the house of Israel, and with the house of Judah; not according to the covenant that I made with their fathers, in the day that I took them by the hand, to bring them out of the land of Egypt; which my covenant they brake, although I was an husband unto them, saith the Lord; but this shall be the covenant that I will make with the house of Israel; After those days, saith the Lord, I will put my law in their inward parts, and write it in their hearts; and will be their God, and they shall be my people. And they shall teach no more every man his neighbour, and every man his brother, saying, Know the Lord: for they shall all know me, from the least of them unto the greatest of them, saith the Lord: for I will forgive their iniquity, and I will remember their sin no more.[4]

The words spring from the shattering events of the Babylonian Exile in which the prophet discerned the judgment of the Living God. The People of God had forsaken the Holy

---

[1] See II Kings xxiii, 1–3.   [2] Jeremiah xxxi, 31–4.
[3] *Jeremiah: A Prophet to the Nations*, p. 77.   [4] Jeremiah xxxi, 31–4.

One of Israel. " They had violated all the terms upon which they had been recognized as His people; they had broken His ' covenant.' They had no longer any standing before Him, as of right."[1] Jeremiah saw plainly that their only hope lay in the mercy of God, in His " covenant-love " (hesedh),[2] which had never failed. That love must once more take the initiative if they were to be restored. The significance of this prophecy of the New Covenant, therefore, is that it offers a fresh start to a people who have forfeited the very basis of their relationship with God. As George Adam Smith observes, it is " a prophecy of Christianity which has hardly its equal in the Old Testament."[3]

The conception of the Covenant has as its basis the forgiveness of sins; the Covenant is a Covenant of grace. It is within this context that the sacrificial system of Israel operated as a means whereby the Covenant relationship, which already existed, might be maintained. Through sacrifice sin was " covered "[4] so that it was no longer a barrier between man and God. And the New Covenant, like the Old has its basis in forgiveness: " I will forgive their iniquity, and I will remember their sin no more (Jeremiah xxxi, 34)."

Jeremiah, however, gives no hint as to how this will be accomplished. " There was one feature in the case," says T. H. Robinson, " which he had failed to enunciate. That was the medium whereby this new law was to be communicated. For leather or papyrus, ink would do; for clay or wax, the stylus. But the only instrument which would impress the truth on men's hearts was blood. And so, for the full realization of Jeremiah's message, the world had to wait till that night when Jesus, having supped, ' took the cup also, saying, This cup is the New Covenant in my blood.' There is no fulfilment of the highest truth the Prophets had to offer, apart from the Cross."[5]

[1] C. H. Dodd, The Bible To-day, p. 45.
[2] See N. H. Snaith, The Distinctive Ideas of the Old Testament, ch. v.
[3] Jeremiah, p. 380.
[4] The Hebrew verb translated " to atone " comes from a root meaning " to cover."
[5] Prophecy and the Prophets, p. 142. The fact that the Last Supper is set in the context of the Passover links the inauguration of the New Covenant with the Exodus. See H. H. Rowley, The Unity of the Bible, p. 112, and J. K. S. Reid, The Authority of Scripture, p. 253.

The restoration of the broken relationship, the ratification of the New Covenant, could be achieved only through the death of Him who was God manifest in the flesh. " It is *necessary*," said Jesus, " that the Son of man should suffer many things."[1]

2. *The Covenant People*

Closely linked with the idea of the Covenant is the kindred conception of the Covenant People—the *qāhāl*, the " assembly " or " congregation " of Israel, which is usually rendered in the Septuagint, from Deuteronomy onwards, by the Greek ἐκκλησία, or Church.

Israel was a chosen people in the sense that it was the Covenant People of Jehovah, and the outward and visible sign of that Covenant was the rite of circumcision.[2] " Membership in Abraham's covenanted race, of which circumcision was the sign (Genesis xvii, 9), brought the Israelite into relation with Jehovah. The sacrifices covered the whole ' church in the wilderness ' (Acts vii, 38), and each worshipper approached God in virtue of his inclusion in the holy people. No foreigner might eat of the Passover (Exodus xii, 45). The propitiatory ritual of the Day of Atonement was expressly designed for the consecration of the whole nation (Leviticus xvi)."[3]

This social aspect of the Covenant persists throughout the whole Bible, both the Old Testament and the New. It is present in Jeremiah's prophecy of the new Covenant, intensely personal though that is. God, says the prophet, will make his Covenant with men by writing His Law, not on tables of stone, nor in a book, but in each man's heart: " They shall all know me." In other words, the New Covenant will be a personal relationship between man and God. But if it is personal, it is not individualistic. The New Covenant is what Ryder Smith calls a " societary " concept. Like the Old Covenant at Sinai, it is made, not with individuals, but with a people—the Covenant People of God: " Behold the days come, saith the Lord, that I will make a new covenant *with the house of Israel, and with the house of Judah*." " The Bible," says Phythian-Adams, " is throughout the book of a Covenant People—this first and

[1] Mark viii, 31.   [2] See Genesis xvii, 9–14.
[3] J. G. Simpson, " Church," in Hastings' one volume *Dictionary of the Bible*, p. 140.

foremost. It is not simply God's Revelation of Himself in general terms: it is a Revelation which follows one clearly defined channel. . . . Where there is a Covenant, a solemn pact by which two parties are joined together, then, though one Partner may be incomparably the greater, there must be a sense in which the other is equally important. It is this second factor, namely Israel, which we are gravely tempted to overlook." And hence he concludes: " We have almost lost our vision of the Church, the New Israel."[1]

The Greek name ἐκκλησία, translated as " church," which the primitive Christian community adopted, indicates that these early Christians regarded themselves as being the spiritual successors of the Chosen People, the true Israel of God. In the Greek city-state the ἐκκλησία was the assembly of citizens, comprising the whole adult male population—with the exception of slaves—to conduct political business. But the only New Testament example of this purely Greek sense is the assembly of craftsmen in the theatre of Ephesus.[2] In all other cases the meaning of the word must be sought in the Greek version of the Old Testament, the Septuagint. Here, as we have seen, ἐκκλησία translates the Hebrew qāhāl—the " assembly " or " congregation " of Israel. The strict connotation of the word was the people of Jehovah assembled together for some special purpose or some common action, but in later usage it came to mean simply the people of God.[3]

The fact, then, that this term was adopted by the primitive Christian community is significant because it implies a sense of continuity with " the Church in the wilderness " (Acts vii, 38). Moreover, phrases used in the Old Testament of Israel are boldly applied by New Testament writers to the Church. In I Peter ii, 9–10, for instance, Christians are addressed as " a chosen generation " (cf. Deuteronomy x, 15; Isaiah xliii, 20), " a royal priesthood " (cf. Exodus xix, 6), " an holy nation " (cf. Exodus xix, 6; Deuteronomy vii, 6; Isaiah lxii, 12), " a

---

[1] W. J. Phythian-Adams, *The Fulness of Israel*, pp. 43–4.

[2] See Acts xix, 32.

[3] Cf. F. J. A. Hort, *The Christian Ecclesia*, p. 7: " Thus ἐκκλησία, as the primary Greek representative of qāhāl would naturally for Greek-speaking Jews mean the congregation of Israel quite as much as an assembly of the congregation."

people for a possession " (cf. Exodus xix, 5; Deuteronomy vii, 6; Isaiah xliii, 21; Malachi iii, 17), " the people of God that has now obtained mercy " (cf. Hosea i, 6, 9, 10; ii, 23). The twelve apostles of the Lamb in Revelation xxi, 4, are reminiscent of the twelve patriarchs (cf. Ephesians ii, 20; Matthew xix, 28; Luke xxii, 30), and the " true vine " of John xv recalls the vine brought out of Egypt of Psalm lxxx, 8, and Isaiah v, 1–7 (cf. Mark xii, 1 ff.). Furthermore, the New Covenant, though it supersedes and replaces, nevertheless corresponds with the Old (cf. I Corinthians xi, 25, and Synoptic parallels, Exodus xxiv, 8); and both these Covenants, as we have noted, are made not with individuals but with a people.

The Christian Church is thus viewed as the successor of " Israel after the flesh," because the Jewish nation had forfeited its inheritance of the divine promises through unbelief. They were not all Israel which were of Israel (Romans ix, 6); only a remnant which walked in the faith of Abraham were the true People of God. But this faithful remnant gradually diminished until it consisted of only one Man— Jesus Himself.

When the Messiah, in and through whom alone the vocation of Israel as the people of God could be realized, stands alone before the high priest, deserted even by the chosen disciples, His rejection is a turning-point, decisive both for the Messiah Himself and for Israel who rejected Him. He is the sole representative at that moment of God's holy people; He bears in His own Person the whole burden of Israel's appointed destiny. His activity thus constitutes plainly a new beginning, transforming as well as fulfilling the old order. The ἐκκλησία of God was among the things that in Him " have become new " (II Corinthians v, 1–17).[1]

There is, therefore, a very real continuity of the Christian Church—those who are " in Christ "—with the chosen people of Israel, a continuity which St. Paul represents by his metaphor of the branch grafted into the olive tree.[2]

Thus the New Testament Christians regarded themselves as the elect (I Peter), the children of Abraham (Galatians iii, 7), the Israel of God (Galatians vi, 16), and as such they laid claim to the spiritual inheritance of " Israel after the flesh."

[1] *Doctrine in the Church of England*, p. 102.   [2] Romans xi, 13–24.

Theirs was " the adoption, and the glory, and the covenants, and the giving of the law, and the service of God, and the promises " (Romans ix, 4); since " the promise, that he should be the heir of the world, was not to Abraham, or to his seed, through the law, but through the righteousness of faith," and this was written " for us also, to whom it shall be imputed, if we believe on him that raised up Jesus our Lord from the dead " (Romans iv, 13, 23–4).

Hence the early Church was from the first rooted in history; it shared in the growing prestige of the Hebrew Scriptures to which it laid claim, and it appropriated all that was best in the Jewish faith with its high ethical standard. " Israel of the Old Testament," says C. H. Dodd, " is the people of God in bondage; the Church is the people of God redeemed and set free." This New Israel transcended all racial bounds and man-made limitations. It acknowledged that God had " made of one blood all nations of men " (Acts xvii, 26; cf. Ephesians iii, 6): in it was neither Jew nor Greek, bond nor free, male nor female, but all were one in Christ Jesus (Galatians iii, 28; Colossians iii, 11). Neverthelesss it recognized its continuity with " Israel after the flesh," being linked to the ancient People of God through the Person of its Founder and Lord, Jesus Christ: " If ye be Christ's, then are ye Abraham's seed, and heirs according to the promise " (Galatians iii, 29).

3. *The Servant of the Lord*

The Hebrew had very strong ideas about racial superiority. He was conscious of belonging to a chosen people, of being a member of a nation which was in some way unique. In one sense, of course, he was right. God had indeed chosen the Hebrew people out of all the nations of the earth to be the medium of His revelation to men. He had endowed them with special susceptibilities; He had spoken through their prophets and wrought mighty acts in their midst. They had been the vehicle through which He had revealed His will.

But this sense of vocation, of destiny, which the Hebrew had in his very bones, was wrongly interpreted by him in terms of political domination. He came to regard himself as belonging to a *Herrenvolk*—a superior race. But here he encountered an obstacle. Palestine, situated as it is between the two oldest civilizations of the Euphrates and the Nile, had through the centuries been a battle-ground possessed by one or other of these rival Powers. True, it enjoyed seasons of independence, but these were infrequent and short-lived. During the greater part of his history, the Hebrew was subservient to a foreign Power— Egypt, Assyria, Babylon, Greece, and finally Rome. Hence there arose in the Hebrew mind what modern psychology calls an " inferiority complex," which found compensatory expression in the hope that one day the nations would lick the dust before Israel's feet. Jehovah, they believed, would vindicate His people by making them the lords of the earth.

There were, however, voices raised against this popular view. Amos warns his people that the Day of the Lord for which they hope will be for them a day of darkness and not of light. The Books of Jonah and Ruth are protests against this narrow nationalism. Israel's vocation, her people are reminded, is not to dominate but to serve; she is called to be a missionary nation, to spread the knowledge of the true God throughout the earth.[1]

Israel's mission is portrayed supremely in the figure of the Suffering Servant of Jehovah which we find in a portion of the Book of Isaiah ascribed to a great unknown prophet of the exile.[2] This conception is embodied in four Servant Songs consisting of Isaiah xlii, 1–4; xlix, 1–6; l, 4–9 and lii, 13–liii, 12. The precise identity of the Servant is one of the unsolved problems of Old Testament scholarship. Is the writer describing an individual—past, present or future—actual, mythical or divine? or the nation as a whole considered empirically, or ideally? or the godly remnant within the nation? The difficulty arises from the fact that in the songs themselves sometimes one and sometimes another of these alternatives seems to be implied. In Deutero-Isaiah as a whole, the Servant is clearly identified as Israel and the close interweaving of the songs themselves with what precedes and follows them suggests that

[1] See H. H. Rowley, *The Missionary Message of the Old Testament*.
[2] Chapters xl–lv are the work of this prophet, who is referred to as Second or Deutero-Isaiah.

they are from the same hand; but the individual nature of the fourth song is undeniable.

The solution of this enigma seems to be that the individual and corporate aspects are inseparable. " Recent exposition . . . suggests that to insist on sharp alternatives is here a mistake, for the thought of a Hebrew writer would readily pass from an individual Hebrew to the Godly Remnant to which he belonged, and again to the whole nation of which the Remnant was part."[1] There is thus, in the words of Wheeler Robinson, " a fluidity of conception, a possibility of swift transition from the one to the many, and vice versa, to which our thought and language have no real parallel."[2] And, as T. W. Manson points out, " where the conception of corporate personality is dominant there is often a tendency to see the corporate personality as embodied in a person."[3]

H. H. Rowley traces such a development in thought through the Servant Songs. He believes that the author, beginning with the Servant as a personification of Israel as a whole, comes to see that only a purified Israel can carry out this vocation, and finally " contemplates an individual who will supremely fulfil the mission of Israel through the organ of his own innocent and vicarious suffering, and who will pass through shame and death to exaltation and triumph."[4] While therefore the Servant is not to be identified with Israel *simpliciter*, it is the vocation of Israel which is portrayed in the Servant Songs. They pass from " the thought of Israel as the Servant to the thought of an individual Servant *par excellence*, without abandoning the thought of Israel as still the Servant. If the fourth song is dominantly individual, the mission which the Servant fulfils is still not merely his own, but Israel's, and Israel is still called to enter in some measure into it, so that the Servant may really be Israel's representative."[5]

Israel as a whole could not rise to such heights. This, the highest conception of the nation's divine vocation, remained

---

[1] C. Ryder Smith, *The Bible Doctrine of Salvation*, pp. 53–4.

[2] *The Cross of the Servant*, pp. 33 ff.

[3] *Bulletin of the John Rylands Library*, xxxii, 1949–50, p. 190.

[4] *The Servant of the Lord*, pp. 51–2. See *ibid.*, pp. 1–57 for an admirable survey of the discussion.

[5] H. H. Rowley, *ibid.*, p. 54. Cf. J. Pedersen, *Israel*, III–IV, pp. 603 ff.

unfulfilled until it found its fulfilment in Christ.[1] He, the sole Representative of the true People of God, deliberately interpreted His life and ministry in terms of it.

The story of Christ's baptism makes it clear that the thought of suffering and death was present in His mind from the very beginning of His ministry. Whatever else the baptism may have been, it was certainly the occasion of a great spiritual experience for Jesus. A description of this experience—which must surely have come originally from His own lips—says: " A voice came from heaven, Thou art my Son, the beloved, in thee I am well pleased."[2] It is noteworthy that the voice of God speaks to Jesus in the language of the Old Testament; it is mediated through the words of a psalm and a prophecy. These two Old Testament passages were singularly relevant because, as John Marsh points out, " they were in fact objectifications of His

---

[1] From the evidence of the Dead Sea Scrolls, the Qumran community appears to have regarded its vocation as the fulfilment of the role of the Servant. According to the *Manual of Discipline*, the community is to be " a holy house for Israel, a foundation of the holy of holies for Aaron, true witnesses for justice and the elect by God's will, to make atonement for the land . . . a house of perfection and truth in Israel to establish a covenant for eternal statutes. And they shall be accepted to make atonement for the land." The covenanters " shall be separated from the midst of the session of the men of error to go to the wilderness to prepare there the way of the Lord. . . . This is the study of the law." Their discipline is to be " for a ransom for the guilt of transgression and sinful faithlessness, and for acceptance for the land more than the flesh of whole burnt offerings and the fats of sacrifice, and an offering of the lips for justice . . . and perfect conduct like a willing gift of an acceptable offering." They are thus to be " a house of community for Israel, those who conduct themselves blamelessly." Cf. F. F. Bruce, *Second Thoughts on the Dead Sea Scrolls* (1956), p. 102: " Their devotion to the divine law, their endurance of suffering, their submission to severe discipline—all this, they hoped and believed, would be accepted by God as an atonement for the sins of the nation which had gone so far astray from the path of His will. Their duty, as they conceived it, was nothing less than the fulfilment of the role appointed for the obedient and suffering Servant of the Lord in Isaiah lii, 13–liii, 12."

W. H. Brownlee and I. Sonne suggest that this vocation of the community was regarded as realized in the person of the Teacher of Righteousness, who was himself identified with the Servant. There is, however, no conclusive evidence for any such identification; nor were any of their messianic figures regarded as fulfilling this role. Indeed, T. H. Gaster maintains that the title " Teacher of Righteousness "—better rendered as " right-teacher," i.e. the true exponent of the Law—does not denote any one particular person but rather a continuing office. See *The Scriptures of the Dead Sea Sect* (1957), pp. 6, 15, 35–6.　　[2] Mark i, 9–11.

own understanding of the experience He was undergoing."[1] The first phrase, " Thou art my Son," is from Psalm ii and refers to the Messianic King; the second, " the beloved, in thee I am well pleased," is from the Septuagint rendering of Isaiah xlii and refers to the Suffering Servant.

The significance of the quotation consists in the fact that this passage in Isaiah represents the *ordination formula* of the Suffering Servant of the Lord. By combining the two passages, accordingly, the voice succeeds in at once anointing the unique Son as the Messiah and ordaining Him as the Suffering Servant! Or, to express the same thought in slightly different terms, it not alone confirms to Jesus' consciousness the fact of His Messiahship, but it serves at the same time to define the nature of that Messiahship as one issuing in suffering, trial, death—the cross.[2]

The fact that these two lines of anticipation are combined in the mind of Jesus means that He cannot have begun His public ministry with high hopes of success which were only later crushed. It indicates that from the beginning He saw tragedy ahead; perhaps only dimly at first, but gradually assuming more definite form. This alone explains the prediction made in the midst of His early popularity: " The days will come, when the bridegroom shall be taken away "[3] and the later saying on the Mount of Transfiguration: "How it is written of the Son of man, that he must suffer many things."[4]

Not only, however, is the thought of suffering and death in the mind of Jesus when He begins His public ministry; He

[1] See *The Fulness of Time*, pp. 91–2.
[2] J. W. Bowman, *The Intention of Jesus*, p. 42. Cf. James Denney, *Jesus and the Gospel*, pp. 203–4: " It is impossible to suppose that this combination is accidental, and it is quite unnecessary to suppose that it is the work of the apostolic Church looking back on the way in which Old Testament ideals were united in the life of Jesus. The ideals of the Old Testament were far more vivid to Jesus than they were to the apostolic Church, and we fail to do justice to Jesus unless we recognize this. Further, they were much more than ideals to Him; they were promises of God which came to have the virtue of a call or vocation for Himself. Often He had steeped His thoughts in them, but at last, in this high hour of visitation by the living God, they spoke to Him with direct, identifying, appropriating power. It was His own figure, His own calling and destiny, that rose before Him in the ideal King of the Psalmist, and the lowly Servant of the Prophet; it was His inmost conviction and assurance from this hour that both ideals were to be fulfilled in Himself. The voice of God addressed Him in both characters at once."   [3] Mark ii, 19–20.   [4] Mark ix, 12.

regards His death as necessary for His vocation. One of the most important crises of His ministry occurs at Caesarea Philippi.[1] When they have retired for a while into the seclusion of Phoenicia, Jesus asks His disciples: " Whom do men say that I am? " They reply: " John the Baptist: but some say, Elijah; and others, One of the prophets." " And he saith unto them, But whom say ye that I am? And Peter answereth and saith unto him, Thou art the Christ." After accepting from His disciples this confession of His Messiahship, Jesus immediately begins to teach them that it involves for Him death. " It is necessary," He says, " for the Son of man to suffer many things."[2] All our narratives agree in recording His insistence that He must go up to Jerusalem to die. St. Mark, especially, emphasizes His repeated attempts to acquaint the disciples with what lay ahead.[3]

When we say that Jesus *must* go up to Jerusalem to die, we may mean one of two things: the constraint which He feels may be, as James Denney puts it, either external or internal. On the one hand, we may mean that in these particular circumstances death for Him is inevitable. The enmity of His foes is implacable, their net is closing around Him, escape He cannot; therefore He must reconcile Himself as best He can to His inevitable doom. But, on the other hand, when we say that Jesus must die, we may mean that death was not merely necessitated by force of circumstances, but that it belonged to the very essence of His vocation, that it was included in the work which He came to do; that it was the supreme goal of his life.

This was most certainly the conception of Jesus himself. If language means anything at all, He saw His vocation throughout His ministry in terms of the Suffering Servant of Deutero-Isaiah, and this thought was uppermost in His mind as the Cross drew near. The phrase " ransom for many " in Mark x, 45, recalls the Servant of Isaiah liii, 11, who shall " justify many; for he shall bear their iniquities." And in Luke xxii, 37, Jesus actually quotes verse 12 of Isaiah liii and explicitly applies it to Himself: " For I say unto you, that this that is written

---

[1] Mark viii, 27–33.   [2] Mark viii, 31.
[3] See Mark ix, 31, and x, 32–4. Note the imperfects, ἐδίδασκεν and ἔλεγεν.

must yet be accomplished in me, And he was reckoned among the transgressors: for the things concerning me have an end."[1]

As we have seen, there is a fluidity of thought in the Old Testament conception of the Suffering Servant: it readily passes from the collective to the individual, and *vice versa*. This same fluidity, as Wheeler Robinson points out, is present also in the New Testament fulfilment: " Though the collective idea contracted into a primary reference to Jesus, yet its virtual presence is seen in the readiness with which it expanded into the doctrine of the Church."[2] This collective element in the fulfilment is emphasized by H. H. Rowley: " If, then, the Church is called to carry to the world the message of the fulfilment of the prophecy of the Servant in the Cross of Christ, it is also called to enter into the experience of the Cross, and to share in some measure in the fulfilment of the prophecy."[3] " For if our Lord is the Supreme Suffering Servant, He gathers His Church unto Himself that it may be His body, that He may so fill it with His own spirit that it may become the extension of His personality and organ of the continuation of His message to the world. The Church believed that it had inherited the mission of Israel, and it is therefore called to be the Servant. It is true that it cannot attain the peak of service attained by its Lord, but it is called to enter into that service to the fullest degree possible, so that the Saviour and Lord of the Church may be indeed its representative."[4]

4. *The Rule of God*

" Some," says Josephus, " have entrusted the government of their states to monarchies, others to oligarchies, others, again, to democracies. But our law-giver would have none of these systems, but, as one may say by a slight violence to language, he put forward a *Theocracy* as the form of government, assigning the rule and power to God."[5]

This conception is expressed in the familiar phrase, " the kingdom of God." But the term " kingdom " is ambiguous,

---

[1] The last phrase, τέλος ἔχει, means literally " is having its end," i.e. " is being fulfilled."   [2] *The Cross of the Servant*, pp. 75 ff.
[3] *The Missionary Message of the Old Testament*, p. 82.
[4] *The Servant of the Lord*, p. 55.   [5] *Contra Apionem*, ii, 16.

as is also the Greek βασιλεία which it translates. It may mean the rule or sovereignty of a king, but we usually understand by it the territory over which he rules. The New Testament expression, " the kingdom of God," however, represents a well-established Aramaic phrase, *malkuth shāmaîm*, or *malkuth Yahweh*, in which " kingdom " (*malkuth*) means " kingship."[1] The expression, therefore, denotes the rule or sovereignty of God rather than, as is naturally suggested to us, a territory ruled by God. " No doubt can be entertained," says Dalman, " that both in the Old Testament and in Jewish literature, *malkuth* when applied to God means always the ' kingly rule,' never the ' kingdom ' as if it were meant to suggest the territory governed by Him."[2] It must be recognized, however, that a community which is subject to God's kingly rule is implied. As Archdeacon Harrison rightly insists, " Kingdom means more than sovereignty; it means a realm of sovereignty: it implies the coming into being of a people of God."[3] But the fundamental fact is that God reigns as King, and " the term ' kingdom ' indicates that specific aspect, attribute or activity of God, in which He is revealed as King or sovereign Lord of His people, or of the universe which He created."[4]

The declaration of the sovereign rule of God runs through the whole of the Old Testament: " The Lord is King, be the people never so impatient: he sitteth between the cherubims, be the earth never so unquiet."[5] C. F. Burney points out that " the fact that Yahwe could be and was conceived and spoken of as *King* in early times . . . is illustrated by popular usage in compound proper names, in which the title ' King ' without nearer definition is referred to Yahwe; and also by the title *Yahwe Sebhā'ōth*, which implies that Yahwe actually fulfils the kingly office as leader of His armies against the foe. Yahwe is said to have assumed the kingship at the commencement of Israel's national life:

He became King in Jeshurun
When the heads of the people were gathered,
All the tribes of Israel together (Deuteronomy xxxiii, 5).

[1] See C. H. Dodd, *The Parables of the Kingdom*, pp. 34 ff.
[2] Gustaf Dalman, *The Words of Jesus*, p. 94.
[3] D. E. W. Harrison, *The Book of Common Prayer*, p. 18.
[4] C. H. Dodd, *op. cit.*, p. 35.   [5] Psalm xcix, 1, Coverdale's version.

His mighty act of redemption, by which He delivered His people out of Egypt, established Him as ' King for ever and ever ' (Exodus xv, 18 E). Thus He is ' the King of Israel ' (II Isaiah xli, 21), or ' the King of Jacob ' (II Isaiah xliv, 6)."[1]

This conception of the national God as the national King was not, of course, peculiar to Israel but was shared by other Semitic peoples. As Robertson Smith observes, the word " theocracy," far from describing something unique and peculiar to Israel, as Josephus supposed, " expresses precisely that feature in the religion of Israel which it had in common with the faiths of the surrounding nations." Nevertheless, as he goes on to say, " There was a great difference between the religion of Israel and other religions . . . it lay in the personal difference, if I may so speak, between Jehovah and the gods of the nations, and all that lay in it only came out bit by bit in the course of a history which was ruled by Jehovah's providence, and shaped by Jehovah's love."[2]

C. H. Dodd points out that we may distinguish two ways in which the Kingdom of God is spoken of in Jewish usage. First, God is King of His people Israel here and now. " His kingly rule is effective in so far as Israel is obedient to the divine will as revealed in the Torah. To submit oneself unquestioningly to the Law is ' to take upon oneself the *malkuth* of heaven.' In this sense ' The Kingdom of God ' is a present fact."[3]

But in another sense " The Kingdom of God " is something yet to be revealed. God is more than King of Israel; He is King of all the world. But the world does not recognize Him as King. His own people is in fact subject to secular powers, which in the present age are permitted to exercise *malkuth*. Israel, however, looks forward to the day when " The saints of the Most High shall take the kingdom " (Daniel vii, 18), and so the kingship of God will become effective over the whole world. . . . In this sense " The Kingdom of God " is a hope for the future. It is itself the *eschaton*, or " ultimate," with which " eschatology " is concerned.

As such, the idea is capable of entering into association with various views of the " good time coming " as set forth in prophecy and apocalyptic. The hope may be a temporal and political one. Thus in the Eighteen Benedictions we have the prayer,

---

[1] *Outlines of Old Testament Theology*, pp. 77–8.
[2] *The Prophets of Israel*, pp. 52–3.
[3] *The Parables of the Kingdom*, p. 35.

" Bring back our judges as at first, and our rulers as afore-
time, and be thou King over us, O Lord, thou alone."

On the other hand, it may be associated with the final and
absolute state of bliss in a transcendent order, as in the *Assumption
of Moses*, ch. x:[1]

" And then His Kingdom shall appear throughout all His
     creation,
And then Satan shall be no more,
And sorrow shall depart with him. . . .
For the Heavenly One will arise from His royal throne,
And He will go forth from His holy habitation
With indignation and wrath on account of His sons. . . .
For the Most High will arise, the Eternal God alone,
And He will appear to punish the Gentiles,
And He will destroy all idols.
And thou, Israel, shalt be happy. . . .
And God will exalt thee,
And He will cause thee to approach to the heaven of the stars."

Where a personal Messiah is looked for, the kingly rule of God is
thought of as exercised by the Messiah, whether He is a human
prince of the house of David, or a supernatural personage.[2]

From this comprehensive survey of the use of the phrase,
Dodd concludes that " in all these forms of belief the common
underlying idea is that of God's sovereign power becoming
manifestly effective in the world of human experience. When it
pleases God to ' reveal ' or to ' set up ' His kingly rule, then
there will be judgment on all the wrong that is in the world,
victory over all powers of evil, and for those who have accepted
His sovereignty, deliverance and a blessed life in communion
with Him."[3]

One of Dodd's most important contributions, however, is
found in a footnote commenting on Rudolph Otto's book,
Reich Gottes und Menschensohn (1934). Here, with characteristic
brilliance, he shows the derivation of this distinctively " eschatological " idea of the Kingdom of God. He points out that the
idea of God as king is characteristic of Semitic religion: " The
god is king of his tribe; its leader in war, its judge in peace,

---

[1] This is the view of R. H. Charles, *The Assumption of Moses*, and H. H.
Rowley, *The Relevance of Apocalyptic*, p. 89. T. W. Manson, however, denies
that the reference is to the transcendent Kingdom. See *The Servant-Messiah*,
pp. 31–2.   [2] C. H. Dodd, *op. cit.*, pp. 36–7.   [3] *Ibid.*, p. 38.

the source of its law as well as the object of its worship." He then goes on to show how in Israel this primitive Semitic belief in the kingship of Jehovah was influenced by the emergence of ethical monotheism in the teaching of the great prophets. " On the one hand, Jehovah is the King of Israel; on the other hand, He is the only God, and His will is universal righteousness. His Kingship therefore extends over the whole earth, and where He is King righteousness prevails. But, in fact, the people whose King was the Lord came to be subject to the ' unrighteous,' who worshipped other gods. On the naïve view, this ought to mean that Jehovah is subject to these other gods. But the higher faith stoutly maintained, in the face of all discouragement, that ' the most High ruleth in the kingdom of men, and giveth it to whomsoever he will ' (Daniel iv, 17). Sooner or later He will reveal His sovereignty. He will be King of all the world, not only *de jure* but *de facto*: ' the saints of the most High shall take the kingdom ' (Daniel vii, 18)." Dodd concludes therefore that " the eschatological idea of the Kingdom of God seems to arise naturally from primitive Hebrew conceptions, under the influence of prophetic teaching and of outward events."[1]

The dominant conception of the New Testament is that this future hope has been realized; in Jesus of Nazareth the Kingdom of God has come. The Kingdom " is the central theme of the teaching of Jesus, and it involves His whole understanding of His own person and work. . . . The fundamental message of Jesus' proclamation was that that day had now dawned. The things which many prophets and righteous men had long desired to see and hear are now present before the eyes and ears of Jesus' disciples (Matthew xiii, 16 ff.; Luke x, 23 ff.). God's reign is here, or at least is so near at hand that already the signs of its activity are manifest; and men must make some response to the claims which it lays upon them."[2]

" Now after that John was put in prison," says St. Mark, " Jesus came into Galilee, preaching the gospel of the kingdom of God, and saying, The time is fulfilled, and the kingdom of

---

[1] *Ibid.*, pp. 38–9, note 1.
[2] Alan Richardson, " Kingdom of God," in *A Theological Word Book of the Bible*, pp. 119–20.

God *has come.*" That is what the Greek really means.[1] The
Kingdom comes with and in Jesus. This is the way to understand His Messiahship: this was the new note in His teaching:
the Kingdom of God is beginning *now.* In Jesus the kingship of
God was embodied; in Him the sovereign rule of God was
already breaking into this world of sin and pain and death.
Its presence was shown in mighty works; the blind received
their sight, the lame walked, the lepers were cleansed, the deaf
heard, the dead were raised up.[2] Good news was proclaimed
to the poor by Him who spake as never man spake. For centuries those great Hebrew preachers, the prophets, had foreseen
the dawning of a new era, the coming of a new age when the
power of God would triumph over the sin and suffering of this
world. But the Good News proclaimed by the Apostolic Church
was that this new age had come. The rule of God had been
inaugurated through Jesus Christ and His followers shared in
that Kingdom which He embodied.

The New Testament teaching concerning the Kingdom of
God must therefore be seen against the background of both the
Old Testament and contemporary Jewish usage if its full
significance is to be grasped. " The Rabbinic expression ' to
take upon oneself the *malkuth* of heaven ' finds a parallel in
the saying of Mark x, 15: ' whosoever does not *receive the
Kingdom of God* as a little child will never enter into it.' The
Rabbis meant by this the scrupulous observance of the Torah.
Jesus was evidently understood to contrast the way of the
' little child,' or the ' babe ' (Matthew xi, 25: Luke x, 21)
with the way of the ' wise and prudent,' "[3] the " disciples
of the wise " being in the Talmud, as Dodd points out, the
members of the Rabbinic schools of Torah. Again, Jesus speaks
of His " yoke " (Matthew xi, 29), " no doubt in contrast with
' the yoke of Torah,' which was also spoken of as ' the yoke of
the *malkuth* of heaven.' "[4] For Jesus, comments Dodd, " to
accept the sovereignty of God is something other than scrupulous observance of the Torah."[5] The Kingdom is present

---

[1] ἤγγικεν Mark i, 14–15. See C. H. Dodd, *op. cit.,* pp. 44 ff.
[2] See Chapter V for a discussion of the miracles of the Gospels as " signs "
of the Kingdom of God.   [3] C. H. Dodd, *op. cit.,* pp. 41–2.
[4] *Ibid,* p. 42, note 1.   [5] *Ibid.,* p. 42.

in His own Person and ministry and may be accepted here and now.[1]

Such a conception of the ministry of Jesus as "realized eschatology" is quite compatible with the recognition of a future aspect of the Kingdom of God, of which Jesus also spoke —the consummation, catastrophic and glorious. Indeed, as Dodd himself observes, "the tension . . . between realization and unfulfilled expectation is thoroughly characteristic of the early Christian outlook."[2] For this future consummation of the Kingdom a distinct phraseology is employed in the New Testament: it is the παρουσία the ἀποκάλυψις, the coming of the Son of Man with power, or glory, or on the clouds of heaven. Jesus would give no precise information about this; He was content to describe it, as was also St. Paul, in terms made current by the apocalyptic writers. The divine rule would be consummated only at the end of time when Christ should return as Judge and the kingdom of this world become the Kingdom of our God. Nevertheless, the Kingdom was— and is—for His followers a present possession, something in which they share here and now through their union by faith with Jesus Christ. Christians have tasted the powers of the age to come (Hebrews vi, 5).

5. *The Messianic Hope*

The Hebrew word "Messiah" (*māshîah*), like its Greek equivalent "Christ" (χριστός), means "the anointed one."

[1] This is the purport of the much-discussed saying of Luke xvii, 21, if ἐντὸς ὑμῶν be rendered "in your midst" or "among you" as in the Old-Syriac version, the Revised Version margin, Moffatt's New Translation and the Revised Standard Version. Such a rendering, which is supported by Weiss, Adeney, Plummer and William Manson, gives a sense more in harmony with the context and with the general usage of the Gospels than "within you."

There is, however, no other instance, either in the New Testament or in the Septuagint, of such a rendering of ἐντὸς ὑμῶν and C. H. Dodd gives cogent linguistic arguments against it. See *The Parables of the Kingdom*, pp. 84–5, note 1. Indeed, in a private letter, he says, "I still wait for someone to produce a genuine example of ἐντὸς ὑμῶν, meaning 'in your midst': I have never seen one."

Tertullian suggests that the phrase means "within your grasp" and Cyril of Alexandria similarly renders it "lies in your power to appropriate it." This view has recently been advocated, with Hellenistic parallels, by Colin Roberts.   [2] See *According to the Scriptures*, pp. 73–4.

Its use in the Old Testament is confined to present or past personages, and it is only in later literature that it is applied to a future king.[1] The term is first used of Saul, who is designated as the Lord's anointed (I Samuel xxiv, 6). Leviticus iv, 3, applies it to a priest and Isaiah xlv to the Persian king Cyrus. In Psalm cv, 15, it is applied to prophets, as the parallelism of the couplet clearly shows. It signifies, therefore, one who is set apart by God for a special work. Moreover, since the ceremony of anointing with oil was the normal procedure by which Hebrew kings were instituted, the designation of " Messiah " or " Anointed One " could be used of any or all of them. This fact is of interest in its bearing upon the covenant relationship between Israel and God: the king was appointed by Jehovah himself for His Covenant People. In general, then, the term " Messiah " is applied in ancient Israel to the three types of person who acted under the commission of God—prophet, priest and king.

" It is important," says H. H. Rowley, " that we should distinguish clearly between the term ' Messiah ' and the messianic concept."[2] Although the term is not used in its present sense in the Old Testament, the conception of a coming Deliverer, to which it was later linked, is prominent.

> The conception of the Messiah is logically implicit in all the expectations of the Hebrew people that Jehovah would deliver Israel and turn it into a glorious empire to which all the heathen would be subjected. But it is not always explicit. The expectation of the coming Kingdom is more in evidence than the expectation of the coming King. But in the same proportion as the conception of the personal Messiah emerges from the general Messianic hope these elements appear within it: (1) the Deliverer; (2) the presence of God's Spirit in His own personality as the source of His power; (3) His work as the salvation of God's people, at first the Jewish nation, but ultimately all those who join themselves to Him.[3]

That summarizes succinctly this Old Testament theme: it was at first concerned with a hope of national deliverance rather

---

[1] Cf. W. O. E. Oesterley, *The Gospel Parables in the Light of Their Jewish Background*, p. 24: " In the Old Testament the Messiah as a technical term does not occur."   [2] H. H. Rowley, *The Relevance of Apocalyptic*, p. 25.

[3] Shailer Mathews, " Messiah," in Hastings' one volume *Dictionary of the Bible*, p. 607. For an important recent discussion of the Messianic idea, see Sigmund Mowinckel, *He That Cometh* (Eng. trans. 1956).

than with any personal Deliverer. The great hope of every pious Israelite was for some future period of peace and prosperity—the " good time coming " when all evil should be swept away; when oppression should cease and wrong be banished; when men would beat their swords into ploughshares and their spears into pruning-hooks and learn war no more; when the lion would lie down with the lamb. But this Utopia was not to come gradually as the result of social progress; it was to be inaugurated catastrophically by a Day of the Lord when Jehovah would subdue the nations and vindicate His own people.

We do, however, find the beginnings of the conception of a personal Deliverer at a very early time. Genesis xlix, for instance, incorporates an ancient poem about the Blessing of Jacob in which it is said: " The sceptre shall not depart from Judah, nor a lawgiver from between his feet, until Shiloh come; and unto him shall the gathering of the people be " (verse 10). The meaning of " Shiloh " is obscure. There is no ground for regarding it as a title for the Messiah, as does the Talmud. The most likely rendering of the verse is that of the Syriac Peshitta Version: " until he comes whose it is "—i.e. " to whom it [the sceptre or rule] belongs " (Revised Standard Version).[1] But although it is not easy to determine the precise meaning of " Shiloh " the reference is clearly to a Messianic King.[2] With this we may compare the Balaam poem in Numbers xxiv which declares: " There shall come a Star out of Jacob, and a Sceptre shall rise out of Israel, and shall smite the

[1] This rendering is supported by other second-century versions and by the Samaritan Pentateuch (fourth century B.C.). It presupposes, however, a linguistic usage which is confined to late Hebrew and to passages with a North Palestine colouring. " Shiloh " is taken as the equivalent of *shelô* (from *she* = *'asher* and *lô*), literally, " whose to him," i.e. " he whose it is."

[2] Since the above was written, J. M. Allegro has published his Pelican book, *The Dead Sea Scrolls* (1956), in which he mentions that " this Genesis passage is quoted and given a messianic significance in a Qumran document, where, instead of ' until Shiloh come,' it has ' until the Messiah of Righteousness come,' and goes on to say that this refers to the ' shoot of David,' to whose seed would be given the kingdom of his people " (pp. 152–3). Cf. T. H. Gaster, *The Scriptures of the Dead Sea Sect* (1957), pp. 351 and 355.

corners of Moab, and destroy all the children of Sheth"
(verse 17). Both of these poems are early and much older than
the complete books into which they have been incorporated.
Again, the "J" account of the Fall in Genesis iii speaks of the
Seed of the woman who shall bruise the serpent's head (verse
15).[1]

With the prophet Isaiah, however, a new development of the
Messianic hope begins—it is definitely associated with a Davidic
king who shall deliver the nation.[2] The promise to David was
that Jehovah would establish his house; " eternity was promised not to any individual descendant, but to the dynasty."[3]
This fact is stressed by the earlier prophets but Isaiah is the first
to proclaim the coming Deliverer as a Davidic prince. Micah
looks for the same ruler and in hailing Bethlehem as his home
indicates that he will be of Davidic descent.[4] The Deliverer,
as the Anointed One, would be a king; but since none of
the dynasties of the Northern Kingdom had done that which
was right in Jehovah's eyes, the Messiah must be of David's
line.

So far the Messianic King is conceived of only as a temporal
ruler; there is no idea yet of a supernatural Being. But the
Messiah is to be endowed with special divine gifts; he is to
possess in some measure the Spirit of God, so that the Child
of which Isaiah vii, 14, speaks may be called Emmanuel—God
with us.[5] Upon this Child's shoulders the government shall
rest and he is given a fourfold name: Wonderful-Counsellor,
the Mighty God, the Everlasting Father, the Prince of Peace.[6]
That, on the face of it, seems to contradict the statement that

---

[1] We have no grounds for thinking that the "J" writer regarded this
statement as a clear-cut Messianic *protevangelium*, as early Christian commentators supposed. Nevertheless, as Alan Richardson observes, " perhaps
he is here hinting in his parable at the ultimate redemption of the human
race, and Christians will rightly interpret his unformulated hope as having
found its realization in Christ's victory over sin and death."—*Genesis* i-xi,
(Torch Comm.), p. 75.

[2] See Isaiah xxxii, 1; ix, 6-7; xi, 1-10.

[3] G. A. Smith, *The Book of Isaiah*, p. 131. See II Samuel vii, 4-17;
cf. xxiii, 1-5.   [4] Micah v, 2.

[5] The name Emmanuel does not necessarily mean that the Child is
himself a *praesens numen*.   [6] Isaiah ix, 6.

we have just made—that so far only a temporal ruler is implied. But, as George Adam Smith points out:

> Two of the names are capable of being used of an earthly monarch: *Wonderful-Counsellor* and *Prince-of-Peace*, which are, within the range of human virtue, in evident contrast to Ahaz, at once foolish in the conception of his policy and warlike in its results. It will be more difficult to get Western minds to see how *Father-Everlasting* may be applied to a mere man, but the ascription of eternity is not unusual in Oriental titles, and in the Old Testament is sometimes rendered to things that perish. When Hebrews speak of any one as everlasting, that does not necessarily imply Divinity. The second name, which we render *God-Hero*, is, it is true, used of Jehovah Himself in the very next chapter to this, but in the plural it is also used of men by Ezekiel (xxxii, 21). The part of it translated *God* is a frequent name of the Divine Being in the Old Testament, but literally means only *mighty*, and is by Ezekiel (xxxi, 11) applied to Nebuchadnezzar. We should hesitate, therefore, to understand by these names " a God in the metaphysical sense of the word."[1]

The Messianic kingdom is characterized as a time of universal justice and peace (Isaiah ix, 6–7). Jeremiah reiterates this theme (Jeremiah xxv, 5; cf. xxxiii, 15). His metaphor of the Branch growing out of the stock of David is also used by Zechariah (Zechariah iii, 8; vi, 12). Zechariah, however, carries the Messianic conception a step further. Hitherto the Messiah's reign of peace has been conceived of as the result of successful war. Now, however, the Messiah himself is portrayed not as a warrior but as a man of peace (Zechariah ix, 9–10). " The remarkable part of the passage," comments Ryder Smith, " . . . is the verse that tells of a Hebrew king who shall be ' righteous and having salvation; lowly, and riding upon an ass, and upon a colt, the foal of an ass.' While the context requires that Jehovah is the warrior-god, here alone clearly the coming king is not to be a warrior-king. It is a surprising concept. In effect the writer says, ' The true king will not be an Alexander.' "[2]

The Old Testament itself never actually pictures the Messiah

[1] *The Book of Isaiah*, i, pp. 136–7. Adam Smith makes it clear that he himself firmly believes that Jesus Christ was God Incarnate. He is merely pointing out that these names are not be be regarded as prophecies of His divinity. They are, however, capable of being charged with a fuller content than they originally possessed. [2] *The Bible Doctrine of Salvation*, p. 42.

as a pre-existent supernatural Being, but later Jewish literature does portray such a Being under another name, a name which Jesus himself adopted—" the Son of Man." This name occurs in the Old Testament, but with a significant difference, in the Books of Ezekiel and Daniel. The term is a common Aramaic phrase, *bar nāshā*, meaning simply " man." In Ezekiel it is used purely as a synonym for " man."[1] In Daniel vii, 13, however, " Son of Man " " is a figure representative of a community ":[2] it denotes the community of the saints, i.e. the nation of Israel, as is clear by a comparison with verse 18 where " the saints of the most High " take the kingdom. Other kingdoms, symbolized by wild beasts, are contrasted with the kingdom of the saints, symbolized as a man.[3] But in the Similitudes of Enoch (Enoch xxxvii–lxxi) the phrase has come to mean an individual, a pre-existent supernatural Being, the representative and head of the kingdom of the saints, who comes as God's vicegerent to the earth. Nevertheless, as H. H. Rowley points out, " there is no evidence that the Son of Man was identified with the Messiah until the time of Jesus."[4]

At the beginning of the first century A.D. Jewish Messianic

---

[1] E.g. Ezekiel ii, 1, 3, 6.

[2] C. H. Dodd, *According to the Scriptures*, p. 117.

[3] See H. H. Rowley, *The Relevance of Apocalyptic*, p. 29: " To select a human figure instead of a beast was to differentiate its character from theirs at once, and to bring it from above instead of from the sea was to emphasize its higher origin and nature."

[4] *Ibid.*, p. 29. T. W. Manson believes that the Son of Man in the Gospels " is the final term in a series of conceptions, all of which are found in the Old Testament. These are: the Remnant (Isaiah), the Servant of Jehovah (II Isaiah), the ' I ' of the Psalms, and the Son of Man (Daniel)." It is " an ideal figure and stands for the manifestation of the Kingdom of God on earth in a people wholly devoted to their heavenly King." The mission of Jesus is " to create the Son of Man, the Kingdom of the saints of the Most High, to realize in Israel the ideal contained in the term. . . . When it becomes apparent that not even the disciples are ready to rise to the demands of the ideal, He stands alone, embodying in His own person the perfect human response to the regal claims of God." See *The Teaching of Jesus*, pp. 227 ff.

H. H. Rowley, however, argues that " the concept of the Son of Man began as a personifying of the saints, . . . and later the personification became a person." See *The Relevance of Apocalyptic*, pp. 28 ff. And C. H. Dodd also maintains that " the New Testament use of the title ' Son of Man ' for Christ results from the individualization of this corporate conception." See *According to the Scriptures*, pp. 116 ff.

hope was strong. But it had come to be interpreted politically.
They looked for a warrior-king who would deliver the land
from the hated invader and drive Rome into the sea:[1]

> They all were looking for a king
> To slay their foes and lift them high,
> Thou cam'st, a little Baby Thing,
> That made a woman cry.

Jesus deliberately led His disciples to recognize Him as the
promised Messiah, but He just as deliberately repudiated all the
political and military implications which had come to be
associated with that name. The story of His temptation is a
symbolic account, no doubt from the lips of Jesus Himself,
of how He had been assailed by this popular view but had
consciously laid it aside.[2] One of the things which He refused
to do was to submit to those who would have taken Him by
force and made Him a king.[3] On the other hand, He deliberately
fulfils the prophecy of Zechariah ix by riding into Jerusalem
upon the colt of an ass.[4]

But this was not the only way in which Jesus broke with
popular Messianic expectations. More significant still is the
fact that He revolutionizes the whole Messianic conception
by linking the role of the Messianic King with that of two other
Old Testament figures. There is clearly in Christ's own conception of His Messiahship a fusion of three different lines of
Jewish expectation; the ancient Messianic hope is interpreted
in terms of both the apocalyptic Son of Man and the Suffering

---

[1] In *The Testaments of the Twelve Patriarchs*, a pre-Christian Jewish work
containing some Christian interpolations, two Messiahs take part in the
final restoration—a Priestly Messiah of the tribe of Levi and a Davidic
Messiah of the tribe of Judah. Both these figures appear also in one of the
Dead Sea Scrolls, the *Manual of Discipline*, which lays down that the Qumran
community shall live under its original rule "until there shall come a
prophet and the anointed ones (Messiahs) of Aaron and Israel." Cf. the
references to "the Messiah of (or from) Aaron and Israel" in the *Damascus
Document*. Although here the word is in the singular, two messianic figures
seem to be implied. T. H. Gaster, however, argues that the term "Messiah"
has no divine eschatological significance in the Qumran documents and the
references mean nothing more than a duly anointed high priest and a duly
anointed king. See *The Scriptures of the Dead Sea Sect*, pp. 15, 29 and 36.

[2] Matthew iv, 1–11; Luke iv, 1–13.   [3] John vi, 14–15.

[4] Mark xi, 1–11; Matthew xxi, 1–11; Luke xix, 29–40. Cf. Zechariah
ix, 9.

Servant of Deutero-Isaiah. This gives new content to the idea of Messiahship.[1]

One result of this fusion was the revolutionary conception of a Suffering Messiah. The Messianic King and the Suffering Servant had never before been linked together in Jewish thought. No one had ever entertained the idea that the Messiah should suffer. But the Messiahship of which Jesus is conscious is a Messiahship which fulfils the role of the Suffering Servant. The King to whom it is said: " Thou are my Son " (Psalm ii) is in the mind of Jesus the same person as the Servant who is called " my beloved, in whom I am well pleased " (Isaiah xlii, 1, Septuagint version; cf. Mark i, 11). " When He unfolds Messiahship," says James Denney, " it contains death."[2]

From this fusion there results also an equally revolutionary view of the Messiah's relationship to the People of God. The Messiah of Jewish expectation was an individual set over against Israel as Jehovah's Anointed King. But the Son of Man and the Suffering Servant are, as we have seen, " societary " concepts characterized by a certain fluidity of thought; there is transition from the corporate to the individual aspect of each, and *vice versa*. When, therefore, the Messiah adopts the title " Son of Man " and deliberately fills the role of the Suffering Servant, He places Himself in an entirely new relationship with His people; instead of being set over against them as their Sovereign Lord, He becomes identified with them as their Representative.

C. H. Dodd points out that only three Old Testament passages referring to the Son of Man appear to have been cited

[1] F. F. Bruce maintains that the Qumran community believed that its task was " to realize not only the figure of the Servant of the Lord who makes many to be accounted righteous, but also the figure of that ' one like a son of man ' who, in Daniel's night vision, receives from the Ancient of Days authority to execute judgment and wield eternal and universal dominion (Daniel vii, 13 f., 22)." See *Second Thoughts on the Dead Sea Scrolls* (1956), p. 103. But there is no evidence that the Qumran convenanters thought of these two roles being combined in any of their messianic figures. As Bruce points out, Jesus " was different from any kind of Messiah expected at Qumran or elsewhere in Israel in those days, and all the accompaniments of messianic expectation had their meaning transformed in the light of His messianic achievement." *Ibid.*, p. 134. See further below, Appendix, " The Dead Sea Scrolls and Christian Origins," pp. 309 ff.
[2] *The Death of Christ*, p. 32.

as testimonies by the New Testament writers—Psalm lxxx and Daniel vii which portray the humiliation and deliverance of Israel, and Psalm viii which refers simply to man, weak and insignificant yet " visited " by God who crowns him with glory and honour. " In these three passages, therefore, the ' Son of Man ' is a figure representative of a community, which may be Israel, as the people of God, or mankind, as ' visited ' by God. If we take seriously the universality of the ' eschatological ' people of God, then the idea of humanity as redeemed by God's grace may be recognized in both." He maintains, therefore, that the New Testament use of the title " Son of Man " for Christ, being an individualization of this corporate Old Testament conception, implies that " ' in Christ,' mankind is delivered and exalted by the visitation of God, and becomes a people of the saints of the Most High."[1]

Similarly, it is the vocation and destiny of Israel which is portrayed in the figure of the Suffering Servant. It is as the representative of the People of God that the Servant suffers and is raised to newness of life. Hence Dodd argues that while the role of the Servant in its completeness is personally enacted by Christ crucified and risen, His experience is no less corporate. " In Him the people of God passes through disaster to glory. The possibility of a real (and not either abstract or fictitious) ' representation ' of the many by the one is given in the idea of a voluntary act of self-sacrifice such as is adumbrated in Isaiah liii and made actual in the self-sacrifice of Jesus. As Servant, He deliberately associates Himself with sinful humanity and offers His life as λύτρον ἀντὶ πολλῶν (Mark x, 45)."[2]

C. H. Dodd concludes, therefore, that " it is a central feature of the Christian idea of Messiahship that the Messiah is ' inclusive representative ' of the people of God, which in His person passes through the experience of death and resurrection by which it secures existence as an actual community of living men. Christology . . . is rooted in the understanding of the passion, death and resurrection of Jesus in the light of a combination of the ideas of Son of Man and Servant."[3] The final result is that " in primitive Christian messianic doctrine . . .

[1] *According to the Scriptures*, pp. 117–18. [2] *Ibid.*, pp. 118–19.
[3] *Ibid.*, p. 119.

there are these two inseparable moments: the Messiah is identified with the People of God as their ' inclusive representative ': he is set over against the People of God as sovereign Lord."[1]

The Old Testament means for us what it has come to mean in the light of Christ and His Cross. " If we may use a rough figure," says George Adam Smith, " the Messianic prophecies of the Old Testament are tidal rivers. They not only run . . . to their sea, which is Christ; they feel His reflex influence. It is not enough for a Christian to have followed the historical direction of the prophecies, or to have proved their connection with the New Testament as parts of one Divine harmony. Forced back by the fulness of meaning to which he has found their courses open, he returns to find the savour of the New Testament upon them, and that where he descended shallow and tortuous channels, with all the difficulties of historical explanation, he is borne back on full tides of worship."[2]

6. *Sacrifice*

The popular institutional religion of Israel may be summarized in one word—sacrifice. This was the divinely ordained means of approach to God, the " means of grace " whereby the covenant relationship of Israel with Jehovah was maintained. Yet, ironically enough, it was this very sacrificial system which became the sphere of the gravest abuse, as the prophets so clearly saw. This institution, which embodied elements of imperishable religious worth and was " fulfilled," in the largest sense of the word, in the death of Christ, was also the centre of the most deadly contamination of the religion of Israel by the Canaanite fertility cults and frequently degenerated into an unethical and superstitious ritualism. *Corruptio optimi pessima.* Nevertheless, sacrifice remains a dominant concept in biblical theology, a vital link between the Old Testament and the New.

As Vincent Taylor points out, although as an idea and an institution sacrifice is deeply rooted in Old Testament thought, nowhere is its rationale explained.[3] " The institution is taken

---

[1] *Ibid.*, p. 121.   [2] *The Book of Isaiah*, i, pp. 143-4.
[3] Cf. W. Robertson Smith, *The Religion of the Semites*, p. 3: " Everyone who reads the Old Testament with attention is struck with the fact that the origin and *rationale* of sacrifice are nowhere fully explained."

for granted as a divine ordinance, and the only principle laid down is that ' the blood is the life.' This attitude was maintained in Rabbinical Judaism, and only in comparatively modern times have attempts been made to ascertain its underlying idea."[1]

Two theories have been put forward regarding the essential nature of sacrifice. Robertson Smith finds its essence in a communion meal. It " is not a mere payment of tribute but an act of social fellowship between the deity and his worshippers."[2] This conception is developed at length in his monumental work on Semitic religion in which he maintains that " the leading idea in the animal sacrifices of the Semites . . . was not that of a gift made over to the god, but of an act of communion, in which the god and his worshippers unite by partaking together of the flesh and blood of a sacred victim."[3]

This, however, is denied by G. B. Gray, who argues that sacrifice is essentially a piacular gift. An examination of the terminology of sacrifice leads him to assert that " with one or two possible but scarcely probable exceptions, none of these (specific) terms, or of the general terms, stands related to the ideas of communion or fellowship. On the other hand, of the generic terms two certainly express the idea of gift. . . . But if the general terms clearly mean gifts, though the special terms do not express that idea, they also all refer to what the Jews, as the general terms show, nevertheless regarded as gifts." He therefore concludes that " whenever in later times the Jew sacrificed, he was consciously intending his sacrifice to be a gift to God."[4]

There is no good reason, however, for holding that these two theories are mutually exclusive; indeed it may be doubted whether any such clearly defined purpose was originally present. " Sacrifice," says T. R. Glover, " was a language used by all men, but understood by none."[5] The " J " narrative of Genesis iv, 2, regards it as being as old as the human race and it appears here as the spontaneous expression of man's

---

[1] Vincent Taylor, *Jesus and His Sacrifice*, p. 49.
[2] *The Religion of the Semites*, p. 224.   [3] *Ibid.*, pp. 226–7.
[4] *Sacrifice in the Old Testament*, pp. 19–20.
[5] *Jesus in the Experience of Men*, p. 63.

need of God. It seems, therefore, as Vincent Taylor suggests, that we must be content to define the original purpose of sacrifice more vaguely as the establishing and maintaining of healthful relations with the gods.[1]

The sacrificial system of Israel, however, is not to be placed in the same category as those of other primitive peoples; it stands in a class apart. Whereas in pagan sacrifice the emphasis is upon what man can do to win the favour of God, Hebrew sacrifice is based upon what God does for man: it presupposes the divine initiative in redemption.

> This divine initiative in redemption is the characteristic thought not only of Paul the great apostle of grace, but also of the whole Bible. Grace means love in action; love which takes the initiative, invasively and creatively. . . . It should be noticed that this is the dominant conception of the Old Testament, where all Israel's religious institutions, practices and ideas express the redeeming activity of God. For example, Israel's history began with a mighty act of deliverance which Israel owed, not to its own exertions or merits but to the mercy of God alone; the relation between God and his people was not a legal but a covenant relation. " He hath not dealt with us after our sins; nor rewarded us according to our iniquities." Indeed it is Israel which first teaches the world that redemption is God's way of being moral. The shocking and wonderful fact is that forgiveness is the divine way of doing right. . . . All Israel's characteristic religious institutions operate within this context or covenant of grace. The sacrifices themselves were offered to a God already and always in a relation of grace with his people. As a great Old Testament scholar once put it: " they were not offered in order to attain God's grace, but to retain it." Indeed, strange and even repulsive though Israel's sacrificial system is to us, its essential meaning and genius was that it was the vehicle of God's revelation to that Semitic people and through them to the world. It was the means of grace, the way provided and used by God himself, whereby he might say to Israel and to the world " I have redeemed thee; thou art mine."[2]

Old Testament sacrifices are expiatory, not propitiatory. " They are appointed means whereby sin is *covered*, so that it no longer stands as an obstacle between the worshipper and God ";[3] they are never the means of placating an angry deity. This is clear from a striking peculiarity in the use of the Hebrew verb

[1] *Jesus and His Sacrifice*, p. 50.
[2] J. S. Whale, *Christian Doctrine*, pp. 77–8.
[3] Vincent Taylor, *op. cit.*, pp. 51–2.

which is translated " to propitiate " or " to expiate "[1]—God is never its object. When used in the sense of " to propitiate," it has a manward reference (cf. Genesis xxxii, 21). At other times it means " to cover over " in the sense of expiating or atoning for sin. Where man is the subject, the reference is chiefly to legal rites (cf. Leviticus xvi); where God is the subject, it means " to treat as covered " and hence " to forgive." " It is conceived that God in His sovereignty may Himself provide an atonement or covering for men and their sins which could not be provided by men."[2] In short, it is not man who " propitiates " God, but God who " expiates " or " covers " man's sin in His own appointed way.

C. H. Dodd, in an exhaustive study of the Septuagint use of ἱλάσκεσθαι as translating *kipper* points out that " the LXX translators did not regard *kipper* (when used as a religious term) as conveying the sense of propitiating the Deity, but the sense of performing an act whereby guilt or defilement is removed, and accordingly rendered it by ἱλάσκεσθαι in this sense. . . . While the translators were aware of the meaning of ἱλάσκεσθαι = ' to propitiate the Deity,' they regarded it as inappropriate to the religion of Israel." Hence he concludes that "Hellenistic Judaism, as represented by the LXX, does not regard the cultus as a means of pacifying the displeasure of the Deity, but as a means of delivering man from sin, and it looks in the last resort to God himself to perform that deliverance."[3]

The significance of this fact was pointed out half a century ago by A. B. Davidson: " The fact that He Himself is represented as the subject who performs the covering or atonement, shows how profoundly the feeling had taken possession of the people's mind that in whatever way sin was to be invalidated, and its effects neutralized, ultimately its removal must be due to God; that He was not moved by something or anything outside of Him, but that the movement came from within Himself, whatever the immediate means were of which He made use."[4]

---

[1] *Kipper*, the Piel form of *Kaphar*.
[2] Brown, Driver and Briggs, *Hebrew and English Lexicon*, ' kipper '.
[3] *The Bible and the Greeks*, p. 93.
[4] *The Theology of the Old Testament*, p. 322.

The whole point of the sacrificial system was that it provided the means of which God made use. The cultus was the symbolic and sacramental means of grace through which the covenant fellowship of Israel with Jehovah was maintained and restored. Besides being the sign and seal of the divine forgiveness, the sacrifices "are vehicles of self-expression; they make possible religious activities with which the worshipper can associate himself, and so in a very real sense make his own."[1] This is seen in the six stages of the ritual.[2] The worshipper "draws near" with his offering; he lays his hands on its head; he himself kills the animal; the priest offers the blood to God; the flesh, in part or whole, is burnt—"not destroyed but transformed, sublimated, etherealized, so that it can ascend in smoke to the heaven above, the dwelling-place of God";[3] and finally, except in the case of burnt-offerings when the entire carcass is burnt, a portion of the flesh is eaten.

Bishop Hicks has set out the underlying ideas of this sacrificial ritual:

> The offerer . . . makes his own approach to the presence of God: it is his own free act. He identifies himself with the victim in the pressing on its head of his hands: what happens thereafter to the animal happens symbolically to himself. He kills the animal: "the soul that sinneth, it shall die": the death is his own death, accepted by him as the consequence of sin. The life is now set free: it is for this that the death was effected: and as set free it is taken by the priest into the presence of God. The atonement—at-one-ment—has been made; and the substance of the offering, the flesh, can now be offered, and, so offered, God accepts it by His fire, and, in accepting, transforms it. In the common meal on the flesh of the victim, now that atonement has been effected, the life of the offerer has been brought before the face of God, and his offering made and accepted, God and man become at one, and man finds his fellowship with man.[4]

It should be noted that the emphasis is not, as is popularly supposed, upon the destruction of the victim, but upon the offering of its life, released in the form of blood, to God. This is true of sacrifice generally. "The fundamental principle

---

[1] Vincent Taylor, *Jesus and His Sacrifice*, p. 53.
[2] I am indebted here to the illuminating analysis of Bishop Hicks in his *Fulness of Sacrifice*.   [3] F. C. N. Hicks, *The Fulness of Sacrifice*, p. 13.
[4] *Ibid.*, pp. 13–14.

THE OLD TESTAMENT AND THE NEW

throughout is the same; the giving of life to promote or preserve life, death being merely a means of liberating vitality. Consequently, the destruction of the victim, to which many writers have given a central position in the rite, assumes a position of secondary importance in comparison with the transmission of the soul-substance to the supernatural being to whom it is offered."[1] By laying his hands upon it, and afterwards by eating its flesh, the worshipper identifies himself with his offering and so through it presents himself to God.

The interpretation of the death of Christ in terms of sacrifice forms part of the common stock of apostolic teaching and is deeply embedded in the New Testament. Indeed, as C. R. North maintains, "it is coming to be realized that what the New Testament says about the Cross cannot be interpreted without violence to its plain meaning, if we read it without reference to ideas about sacrifice."[2]

The facts may be summarized thus. Very early in His ministry Jesus was aware that suffering and death awaited Him. There is conclusive evidence that He interpreted His mission as Son of Man in terms of the Suffering Servant of Isaiah liii and thus saw His sufferings and death as necessary for the fulfilment of the divine purpose in His ministry. Hence our Lord regarded His death, not as a mere martyrdom, but as a decisive act which had a significance in itself. His sufferings were vicarious in that they were a service through which deliverance would come to many. He identified Himself so completely with men " as to feel in His spirit the shadows of the Divine judgment upon sin."[3] Now the conception of sacrifice, as the divinely appointed means of restoring communion between man and God, includes within itself the ideas of the necessity of Christ's death, of its relation to sin and forgiveness, and of its final efficacy. Jesus, through His death, has accomplished all that was required to be done for the reconciliation of man to God.

Furthermore, as Vincent Taylor has made clear,[4] Jesus

---

[1] E. O. James, *Origins of Sacrifice*, p. 256.

[2] "Sacrifice," in *A Theological Word Book of the Bible* (ed. Alan Richardson), p. 213.

[3] Vincent Taylor, *op. cit.*, p. 163.   [4] See *ibid.*, Parts II and III.

Himself regarded His surrendered life as a sacrificial offering in which men might share, and He instituted the sacrament of Holy Communion as a means whereby His disciples might partake in His broken body and shed blood.

> The Messianic, redeeming, sacrificial significance which the whole primitive jewish church unhesitatingly saw, first in His death, and then in His Person and whole action towards God, is the proof that this meaning was grasped by that church primarily through the eucharist, which arose directly out of what He had said and done at the last supper. There, and there alone, He had explicitly *attached* that particular meaning to His own death and office.[1]

" The fraction of the loaf is symbolic and recalls the practice of the Old Testament prophets who sometimes in similar ways dramatized their words. . . . The intention is to suggest that, as the loaf is broken, so His body will be broken in the near future."[2] The passing of the bread to the disciples is, as Otto has said, " the gift of a share in the power of that which is represented, namely, the expiatory power of the broken Christ."[3] Dalman has pointed out that in Semitic idiom to give the body for someone means to die;[4] hence the phrase, " this is my body," suggests Christ offering Himself in death, and we are powerfully reminded of " the sacred meal which normally was the final stage in the Old Testament sacrifices, when the worshipper participated in that which he offered or in that which was offered on his behalf."[5] Jesus clearly " intends the bread to be a means whereby the disciples may participate in the power of His surrendered life."[6]

Similarly, He speaks of His blood as " covenant blood," thus recalling Exodus xxiv, 8, with its accompanying sacrifices. " Jesus does not invite His disciples to drink blood, or to drink blood symbolically, but to drink wine as representing His life surrendered for many."[7] As at Sinai " dedicated blood was

---

[1] Gregory Dix, *The Shape of the Liturgy*, p. 77. Cf. A. E. J. Rawlinson, *Mysterium Christi*, p. 241: " The doctrine of sacrifice (and of atonement) was not . . . read *into* the last supper; it was read out of it."

[2] Vincent Taylor, *op. cit.*, p. 118. Cf. P. T. Forsyth, *The Church and the Sacraments*, pp. 214–5.

[3] Rudolph Otto, *Reich Gottes und Menschensohn*, p. 257.

[4] *Jesus-Jeshua*, p. 145.   [5] Vincent Taylor, *op. cit.*, p. 121.

[6] *Ibid.*, p. 124.   [7] *Ibid.*, p. 135.

applied in blessing to the people of Israel, so now His life, surrendered to God and accepted by Him, is offered to, and made available for men."[1] This is in full accord with the Pauline narrative of the Lord's Supper in I Corinthians xi, 23–5.

Clearly, the death of Jesus, in His own eyes, did have the significance of a great deed, and the only interpretation of it which is adequate to cover all the implications both of His recorded sayings and of the varied conceptions of the Apostolic Church is that which views His work as sacrificial. There can be no doubt that our Lord regarded His passion and death as a sacrifice of Himself on behalf of men, and, by instituting the Eucharist, He provided a means whereby His disciples through the ages might associate themselves with His offering and share in the self-oblation of His surrendered life.

[1] *Ibid.*, p. 138.

CHAPTER VII

DIFFERING LEVELS OF TRUTH

ALL parts of the Bible are not equally authoritative. It cannot therefore be read in the flat. The Book of Judges and the Gospel of John, for instance, are far from equal in the value of the portrait of God which each gives. Leviticus belongs to a different stage of religious development from that of Luke; and we must see each in its proper perspective if we are rightly to assess its permanent value as revelation and truth. It is also necessary to differentiate between the record and the revelation which it records. The revelation is given objectively in the stuff of history: God is known for what He is by what He does. The record is the work of fallible, sinful men, inspired admittedly, but not thereby rendered free from error. There is no biblical warrant for making inerrancy a corollary of inspiration: we have this treasure in earthen vessels. " The principle that God has revealed Himself through human instruments makes it inevitable that there should be imperfections in the Bible."[1]

The divine word is, as Florovsky puts it, " always inescapably ' situation-conditioned.' "[2] Although, " it was ever the same God, and His ultimate message was ever the same," He was nevertheless " leading His people from truth to truth. There were stages in His revelation: *per incrementa*."[3] " Many were the forms and fashions in which God spoke of old " (Hebrews i, 1, Moffatt).

To maintain thus, as does St. Thomas Aquinas, that there are " degrees of prophecy "[4] is not the same thing as the

---

[1] A. G. Hebert, *The Authority of the Old Testament*, p. 10. Cf. H. H. Rowley, *The Authority of the Bible*, p. 10: " Once we recognize a human element we recognize a fallible element."

[2] " Revelation and Interpretation," in *Biblical Authority for Today*, p. 173.

[3] *Ibid.*, p. 165.   [4] *Summa Theologica*, iia–iiae, clxxiv, 3; cf. *ibid.*, clxxi, 4.

nineteenth-century Liberal notion of " progressive revelation "
which attempted to fit the biblical revelation into evolutionary
categories; it was assumed that primitive ideas must be early
and higher conceptions late. It is rather to assert that within
the Bible there are to be found different levels of truth.[1] They
are not necessarily apprehended successively, however; they
may be apprehended contemporaneously. C. H. Dodd recently
recalled to the writer how S. A. Cook used to pull up the critics,
who neatly arranged the ideas of the Old Testament in a strictly
chronological order of development, and insist that in the
Judaism of the sixth century B.C. you could find ideas co-existing
which belonged to any period since the Exodus or before.

Nor can the " degrees of prophecy " be brought into the
" transient " and " permanent " categories. Here again
nineteenth-century Liberalism was too facile in distinguishing
between the abiding kernel of truth and its transient " husk."
The eschatology of the Bible, for example, was confidently
dismissed as part of the latter until Albert Schweitzer insisted
that it could not be so easily disposed of. In recent years it
has come to occupy a central position. T. W. Manson's warning
is therefore salutary: " We have to avoid, like the plague, the
fault of Liberalism which, by using the distinction between
passing and permanent, or kernel and husk, succeeded in
watering down the plain meaning until all the characteristic
flavour of the biblical teaching had disappeared."[2] The
danger of any such antithesis is that it may be used to dismiss
anything which the individual critic happens not to like. " The
Bible," says Barth, " gives to every man and to every era such
answers to their questions as they deserve. We shall always find
in it as much as we seek and no more: high and divine content,
if it is high and divine content that we seek; transitory and
' historical ' content, if it is transitory and ' historical ' content that we seek—nothing whatever, if it is nothing whatever
that we seek."[3]

[1] Cf. H. H. Rowley, *op. cit.*, p. 11: " Because inspiration works through
fallible men, there are different levels of inspiration even where all are
inspired."
[2] " The Failure of Liberalism to Interpret the Bible as the Word of
God," in *The Interpretation of the Bible* (ed. C. W. Dugmore), p. 106.
[3] *The Word of God and the Word of Man*, p. 32.

I. HISTORICAL CORE AND UNHISTORICAL ACCRETIONS

A sounder line of approach is taken by Phythian-Adams and A. G. Hebert, who distinguish between the central historical core of the Bible and the unhistorical accretions which have become attached to it. These latter are regarded as " Sacred Stories (ἱεροὶ λόγοι) designed for specific purposes; and in no one absolutely clear instance is the purpose to be recognized as what *we* should call historical."[1] But " the original historical kernel can still be discerned in spite of contradictions and inconsistencies and the manifold embellishments of tendentious editors."[2] " However much they may embellish the facts, or even obscure them in the interests of their particular purpose, at the heart of their narrative these facts remain as a solid, resistant core, the indestructible nucleus of historical reality."[3] From these premises Father Hebert reasons that " if this distinction between the core of the tradition and its elaboration is a sound one, it is no more legitimate to argue that the unhistorical character of the additions casts doubt on the central events themselves, than it would be to argue that our Lord probably did not die on a cross because some early medieval crucifixes represent the Crucified as robed and crowned, or because some Italian painters put the Crucifixion on the background of a Tuscan landscape, or because Dorothy Sayers gives St. Matthew a cockney accent. . . . As the historical fact that our Lord was crucified is in no way endangered by the various ways in which Christians through the ages have expressed their devotion to the Passion, so the diversity of the documents in which the Israelites told the story of the events of the Exodus and the Covenant only throws into stronger relief the historical actuality of those events."[4]

In dealing with any biblical statement, therefore, we need to ascertain, as far as modern critical method makes possible, whether it belongs to the historical core or to an unhistorical accretion. For example, although there is no contemporary evidence (with the possible exception of the Song of Miriam),

[1] W. J. Phythian-Adams, *The Call of Israel*, p. 63.
[2] W. J. Phythian-Adams, *The Fulness of Israel*, p. 36.
[3] W. J. Phythian-Adams, *The Call of Israel*, p. 64.
[4] *The Authority of the Old Testament*, pp. 60–1.

there can be little doubt about the historicity of the Exodus and the Deliverance at the Red Sea. Not only are these events directly attested by the chief historical sources;[1] they are presupposed throughout the entire range of Old Testament literature and by the traditions and institutions of Israel. " While then the details of the great events of the Plagues of Egypt, the Passover, the Crossing of the Red Sea, and the Covenant at Horeb must remain in large measure uncertain, it is possible to affirm with much confidence that the core of the tradition is substantially sound."[2]

The same thing is true of the Gospel tradition in the New Testament, with the added consideration of a considerably smaller interval of time between record and event. Indeed few events of the ancient world are better attested than is the general outline of the life and ministry of Jesus of Nazareth.

The fact, however, that a period of thirty-five years separates the events of the life of Jesus and the first written Gospel raises for many people the question, Are our records reliable? Can we really know what Jesus said and did? Several things may be said in reply. In the first place, this gap of thirty-five years is not so formidable as its mention might suggest. As C. H. Dodd points out, its seriousness is in inverse proportion to your age. " When I was a young teacher of the New Testament," he says, " I remember, I used to feel this gap between event and record to be a very serious matter. Later on I realized, quite suddenly, that in my own memories thirty-five years did not seem at all a long time. . . . When Mark was writing, there must have been many people about who were in their prime under Pontius Pilate, and they must have remembered the stirring and tragic events of that time at least as vividly as we remember 1914. If anyone had tried to put over an entirely imaginary or fictitious account of them, there would have been middle-aged or elderly people who would have said (as you or I might say) ' You are wasting your breath: I remember it as if it were yesterday! ' "[3]

[1] " The fact that the written narratives can be analysed into various sources constitutes evidence far stronger than would be that of one single narrative."—A. G. Hebert, *op. cit.*, p. 56.

[2] *Ibid.*, p. 57. Cf. above p. 163.   [3] *About the Gospels*, pp. 11–12.

Secondly, there were certain factors which safeguarded the growth of the Gospel tradition during the oral period. It took shape among a people whose memories had been schooled by Rabbinic method. The disciples of a Jewish Rabbi were not allowed to make a written record of his teaching; it must be preserved and transmitted by word of mouth. Hence it was given in a crisp epigrammatic form that was easily retained in the mind. It was not otherwise with the teaching of Rabbi Jesus; and we have no reason to think that his disciples were less careful than those of any other Rabbi in preserving their Master's words. Furthermore, as Dodd points out, " the oral tradition behind the Gospels is anything but irresponsible gossip. It is the sifted and certified tradition of a community " which " had a strong sense both of its duty to publish its faith, and of responsibility for the truth of what it published." "The Christian community, acting through its accredited agents—apostles, evangelists and teachers—knew that it was on its honour to speak the truth, like a witness in court. That is the atmosphere in which the oral tradition took shape."[1]

In the third place, behind the synoptic tradition of the first three Gospels are four distinct formulations of oral tradition, each going back to the testimony of eye-witnesses: Mark, written in Rome in A.D. 65 and embodying, on the unanimous testimony of the early Church, the preaching of St. Peter; the sayings-document " Q " which Vincent Taylor describes as " perhaps the most valuable source used by the Evangelists "[2] and which T. W. Manson dates about the middle of the first century, " probably rather before than after A.D. 50," and connects with Antioch, the headquarters of Gentile Christianity;[3] the special source of Matthew, representing the tradition of the Jerusalem Church; and Luke's special source derived from Caesarea. To these must be added the testimony of the Fourth Gospel emanating from Ephesus round about A.D. 95.

Finally, just as the events of the Exodus and the Deliverance at the Red Sea are presupposed in those parts of the Old Testament which do not bear direct witness to them, so the events of the Gospel story are presupposed throughout the rest of the

[1] *Ibid.*, p. 13.   [2] *The Gospels*, p. 24.
[3] *The Mission and Message of Jesus*, p. 312.

New Testament. The Pauline Epistles, in particular—all of which were in circulation before the earliest of the Gospels was written—are full of allusions to the life and character, the death and resurrection of Christ. So much so that, as Anderson Scott used to maintain, if the Gospels had been lost, it would have been possible to reconstruct a picture of Jesus from the information given incidentally in the writings of St. Paul.[1]

In this connection one Pauline passage is particularly important. I Corinthians xv, verses 3 ff., contains the oldest testimony that we have to the death and resurrection of Christ. St. Paul, writing in A.D. 54–5, recalls that what he taught in Corinth was the basic Christian tradition which had been passed on to him when he himself became a Christian: " I delivered unto you first of all that which I also received (παρέλαβον)." The verb παραλαμβάνω is used of disciples receiving something transmitted by the instruction of a teacher. The crucial question is, When did St. Paul " receive " this Christian tradition? Harnack dates his conversion at only a year after the death of Christ; Ramsay would put it at three or four years; Lightfoot estimates it at six or seven years.[2] C. H. Dodd maintains that it cannot, on St. Paul's own showing, be dated later than about A.D. 33–4.[3] Three years later he visited Jerusalem and spent a fortnight with St. Peter; and, as Dodd remarks, " we may presume they did not spend all the time talking about the weather."[4] These were the only opportunities for instruction in the Christian tradition that St. Paul had prior to his preaching in Corinth. His testimony in I Corinthians xv is therefore of primary historical importance. Not only was it written down at least ten years before St. Mark's

---

[1] See Anderson Scott, *St. Paul the Man and the Teacher*, pp. 65–6: " He refers to the ' grace '; . . . to His ' deference,' and ' considerateness ' or ' magnanimity ' (II Cor. x, 1); to His ' disinterestedness ' and ' purity ' (II Cor. xi, 3); to His ' obedience ' (Philippians ii, 8; cf. II Cor. x, 5); to His ' heroic endurance ' (II Thessalonians iii, 5); to the fact that ' He pleased not Himself ' (Romans xv, 3)."

[2] See the article on " Chronology," in Hastings' *Dictionary of the Bible*, i, p. 424.

[3] Article on " Chronology of the Acts and the Pauline Epistles," in the Oxford *Helps to the Study of the Bible*, 1931, pp. 195–7.

[4] *The Apostolic Preaching and its Developments*, p. 16.

Gospel appeared, but it takes us back to within not more than seven years, and probably only four years, of the events themselves.

The presence of discrepancies and contradictions in matters of detail in no way invalidates the witness of all our sources to the central events of the Gospel tradition. Indeed the very fact that there are minor discrepancies in the various accounts only throws into relief their common attestation of the central events.

Our sources differ, for example, in regard to the date of the Last Supper and the Crucifixion. For Mark the Last Supper is the Passover meal (Mark xiv, 12–26) and Jesus is crucified the following day. The same is true of Matthew, whose Passion narrative follows Mark very closely (Matthew xxvi, 17–30). Luke, who definitely states that it was the Passover which the disciples were sent to prepare (Luke xxii, 7–13), does not make it clear whether Jesus partook of the actual Passover meal or not. The words in verse 15, " With desire I have desired to eat this passover with you before I suffer," are ambiguous. They may mean—as the context seems to imply—that Jesus, in realization of a great wish, was able to share in the Passover meal with his disciples before his arrest. On the other hand, they may equally well mean that He did not: although everything had been prepared, He knew that the one thing He had longed for—the eating of the Passover meal—would be impossible; at the time it was held He would be dead. In that case, the meal of which He partook would be the Kiddush, a simple weekly meal shared by a Rabbi and his disciples on the eve of a Sabbath or a festival and closely connected with the Passover celebrations. John, however, is quite definite that the Last Supper was not the actual Passover. It was held " before the feast of the passover " (John xiii, 1). At the trial before Pilate, the high priest and his company " went not into the judgment hall, lest they should be defiled, but that they might eat the passover " (John xviii, 28). It was then " the preparation of the passover " (John xix, 14; cf. verses 31 and 42), and Jesus' death coincided with the killing of the Passover lambs.

It seems clear that the author of the Fourth Gospel is here

deliberately clearing up, for the sake of his Hellenistic readers, an ambiguity in the Synoptic tradition and correcting an error of detail in St. Mark's account. As W. D. Maxwell observes, " If the Passover had begun on ' the night on which He was betrayed,' our Lord could not have been tried and executed that day, for it was against the law of the Jews to hold a trial or execution during the Passover. But the Last Supper took place, according to Jewish reckoning, on the same day as the trials and crucifixion. This alone is really sufficient to prove that it was a pre-Passover meal that our Lord shared with His disciples, and not the Passover proper; although, being closely associated with the Passover as a normal part of its celebration, it is not unnatural to find it called the ' Passover ' in the narratives: it would be clear enough to a Jewish reader what was meant."[1] The very fact, however, that the later writer deliberately corrects what he knows to be an error of detail in the earlier account only serves to strengthen the evidence for the historicity of the events to which both accounts bear witness.

It is easy to see how accretions which are, strictly speaking, unhistorical can gather around a core of well-attested historic events. A good story usually improves in the telling. Legends soon grow up around great men. But a legend although " unhistorical " is not necessarily valueless; it may embody penetrating insights into the character and personality of the man. A comparison of one of the later Synoptic Gospels— Matthew or Luke—with Mark shows the kind of tendencies which modified the details of the Gospel tradition as the events receded more and more into the past. For example, the various human emotions of Jesus—anger, annoyance, amazement— are suppressed and the misunderstandings and failures of the Apostles either omitted or toned down. On the other hand, there is the tendency to heighten the miraculous, as a comparison of Matthew's with Mark's account of the Resurrection will show. The setting, and subsequent bribing, of the guard; the earthquake and dramatic descent of the angel—these have all the characteristics of embellishments of the Marcan narrative. Even in Mark, however, a story like that of the Gadarene

[1] *An Outline of Christian Worship*, p. 6.

swine (ch. v.) in its present form is held by many scholars to be more of the nature of an accretion than a part of the central historical core. The same is true of Matthew's account of the coin in the fish's mouth (Matthew xvii, 24–7). The critical method of modern biblical study both enables us to discriminate between the accretions and the core, and establishes the substantial accuracy of the latter beyond reasonable doubt.

II. Time-Relativity and Historical Perspective

The temporal distinction of " transient " and " permanent " is, as we have seen, inadequate when dealing with the contents of the Bible. Permanence belongs only to truth, which is eternal. The primary distinction that we have to make therefore is not between what is transient and what is permanent, but between what is *true*—at any time and any place—and what is *false*, at any time and at any place. This is a distinction that we need to recognize, even though we cannot discriminate in any final or dogmatic way. And of some statements in the Bible we may have to say that they are just not true, not that they are transient. Having made this distinction, as far as it is possible, we must then go on to ask, On what level of truth does this statement stand, in so far as it is true?

Nevertheless, the question of time-relativity is an element in the situation: the divine Word given in the Bible is not only " situation-conditioned "; it is frequently " time-conditioned " also. " In the process, . . . comparatively crude and inadequate ideas are gradually replaced by ideas more worthy of their objects. We may think of it as a process of education. God, who is the source of all truth, communicated to men, stage by stage, as they were able to digest it, an increasing measure of knowledge about Himself."[1] This is the truth behind the idea of " progressive revelation." The revelation is to some extent conditioned by the receptiveness of those to whom it is given. " When God speaks to babes," says Calvin, " He babbles." T. H. Robinson reminds us that " our mathematical teachers

---

[1] C. H. Dodd, *The Bible To-day*, p. 98.

started us with the multiplication table, not with quadratic equations."[1]

We must, however, be on our guard against relapsing into the propositional view of revelation. Revelation does not consist of a series of statements about God: it is the self-disclosure of God. And God's revelation of Himself is not to be equated with man's apprehension of it. God is ever the same and His relationship with men does not change. The fact that there is growth and development in men's *ideas* about God does not mean that God deliberately gave men false or unworthy conceptions of Himself which had later to be discarded, but that men failed to apprehend the self-disclosure of God and sometimes distorted the revelation that He gave. Nevertheless, there is a sense in which, just as a mother cannot disclose her whole personality to her immature child, God's own self-disclosure is to some extent limited by the receptiveness of men.[2]

> Just as the history of revelation itself is disclosed as a divine economy, or a kind of education, so is it with the record of the revelation. God Himself moved with His people Israel from the primitive stage to the higher forms of belief and worship, and finally to the highest of all, and this " divine economy " is visible in the Old Testament.[3]

1. *Sub-Christian Morality in the Old Testament*

A recognition of this fact will resolve the question raised by the sub-Christian morality of parts of the Old Testament. It must be frankly admitted that the Old Testament does create certain problems for the Christian mind. It contains conceptions of God and standards of human conduct which stand in

[1] *An Introduction to the Old Testament* (Merlin Books), p. 14. Cf. W. Sanday, *Inspiration*, pp. 417–8: " We observe that there is a law running through the whole of Revelation which, after the example of the logicians, we might call perhaps the Law of Parsimony; the law, I mean, that all revelation is suited to the condition of those who are to receive it, that it starts from the actual circumstances in which they are placed, and that it tells them what is essential for them to know and not really more—for although there may be a latent meaning which comes out in the wider survey of God's purposes, we certainly cannot lay down beforehand how far this meaning shall extend."

[2] J. K. S. Reid fails to realize this in his otherwise excellent discussion of " progressive revelation." See *The Authority of Scripture*, pp. 182 ff.

[3] Emil Brunner, *Revelation and Reason*, pp. 133 f. Cf. St. Paul's conception of the Law as a παιδαγωγὸς εἰς Χριστόν. See Galatians iii, 24.

marked contrast to the life and teaching of Jesus. If the latter be normative for the Christian, if it be the plumb-line by which he proves all things and holds fast to that which is good, what is he to make, for instance, of the hewing of Agag in pieces[1] or the utter extermination of Canaanite women and children at the command of Israel's God?[2] How can he at one and the same time accept the Old Testament as authoritative Scripture and be true to the light which he has seen in Christ?

The answer is that each part of the Bible must be seen in its true historical perspective. As E. P. Gould reminds us, the " principle of accommodation to the time in Scripture is of inestimable importance, and of course limits finally the absoluteness of its authority. We find that the writers were subject to this limitation, as well as their readers."[3] The books of the Bible, since they are historical documents, must be studied historically and critically, just as other ancient documents are studied; because we can fully apprehend the revelation which they contain only as we understand the people to whom it was given and the conditions in which they lived. Man is not an automaton but a free spirit, and God will not rob him of the freedom with which he has endowed him by using him as a dictaphone which automatically records whatever He speaks. Just because God's co-operation with man has its basis in human freedom, man may distort the revelation that is given.[4] Revelation is apprehended according to man's capacity to receive it. When therefore we find in the Books of Samuel or Judges vindictiveness and cruelty perpetrated in the name of God, we must remember that the people of that day saw through a glass darkly; they only dimly discerned God's will; sometimes they were just plain wrong; but they did carry out what they believed to be God's will, however terrible it might be. To us it has been given to see the Holy One of Israel as the God and Father of our Lord Jesus Christ.

The Old Testament is not a collection of infallible oracles.

---

[1] I Samuel xv, 32–3.   [2] Joshua vi, 21.
[3] *St. Mark* (I.C.C.), p. 184.
[4] Cf. H. H. Rowley, *The Authority of the Bible*, p. 10: " Even God Himself is limited by the spiritual maturity and sensitiveness of those He uses, and that is why the Incarnation was necessary for the supreme revelation."

It was never intended as such, and to treat it as if it were is to subject it to misunderstanding and abuse. It is rather the account of God's redemptive dealings with Israel—a nation, not of religious geniuses, but of very ordinary men and women who were frequently wilful and disobedient. Consequently they often misunderstood and distorted the divine will for them. Just because the Old Covenant was imperfect and incomplete, it had to be superseded by the new. " For the Christian the test whereby the level of inspiration and authority is to be judged is Christ, Who is the supreme medium of divine revelation and by Whom all other revelation is to be tested."[1] The Old Testament therefore must be both interpreted and judged in the light of Christ. " In so far as it accords with the revelation in Christ it is enduringly valid, while in so far as it falls short of that revelation it shows the mark of the imperfections and fallibility of the persons through whom it was given and is superseded."[2]

2. *St. Paul and his Times*

The question of time-relativity does not apply only to the Old Testament; it has a bearing on the New Testament also, particularly in regard to certain elements in the writings of St. Paul.

Paul is by far the greatest interpreter of Christ. As James Denney observes, " He did more than any of the apostles to win for the Christian religion its place in the life of the world, and he has done more than any of them in always winning that place again when it seemed in danger of being lost."[3] Although an original thinker, he was no innovator. " He did not invent Christianity; there were apostles and preachers and men in Christ before him. And he tells us expressly that in the fundamentals of Christianity he not only agreed with them, but was indebted to them."[4] He preached the same Gospel that was handed on in the primitive apostolic Church. There is no ground whatever for the accusation which has sometimes been made against him that he perverted the simple religion

---

[1] H. H. Rowley, *ibid.*, p. 11.   [2] *Ibid.*, p. 12.
[3] *Jesus and the Gospel*, p. 22.
[4] J. Denney, *The Death of Christ*, p. 112.

of Jesus into a complicated theology about Jesus.[1] Whatever opposition he had to face from the Mother Church at Jerusalem, he was never accused of innovating here—not even by his bitterest enemies. " Though Paul clashed with the Jerusalem leaders on other issues (e.g. table-fellowship: Galatians ii, 11 ff.) there is no evidence that they ever disagreed on the capital issue of Christianity."[2] As C. H. Dodd observes, " Paul himself at least believed that in essentials his Gospel was that of the primitive apostles."[3] He shared in the common stock of Christian tradition and his atonement theories are but the drawing out and developing of what was implicit in the life and teaching of Jesus and in the thought of the early Church concerning his death and resurrection. " Paul's essential Christology is not fundamentally different from that of the Primitive Church."[4]

But St. Paul is not to be regarded as an infallible oracle. As Anderson Scott remarks, " He did not think of himself as infallible or of his writing as infallible. In much of what he

[1] A. Powell Davies has recently attempted to resurrect the long-discarded theory that it was Paul " who first conceived the purpose of binding Israel to Athens, the dying Temple of Jerusalem with the Mithraic sacrifice, the Essenic Jehovah with the Unknown God of the Areopagus " and he " saw that Apollos, Mithras and Osiris could be made to bow before his own Hebraic Adonai, and that by absorption of their saviorhoods and blood redemptions, the Messiah of Israel could become the world-Christ." Davies maintains that " the view eventually taken of Jesus as a Redeemer was not a Judaic concept; nor was it held by the first Christians in Palestine " and " the extent of the indebtedness of Christianity to Pagan religion is so great that, provided there was a Judaic-Christian nucleus at all, very little indeed need have been supplied by the Palestinian Christians." He goes on to say that " whether it has been he (Jesus) or the Lord Mithras would have made very little difference in the redemptionist doctrines, the sacraments and observances of the church that at last declared that ' Christ ' was the Savior God." " The one essential nexus for making the Judaic Christ the victor in the struggle of salvationist religions was Paul of Tarsus. . . . But it could have happened otherwise and still have borne the name of Christianity." See The Meaning of the Dead Sea Scrolls (Signet Key book, 1956), pp. 89–92.
The truly astonishing thing is Davies' categorical assertion: " That is what the scholar knows but not the layman " (p. 92). The plain fact is that such theories of Christian origins are now completely discredited and were discarded long ago by the best biblical scholarship.
[2] A. M. Hunter, The Unity of the New Testament, p. 36.
[3] The Apostolic Preaching and its Developments, p. 13.
[4] A. M. Hunter, op. cit., p. 37.

wrote he believed he had behind him the authority of Christ or of the Holy Spirit, but not in all."[1] His utterances, like those of any other biblical writers, are frequently coloured by his prejudices, early training, environment, and the intellectual climate of his time. Furthermore, he himself is careful to distinguish between what he can declare as a commandment of Christ and what is his own opinion. When the Corinthian Church consults him on some disputed question of Christian behaviour regarding marriage and the relations of the sexes, he settles some points by citing what he calls " a commandment of the Lord " : " And unto the married I command, yet not I, but the Lord, Let not the wife depart from her husband . . . and let not the husband put away his wife " (I Corinthians vii, 10–12). On other matters he frankly points out that what he is giving is his own opinion: " I speak this by permission, and not of commandment " (I Corinthians vii, 6); " But to the rest speak I, not the Lord: If any brother hath a wife that believeth not, and she be pleased to dwell with him, let him not put her away " (I Corinthians vii, 12; cf. II Corinthians xi, 17). On at least one occasion he has to correct himself whilst writing (I Corinthians i, 14–16). He is mistaken when he questions that God cares for oxen (I Corinthians ix, 9) and " evades the true meaning of a command in Deuteronomy by allegorizing it."[2]

St. Paul's attitude to women causes a good deal of perplexity among thinking people today. What are we to say about his prohibition of women's public speaking in church, his demand that their heads be covered in worship, and his subordination of woman to man?

It must be pointed out, in the first place, that the passage in which women are forbidden to speak in church consists of only two verses (I Corinthians xiv, 34–5) which are of doubtful authenticity. In one important group of manuscripts they follow verse 40, which suggests that they may be a later interpolation and not part of the original text of the epistle. This impression is confirmed by several facts: first, the verses, as they now stand, break the flow and continuity of the chapter;

[1] *St. Paul the Man and the Teacher*, p. 67.
[2] Anderson Scott, *ibid.*, p. 68.

secondly, they are inconsistent with chapter xi, 5 ff., where Paul speaks, apparently with approval, of women praying and prophesying in church, which seems to have been the normal practice; and thirdly, in the words of Anderson Scott, " he freely acknowledges the services of women as fellow-workers in the Gospel."[1] Some scholars therefore regard these two verses as a marginal note by a later scribe which has become incorporated into the text.

Even if the passage be accepted as authentic, however—as C. H. Dodd believes it to be—it cannot, in view of chapter xi, 5 ff., be regarded as a complete prohibition of women taking an active part in the leading of public worship. We must surely conclude, with James Moffatt, that " in reality he never vetoed a devout women from exercising, even at public worship, the prophetic gift which so many women in the primitive Church enjoyed "; but that what St. Paul objected to was " a practice, evidently popular at Corinth, of matrons taking part in the discussion or interpretation of what had been said by some prophet or teacher during the service."[2]

The question of women having their heads covered in church (I Corinthians xi, 5 ff.) was, as T. T. Shore remarks " of ephemeral moment, and as we all now would regard it, of trivial importance."[3] Here in this chapter we do find the " transient-permanent " antithesis writ large. " The contrast between this piece on women's attire in worship and the following directions upon the Lord's Supper (17–34) is as dramatic as anything in Paul's correspondence. In the former he is of his age; the watermarks of contemporary prejudice are visible in arguments and conclusion. But in the next passage his message has proved to be permanent."[4]

The question here is largely one of contemporary social etiquette. Among the Greeks it was not done for a woman to appear in public unveiled. The veil was the distinctive part of a woman's dress. It was " the recognized badge of seclusion; it was the badge which proclaimed that she who wore it was a

[1] *Ibid.*, p. 133.
[2] See *The First Epistle of Paul to the Corinthians*, pp. 232–4.
[3] *I Corinthians* (*The Commentary for Schools*), p. 98.
[4] J. Moffatt, *op. cit.*, pp. 155–6.

private, not a public, person, finding her duties at home, not abroad, in one household, not in the city."[1] The absence of a veil, therefore, was a virtual repudiation of this private nature of the woman's person; it marked her out as a " public " person, a woman of easy virtue. St. Paul asserts the spiritual equality of women and men, but he is rightly anxious to ensure that the exercise of Christian freedom does not outrage the conscience of the pagan world. For a woman to take an active part in public worship unveiled was " a rash defiance of those established rules of decorum that were rooted in the feelings of the country. . . . To pray unveiled was to insult all the conventional feelings of Jew and Gentile."[2]

It frequently happens, however, that what is essentially a practical concern becomes invested with theological significance. So here, St. Paul bolsters up his requirement with a theological argument: " a woman praying or preaching bareheaded was contravening the divine order which made man supreme over her and therefore entitled alone to appear bareheaded."[3] At marriage a woman assumed the veil as a symbol of her acceptance of her husband as her head and of her dependence upon him. She must therefore display this sign of her husband's authority when in church she joined in worship " with angels and archangels and with all the company of heaven," lest by appearing to defy the divine order of creation she incite the heavenly beings to transgress that order as did the angels who cohabited with women in the story of Genesis vi.

This apparently trivial matter will serve to show the kind of discrimination which is necessary in dealing with the Bible. In some things here we must acknowledge quite frankly that St. Paul was wrong; not merely that his statements were " time-conditioned." As Ernest Evans remarks, " Some of his reasons will hardly appeal to a generation whose male ancestors two centuries ago wore long hair, and which has raised no objection to women being shorn; nor will his arguments from the Old Testament have much weight with those who find difficulty

---

[1] Marcus Dods, *The First Epistle to the Corinthians*, p. 247.
[2] F. W. Robertson, *Expository Lectures on St. Paul's Epistles to the Corinthians*, pp. 161–2.   [3] J. Moffatt, *op. cit.*, p. 151.

in attaching any historical value to the stories of the creation of woman (Genesis ii) and of the fall of the angels (Genesis vi)."[1] Most educated Christians, therefore, would agree with C. H. Dodd's observation[2] that when Paul says a woman should have ἐξουσία on her head διὰ τοὺς ἀγγέλους he is just plain wrong, whether for the first century or for the twentieth.

When, however, he links the question with civilized usage, in order to avoid offending the conscience of the pagan world,[3] he is saying something which *on that level* is still true in principle, though " time-conditioned " in application and not therefore directly applicable today. He is declaring that the Christian woman " appears as a woman with certain social relations. Her relation to Christ does not dissolve her relations to society. Rather does it intensify them."[4] " Although there is in Christ an absolute levelling of distinctions . . . yet these distinctions remain and are valid in society. A woman is a woman still though she become a Christian."[5] T. C. Edwards sums up this aspect of the question in a sentence when he says, " The Apostle maintains the perfect consistency of personal equality and social subordination, and shows that Christianity conse-crates both to the service of Christ, by elevating personal into spiritual equality and converting social difference into Church order."[6]

On the deepest level the truth is that in Christ there is neither male nor female, as St. Paul himself maintains in Galatians iii, 28. This underlies his assertion here of men and women being essential to one another in the Lord which Moffatt describes as " the one lasting sentence in the whole discourse."[7] But to attempt to apply that truth on *every* level would put an end to civilization; indeed, its literal application on the biological plane would lead to race suicide.

[1] *Corinthians*, The Clarendon Bible, p. 116.
[2] In a letter to me from Cambridge dated April 22nd, 1953.
[3] See T. T. Shore, *op. cit.*, p. 99: " In ruling that men taking part in religious ceremonies are to have their heads *uncovered*, St. Paul puts aside his Jewish prejudice in favour of the Greek practice which was the national custom of the country."   [4] Marcus Dods, *op. cit.*, p. 249.
[5] *Ibid.*, p. 257.
[6] *A Commentary on the First Epistle to the Corinthians*, p. 272.
[7] *Op. cit.*, p. 153.

3. *The Teaching of Jesus*

The norm of truth in the Bible is Christ himself. It is by reference to Him that all its diverse contents must be judged. The test of truth is to be found in Him who is the Way, the Truth and the Life. Hence the teaching of Jesus has final and absolute authority. " In His life and words will be found the standard and norm of Christian behaviour "[1] and " no doctrine concerning Him which fails to take full account of the things He said Himself can satisfy Christian faith."[2]

The teaching of Jesus, however, is not to be examined in isolation; it is vitally and indefeasibly associated with who He is and what He came to do. It must be seen, therefore, in relation to His Person and Work. As Dale reminds us, " He came not to preach the Gospel, but that there might be a Gospel to preach." Hence a statement like that of W. A. Curtis that " the Teaching of Jesus, with the Spirit which it breathes, remains the charter of the Church's liberty, the savour of its Gospel, and the essence of its faith "[3] must be treated with caution. The essence of the Church's faith is to be found not in the teaching of Jesus but in what He has done for us men and for our salvation. It is not His sayings which constitute the Gospel but His Incarnation and Death and Resurrection. " Great teacher that He was," says Archdeacon Harrison, "our Lord was not primarily a teacher. He was the Word made flesh, and therefore both the embodiment and the preacher of the saving activity of God."[4] " What Jesus says is, if not meaningless, at least useless, apart from what Jesus is. His teaching is wholly concerned with life in the Kingdom of God: but men and women come into the Kingdom as Peter did at Caesarea Philippi, by accepting the Lordship of Jesus."[5] Nevertheless the teaching of Jesus is of supreme importance and Christians " have the commands of the Lord Jesus Christ Himself graven upon their hearts."[6] As Cave observes, " He cannot be understood merely as a teacher. And yet that teaching may not be ignored."[7]

[1] T. W. Manson, *The Mission and Message of Jesus*, p. 301.
[2] W. A. Curtis, *Jesus Christ the Teacher*, p. 13.   [3] *Ibid.*, p. 205.
[4] D. E. W. Harrison, *Christian Ethics and the Gospel*, p. 10.
[5] *Ibid.*, p. 13.   [6] Aristides, *Apology*,
[7] S. Cave, *The Christian Way*, p. 44.

It is in this perspective that the Sermon on the Mount is to be seen. It is not the Gospel: " For the primitive Church the central thing is the Cross on the Hill rather than the Sermon on the Mount."[1] Neither is it a new law in the sense in which we usually understand the term. Laws are determined by the moral standards and capacities of those for whom they are made; they are based on the assumption that their requirements are reasonable and that they will be kept.[2] But what man is sufficient for this ethic of perfection? " It is a mistake," says T. W. Manson, " to regard the ethical teaching of Jesus as a ' New Law ' in the sense of a reformed and simplified exposition of the Old, or as a code of rules to take the place of the code of Moses and his successors. What Jesus offers in his ethical teaching is not a set of rules of conduct, but a number of illustrations of the way in which a transformed character will express itself in conduct."[3] His purpose is " to introduce principles of conduct which would gradually supersede the necessity of legal restraints."[4] Indeed, the Sermon on the Mount is " the *reductio ad absurdum* of the whole legal conception of God's relationship with men."[5] It is not therefore to be regarded as a programme of social action, a blueprint for Utopia, which may instantly be put into general practice, as Tolstoy thought.[6]

We cannot properly understand the Sermon on the Mount unless we realize that it is bound up in a threefold relationship. In the first place, it is related, as we have seen, to the Person and Work of the Teacher. The author of St. Matthew's Gospel portrays this scene in a way that could not fail to remind his Jewish readers of the Giving of the Law at Mount Sinai: Jesus is represented as the New Moses giving a New Law to the New Israel. But the contrast as well as the similarity of the two occasions is clear. Not only is the New Law not " law " at all in the strict sense of the word; it is given with an authority which is direct and unmediated: " Ye have heard

---

[1] T. W. Manson, *op. cit.*, p. 301.
[2] See A. D. Lindsay, *The Moral Teaching of Jesus*, pp. 96 ff.
[3] *The Teaching of Jesus*, p. 301.
[4] H. B. Swete, *Studies in the Teaching of Our Lord*, p. 30.
[5] S. Cave, *op. cit.*, p. 61.
[6] See Leo Tolstoy, *Christ's Christianity*, Part II, " What I Believe."

that it was said . . ." is contrasted with, " But I say unto you. . . ."
" The distinguishing note of His teaching was ' authority '
(ἐξουσία), not so much unusual capacity as the consciousness of a Divine right to teach."[1] It was given with " the
irresistible force of a Divine message, delivered under the
sense of a Divine mission."[2]

Secondly, the Sermon is related to the central theme of
the teaching of Jesus—the Kingdom of God which Wendt
describes as " an ideal religious relation of fellowship between
God and man."[3] As C. H. Dodd maintains, " The implied
major premiss of all His ethical sayings is the affirmation ' The
Kingdom of God has come upon you,' "[4] and the subject of the
Sermon on the Mount " is neither righteousness, nor yet the
New Law (if such designation be proper in regard to what is in
no real sense a Law), but that which was innermost and uppermost in the mind of Christ—the Kingdom of God."[5] The
Sermon describes the quality of life peculiar to the Kingdom:
this is how men and women live together under the sovereign
rule of God. It implies a community which acknowledges the
divine sovereignty by submitting to the Lordship of Christ and
living in dependence upon His grace.

In the third place, then, the Sermon on the Mount is related
to the Church; it is addressed not to the multitudes but to
the disciples (Matthew v, 1–2), although Matthew vii, 28,
implies that others listened to it. As Gore says, " It was spoken
to the Church, not to the world; . . . it was spoken into the
ear of the Church and overheard by the world."[6] The character
of the Sermon thus becomes clear: it " is essentially *disciple-
teaching*, teaching for those who, though they must live in this
world, have their true citizenship elsewhere."[7] " It was given
as a way of life for the men of the Kingdom, not for mankind at

---

[1] H. B. Swete, *Studies in the Teaching of our Lord*, p. 18.
[2] *Ibid.*, p. 19; cf. J. Denney, *Jesus and the Gospel*, p. 245: " The sovereign
legislative authority which breathes throughout the Sermon on the Mount
stands absolutely alone in scripture."
[3] H. H. Wendt, *The Teaching of Jesus*, p. 393.
[4] *History and the Gospel*, p. 125.
[5] A. Edersheim, *The Life and Times of Jesus the Messiah*, i, p. 528.
[6] C. Gore, *The Sermon on the Mount*, pp. 15–16.
[7] A. M. Hunter, *The Work and Words of Jesus*, p. 67.

large."[1] The teaching concerning the Rule of God is given to those who constitute the Realm of God. These two things— Rule and Realm—are correlative since, as H. H. Rowley remarks, the Kingdom " embraced the idea of a new world era, in which God should rule over men and His will be embodied in their life, but the totality of those who accepted His rule would form His realm."[2]

The Sermon on the Mount is thus, in C. H. Dodd's phrase, " a design for life in the kingdom of God."[3] " What Jesus does is to set before men the character, the transformed character of the citizens of God's Kingdom, not by negative enactments, or even literal enactments at all, but by principles embodied in proverbs which must be apprehended in their inner spirit; by illustrations of how transformed character expresses itself in action. Our Lord does not require us to do such and such things, but to be this kind of people."[4]

There are two approaches to the problem of ethics: the legalist way attempts to determine character by regulating conduct; the prophetic way regards right conduct as the fruit of a transformed character. The former was the method of Judaism, the latter the teaching of Jesus. " For Judaism good conduct is a part of religion; for Jesus it is a product of religion."[5] " He refuses to legislate, because He is concerned with the springs of conduct rather than with the outward acts. . . . For Jesus all legal questions, all questions of behaviour, all questions about the relations of man to man, are questions of character, questions affecting, not merely the life and property, but the souls of the persons concerned; and therefore they are at bottom religious questions in the strictest sense, questions concerning the relation of the individual soul to God and to God's Kingdom and righteousness."[6]

There is a complete lack of casuistry in the Gospels. We find there no explicit directions for Christian conduct such as are

[1] A. M. Hunter, *Design for Life*, p. 109.
[2] *An Outline of the Teaching of Jesus*, p. 13.
[3] Quoted by A. M. Hunter, *The Work and Words of Jesus*, p. 64.
[4] D. E. W. Harrison, *Christian Ethics and the Gospel*, p. 18.
[5] T. W. Manson, *The Teaching of Jesus*, p. 305; cf. D. E. W. Harrison, *op. cit.*, p. 18: " The pre-requisite of right conduct is a change of heart."
[6] T. W. Manson, *The Teaching of Jesus*, pp. 301–2.

given in the Epistles. Jesus consistently refuses to legislate for precise situations; He lays down certain guiding principles and leaves men to apply them to their own situation. This is His characteristic method and we have no reason to believe that He ever departed from it. What B. W. Bacon says of the Sermon on the Mount applies equally to the teaching of Jesus as a whole: it " is not legislative, but prophetic. It does not enact but interprets. It does not lay down rules, but opens up principles."[1]   Christ will not do men's thinking for them, neither will He judge for them in their moral choices. He " insists that men must perceive the real issues themselves and decide for themselves."[2]

That is why Jesus gave so much of His instruction in the form of parables, which C. H. Dodd describes as the most characteristic element in His teaching.[3] " He sets up before us aspects of real life, not asking in the first place whether this or that action is to be morally approved or reprobated, but noting that men do as a matter of fact so and so—the shepherd seeks his sheep; the pearl-merchant knows a good bargain when he sees it; people often do a service not out of pure kindliness but to save themselves trouble; clever rogues use their advantages without scruple and profit by it. We are asked simply to observe that life is like that. When we have looked at life as it is, then the meaning of the parable suggests itself to the mind."[4] Thus the parables, by portraying some critical situation demanding action, are intended to tease the minds of the hearers into active thought and challenge them to pass a judgment upon the situation portrayed. " Was the peasant a fool to impoverish himself for the sake of buying the field? Was it unpardonable rashness in the merchant to realize all his assets to buy a single pearl? At first sight, yes. But to know when to plunge makes the successful financier. Only, you must feel quite sure of the value of the property you are buying."[5]

The parables, like the Sermon on the Mount, are related to the central theme of Christ's ministry—the Kingdom of God.

---

[1] *The Sermon on the Mount*, p. 109.
[2] D. E. W. Harrison, *op. cit.*, p. 13.
[3] See C. H. Dodd, *The Parables of the Kingdom*.
[4] C. H. Dodd, *The Authority of the Bible*, pp. 147–8.
[5] C. H. Dodd, *The Parables of the Kingdom*, pp. 112–3.

But whereas the teaching of the Sermon on the Mount was given to the inner circle of disciples, the parables are spoken to the mixed multitude with the object of evoking repentance and faith. Those who respond are received into the inner circle where they receive more explicit teaching concerning the Messiah and the Kingdom: " To him that hath shall be given and he shall have abundance." By thus separating the responsive hearers from the unresponsive the parable becomes, not only a mode of preaching the Kingdom of God, but also a test for admittance to discipleship.

Since their object is to evoke both repentance and faith, the Gospel parables, like those of the Old Testament, fall into two distinct classes:[1] some—like the Two Sons, the Pharisee and the Publican, the Good Samaritan, and the Rich Fool— present a type of human conduct in such a way that a direct appeal is made to the conscience calling for repentance; others—like the Hidden Treasure or the Pearl of Great Price, the Labourers in the Vineyard, the Lost Sheep or the Lost Coin, the Mustard Seed, and the Leaven—set forth some principle or aspect of God's government so as to appeal to the religious insight of the hearers with the object of evoking faith. There is, however, a group of parables—such as the Vineyard, the Talents, the Great Feast, and the Prodigal Son—which combine a type of human conduct and a principle of divine government and so call for a response of both repentance and faith. In each of these three groups there is portrayed " in vivid and variable imagery the arrival of a ' zero hour ' in human experience."[2] All the parables " depict the ministry of Jesus Christ as the great moment when the relations between God and man were put on a new footing, when the great moral issues could no longer be shirked, and when the possibilities of human life were indefinitely enlarged."[3] They thus challenge men to decision.

" The greatest teachers," says F. H. Ballard, " usually have only a few things to say, though they say them in such a variety of ways that there is no monotony in the repetition."[4]

---

[1] See T. W. Manson, *The Teaching of Jesus*, p. 57 ff.
[2] C. H. Dodd, *Gospel and Law*, p. 56.   [3] *Ibid.*, p. 58.
[4] *The Desire of all Nations*, p. 25.

This is certainly true of Jesus. On many great themes He is silent. We never find Him arguing for the existence and sovereignty of God, for example, or for social righteousness. He had no need to: His hearers, being Jews, were well schooled in the Old Testament and He could at least presuppose its high religious and moral teaching. And when we examine the content of His own teaching we find little that is really new. Much is anticipated in the sayings of Plato, Seneca, Buddha, Lao Tsze and the Stoics, to say nothing of the Jewish Fathers.[1] Klausner, indeed, maintains that " *throughout the Gospels there is not one item of ethical teaching which cannot be paralleled either in the Old Testament, the Apocrypha, or in the Talmudic and Midrashic literature of the period near to the time of Jesus.*"[2] That this is too sweeping a statement other Jewish scholars like Montefiore would admit,[3] and even Klausner has later to allow that " there is a new thing in the Gospels " which stamps all their ethical teachings with a peculiar hallmark, and that " a man like Jesus . . . was something hitherto unheard of in the Judaism of the day."[4] Even so, Sanday's description of the teaching of Jesus as " the distilled essence of the Old Testament "[5] is not far short of the mark.

This, however, in no way detracts from the originality of Christ's teaching. As A. M. Hunter reminds us, " originality is not a matter of utter newness but rather the power of seeing old things in a new light. . . . It is not a case of wiping the slate clean and beginning *de novo*, as though all that had been said and thought by man about God and man and good and evil had

---

[1] Cf. C. Gore, *The Sermon on the Mount*, pp. 6–7: " Christ is the Word; and it is through fellowship in the Word, who is also the Reason of God, that all men are rational. Christ, therefore, is the light which in conscience and reason lightens every man from end to end of history." Hence, " the whole moral development of mankind, the whole moral education of the human race, is of one piece from end to end. There moves in it the same Spirit, there expresses itself the same Word."

[2] *Jesus of Nazareth*, p. 384.

[3] See Montefiore, *The Beginnings of Christianity*, i, p. 79: " The summons not to wait till they meet you in your sheltered and orderly path, but to go forth and seek out and redeem the sinner and the fallen, the passion to heal and bring back to God the wretched and the outcast—all this I do not find in Rabbinism; *that* form of love seems lacking."

[4] *Op. cit.*, p. 389.

[5] W. Sanday, *Outlines of the Life of Christ*, p. 66.

been false and futile. It is rather the power to take the old truth, to transform it, to perfect it: to turn the lead into gold, the carbon into diamond, and in so doing to discard much that was accidental, transient and for a day."[1]   Over the teaching of Jesus there might be written the motto of a North of England college: *Non nova sed novae*.

It will be obvious that Chris'ts teaching, as the norm of Christian faith and life, needs to be seen in its true historical perspective. Jesus was an Oriental, a Jew of the first century; not a Westerner of the twentieth.[2] The conditions in which He lived and taught were vastly different from those of Britain or Australia today. " He addressed Jews who had no responsibility for the government of their land and who lived in an agrarian society quite unlike the complex industrial order in which we live."[3]   Hence we look in vain to His words for explicit directions concerning many of the burning questions of the modern world. Indeed His teaching as a whole, high and searching as it is, may seem at first sight to bear little relationship to some of the problems which perplex us most.[4] What does Jesus think about an industrial combine, or a lottery? What is His attitude to birth control, and euthanasia, and compulsory trade unionism? Would He approve of the sterling block or the Pacific Pact? The plain fact is that the

---

[1] *Design for Life*, pp. 22–3.
[2] This fact has a bearing upon Christ's use of current Jewish ideas and phraseology. Cf. Sanday, *Inspiration*, p. 419: " Is there not what we might perhaps call a *neutral zone* among our Lord's sayings? Sayings, I mean, in which He takes up ideas and expressions current at the time and uses without really endorsing them." Even so conservative a scholar as Professor G. C. Aalders admits this in connection with the New Testament references to " Moses and the prophets ": " In such phraseology our Lord Jesus Christ and His apostles follow the usage of the Jews; they call the Pentateuch simply by the name generally employed in their day. . . . Such common parlance, which does not aim at scientific accuracy, has nothing to do with the personal opinion of those who make use of it." *A Short Introduction to the Pentateuch*, pp. 139–40.   [3] S. Cave, *The Christian Way*, p. 32.
[4] Cf. Shirley Jackson Case, *The Social Triumph of the Ancient Church*, p. 12: " There is a wide range of social tasks that were but dimly, if at all, perceived in ancient times. However loyal the individual may be to the Christian heritage, he frequently finds it deficient as a guide to all his conduct when he is faced with the more crucial issues of the present. Even the problems of personal conduct have taken on many new aspects in the history of social evolution since the time of Jesus."

ethic of Jesus " has nothing to say about the relativities of politics and economics, nor of the necessary balances of power which exist and must exist in even the most intimate social relationships. . . . It does not establish a connection with the horizontal points of a political or social ethic or with the diagonals which a prudential individual ethic draws between the moral ideal and the facts of a given situation. It has only a vertical dimension between the loving will of God and the will of man."[1]

This does not mean, however, that it is irrelevant in the modern world; it does mean that it may not be used as a rule of thumb. It must be applied with spiritual insight and moral earnestness and in humble dependence upon the guidance of the Spirit of Truth. It had so to be applied to their own situation by the people to whom it was first given; it must be similarly applied to our situation today. Jesus, says Gore, " teaches in a way which leaves us a great deal to do for ourselves, and requires of us a great deal of moral thoughtfulness."[2]

The significance of the teaching of Jesus for the modern man is threefold. In the first place, it discloses an absolute standard at which we are to aim and by which we are judged—" the unattainable which yet we are bound to attain."[3] This is the divine intention for man, realized in the Person of Him who proclaims it, and this alone is relevant for those who acknowledge the sovereign rule of God. Such a standard, as Dodd points out, is " not defined in general and abstract propositions, but in dramatic pictures of action in concrete situations." It is " intended to appeal to the conscience by way of the imagination."[4]

In the second place, the teaching of Jesus is a signpost which indicates the direction in which human life moves when it is submitted to the Lordship of Christ. Direction is more

[1] Reinhold Niebuhr, *An Interpretation of Christian Ethics*, p. 49.
[2] C. Gore, *The Sermon on the Mount*, p. 61.
[3] W. Manson, *Jesus the Messiah*, p. 87. Cf. R. Niebuhr, *op. cit.*, p. 130. " In Christian theology, at its best, the revelation of Christ, the God-man, is a revelation of the paradoxical relation of the eternal to history, which it is the genius of mythical-prophetic religion to emphasize. Christ is thus the revelation of the very impossible possibility which the Sermon on the Mount elaborates in ethical terms."   [4] C. H. Dodd, *Gospel and Law*, p. 61.

important than attainment. A person's character may be very imperfect, but if his life is moving in the direction of the divine perfection it will approximate more and more closely to its goal. This interrelation of direction and character is finely stated by A. D. Lindsay: " On any road you take from inner desire," he says, " you will not get what you want without becoming a different person in the process."[1] Hence " Jesus supplied, not so much new ethical precepts, as a new *direction* to the ethical life of man, and invested it with a new power."[2]

Thirdly, Christ gives us " not literal enactments, but rather principles or motives for action."[3] This is a point which we have already noted in another connection. It underlies both the universality and the timelessness of the teaching of Jesus. " Vast as it is in its significance, and wide as it is in its range, it rests on principles which are intellectually simple to grasp, but spiritually profound and challenging."[4] Jesus sums up the whole duty of man in the words of two great Old Testament passages: " Thou shalt love the Lord thy God with all thy heart, and with all thy soul, and with all thy mind, and with all thy strength " and " Thou shalt love thy neighbour as thyself " (Mark xii, 28–31; cf. Deuteronomy vi, 4–5, and Leviticus xix, 18). To these He adds the Golden Rule: All things whatsoever ye would that men should do to you, do ye even so to them " (Matthew vii, 12) which A. M. Hunter describes as the capstone to the Sermon on the Mount.[5] It must be emphasized, however, that these principles are not the Gospel; rather they themselves spring out of the Gospel. They are the response by man to what God in Christ has done for man.[6] The divine imperative of the Law of Love arises out of the divine indicative of the Gospel of Love: we love because He first loved us. " The practice of the Golden Rule springs out of love for one's

[1] *The Moral Teaching of Jesus*, p. 66.
[2] L. H. Marshall, *The Challenge of New Testament Ethics*, p. 8.
[3] C. Gore, *op. cit.*, p. 109.
[4] H. H. Rowley, *An Outline of the Teaching of Jesus*, p. 44.
[5] *Design for Life*, p. 86.
[6] See C. H. Dodd, *op. cit.*, p. 83: " The Christian ethic, in short, can as little make itself good in the world apart from the Gospel as the Gospel can be understood apart from its ethical implications."

neighbour; and love for one's neighbour out of love for God; and that love is man's response to God's prior love."[1]

There are two practical issues upon which especially modern Christians are divided in their interpretation and application of the teaching of Christ—military service and divorce.

(1) *Military Service.* The Lambeth Conference of 1930 states categorically that " war is incompatible with the life and teaching of our Lord Jesus Christ," and H. E. Fosdick calls it " the world's greatest collective sin." What, then, should be the Christian's attitude when he is called upon to bear arms or train for military service? Some, on the basis of the Sermon on the Mount, take the pacifist position and maintain that Christ's word, " But I say unto you, That ye resist not evil " (Matthew v, 39) precludes the Christian from taking any part in military service. Others hold the traditional view of the Church as stated in Article XXXVII of the Anglican *Articles of Religion*: " It is lawful for Christian men, at the commandment of the Magistrate, to wear weapons, and serve in the wars."

On the face of it, this saying of Christ about non-resistance seems to support the pacifist's case. Several factors need to be taken into account, however. In the first place, we must remember that Jesus is not laying down a piece of general legislation which is applicable to every situation; He is concerned with personal relationships in which His disciples are involved. This is clear from the concrete examples which He cites:

> The principle therefore which He enunciates is that of *non-retaliation in cases of personal wrong*, and He drives it home with four picturesque illustrations. One is a personal assault; another, a suit at law; a third, an official demand; and the fourth, a request for help. Interpret these illustrations as laws to be obeyed to the letter, and we miss the point. Literal obedience to them would only result in violence, robbery and anarchy. For Jesus is here talking to disciples, and speaking of personal relations: He is not

[1] H. H. Rowley, *op. cit.*, pp. 29–30. Cf. R. Niebuhr, *Why the Christian Church is not Pacifist*, p. 8: " The good news of the Gospel is not the law that we ought to love one another. The good news of the Gospel is that there is a resource of divine mercy which is able to overcome the contradiction within our own souls, which we cannot ourselves overcome."

laying down moral directions for states and nations, and such issues as the work of the police or the question of a defensive war are simply not in His mind.[1]

Secondly, we must beware of over-simplifying the problem of moral choices in a world which does not acknowledge the sovereign rule of God. Non-retaliation in the case of a malicious personal wrong is one thing: our attitude as Christian citizens towards deliberate national aggression is another. The moral dilemma of the Christian results from the fact that he is faced with a choice between evils. It is not a simple question of choosing between black and white but between different shades of grey. And sometimes war, terrible as it is, may be the lesser of two evils. This was clearly the situation in the second world war. The choice was between resisting Nazi Germany in the only way that a nation can be resisted—by force of arms— or capitulating to a system which enslaved not only the bodies but the minds and souls of men. An Allied victory—in spite of all the moral and physical devastation involved—did at least make possible the continuance of a civilization shaped by centuries of Christian teaching: an unresisted Nazi advance would have plunged Europe into a new Dark Age.

Thirdly, we must avoid confusing individual and social ethics. The Christian is a citizen as well as a churchman and as such he has a responsibility to the society to which he belongs. Our Lord's word concerning non-resistance to evil means that " we are to be ready not to give up our public concern for law, but to modify our private resentments. We are to go a long way in not standing up for our rights at those times when without danger to society we are free to do so."[2]

But in addition to our personal relationships with other individuals as members of a society, we exist in national groups each of which functions as a whole with its own sense of solidarity and its own collective responsibility. Now group or social ethics are not in all respects identical with individual ethics. As Jessop reminds us, " We, like all other peoples, believe that the State may rightly do what the individual may not rightly do, e.g. that it may take people's money away

---

[1] A. M. Hunter, *Design for Life*, pp. 53–4.
[2] A. D. Lindsay, *The Moral Teaching of Jesus*, pp. 104–5.

whether they want to give it or no (in taxation), and that it may deprive wrongdoers of estate and liberty."[1] The State exists in the providence of God for the preservation of law and order and the promotion of the welfare of its members. It must therefore resist whatever makes for anarchy and disorder and suppress, if needs be by force, whatever threatens its members' welfare. It is " a servant and instrument of God for the preservation of justice."[2] But the actions of the State are the collective responsibility of the individuals who compose it and on whose allegiance and obedience it has a lawful claim. Hence, as Gore maintains, " when our own personal feeling has been utterly suppressed, then it is quite possible that another duty, the duty of justice, the duty of maintaining the social order, may come into prominence again."[3]

Christ Himself recognized the lawful claims of the State upon the individual: Caesar, as well as God, must be given his rightful due.[4] Nor was He indifferent to social justice: every possible effort must be made to bring home to the offending brother his fault;[5] and He Himself at His trial before the high priest claims justice from the officer who strikes Him.[6]

" We observe therefore," says Gore, " two opposite duties. There is the clear duty, so far as mere personal feeling goes, of simple self-effacement. Only then, when we have got our own wills thoroughly subordinated to God's will, when all the wild instinct of revenge is subdued, are we in a position to consider the other duty and to ask ourselves what the maintenance of the moral order of society may require of us."[7]

(2) *Divorce.* " The crisis in marriage," says Emil Brunner, " presents the Christian ethic with the most serious and the most difficult problem with which a Christian ethic has to deal. . . . What an ethic has to say on *this* question shows whether it is any use or not."[8] On the sanctity of marriage and its ideal of a lifelong union of one man and one woman, all Christians

---

[1] T. E. Jessop, *Social Ethics: Christian and Natural,* p. 43.
[2] W. Temple, *Citizen and Churchman,* p. 36; cf. Romans, xiii, 1–4.
[3] C. Gore, *The Sermon on the Mount,* pp. 89–90.
[4] Mark, xii, 14–17.   [5] Matthew xviii, 15–17.
[6] John xviii, 22–3.   [7] *Op. cit.,* p. 91.
[8] *The Divine Imperative,* p. 341.

are agreed; on the possibility of its dissolution, however, should the marriage break down, Christian opinion is sharply divided. Broadly speaking, Catholics—both Roman and Anglican—maintain that marriage, once validly contracted, can be dissolved only by the death of one of the partners. Divorce is therefore a contradiction in terms and the remarriage of one partner, during the lifetime of the other, adultery. In practice, however, the Roman Church, though not recognizing divorce, has shown great ingenuity in finding grounds for declaring a broken marriage null and void. Protestants, on the other hand, while acknowledging the possibility of divorce in certain circumstances, vary considerably in the extent to which they recognize grounds for it other than infidelity.[1]

The precise attitude of Jesus to the question of divorce is not nearly so clear as some " Catholic " theologians would have us believe. Such records as we have of His teaching on this matter present certain ambiguities when taken as a whole, so that it is not easy to decide whether He is speaking of divorce *per se* or divorce on certain assumed grounds. The extent to which His discussions were related, directly or indirectly, to contemporary happenings and disputes must be taken into account. Again, was Jesus laying down a general principle for human relationships among those who acknowledge the rule of God? or was He " legislating " for a particular time and place?—or for all time? Even if we are able to reach certain conclusions regarding the precise meaning of His words, are we justified in applying literally what was said in the context of a first-century Palestinian society, in which women had little independent status, to our twentieth-century industrial society in which men and women meet on equal terms?

Christ's teaching on divorce is found in two primary Synoptic sources—Mark and the Sayings Document " Q." In the former it is given in reply to a test question of the Pharisees (Mark x, 2–12). St. Matthew, as we shall see, expands this Marcan account but alters substantially the form of the question (Matthew xix, 3–12). The " Q " teaching is given by St. Matthew in the context of the Sermon on the Mount

---

[1] The Eastern Orthodox Churches allow divorce and remarriage on certain grounds other than adultery.

(Matthew v, 31–2) and by St. Luke in another context after a saying about the permanence of the law (Luke xvi, 18).

We shall look first of all at the Marcan account of the discussion with the Pharisees and its expansion in St. Matthew's Gospel. According to St. Mark, the question of the Pharisees was simply: " Is it lawful for a man to put away his wife? " The issue raised is that of divorce in principle: is it, or is it not, permissible? It was a test question (πειράζοντες αὐτόν) intended to elicit from Jesus an answer calculated to discredit His teaching. As T. W. Manson points out, the same verb is used in the Septuagint translation of I Kings x, 1, for the questioning of Solomon by the Queen of Sheba.[1] F. C. Burkitt calls attention to the significance of the contemporary background of the discussion—the recent divorce by Herod Antipas of his Arabian wife in order to marry Herodias who had herself divorced her husband Philip, the half-brother of Antipas.[2] The protest of John the Baptist had cost him his life. " Jesus in the eyes of many was first and foremost the successor of the Baptist. For months He had been in hiding; now He was again upon the scene, and the question about Divorce could not fail to draw from Him a decisive pronouncement."[3] Christ's reply, as reported in Mark, " clearly implies a reference to Herodias, a reference which is singularly appropriate in the time and place."[4]

According to Jewish law, the right of divorce belonged only to the husband: " it seems as if the husband, without further ado, can dissolve the marriage—whereas we hear nothing of women possessing the same freedom."[5] Herodias, it appears, had taken advantage of the Roman procedure which allowed

---

[1] See *The Teaching of Jesus*, p. 292, note 4.
[2] See Mark vi, 17–18; Matthew, xiv, 3–4; Luke iii, 19. Cf. Josephus, *Antiquities*, XVIII, v, 4.
[3] F. C. Burkitt, *The Gospel History and its Transmission*, pp. 98–9.
[4] *Ibid.*, p. 101.
[5] J. Pedersen, *Israel*, I-II, p. 71. While the present work has been in the press, S. B. Gurewicz has sent me a copy of his article, " Divorce in Jewish Law," in which he points out that by the Talmudic period, and by means of an interesting legal fiction, " provision was made whereby the wife could petition for a divorce, and the husband was then compelled by the courts to issue a ' Get ' (i.e. Bill of Divorcement) to his wife." See *Res Judicatae*, Vol. 7, No. 4 (The Journal of the Law School of Melbourne).

women the right of divorce.[1] Jesus, as was expected, appeals first of all to the Law: " What did Moses command you? " In reply, they cite the provision of Deuteronomy xxiv, 1–4, which permitted the husband to dissolve the marriage by giving to the wife a bill of divorcement. Jesus then points out that this Deuteronomic legislation was merely a concession to human weakness and appeals behind it to the divine ideal of a permanent, lifelong union of man and woman in marriage, as portrayed in the Genesis creation story.[2] This, and not the Deuteronomic concession, represents the divine intention for man.

Christ's reply to the private enquiry of the disciples, which follows the discussion, is significant because He puts the two sexes on exactly the same level. This was something unheard of before among the Jews. Just as the man could divorce the woman but not the woman the man, so the woman could commit adultery against the man but not the man against the woman. " The operation of both of these principles was entirely one-sided; that is to say, there was no such thing as adultery of the husband against his wife, and a wife had no power to divorce her husband."[3] According to Jewish law, " a husband retains full liberty of intercourse with women other than his wife; he does not thereby commit adultery. . . . He cannot sin against his own marriage, but only against the marriage of another man, whereas the wife sins only against her own; that is to say, we can only speak of adultery by a man in so far as, by intercourse with another man's wife, he inter-feres with that man's marriage."[4] Thus, as A. M. Hunter points out, " the new feature in Jesus' reply is His declaration that a husband can commit adultery against his wife."[5]

[1] Her great-aunt Salome had done this. See Josephus, *Antiquities*, XV, vii, 10.

[2] A close, and indeed unique, verbal parallel to this appeal of Jesus to the Genesis creation story is found in the *Damascus Document* or *Zadokite Work*, fragments of which appear among the Qumran texts. Here the covenanters are warned against " taking two wives during their lifetime, whereas the basic principle of the creation is, ' male and female He created them.' " But the similarity is only verbal, since the passage is concerned not with divorce but with polygamy.   [3] D. R. Mace, *Hebrew Marriage*, p. 241.

[4] A. Bertholet, *History of Hebrew Civilization*, p. 154.

[5] *The Gospel According to St. Mark* (Torch Bible Commentaries), p. 100.

It is only in St. Mark's account that the woman's offence is mentioned, and in the Old Syriac version and one of the Greek manuscripts she is mentioned first. It may well be, as Burkitt suggests, that we have here, not an addition to the words of Jesus based on Roman law, as Schmiedel thinks, but a primitive feature of St. Mark's Gospel—an allusion, indeed, to Herodias' desertion of her husband in order to marry Herod Antipas.[1] " There are certain variations of order and wording in the transmitted text of these words, but all MSS and versions agree in the main point, which is, that the woman that deserts her husband to marry someone else is blamed as well as the man who divorces his wife."[2]

According to the Marcan account, then, Jesus regards marriage as one of the Orders of Creation which is intended by God as the union of husband and wife in an unbreakable relationship that takes precedence over even the closest natural ties. In the divine intention " the man in the image of God is not an individual, but a society of two."[3] Divorce and remarriage therefore—by either the man or the woman—is a frustration of the divine intention and as such is equivalent to adultery.

In St. Matthew's account, the whole complexion of the discussion is changed by the different form of the question put to Christ. It is not just, " Is it lawful for a man to put away his wife? " but, " Is it lawful for a man to put away his wife *for every cause* ? "—which is a different matter. The additional clause links the discussion with a contemporary debate between two rabbinical schools—the school of Shammai and the school of Hillel. Both based their teaching on the legislation of Deuteronomy xxiv, 1 ff.: " When a man taketh a wife, and marrieth her, then it shall be, if she find no favour in his eyes, because he hath found some unseemly thing in her, that he shall write her a bill of divorcement, and give it in her hand, and send her out of his house. And when she is departed out of his house, she may go and be another man's wife."[4] The point at

---

[1] It must be remembered that St. Mark's Gospel was written in Rome for Roman Christians.   [2] F. C. Burkitt, *op. cit.*, p. 100.

[3] S. Cave, *The Christian Way*, p. 189.

[4] It is noteworthy that Jesus corrects the Pharisees' ἐνετείλατο to ἐπέτρεψεν (Matthew xix, 7–8): Moses *allowed* divorce; he did not *command* it.

issue between them was the interpretation of the " unseemly
thing " which caused the wife to " find no favour " in her
husband's eyes. The school of Shammai restricted its meaning
to infidelity; that of Hillel widened it to include trivial matters
such as bad temper and " letting his food burn." Rabbi
Akiba goes so far as to say, " Even if he finds another woman
more beautiful than her, for it is said: ' It shall be if she find no
favour in his eyes.' "[1] The question, therefore, according to the
Matthaean account, is not the permissibility of divorce as such
but the grounds of divorce. That a wife's infidelity is a valid
ground is taken for granted; was it also permissible " for every
cause "? In other words, did Jesus side with Hillel or
Shammai?

In line with this general tenor of the discussion is the exception which St. Matthew inserts into Christ's pronouncement:
" Whosoever shall put away his wife, *except it be for fornication*,
and shall marry another, committeth adultery; and whoso
marrieth her which is put away doth commit adultery "
(Matthew xix, 9). The precise meaning of this " excepting
clause," μὴ ἐπὶ πορνείᾳ, is not clear. Does it refer to a single
act of infidelity, or to persistent adultery or promiscuity, or to
a relationship within the prohibited degrees, or to pre-marital
unchastity? We just do not know.[2]

Here, then, we have two accounts of the same incident and,
while the reply of Jesus is *substantially* the same in both, the
differences that we have noted obscure His precise attitude
towards the permissibility of divorce on any grounds whatsoever. Central in both accounts is His positive, unambiguous
assertion that marriage in the divine intention is an indissoluble,
lifelong union, so that formal divorce and remarriage amount
essentially to adultery. His only concession—if He made one at
all—is on the ground of infidelity. But did He in fact make any
such concession?

The opinion of most New Testament scholars is that He did
not. There are good reasons for holding that St. Mark's

---

[1] See Mishnah *Gittin*, ix, 10.

[2] Ernest Evans maintains that, in the case of a married woman, πορνεία
can only mean promiscuous misconduct. See *Corinthians* (Clarendon Bible),
p. 95.

account is the more accurate of the two. Not only is it earlier; it is more in accord with our Lord's general method of enunciating great principles rather than legislating for particular situations. And if, as G. E. P. Cox points out, "Jesus cites the divine ordinance concerning ' one flesh ' (v, 5) in all its primitive rigour only to side finally with Shammai," " the sense of anticlimax is inescapable."[1] Hence T. W. Manson assumes that " it is as certain as anything can be in New Testament criticism that the qualifications παρεκτὸς λόγου πορνείας and μὴ ἐπὶ πορνείᾳ (Matthew v, 32; xix, 9) are not part of the genuine teaching of Jesus on this point."[2]

But Manson's assumption is too sweeping, and other outstanding New Testament scholars would agree with R. H. Charles that St. Matthew's account defines the issue in question more specifically and is to be preferred.[3] There is ground for maintaining that adultery did not come into the question since it was covered by separate legislation. In that case, the reply of Jesus in Mark x, 10–12, would refer to cases of divorce on all grounds other than adultery. This was regarded as automatically terminating the marriage, the penalty prescribed by the Law being death (Deuteronomy xxii, 22; cf. John viii, 5). According to Abrahams, " it is not probable that the death penalty for adultery was inflicted at all in the age of Jesus."[4] Mace, indeed, maintains that " the Old Testament provides us with not a single instance of the legal penalty for adultery being enacted " but admits in a footnote that cases are recorded elsewhere.[5] However, as Abrahams points out, when the death penalty ceased to be applied, adultery was still regarded as breaking the marriage tie and later Jewish law compelled a man to divorce his unfaithful wife.[6] Thus adultery " dissolved a marriage by theoretically bringing about the execution of the wife. But even when this was modified, and divorce became the penalty, adultery still meant the end of the union."[7] Vernon Bartlett maintains that this was " a ground admitted in all Jewish circles as making divorce a positive duty, and one

---

[1] *The Gospel According to St. Matthew*, p. 122.
[2] *The Teaching of Jesus*, p. 200, note 5.
[3] See R. H. Charles, *The Teaching of the New Testament on Divorce*, pp. 85 ff.
[4] I. Abrahams, *Studies*, p. 73.   [5] *Hebrew Marriage*, p. 249.
[6] *Op. cit.*, p. 74.   [7] D. R. Mace, *op. cit.*, p. 250.

therefore which is *presumably taken for granted* both by Jesus and His questioners."[1]

Thus Streeter regards the Matthaean account as being " more naturally told and more closely related to Jewish usage than the parallel in Mark,"[2] and Creed, although regarding the " excepting clause " in Matthew xix, 9, as an interpretative gloss, maintains that " it seems on the whole probable that it preserves the actual purport of the teaching of Jesus."[3] H. G. Wood, commenting on Mark x, 1–12, is even more definite: " The case of the breaking of marriage by adultery is not directly considered. The exception introduced in Matthew xix, 9, probably interprets the teaching of Jesus aright. This passage does not establish the absolute indissolubility of marriage. There is no reason to suppose that Jesus differed from Shammai in regarding adultery as justifying divorce."[4]

Against this it may be urged that St. Matthew's version bears all the marks of the Jewish legalism which colours the First Gospel. Jesus is there portrayed as a second Moses giving a new Law and St. Matthew is at pains to tone down anything in Christ's teaching which may appear disparaging to the Mosaic Law. Hence W. C. Allen's comment that " in view of other features of the Gospel, it is probable that the editor was a Jewish Christian who has here judaized, or rather rabbinized, Christ's sayings " and " so shaped Christ's teaching about divorce as to make it consonant with the permanent validity of the Pentateuchal law, and harmonious with the stricter school of Jewish theologians."[5] The same view is held by Vincent Taylor, who suggests that " the exceptive clauses in Matthew represent the first stage in a process by which His sayings have been treated as enactments,"[6] and by A. M. Hunter, who sees in them " the mind, not of Jesus, but of a section of the early Church who shrank from the rigour (as some of us do) of Christ's ruling."[7]

[1] *St. Mark*, p. 287.   [2] B. H. Streeter, *The Four Gospels*, p. 259.
[3] J. M. Creed, *The Gospel According to St. Luke*, p. 208.
[4] " Mark," in *Peake's Commentary on the Bible*, p. 693.
[5] *St. Matthew* (I.C.C.), pp. 202–3. Cf. S. Cave, *op. cit.*, p. 201: " It is probable that the exception of fornication in Matthew reflects the transition from an ideal into the law of that Jewish Christianity which that Gospel reflects."   [6] *The Gospel According to St. Mark*, p. 421.
[7] *The Gospel According to St. Mark* (Torch Bible Commentaries), p. 100.

The teaching derived from the " Q " source is given in Matthew v, 31–2, and Luke xvi, 18. There are, however, certain differences between these two passages which we must note. As A. J. Grieve points out, Luke xvi, 18, " combines the first case of Mark x, 11, with the second case of Matthew v, 32, and may be the original form ":[1]

> Everyone who divorces his wife and marries another commits adultery, and he who marries a woman divorced from her husband commits adultery.

The Matthaean passage says, not that the man who divorces his wife and marries another commits adultery, but that " everyone who divorces his wife . . . makes her an adulteress." The assumption is that she will marry again, as indeed the law of Deuteronomy xxiv, 1–4, explicitly permits. Hence the phrase " appears to mean ' drives her into the arms of another man ' as the only alternative to destitution."[2] But the implication is that the first marriage cannot be dissolved by formal divorce; it still stands and her second marriage is therefore essentially adultery.[3] Here, as in xix, 9, St. Matthew inserts an " excepting " clause. The wording, however, is different, and as F. W. Green points out, there is a subtle difference of meaning.[4] παρεκτὸς λόγου πορνείας means, not " except on the ground of unchastity," but "apart from a charge of unchastity." In other words, leaving aside the question of whether or not she is guilty of misconduct, the divorced wife is inevitably driven into a situation which is essentially adulterous. Green maintains therefore that " the words in themselves do not give an innocent party in a divorce suit a general permission to remarry but merely reserve the case of an adulterous wife for special consideration. Jesus does not in this place say what ought to be done in the case of adultery."[5]

[1] " Luke," in *Peake's Commentary on the Bible*, p. 736.
[2] F. W. Green, *The Gospel According to St. Matthew* (Clarendon Bible), p. 134.
[3] The Provost of Sheffield maintains that there is no need to suppose the necessity of the woman's remarriage. " The divorce as such has made it impossible for her to be faithful to the marriage bond. She, who should have belonged to her husband, is no longer bound to him. The innocent partner is made to share in the sin of the other." See J. H. Cruse and Bryan Green, *Marriage, Divorce and Repentance in the Church of England*, p. 22.
[4] *Op. cit.*, p. 133.   [5] *Ibid.*, p. 133.

When the records are examined in this way, it is clear that there is no simple answer to the question of Christ's attitude to the precise problems of divorce. We do not know what His actual words were.[1] All we can say for certain is that He appealed behind the divorce legislation of Deuteronomy to the divine intention of lifelong indissoluble marriage and described as adulterous breaches of God's creative will. But are His pronouncements to be regarded as law or ideal? Is He imposing an inflexible marriage rule upon His followers, or is He describing the "idea" of marriage in the purpose of God?

Four observations may help to clarify this issue:

(1) As we have seen, legalism is contrary to the genius of Christ's teaching which is not legislative but prophetic. "It is generally agreed that Our Lord did not legislate or provide a new moral code of detailed precepts or rules which must be invariably followed. Rather He flung down uncompromising principles of right conduct, absolute and unqualified in their demands, and left it to His followers to work out the application in the relativities of their daily lives."[2]

Is it likely then that on this one occasion Jesus departed so far from His own practice as to give precise directions in the matter of divorce? Have we here the one isolated instance of casuistry in His teaching? E. F. Scott believes that we have: "The pronouncement on divorce is notable as the one exception to the rule that Jesus did not lay down laws, but only guiding principles."[3] But why should it be? The onus of proof is upon those who maintain that it is. Brunner is surely right when he observes that "the theological ethic of marriage is the point at which Protestant Ethics has remained either Anabaptist or Catholic, since it here applied the Sermon on the Mount as a 'law.'"[4] But what right has it to do this? Does not such an application impose upon this pronouncement

---

[1] For an attempt to resolve the differences between the various accounts by distinguishing between divorce in the sense of separation *a mensa et toro* and absolute divorce *a vinculo* with the possibility of remarriage, see Ernest Evans, *Corinthians* (Clarendon Bible), pp. 93-6.

[2] J. H. Cruse and Bryan Green, *op. cit.*, p. 27.

[3] *The Ethical Teachings of Jesus*, p. 98.

[4] *The Divine Imperative*, p. 341, note 1.

of Jesus a character which is alien to the essential nature of the teaching in which it occurs? " While phrased in terms of a legal prohibition, it is obviously not a law which can be forced upon people who live in a state of sin. . . . Jesus' absolute prohibition of divorce on any grounds cannot be interpreted in a juridical sense, for it is not meant for the court-room."[1]

(2) May not the will of God be expressed in the accommodations of both the Old Testament and the New? When the Pharisees cite the provision of the Deuteronomic law for divorce, the comment of our Lord is: " Moses because of the hardness of your hearts suffered you to put away your wives: but from the beginning it was not so." As J. H. Cruse points out, " He does not censure Moses for making this concession and probably regarded Moses as having done so under Divine guidance. It was in fact part of the Divine Law, given as a limitation to a great laxity which was common at the time. It was a temporary lowering of the ideal because of man's sinfulness, but its purpose was to safeguard marriage, not to destroy it."[2]

Similarly, even if the " excepting " clause in Matthew v, 32, and xix, 9, is not ascribed to Jesus, " the presence of these words in Scripture has still . . . to be explained."[3] If they represent an accommodation which the Apostolic Church found it necessary to make, it may still be claimed that " there is scriptural authority for marriage being dissolved under certain conditions."[4] As. E. G. Wright observes, biblical men who knew the will of God " in both Old and New Testaments were faced with the necessity of accommodation and compromise because they were children of faith in a world of sin. . . . There is no doubt that the writers of both Deuteronomy and Matthew believed that the will of God was also expressed in the accommodation."[5]

[1] E. G. Wright, " From the Bible to the Modern World," in *Biblical Authority for Today*, pp. 231–2. Cf. P. T. Forsyth, *Marriage its Ethic and Religion*, pp. 44–5: " Considering, further, that Christ's words referred only to arbitrary dismissal by the man, and not to the solemn decision of a court of justice (which did not exist for such cases), they should no more be applied to that decision than ' Swear not ' applies to oaths in court, or ' Thou shalt not kill ' to judicial executions."

[2] J. H. Cruse and Bryan Green, *op. cit.*, p. 20.   [3] *Ibid.*, p. 19.
[4] *Ibid.*, p. 19.   [5] *Op. cit.*, p. 233.

This appears to have been the attitude of St. Paul towards the problems arising from mixed marriages in the Corinthian Church (I Corinthians vii, 10–15). On the one hand, he cites the teaching of Jesus regarding the indissoluble nature of the marriage bond: " Unto the married I command, yet not I, but the Lord, Let not the wife depart from her husband: but and if she departs, let her remain unmarried, or be reconciled to her husband: and let not the husband put away his wife " (cf. Romans vii, 2–3). But on the other hand, in the situation at Corinth " the intimate connection of heathenism with the details of social life made the position of Christians married to heathens so peculiar that it could not be dealt with on the grounds of words spoken by Christ to those only who were worshippers of the true God."[1]

Since, therefore, he can cite no word of Jesus which is directly applicable to the situation, St. Paul feels free to deal with this particular case on its merits,[2] " not as speaking by God's command, but as having the Spirit of God."[3] And so he accommodates the absolute divine requirement to the pressing human needs of hard cases which arise through the clash of Christian ideals with a pagan environment. Mixed marriages are valid marriages which the Christian partner must strive to maintain. But if the non-Christian partner is bent on dissolving the marriage (χωρίζεται), let him (or her) be gone (χωριζέσθω). Such deliberate, final desertion releases the Christian from the marriage bond (οὐ δεδούλωται). As Hodge observes, " this seems to be the plain meaning. . . . In other words, the marriage is thereby dissolved,"[4] and the implication is that the Christian may marry again. T. C. Edwards rightly urges

[1] J. Agar Beet, *St. Paul's Epistles to the Corinthians*, p. 116.

[2] " Casuistry " is legislating for particular " cases " in the light of general principles.

[3] F. W. Robertson, *Expository Lectures on the Corinthians*, p. 104. Cf. P. T. Forsyth, *Marriage its Ethic and Religion*, pp. 49–50: " Paul did not feel prevented, in dealing with his infant churches, from meeting the actual situation in a casuist way; in doing which he allows a freedom that Christ was not called on expressly to name . . . Paul had to legislate for the Church as Christ had not—for special cases in it at least. And he uses the flexibility of the spirit and not the stiffness of the letter."

[4] Charles Hodge, *Systematic Theology*, iii, p. 395.

that " no other explanation does justice to the words 'is not enslaved.' "[1]

" Hardness of heart " is not peculiar to the time of Deuteronomy or of Matthew; it is with us still. Nor is it confined to irreligious people; it is found inside, as well as outside, the Church. Neither are the problems of mixed marriages confined to the Corinth of St. Paul's day. The question is, therefore, " What particular laws about divorce, men and women and society being at any time what they are, will at this time help men and women most nearly to achieve the ideal institution of Christian marriage? "[2] since morality " is concerned with the application to historical conditions of the universal principles which Jesus lays down."[3] Hence Brunner maintains that while divorce is a sign of weakness, " cases are possible where not to divorce might be a sign of greater weakness, and might be a still greater offence against the Divine order." And he urges that, while the Church must emphasize the indissoluble character of marriage, " the legalistic misuse of the idea of marriage by the Christian ethic, custom, and ecclesiastical practice makes it necessary today to call attention to the other side of the question, to the moral right of the exceptional case—which indeed is not a rare exception."[4]

(3) Jesus is concerned with attitudes of mind rather than external actions. That is why His teaching is so penetrating and His interpretation of the Law so revolutionary. He goes behind the legal prohibition of a certain line of action to the mental attitude which prompts it and of which it is the expression. The Law treats the symptoms; Christ diagnoses the disease. Symptoms may vary considerably in intensity and yet spring from the same basic disorder. Hence our Lord describes as adulterous not only remarriage after divorce but also the lustful look. Both are symptoms of the same disease—an attitude of mind which is at variance with the divine intention for

---

[1] *A Commentary on the First Epistle to the Corinthians*, pp. 174–5; cf. Wordsworth's comment quoted by Hodge, *op. cit.*, p. 396: " Although a Christian may not put away his wife, being an unbeliever, yet if the wife desert her husband ($\chi\omega\rho\acute{\iota}\zeta\epsilon\tau\alpha\iota$) he may contract a second marriage."

[2] A. D. Lindsay, *The Moral Teaching of Jesus*, pp. 159–60.

[3] *Ibid.*, p. 162.   [4] *The Divine Imperative*, p. 362.

man; and it is with this attitude that Jesus is primarily concerned, whether its symptoms be pronounced or mild. " If this
section [of Christ's teaching, i.e. Matthew v, 17–48] be regarded
as a new and stricter law, then it is a law which most of us can
claim to have obeyed in one respect only; in its prohibition of
divorce. But who can claim never to have been guilty of an
angry thought or a lustful look? "[1] So Brunner rightly concludes, " What Jesus has said of the lustful glance, as the absolute law about adultery, makes every one of us an adulterer."
" We are all ' below the line,' for we are all adulterers, some
within legitimate marriage and others outside it."[2]

This fact cannot be too strongly emphasized. Failure to
recognize it, with all its implications, has vitiated much recent
discussion on the subject. Unless it be grasped, Christ's
teaching regarding divorce will inevitably be seen out of
perspective. To isolate the overt act of infidelity and treat it as
if that alone were adultery is to be guilty of the very legalism
which Jesus implicitly condemns (Matthew v, 27–28). In the
words of A. D. Lindsay, " What Jesus is clearly saying in this
verse is, ' If your attitude, your feeling towards, your thinking
about women is of a certain kind, you are an adulterer. Whether
that attitude actually leads to what the law recognizes as
adultery is, comparatively speaking, an accident.' "[3] It is the
attitude of mind that really matters, and, according to Jesus,
the attitude of the man who gets rid of one wife in order to marry
another is no worse than that of the man who merely desires
physical satisfaction through illicit love: they are essentially the
same.

But divorce in the modern world may be prompted by very
different motives and " licit " as well as "illicit" love may be
nothing more than the expression of lust. Furthermore, the
desire for so-called " illicit " love does not always spring from
lust. " There can be adulterous relations between men and
women," says Lindsay, " inside marriage, as Milton recognizes
in *Paradise Lost*. It is, I think, also true that there may be

---

[1] *Report of the Commission on the Marriage of Divorced Persons* appointed by the
General Purposes Committee of the Congregational Union of England and
Wales, p. 5.

[2] *The Divine Imperative*, pp. 350 and 353.   [3] *Op. cit.*, p. 140.

relations between men and women which the law condemns as adulterous which do not fall under the condemnation of this verse."[1] " The essential evil is to regard a woman as a means to the gratification of our desires—as an object, a thing, and not as a person."[2]

Lindsay maintains that Christ's teaching regarding divorce must be interpreted against the contemporary background of conventional morality. He was speaking to *men* in a situation where *men* determined the relation of the sexes and in which it was taken for granted that a woman must belong to some man.[3]

> Clearly the assumption that women are to be regarded, not as persons or individuals in their own right, but as means only for the gratification of men's sexual desires or for their utility, was stamped upon the Mosaic law which He is criticizing. Jesus is in effect saying, " Moses set some limits to your right to regard women as your property and to get rid of them when you are tired of them or have no further use for them or when they are childless. Moses said there must be a certain amount of decency about it. You must give them a writing of divorcement. But I say the whole thing is wrong. You have under no circumstances a right to dispose of women in that way, whatever the excuse may be.". . .
>
> If this interpretation is correct, what Jesus was denouncing was the fact of the man having this power over the woman and of men holding this view of women. He was denouncing all that divorce must mean whilst this power and this view held. And we need not necessarily suppose that if this evil is avoided, the prohibition of any kind of divorce must still remain unchanged. What does remain is the ideal of marriage as a lifelong partnership. A possibility of divorce is not a repudiation of that ideal, but the giving the power of divorce into the hands of the man is.[4]

(4) Christian Ethics are derived from the Christian Gospel, which is essentially a Gospel of forgiveness and restoration. Its basic principle is not law but grace: " He hath not dealt with us after our sins; nor rewarded us according to our iniquities." Divorce—even though it be the lesser of two evils—is always sinful, to a greater or a lesser degree, because it is a frustration of the divine intention in marriage. But the sin lies in the failure of the marriage which has led to the divorce; for, " when two people propose divorce, to all intents and purposes in the

---

[1] *Ibid.*, pp. 140–1. [2] *Ibid.*, p. 145.
[3] *Ibid.*, pp. 133–4. [4] *Ibid.*, pp. 164–6.

ethical sense, the marriage is already dissolved."[1] The formal legal divorce is merely its death certificate. One of the partners will be held responsible, in the eyes of the law, for the dissolution—the so-called " guilty party," but seldom can the " innocent party " disclaim all responsibility. The inescapable truth is that " a union which is indissoluble by divine institution may in fact be wrecked by sin; and that by the sin of one or both partners, the personal relationships in marriage can be completely destroyed."[2]

But the Christian Gospel of forgiveness and restoration through repentance either applies to all sins—including sins in marriage—or it is not a Gospel of forgiveness at all. As Cave observes, " we all alike need the divine forgiveness, and it is difficult to see on what grounds failure in marriage should be treated as if it was the one failure for which the penitent cannot be forgiven."[3] Our Lord's attitude towards the woman taken in adultery (John viii, 1–11) is certainly far removed from that of many ecclesiastics.[4] Indeed the traditional Christian ethics of sex and marriage appear at many points to have been shaped more by the influence of Platonic Hellenistic mysticism and Manichaeism than by the Spirit of Christ. This fact has contributed in no small measure to the Church's failure in the present marriage crisis. " Even in matters of marriage," says Brunner, " God is more merciful than the usual theological ethic. . . . Were it not for the fact that pastoral practice has at all times acted with far more insight than the official doctrine would have permitted, the disaster would have attained greater proportions, and the crisis would have supervened much earlier."[5]

If we may judge by His reply to Pharisaic legalism on the question of Sabbath observance, the essential attitude of Jesus would be that marriage was made for man, and not man for marriage.

---

[1] Emil Brunner, *The Divine Imperative*, p. 363.
[2] *The Lambeth Report*, 1948.   [3] *The Christian Way*, p. 203.
[4] See J. R. Seeley, *Ecce Homo*, pp. 96–9.   [5] *Op. cit.*, pp. 354–5.

Chapter VIII

THE WORD OF GOD

"THE consciousness of authority is doubtless human," says Martineau, " but conditional on the *source* being divine."[1] The only final authority is the authority of God Himself. The Bible therefore is authoritative in so far as it mediates this divine authority. In the words of C. H. Dodd, " Authority in the absolute sense resides in the truth alone, or, in religious language in the mind and will of God. In so far as the Bible possesses authority in religion, it can be only as mediating the truth, or as ' the Word of God.' "[2]

But can we speak of the Bible as the Word of God? And if so, in what sense? Because clearly the authority for us of what the Bible says is ultimately determined by our conception of what the Bible essentially is. " It is clear," says Leonard Hodgson, " that whatever we may mean by ' the Word of God,' we are referring in some sense or other to the Bible. The question is, in what sense? "[3]

This Book has been variously regarded. Some have seen in it a collection of literature, much of which is unsurpassed; others have found here a volume of historical documents differing in their degrees of value. For some it is a quarry of anthropological data; for others a compendium of ethical rules. But the Christian view of the Bible is something quite different. It is seen as the record and the instrument of God's revelation of Himself to man. Through it His Word of judgment and mercy, of demand and succour, of reproof and grace is given. In the words of Article VI in the *Thirty-Nine Articles of Religion* of the Anglican Church, " Holy Scripture containeth all things

---

[1] *The Seat of Authority in Religion*, preface, vii.
[2] *The Authority of the Bible*, p. 289.
[3] *Towards a Christian Philosophy*, p. 128.

necessary for salvation." This affirmation is expressed more
fully in a paragraph which is common to two classic documents
of Orthodox Dissent—the Presbyterian *Westminster Confession*
of 1646 and the Congregationalist *Savoy Declaration* of 1658:

> The whole Counsel of God concerning all things necessary for
> his own Glory, man's Salvation, Faith and Life, is either expressly
> set down in Scripture, or by good and necessary consequence may
> be deduced from Scripture; unto which nothing at any time is to
> be added, whether by new Revelations of the Spirit, or Traditions
> of men.[1]

That is what Christians believe, and always have believed,
about the Bible. " The Bible," says Father Hebert, " was in its
very origin the Book of the Faith. It is from this point of view,
then, that it demands to be seen, when it is being studied as
Scripture, and as having authority for Christian faith and life."[2]

I. The Significance of Speech

Before we can profitably discuss the significance of the Bible
as the Word of God, it is necessary to clarify in our own minds
the significance of speech. What exactly do we mean when we
talk of a " word "?

One of the most able writers of the modern world is a woman
who in early infancy became blind, deaf and dumb—Miss
Helen Keller. For several years, although her body grew, her
mind remained entirely undeveloped, since, having neither
sight nor hearing, there seemed to be no way of establishing any
communication between her personality and the outer world.
It was only after years of patient and devoted effort that her
nurse finally succeeded in making contact with that isolated
mind by inducing her to respond to gentle pressure on her
hand.[3]

It is, perhaps, only when we are confronted with a case such
as this that we realize how dependent we are upon some sort of
speech. Whether or not some extraordinary people are gifted
with powers of telepathy or thought-transference, it remains
true for the rank and file of us that we can get into touch with

---

[1] See *Westminster Confession*, I, vi.
[2] *The Authority of the Old Testament*, pp. 45–6.
[3] See Helen Keller's autobiography, *The Miracle of a Life*.

one another only through some means of signalling, as it were. Each of us is shut up in a sort of ivory tower. No one, not even our nearest and dearest, can enter into the innermost citadel of our personality; and neither can we come out of it. We can only signal to one another through our senses of hearing and seeing and feeling; and if some of these senses are missing, it will be extremely difficult ever to make contact with the outside world. If they all were missing, it would of course be quite impossible.

It is, then, speech in some form which enables us to come together, really to confront and impinge upon one another. " By means of words, and normally by no other means, one person can affect another without infringing his personal independence."[1] If I want to make contact with you, I can do it only by my word. If you are deaf, I may have to translate that word into a sign; if you are both deaf and blind, I may have to convey it through touch. But the deaf-and-dumb language, the dots and dashes of pressure by which Helen Keller's nurse eventually made contact with the mind of that girl—these are just other forms of speech, other ways of conveying, of getting across, the particular word.

It follows, therefore, that a word is always more than just the communicating of an idea or the conveying of information. It carries with it something of the personality of the one who speaks it. " The words of a man, assuming that they are the deliberate expression of his meaning, command just that measure of authority which we recognize in the man himself."[2] When I speak to you, I myself confront you yourself through my word. My personality stands over against yours, either demanding something of you or giving something to you—I ask for service or information; I offer help or advice. It is this confronting of one another in succour or in demand which is achieved through —and only through—the medium of words. " Human words," says Wheeler Robinson, " are always a body animated by the more or less of vital truth they derive from the speaker and the hearer. The marvellous power they can exert is not in themselves, but in the contact they make between mind and mind."

[1] C. H. Dodd, *The Bible To-day*, pp. 104–5.
[2] C. H. Dodd, *The Authority of the Bible*, p. 17.

And he recalls how, in the early days of wireless, a lady said to Marconi, " How wonderful this wireless is! " " Not half so wonderful," the inventor replied, " as the fact that you and I are talking now." " An intelligible word spoken to me," comments Robinson, " brings my mind and personality into contact with another, and is sacramental through his informing spirit."[1]

This approach will perhaps help to clarify the meaning of the phrase, " the Word of God." Just as the word of John Smith to Mrs. Smith is John Smith communicating, not just his ideas, but *himself* to his wife, so the Word of God is God communicating Himself to man; God making contact with us; God meeting us, coming to us. " The Word, the Logos, is God in His revelatory action."[2] It is " a sacramental means by which God the Holy Spirit makes Himself present to faith."[3] And just as you are dependent upon my word for any real personal knowledge of me—just as you could not know me if I refused to speak to you, so too we know God, we only can know God, through His own communication of Himself to us—that is, through His Word.

II. The Word Incarnate

God thus communicating Himself to man, God in His revelatory action, is what Christian theologians mean by God the Son—the Second Person of the Blessed Trinity. He is the eternal Word by whom all things were made, who spake by the prophets. And in the fulness of time that Word was incarnate in Jesus Christ. " In the beginning was the word," says St. John, " and the word was with God and the word was God. . . . And the word was made flesh and dwelt among us."[4]

That is the very heart of the Christian Gospel, the centre and core of the Christian faith, that God comes to man. That is what revelation really means. " Revelation," says P. T. Forsyth, " does not consist of communications about God. It never did. . . . Revelation is the self-bestowal of the living God. . . . It

---

[1] *Redemption and Revelation*, pp. 189–90.
[2] O. Cullmann, *Christ and Time*, p. 24.
[3] Wheeler Robinson, *op. cit.*, p. 189.   [4] John i, 1–14.

is God Himself drawing ever more near and arriving at last."[1]
Jesus was no mere prophet, like Isaiah, proclaiming the ways
of God to men; He was no mere teacher, like Socrates, apprehending and unveiling eternal truth; He was no mere martyr,
like Joan of Arc, giving His life for some high and noble cause.
He was God manifest in the flesh. He came, not to point to
the way, or to teach the truth, or to exemplify the life; He *is*
the way, the truth, and the life. In the words of Forsyth, " It
was by men that God gave Himself to men, till, in the fullness
of time, He came, for good and all, in the God-man Christ,
the living Word; in whom God was present, reconciling the
world unto Himself, not merely acting through Him but present
in Him, reconciling and not speaking of reconciliation or
merely offering it to us. He acted not only through Christ
but in Christ. He who came was God the Son, and not a sinless
saint dowered and guided by the Spirit. In Christ we have
God Himself, and no mere messenger from God."[2]

It is of the highest importance that Jesus Christ Himself, the
One in whom God imparts Himself to us, is called " the Word."
It is therefore He, this Person, who is really the Word. He Himself is the communication, the self-communication of God; it is
He Himself in whom God proclaims and realizes His will to
Lordship and His will to fellowship. The new point of view in
the New Testament in contrast to the Old is that God proffers
us His Word no longer only in the words of the prophets but in
the Word become flesh. It thus becomes unmistakably clear that
what God wills to give us cannot really be given in words, but only
in manifestation: Jesus Christ, God Himself *in persona* is the real
gift. The Word of God in its ultimate meaning is thus precisely
not " a word from God," but God in person, God Himself
speaking, Himself present, Immanuel.[3]

In the words of John Baillie, " God and His Word are one."[4]
The unknown author of the Epistle to the Hebrews summarizes it all in a classic verse: " God, who at sundry times and
in divers manners spake in time past unto the fathers by the
prophets, hath in these last days spoken unto us by his Son."[5]

[1] *Positive Preaching and the Modern Mind*, p. 16.
[2] *Ibid.*, pp. 16–17.
[3] Emil Brunner, *The Divine-Human Encounter*, pp. 77–8.
[4] *Our Knowledge of God*, pp. 162–3.   [5] Hebrews i, 1–2.

And St. John expresses it in one short sentence: " And the word was made flesh, and dwelt among us."[1]

III. THE WRITTEN WORD

" Because He [Christ] Himself is the Word of God," says Brunner, " all words have only an instrumental value. Neither the spoken words nor their conceptual content are the Word itself, but only its ' frame,' the means of conveying it."[2] The Bible may be spoken of as the Word of God in this derivative sense because it declares Jesus Christ. It is a " mode " of the Word; it is the record of the testimony of saints, apostles, prophets and martyrs concerning Christ, the living Word, and as such it is the means whereby that Word is given to us. For Luther the authority of Scripture is derived from the declaration of Christ: " This is the touchstone by which all books may be tested, to see whether they proclaim Christ or not, since all Scripture witnesses to Christ and St. Paul will know nothing save Christ. Whatever does not teach Christ is not apostolic, even were it taught by St. Peter or St. Paul."[3] Christ is thus *dominus et rex scripturae.* The authority of the Scriptures is therefore, as Brunner rightly maintains, the authority of a norm: " The Scriptures possess this authority because they are the *primary witness* to the revelation of God in Jesus Christ."[4]

Christ is the theme, not only of the Gospels, but of the whole Bible. As Father Hebert reminds us, " the New Testament in no way justifies the notion, widely held today, that God is revealed in Jesus as in an isolated figure, separated from the Old Testament background on the one hand, and from His body the Church on the other."[5]

The Old Testament declares Christ by anticipating Him, by pointing towards Him, by finding its fulfilment, its completion in Him. " It tells of the choosing of a peculiar people, their deliverance, their teaching by the Prophets, their schooling through suffering, their vision and their hardening of heart. It makes clear that the coming of the Son of Man was not unprepared nor unrelated to the past, but the end of its travail

---

[1] John i, 14.   [2] *Op. cit.,* p. 78.   [3] *Erlangen Ausgabe,* 63, 157.
[4] *Dogmatics,* i, p. 45.   [5] *The Authority of the Old Testament,* p. 80.

and the fulfilment of its promise. . . . It tells not ordinary history, but, as the Germans say, *Heilsgeschichte*, the story of our salvation."[1]

The New Testament declares Christ by witnessing to Him, by embodying the testimony of those who trod the streets and lanes of Palestine with Him. It proclaims Good News—the news that the long-expected day has arrived; that the story of the past has reached its fruition; that the hope of the nation has been fulfilled; that the event to which the prophets looked forward has happened; that in Jesus of Nazareth God has visited and redeemed His people.

> This day hath God fulfilled his promised word,
> This day is born a Saviour, Christ the Lord.

" The Bible, therefore, is there as the medium of the Gospel."[2] It mediates the Word.

This is the sense in which the Reformed doctrine of Holy Scripture is to be understood. The Bible *is* the Word of God in the same way as the sacramental bread *is* the Body of Christ. In neither case is logical identity implied. St. Paul speaks of the bread as the *communion* of the Body of Christ (I Corinthians x, 16), but, as Calvin points out, communion is something different from the Body itself.[3]

> As, therefore, the apostle says that the rock from which spiritual water flowed forth to the Israelites was Christ (I Corinthians x, 4), and was thus a visible symbol under which that spiritual drink was truly perceived . . . so the body of Christ is now called bread, inasmuch as it is a symbol under which our Lord offers us the true eating of His body.[4]

Here is the ground upon which He justifies the use of the copula " is ":

> For although the sign differs essentially from the thing signified, the latter being spiritual and heavenly, the former corporeal and visible—yet, as it not only figures the thing which it is employed to represent as a naked and empty badge, but also truly exhibits it, why should not its name be justly applied to the thing?[5]

[1] N. Micklem, *What is the Faith?* pp. 86-7.
[2] P. T. Forsyth. *op. cit.*, p. 16.   [3] *Institutes*, IV, xvii, 22.
[4] *Ibid.*, IV, xvii, 21.   [5] *Ibid.*, IV, xvii, 21.

This is clearly the way in which Calvin, and the Reformers generally, regarded the relationship between the Word of God and the Bible—a fact which fundamentalist theologians like Warfield and Hodge fail to see. The distinction is implied in Calvin's saying that " the Word itself, whatever be the way in which it is conveyed to us, is a kind of mirror in which faith beholds God,"[1] and in the statement of the *Westminster Confession* regarding saving faith by which " a Christian believeth to be true whatsoever is revealed in the Word (i.e. the Bible), *for the authority of God Himself speaking therein*, and acteth differently upon that which each particular passage thereof containeth, yielding obedience to the commands, trembling at the threatnings, and embracing the promises of God for this life, and that which is to come. But the principal acts of saving faith are, accepting, receiving, and resting upon Christ alone. . . ."[2]

Thus, as T. M. Lindsay rightly maintains, " the way in which Reformed creeds and other subordinate standards interpreted the copula by such words as *contains, presents, conveys, records*, all show that there was a real distinction in the minds of the Reformers between the Word of God and Scripture."[3] And Robertson Smith was only making explicit this implicit distinction of classic Reformed theology when he observed that " since Scripture has no other end than to convey to us a message which, when accompanied by the inner witness of the Spirit, manifests itself as the infallible Word of God, we may, for practical purposes, say that Scripture *is* the infallible Word of God. For Scripture *is*, essentially, what it is its business to convey."[4]

It is in the light of this distinction between the Word of God

---

[1] *Institutes*, III, ii, 6. See J. K. S. Reid, *The Authority of Scripture*, p. 38: " If it is permissible to take this metaphorical use as really normative for Calvin's thought, it yields a clear indication of his view of Holy Scripture. For a mirror makes something visible, but the representation is not the thing in itself. Applying this to the case in hand, the Bible conveys the Word of God, but for this very reason is not identical with that word." Cf. *Institutes*, I, viii, 1: " In the Sacred Volume there is a truth divine, a something which makes it immeasurably superior to all the gifts and graces attainable by man."   [2] I, xiv, 2 (my italics).
[3] " The Doctrine of Scripture," in *Expositor*, V, 1, p. 283.
[4] *Answer to Form of Libel*, p. 26.

and the Scriptures which convey it that the " infallibility " of the Bible is to be understood. Infallibility is not to be confused with inerrancy: they are quite different. Infallibility pertains to the message of the Bible—the Divine Word; inerrancy is attributed, wrongly, to the record—the Book. We may frankly acknowledge the presence of contradictions and errors of chronology, for example, in the Bible and yet assent to what the *Westminster Confession* says about " our full persuasion and assurance of the infallible truth and divine authority " of Holy Scripture.[1] " We can rightly say the Scripture is of infallible truth and divine authority," says Lindsay, " but when we say so, we must remember that the more precise statement will be, Scripture records or conveys to us the infallible and authoritative Word of God."[2] " It is this presentation of God Himself and of His will for our salvation which is of infallible truth and divine authority, and the infallible truth and divine authority of Scripture mean simply its infallible truth and divine authority as a record of God's saving revelation of Himself and of His will."[3]

Infallibility and divine authority are descriptive of the religious significance of the Bible; inerrancy is concerned with its form. And to interpret the former in terms of the latter is to empty them of their distinctively religious content.

> Infallibility does not consist in formal inerrancy at all, but in the power which compels me to know that God is through this Scripture speaking to me now as He spoke not merely *by* the prophets and holy men of old, but *to* them and in them, and giving me through them in word and picture the message of His salvation.[4]
>
> Inerrancy, if it exists, is merely a matter of fact to be recognized by the ordinary reason. But the infallibility which compels the conviction that God is speaking to us infallibly, telling us that if we hear and accept this Saviour we shall infallibly be saved, requires faith. And that is the infallibility which the Bible possesses and which man needs.[5]

[1] I, v.
[2] T. M. Lindsay, " Professor W. Robertson Smith's Doctrine of Scripture," in *Expositor*, IV, x. p. 255.   [3] *Ibid.*, p. 256.
[4] T. M. Lindsay, " The Doctrine of Scripture," in *Expositor*, V, i, p. 288.
[5] *Ibid.*, p. 290.

The nature of infallibility, as Marcus Dods points out, is determined by the purpose of that for which it is claimed. To say of anything that it is infallible means that it is not liable to fail. But to fail in what? In that which constitutes its *raison d'être*; not in anything else. " If you say that your watch is infallible, you mean, as a time-keeper; not that is has a flawless case, not that it will tell you the day of the month, or predict tomorrow's weather. The navigator finds his chart infallible as a guide to lighthouses, and shallows, and sunken rocks, but useless to give him the time of day or to inform him of the products and prices of the land he is bound for."[1] Infallibility is limited to the sphere in which the person or thing concerned possesses authority. Hence infallibility in one particular sphere may coexist with ignorance and error in others. " The pilot who has never lost a ship, and who is practically infallible within his own domain, may yet believe in mermaids and sea serpents, may never have heard of Cromwell or Milton or Washington, and may think brandy a cure for every human ill."[2]

Now the Bible exists as the medium of the Gospel. Its purpose is to convey the Divine Word of judgment and mercy, uttered in the mighty acts of Sacred History, proclaimed by the prophets, incarnate in Christ. " By means of the Scriptures the knowledge of God's saving love in Christ is communicated to the world. It was not God's purpose to teach science or ethnology by them, nor to give us knowledge of matters about which men are always curious, such as the conditions of a future life."[3] The discrepancies within the Bible are obvious enough to the unbiased reader; that there are inaccuracies of detail no competent historian will deny; its writers are as ignorant of the findings of modern biology and astronomy as they are of nuclear fission and X-rays—which is what we should expect. But they *are* faithful witnesses of what God has done for us men and for our salvation, and " no errors in Scripture are of importance which do not prevent it from accomplishing God's purpose of preserving for us the knowledge of His revelation in Christ. . . . This object it has infallibly accomplished. . . . The Scriptures have infallibly led men to Christ."[4]

[1] Marcus Dods, *The Bible: Its Origin and Nature*, pp. 151–2.
[2] *Ibid.*, pp. 159–60.   [3] *Ibid.*, p. 152.   [4] *Ibid.*, pp. 154–5.

It is impossible to maintain the infallibility of Scripture on the ground of its literal accuracy in every one of its statements; and it is impossible to deny the infallibility of Scripture as a spiritual guide on the ground that there are found in it certain errors and discrepancies. Our acceptance of Scripture as the Word of God depends, not on its absolute freedom from error of every kind, but on our recognition of God's voice in it.[1]

IV. THE DIVINE-HUMAN ENCOUNTER

It is just because the Word mediated by the Bible is the living and abiding Word of God that God continues to speak to man through the Bible. The words of the Bible become God's message for each one of us. Although it comes to us from so long ago, the Bible is always relevant. Although its words were originally uttered to different people of different times, they have a strange way of speaking to the hearts of men and women in every age. They speak to our condition. The Bible " has indeed an archaeological aspect, for it is bound up with the life of remote epochs in the past; and in another aspect it comes to the believing reader direct from God this moment."[2] As Alan Richardson puts it, " The Bible is and remains the appointed means of God's conversation with men."[3]

God speaks to us through the Bible, not through words miraculously heard by the ears of our minds; *He speaks through the words of the Bible*, and the depth of meaning which we perceive in the Biblical words as we meditate upon them is God's message for us. That is the way which God has appointed as the means of His self-communication. And we know that God has spoken to us by the forceful conviction with which the Biblical truths come home to us; we know that God has " found " us through His Word. Our whole being responds with a deep " Yes " to the word which God has spoken to us. This is conviction, assurance; we know that God has indeed spoken to us. We have seen something of God's will for our world, for our lives and for our salvation, and we know that God has revealed it to us.[4]

Here is the essence of John Baillie's conception of " mediated immediacy." He recalls Rousseau's question to M. de Beaumont.

---

[1] *Ibid.*, p. 158.
[2] C. H. Dodd, " The Relevance of the Bible," in *Biblical Authority for Today*, p. 157.
[3] *Preface to Bible-Study*, p. 13.   [4] *Ibid.*, pp. 15–16.

" Is it simple, is it natural, that God should have gone and found Moses in order to speak to Jean Jacques Rousseau? " And Baillie says of his own childhood: " I could not hear a Bible story read without being aware that in it I was somehow being confronted with a solemn presence that had in it both sweetness and rebuke. Nor do I remember a day when I did not already dimly know that this presence was God. . . . The story told me how God had spoken to Abraham and Moses and the prophets and apostles, but what gave the story its power over my mind and imagination and conscience was the knowledge that ' in, with and under ' this speaking to these others of long ago He was also now speaking to myself. . . . What is it to me that God should have commanded David to do this or that, or called Paul to such and such a task? It is nothing at all, unless it should happen that, as I read of His calling and commanding them, I at the same time found Him calling and commanding me."[1]

This inward authentication of Scripture, the force with which it comes home to the believing Christian as he reads it, is what Calvin means by the *testimonium Spiritus Sancti internum*: God Himself authenticates His own Word in the hearts of those who will receive it.

> For as God alone can properly bear witness to His own words, so these words will not obtain full credit in the hearts of men, until they are sealed by the inward testimony of the Spirit . . . Let it therefore be held as fixed, that those who are inwardly taught by the Holy Spirit acquiesce implicitly in Scripture . . . Enlightened by Him, we no longer believe, either on our own judgment or that of others, that the Scriptures are from God; but, in a way superior to human judgment, feel perfectly assured—as much so as if we beheld the divine image visibly impressed on it—that it comes to us, by the instrumentality of men, from the very mouth of God.[2]

> The same Spirit, therefore, who spoke by the mouth of the prophets, must penetrate our hearts, in order to convince us that they faithfully delivered the message with which they were divinely entrusted.[3]

It may be objected that this line of reasoning makes the criterion of biblical authority purely subjective. How are we to

[1] See *Our Knowledge of God*, pp. 181–9.   [2] *Institutes*, I, vii, 4 and 5.
[3] *Ibid.*, I, viii, 4.

differentiate between the inward testimony of the Holy Spirit and our own predilections? What guarantee have we that what John Calvin, for example, accepts as the Word of God is anything more than the projection of his own wishes and ideals upon the page of Scripture? The objection, it must be admitted, has some force. As C. H. Dodd concedes, " the criterion lies within ourselves, in the response of our own spirit to the Spirit that utters itself in the Scriptures."[1] But we are not thereby reduced to pure subjectivism all the same. As Dodd adds in a footnote, " Christianity recognizes a ' somewhat not ourselves ' in the most inward form of experience: that is the *testimonium Spiritus Sancti internum*. The ultimate ' fact ' is the unity of experience in which ' subjective ' and ' objective ' are one."[2]

This unity of experience is the hallmark of the Bible itself and provides an objective criterion of its authority. Faith and fact are linked indivisibly together. Inner conviction is authenticated by historic event. While neither determines the other, each substantiates the other; and together they form a single complex demanding an origin common to both.

H. H. Rowley has elaborated this point in his Joseph Smith Memorial Lecture.[3] He points out that in the Exodus " we have a complex of human and non-human factors, and neither could determine the other, and *the only possible common source of both was God*. Deliverance was achieved by the timely act of Nature. But that timely act fulfilled the prior promise of Moses, who had no means of knowing how deliverance would be effected. . . . His conviction was justified and his faith vindicated, and the confidence that *God* would not let him down led to the experience that *Nature* came to his aid. Nature could not have given him his commission; his confidence in God could not of itself have stirred the forces of Nature. He therefore found the hand of God in the whole complex, and there is no other hypothesis which is both scientific and adequate."[4]

Similarly, the diverse " messianic " prophecies of the Old Testament are realized, in unsuspected ways, in Christ. " There is the claim that God was speaking through the Israelite voices that announced these hopes and that He was active in the

---

[1] *The Authority of the Bible*, p. 296.   [2] *Ibid.*, p. 297, note.
[3] *The Authority of the Bible*, 1950.   [4] *Ibid.*, p. 13.

fulfilment, which gave a fullness to the meaning of the Old
that it could not otherwise have had, and provided firm ground
for the belief that the Old Testament not alone did lead to
Christ in fact, but was intended by the God Whose partial
revelation it contained to lead to Christ. . . . The hopes of the
Old Testament could not of themselves effect their fulfilment
in the New; on the other hand it is certain that the fulfilment
in the New did not create the hopes which antedated it."[1]

While Jesus did not always fulfil the Old Testament prophecies in a literal way, the deeper meaning of each line of
anticipation—Messianic King, Suffering Servant, Son of Man
—was realized in Him. Of special significance was His interpretation of Messiahship in terms of the Suffering Servant,
and here, as Rowley points out, we have a repetition of the
pattern seen in the Exodus complex. " Jesus believed that His
death would have unique power; in indisputable fact it has had
unique power. Neither of these facts can be explained by the
other. Jesus believed that His death would achieve that which
the death of the Servant was represented as certain to achieve,"
that it " would be unique in its effect, with a uniqueness which
could only be expressed in terms of the Suffering Servant," and
" in objective, historical fact His belief has been justified."
As with Moses and the Exodus, " the source of the confidence
was declared to be God, and here we have the added factor
of the expressed hope of the Old Testament as well as the
confidence of our Lord to take into account with the fulfilment
of the hope. If God was active in all, then all would be
explained. But there is no other explanation which is both
scientific and adequate."[2]

Hence Rowley concludes that " in the Old Testament
there is evidence of the hand of God in the events it records and
in the persons who figure in its story, and especially in the
combination of event and person in a single complex. Similarly there is evidence that the hand of God was in Christ
and in all the fulfilment of His promise in subsequent history."
Thus " each Testament when viewed alone can satisfy objective
tests."   But in addition to this, " there is the response of the
New Testament to the hopes of the Old, and the common

---

[1] *Ibid.*, pp. 14–15.   [2] *Ibid.*, pp. 16–17.

pattern in the crucial complexes of the two Testaments, to bind them together in a profound unity."[1] Rowley claims, therefore, that " there is demonstrable ground to believe that behind the Bible and its record is God, and that therefore its sublimity is not of merely human origin, but charged with a higher authority."[2]

Here, then, is the objective biblical fact which matches the subjective experience of the divine-human encounter through the medium of the Bible.

It is part of the data of religious experience that God does in fact speak to men through this Book. St. Augustine tells how, as a dissolute young man of thirty-two, he walked in the garden wrestling with passions which had held him in bondage for sixteen years. Suddenly he felt an urge to read the Bible, and opening the book at Romans xiii, his eyes fell upon the words: " Not in rioting and drunkenness, not in chambering and wantonness, not in strife and envying: but put ye on the Lord Jesus Christ, and make not provision for the flesh, to fulfil the lusts thereof " (verses 13–14). " No further would I read," he says, " nor was there need; for instantly at the end of this sentence, as though my heart were flooded with a light of peace, all the shadows of doubt melted away."[3]

Martin Luther, having vainly sought for peace of heart and mind in penances and good works, heard the voice of God speaking to him in some other words of St. Paul: " The just shall live by faith " (Romans i, 17). It was while someone was reading Luther's preface to the Epistle to the Romans in the Aldersgate Street Society that John Wesley felt his heart strangely warmed.

To come down to recent times, Dr. Barnardo was led to devote his life to work among waifs and strays through a similar experience. He was a young medical student in London, whose great ambition was to go to China as a medical missionary. A spare-time Ragged School which he started revealed the appalling conditions in which homeless children lived on the streets of London, sleeping under tarpaulins in Billingsgate and on the roof of the Rag Market. Here was a work to which he found himself increasingly urged by the immensity of the need;

[1] *Ibid.*, p. 18.   [2] *Ibid.*, p. 20.   [3] *Confessions*, viii, 12.

but he feared the constant expense which it would involve His biographer tells how he prayed for guidance and found it as he read Psalm xxxii, 8: " I will instruct thee and teach thee in the way which thou shalt go: I will guide thee with mine eye." " I took these words," says Barnardo, " as a definite answer to prayer, and as a promise given to myself. Here was a pledge of personal guidance which came to me then as if God had spoken it in my ears, and to me alone, and had designed it for my peculiar circumstances. . . . At last my fears were quieted, and I was at peace and rest, for had not God spoken? "[1]

V. The Bible and the Church

" The Bible is the Holy Book of a people. It came out of the long history of a community of faith."[2]   The inspired biblical writers were not solitary mystics but members of a community, the Covenant People of God, which received, preserved and transmitted their words. A process of selection by a " Church " underlies the canon of both the Old Testament and the New. The Scriptures " come to us demanding recognition in virtue of their own intrinsic quality of word and thought, and reinforced by the general acceptance of age-old Christian experience."[3]   " The Bible exists to maintain and express the Gospel in one way, as the Church in another."[4]

The authority of the Bible is therefore bound up very intimately with the faith and life of the Church. It is essentially a book for Christians: " It is a *sacred* book addressed primarily to believers."[5]   It can be fully understood therefore only by those who stand within the Covenant of grace, not by those outside. As Florovsky points out, " The Bible, as a book, has been composed in the community and was meant primarily for its edification. The book and the Church cannot be separated. The book and the Covenant belong together, and Covenant implies people. It was the People of the Covenant to whom the

---

[1] See A. E. Williams, *Barnardo of Stepney*, pp. 69–70.

[2] D. D. Williams, *Interpreting Theology, 1918–1952*, pp. 135–6.

[3] J. W. C. Wand, *The Authority of the Scriptures*, p. 62.

[4] J. K. Mozley, " The Bible: Its Unity, Inspiration, and Authority," in *The Christian Faith*, ed. W. R. Matthews, p. 62.

[5] G. Florovsky, " Revelation and Interpretation," in *Biblical Authority for Today*, p. 163.

Word of God had been entrusted under the old dispensation (Roman iii, 2), and it is the Church of the Word Incarnate that keeps the message of the Kingdom. The Bible is the Word of God indeed, but the book stands by the testimony of the Church. The canon of the Bible is obviously established and authorized by the Church."[1] In short, the Bible is not a book whose meaning is always plain and clear: it needs to be read and interpreted in the light of the faith of the Church.

This is so because the Bible is a product of the faith and life of the Church; it springs directly out of it. " The Church read as Scripture those writings which it felt to be most vitally related to the spiritual impulse that created it."[2] The Bible did not produce the Church any more than the Church produced the Bible. Rather, both Bible and Church were " derived from a common source—the experience of those who came into personal contact with Jesus Christ, and felt the inspiration of His saving personality and work."[3] Hence it is only in the context of the life of the Church that the Bible can be rightly understood.

> We receive it from the Church: there is no other source from which we can receive precisely *these* writings in *this* setting, which make up the canon of Scripture. It is also the book which contains the history out of which the Church emerged. The Scriptures are concerned with the continuing life of an historical community—the people of God. This community remains self-identical through many changing historical forms—Hebrew clan, Israelite kingdom, Jewish dispersion, Catholic Church. Every part of that long history—down to the present day—is relevant to the acceptance and understanding of the Bible as the Word of God. Bible and Church are correlatives. The attempt (since the Reformation) to set the authority of the Bible over against that of the Church, and the authority of the Church over against the authority of the Bible, results only in obscuring the nature of this authority, which resides in both together.[4]

Thus, as Father Hebert maintains, the Bible " is read as ' Scripture ' or as ' Bible ' only when it is read in the light of the religious faith which has been held by a certain visible

---

[1] *Ibid.*, p. 164.   [2] C. H. Dodd, *The Authority of the Bible*, p. 196.
[3] E. Griffith-Jones, " The Bible: Its Meaning and Aim," in *Peake's Commentary on the Bible*, p. 7.
[4] C. H. Dodd, " The Relevance of the Bible," in *Biblical Authority for Today*, p. 157.

society, variously called Israel, the *Qahal*, the *Ecclesia*, or the
Church, which has existed for more than three thousand years
and still exists, and which regards it as a divinely inspired
book."[1] This book is essentially the record and interpretation
of the saving acts of God in human history by which a People
of God was brought into being. And it is from these saving
acts of God that the faith of His People springs. It follows,
therefore, as Hebert says, that " if there really have been
such events, they must inevitably be misjudged if the tradition
which describes them is not studied in the light of the faith
which inspired the tradition."[2]

Hence these two things, the record—the Bible—and the faith
of the Church, are indivisibly linked together; they check and
interpret each other. The Bible serves " as the organ of a
religious life lived by a continuous community in its various
historical forms. Its words are laden with power to recall that
which has passed out of this corporate life into the subconscious
mind of the reader."[3] Both are handed down from generation
to generation within the Church: both are necessary for its
continued life, and neither of them can stand alone. How, for
instance, is the saving love of God in Jesus Christ mediated to
men today? An old hymn answers:

> Jesus loves me, this I know
> For the Bible tells me so.

But would it not also be true to say:

> For my mother told me so?

There are the two things—the record of the Bible and the faith
of the Church passed on to us at our mother's knee—the one
confirming and interpreting the other.

Thus, as Cunliffe-Jones reminds us, " The meaning of the
conviction that Jesus is Lord is given by the Bible—but not
by the Bible only but by the Bible as interpreted by a living
faith. . . . At some point or other the Biblical evidence must be
interpreted by a theological conviction, which arises out of the
Biblical material, which sets it all in a new illumination, but is
not strictly given by an objective study of the Bible, but by the
Bible in the light of the present affirmation of faith by an

---

[1] *The Authority of the Old Testament*, p. 7.   [2] *Ibid.*, p. 62.
[3] C. H. Dodd, *The Authority of the Bible*, p. 6.

obedient Church. We are forced to go beyond the Bible to theological truth in order to understand what the Bible itself is saying."[1] Hence Bible and Church must never be separated.

> The Bible can never be rightly understood apart from that tradition of the Israel of God out of which it arose. . . . Further, the whole Bible presupposes the existence of the Israel of God, which is the Church. On the other hand, apart from the Bible and the living Word of God spoken through it, the Church becomes heretical and sacerdotal in the wrong sense, or worldly or pietistic. The Bible is there to recall it to the acts of the Living God, and where the Bible is shut out, the Church lacks the well-spring of life.[2]

This close interrelationship of Bible and Church was accepted as axiomatic until the Reformation. The New Testament grew out of the proclamation of a living faith by the Christian Community. It crystallizes and interprets that faith and applies it to the conditions and problems of the Apostolic Church.[3] The presupposition of medieval preaching was " the Church to teach, the Bible to prove." The scholastic theologians " do not distinguish between the authority of the Church and the authority of the scriptures, any more than the ordinary traveller today draws a clear distinction between the responsibility of the signal-man and that of the engine-driver—these two co-operate to produce in the passenger an almost complete trust. . . . With the writers of the Middle Ages you cannot have one without the other."[4] The laity, it is true, had no first-hand knowledge of Scripture—a fact of which Wyclif frequently complained. But they were by no means completely ignorant of its contents.

> Although the fourteenth-century layman might have no first-hand knowledge of the Bible he was usually acquainted with a number of Biblical incidents and stories. It would be a gross mistake to imagine that Scriptural history became part of the common stock of knowledge only after the Reformation. The everyday speech of the people was not indeed steeped in scriptural phraseology before the Authorized Version appeared, but the popular literature of the fourteenth century—songs, romances, and moral anecdotes—is filled with references to the Bible.

[1] H. Cunliffe-Jones, *The Authority of the Biblical Revelation*, p. 112.
[2] A. G. Hebert, " Which comes first, the Church or the Bible? " in *The Student World*, No. 2, 1949, p. 116.   [3] See above, Chapter II, pp. 51-2.
[4] Conrad Pepler, " The Faith of the Middle Ages," in *The Interpretation of the Bible*, ed. C. W. Dugmore, pp. 44-5.

Noah's Flood, the wives and wisdom of Solomon, the wickedness
of Jezebel and the fate of Nebuchadnezzar were as current in the
common speech of Catholic as of Protestant England. The story
of " man's first disobedience, and the fruit of that forbidden tree "
had provoked popular controversies before Wyclif's followers
translated the first chapters of Genesis; the responsibility of Eve
and the serpent for Adam's fall was as hotly contested in Chaucer's
day as in Darwin's.[1]

The range of such biblical knowledge was admittedly
restricted: " Within certain limits the ground was fairly
familiar, but outside it was almost unexplored."[2] But what
knowledge of the Bible the layman had was mediated to him
through the pictures, stained-glass windows, mystery plays and
sermons of the medieval Church. It all lay within the medieval
schema of interpretation, as C. H. Dodd points out, the Old
Testament being presented as a series of prophecies or " types "
which are fulfilled in the New Testament; and this provided the
key to its understanding. " Broadly speaking, it is probably true
to say that the Church was more concerned to communicate
the *schema* to the laity than the Bible itself; but in doing so it
ensured that whatever of the biblical material became available,
either by direct reading, or through liturgy and offices, through
sermons, hymns or pictures, was seen in a well-defined
perspective."[3] Hence, " the Bible in the Church may be said
to be the source of the faith of the Middle Ages, and thus of the
life of the Middle Ages."[4]

It was unfortunate, if inevitable, that at the Reformation
the authority of the Bible was set over against the authority of
the Church.[5] The result has been an over-emphasis upon one

[1] B. L. Manning, *The People's Faith in the Time of Wyclif*, p. 49.
[2] *Ibid.*, p. 50.   [3] *The Bible To-day*, pp. 19–20.
[4] Conrad Pepler, *op. cit.*, p. 48.
[5] The reason, as T. M. Lindsay points out, was that what the medieval
theologian called the Church " really was the opinions of accredited theologians confirmed by decisions of Councils or Popes. The 'Church' had barred
the way of access to the mind and heart of God in the Scriptures by inter-
posing its authoritative method of interpretation between the believer
and the Bible, as it had interposed the priesthood between the sinner and the
redeeming Saviour."—*History of the Reformation*, i, p. 458. But C. H. Dodd
rightly reminds us that " in thus opening the entire Canon of Scripture
to the free study of the laity, the reformers did not intend to abandon the
ancient framework within which it was to be understood."—See *The Bible
To-day*, pp. 21–3.

or the other in the Catholic and Reformed traditions. Each
side has frequently been right in what it affirmed but wrong
in what it denied. A false antithesis has been set up which is
responsible in no small measure for the ecclesiastical fragmenta-
tion of the last four hundred years. " The claim that the Bible
could be read, just as it stood, without the guidance of tradition,
and with equal authority attaching to all its parts, exposed it
to the dangers of a chaotic individualism."[1] In particular,
the Reformed doctrine of the authentication of Scripture
by the *testimonium Spiritus Sancti internum*, which the Reformers
themselves never held in isolation from their churchmanship,
degenerated into the atomistic and secular idea of the right
of " private judgment " in the interpretation of the Bible. The
result has been the unbridled sectarianism which has produced
in America no less than 256 religious bodies[2] each claiming
biblical support—a *reductio ad absurdum* proof of the fallacy of
attempting to interpret the Bible apart from the Catholic
faith of the Church.

" The Christian religion is founded upon a specific revelation
of God in history. To this revelation Scripture and the Church
alike bear witness." And while Protestantism rightly emphasizes that " the Church has always claimed that its doctrine
is based on Scripture," it is also true that " the faith and doctrine of Christianity are handed down to us in the context
of a living fellowship."[3] This is the truth behind the Roman
Catholic doctrine of the equal authority of Scripture and Tradition—a doctrine which in fact results in the subordination
of Scripture to Tradition.[4] It is not without significance,
however, that the renewed emphasis upon the indivisibility
of Bible and Church comes from Reformed as well as Catholic
and Orthodox scholars. Here Dodd and Florovsky, Cunliffe-
Jones and Hebert speak with one voice. It is not a Catholic
but a Protestant theologian in the Baptist tradition, H. H.
Rowley, who writes: " If the Church is the body of Christ

[1] C. H. Dodd, *The Bible To-day*, p. 22.
[2] According to the 1936 Federal Census. See W. L. Sperry, *Religion in America* (O.U.P.), 1945.
[3] Quotations from *Doctrine in the Church of England*, p. 27.
[4] See J. K. S. Reid, *The Authority of Scripture*, pp. 103–55, for a critical exposition of the Roman Catholic view.

(I Corinthians xii, 27), capable of being guided into all truth by the Spirit of truth (John xvi, 13), it, too, should be the vehicle of inspiration, and vested with an authority beside the authority of the Bible." But it should be noted that Rowley begins from biblical premisses, as his Scripture references show; and he rightly continues: "Neither, however, can be the ultimate authority for Christians. For the authority of both the Scriptures and the Church goes back to the authority of Christ."[1]

VI. The Nature of Biblical Authority

A recent writer expresses a widespread popular view when he says that "the real point about the Bible in the modern world is that it is a fallen oracle."[2] Nevertheless, as Hebert rightly comments, "the ordinary person has a distinct feeling that in thus setting aside the authority of the Bible he has lost hold of something of the greatest value for human life."[3] In many quarters, however, the authority of the Bible has been set aside because it has been misunderstood. The question of the nature of biblical authority is therefore crucial for its rehabilitation. In what sense, then, may the Bible be regarded as authoritative? What is the sphere of its authority? Of what kind is it?

The nature of the authority of the Bible is determined by the nature of the Bible itself. But as Leonard Hodgson observes, "What we find in the Bible depends on the presuppositions with which we come to the Bible."[4] If we regard the Bible as the Mohammedan regards the Koran—as a faultless and inerrant oracle, its authority for intellectually honest men and women will of necessity be contingent upon the accuracy of its factual statements. Should it be proved wrong in any detail of history, physics or astronomy, its status, on such a pre-supposition, must become that of a "fallen oracle." That is the dilemma in which the Fundamentalist finds himself. By beginning with an unbiblical assumption—the inerrancy of the

---

[1] *The Relevance of the Bible*, pp. 50–1.
[2] R. A. Edwards, *Jack, Jill and God*, p. 88.
[3] *The Authority of the Old Testament*, p. 19.
[4] *Towards a Christian Philosophy*, p. 129.

Scriptures—he is ultimately driven either to sacrifice intellectual integrity in an attempt to vindicate every factual statement
of the Bible, or to abandon all belief in biblical authority.
It is not surprising that, in such a dilemma between obscurant-
ism and scepticism, many sincere people who have been brought
up on these views find themselves impaled upon its latter horn.
" The man," says Snell, " who binds up the cause of Christianity with the literal accuracy of the Bible is no friend of Christianity, for with the rejection of that theory too often comes the
rejection of the Bible itself, and faith is shattered."[1]

Marcus Dods reminds us that Renan parted company
with the Church because his own study of the history of Israel
showed that the doctrine of the inerrancy of Scripture in which
he had been brought up was untenable because inconsistent
with the facts.[2]   Similarly, Charles Bradlaugh, " from an
ingenuous and inquiring youth, was turned into a bitter
opponent of the faith because a kind of faith in Scripture was
demanded of him which he could not honestly give." Fundamentalists who make biblical inerrancy an article of the faith
would do well to ponder Dods' penetrating comment that
" those who maintain that we must accept every statement of
Scripture, or none of it, should consider that no doctrine
more surely manufactures sceptics."[3]

The Bible itself, as C. H. Dodd points out, " does not make
any claim to infallible authority for all its parts."[4]   It is no
inerrant oracle; but neither is it merely literature or merely
history.   It is the record and the vehicle of a revelation, an
unveiling, a self-disclosure of God given in an historic process
which finds its climax and its fulfilment in Jesus Christ. The
Bible has authority for us, therefore, " as the record of a divine
Purpose worked out in history."[5]   It is because the written
Word leads us, in a way that no other book can lead us, to the
living Word of God, Jesus Christ, that the Bible has a unique
place in Christian literature and is regarded as authoritative
by all sections of the Christian Church.

[1] *Gain or Loss*, p. 20.   [2] See E. Renan, *Recollections*, pp. 256–7.
[3] See Marcus Dods, *The Bible: Its Origin and Nature*, pp. 139–43.
[4] *The Authority of the Bible*, p. 15.
[5] A. G. Hebert, *The Authority of the Old Testament*, p. 52.

Scripture is not a *formal* authority which demands belief in all it contains from the outset, but it is an *instrumental* authority, in so far as it contains that element before which I must bow in the truth, which also itself awakens in me the certainty of truth. This is what Luther means by the " Word of God," which therefore is not identical with the Word of Scripture, although it is only given to me through the Scriptures, and as the Word of the Scriptures.[1]

Brunner is right, therefore, in maintaining that "the content and the real authority of Scripture is Christ."[2] Hence the Bible, as a "mode" of the Word of God, is "the genuine, supreme criterion of Church proclamation and thereby also of dogmatics."[3]

We must always remember that the Bible is a textbook not of science but of religion. As the Puritan commentator, Matthew Henry, puts it: " The Scriptures were written not to make us astronomers, but to make us saints." The authority of the Bible, therefore, lies not in the realm of biology, or of geology, or of astro-physics, but in the realm of personal relationships between man and God.

It is refreshing to find this fact acknowledged by a self-styled fundamentalist scholar, D. Broughton Knox. " We must be careful not to believe too much," he says. " The Scriptures are authoritative for the purpose for which God designed and gave them: they are not authoritative for every purpose. Thus they are an infallible guide to the Word of God in faith and morals, ' to teach, to reprove, to correct, to instruct in righteousness,' but if we use them for fortuitous guidance as some use a promise box, we must not expect to avoid grave mistakes. Nor were the Scriptures given for the purpose of teaching history, geography or science. They are not a primary or infallible source in these matters."[4]

The authority of the Bible is essentially a *religious* authority which " comes home to us primarily in inducing in us a religious attitude and outlook."[5] This does not mean, as Dodd points out, that the Bible is the " last word " on all religious questions; it is rather " the ' seminal word ' out of which fresh

[1] E. Brunner, *Dogmatics*, i, pp. 110–11.   [2] *Ibid.*, p. 110.
[3] Karl Barth, *The Doctrine of the Word of God*, p. 302.
[4] " The Authority of Scripture," in *The Reformed Theological Review*, Vol. ix, No. 2.   [5] C. H. Dodd, *The Authority of the Bible*, p. 297.

apprehension of truth springs in the mind of man."[1] Pastor
John Robinson's classic words to the Pilgrim Fathers in 1620
are still true: "The Lord hath more light and truth yet, to
break forth out of His holy word."

The Bible, however, is no mere textbook; it is, as we have
seen, the instrument of a divine-human encounter, to borrow
the title of Brunner's book. God not only speaks to us through
it; He confronts us vitally and inescapably in its pages. There
is something sacramental about it. "We may not deny nor
prevent our being led by Bible ' history ' far out beyond what is
elsewhere called history—into a new world, into the world of
God."[2] In this biblical world we become aware of the authority
of God confronting us in succour and demand. But authority,
as J. W. C. Wand points out, is a reciprocal relation: "The
authority of the Scriptures is only completely effective if it
is accepted. . . . When we are ready to listen and to respond,
the authority is overwhelming."[3] Hence the full authority of
the Bible is realizable only within a faith situation; it is
realized "existentially." As Barth puts it, the Bible "becomes"
the Word of God for us when Jesus Christ is disclosed to us
through it and we respond in faith. Faith is *Entscheidung*;
"and it is certain that the Bible, if we read it carefully, makes
straight for the point where one must decide to accept or
to reject the sovereignty of God."[4]

Authority, for the Christian, is a cord of three strands—the
Bible, the Church and the Inner Light. None of these is
inerrant and each requires the augmentation of the other two.
The Church, unless subject to continual repentance and
reformation according to the Word of God, is subject to error;[5]
the Inner Light unchecked may lead to the outer darkness;
the Bible needs to be read in the light of the living faith of the
Church and authenticated in the heart of the believer by the
inward testimony of the Holy Spirit. It is not infallible either

[1] *Ibid.*, p. 300.
[2] Karl Barth, *The Word of God and the Word of Man*, p. 37.
[3] *The Authority of the Scriptures*, p. 110.
[4] Karl Barth, *op. cit.*, p. 41.
[5] Cf. Karl Barth, *The Doctrine of the Word of God*, p. 298: "The Bible found
and the Bible finds utterance in the Church. Thereby the possibility is not
ruled out, that it may also find utterance over against the Church."

in scientific pronouncements or in historical details, since, as Forsyth observes, " the divine authority always reaches us in a human form."[1] Nevertheless, as Marcus Dods maintains, if you follow the teaching of this Book it will *infallibly* lead you to Christ. " The Bible," says James Denney, " is our textbook because it puts us in communication with Him; but He is our authority."[2]

The authority of the Bible, therefore, has to be experienced to be known; it is not finally demonstrable by the laws of logic or open to mathematical proof. But that is no reason for dismissing it as illusory because subjective. The religious experience has validity in its own right: it is akin to the aesthetic, the rational and the moral experiences which point to objective realities beyond themselves. " It is impossible," says Von Hügel, " to see why Plato, Aristotle, Leibniz and Kant, and why again Pheidias and Michael Angelo, Raphael and Rembrandt, Bach and Beethoven, Homer and Shakespeare are to be held in deepest gratitude, as revealers respectively of various kinds of reality and truth, if Amos and Isaiah, Paul, Augustine and Aquinas, Francis of Assisi and Joan of Arc are to be treated as pure illusionists in precisely what constitutes their specific greatness."[3] If this be granted, the Christian experience of divine authority mediated through the Bible may not lightly be denied.

What this experience means has been admirably stated by an outstanding scholar whom no one could accuse of undue subjectivism, W. Robertson Smith: " If I am asked why I receive Scripture as the Word of God, and as the only perfect rule of faith and life, I answer with all the fathers of the Protestant Church, *Because the Bible is the only record of the redeeming love of God, because in the Bible alone I find God drawing near to man in Jesus Christ, and declaring to us in Him His will for our salvation. And this record I know to be true by the witness of His Spirit in my heart, whereby I am assured that none other than God Himself is able to speak such words to my soul.*"[4]

---

[1] *The Principle of Authority*, p. 365.   [2] *Studies in Theology*, p. 46.
[3] " Religion and Illusion; and Religion and Reality," in *Essays and Addresses on the Philosophy of Religion*. First Series, p. 38.
[4] *Answer to the Form of Libel*, p. 21.

APPENDIX

THE DEAD SEA SCROLLS AND CHRISTIAN ORIGINS

IN the Spring of 1947 a number of ancient scrolls were discovered by Bedouin in a cave at Qumran near the north-western corner of the Dead Sea. Their discovery has been described by the Director of Antiquities for the Kingdom of Jordan as perhaps the most sensational and outstanding archaeological event of our time.[1] Subsequent exploration of the neighbourhood revealed other caves containing similar manuscripts and fragments, and the excavation of a ruined monastery nearby, known as Khirbet Qumran, produced important evidence for the dating of the finds.

Seven major manuscripts were found in the first cave:

1. The *St. Mark's manuscript of Isaiah*.[2] This, the largest of the scrolls, is one foot wide and twenty-four feet long and consists of seventeen strips of leather sewn end to end. It contains the book of Isaiah in full[3] and is, with the exception of some of the smaller fragments, the oldest of all the manuscripts. Indeed it is the oldest complete manuscript of any book of the Bible. Significantly enough it is in substantial agreement with the Masoretic text although, in addition to differences in spelling and grammatical forms, there are a number of minor variant readings thirteen of which have been adopted in the Revised Standard Version of the Old Testament.

2. The *Hebrew University manuscript of Isaiah*, which is incomplete, containing only parts of chapters x–lxvi. It is later in date and agrees much more closely with the Masoretic text than does the St. Mark's manuscript.

3. The *Commentary on Habakkuk* consists of a smaller scroll five feet long and five and a half inches wide. Its date is relatively early and one column at the beginning is missing. It contains the text of the first two chapters of Habakkuk with a running commentary which explains the prophecy in terms of the history of the sect to which the

---

[1] G. Lankester Harding in *Picture Post*, 8th August, 1953.

[2] So called because it is one of the four manuscripts bought by Archbishop Samuel and kept for some time at the Syrian Orthodox Monastery of St. Mark in Jerusalem.

[3] No other scroll contains a whole book of the Bible.

writer belongs. There are mysterious allusions to persons and
events which have given rise to much controversy in attempts to
identify the chief *dramatis personae*—the Teacher of Righteousness
and his persecutor, the Wicked Priest. This work has close affinities
with the *Damascus Document* or *Zadokite Work*[1] in which there are
similar allusions and also references to the Teacher of Righteousness.

4. The *Manual of Discipline*, the beginning of which is missing,
consists of two separate pieces which were originally joined to form
a scroll just over six feet in length. It describes the organization,
institutions, beliefs and discipline of the community to which the
manuscripts belonged, with instructions for those wishing to join it,
and concludes with a thanksgiving psalm. Fragments of eleven
manuscripts representing older recensions of the Manual have been
found in other caves. This composition also is closely related to the
Damascus Document.

5. The so-called *Lamech Scroll* is a torn and decayed Aramaic
manuscript which was at first thought to be the lost book of
Lamech. When, however, it was eventually unrolled in Israel at the
beginning of 1956, it proved to be a *midrash* of Genesis v–xv,
embellishing the biblical narrative with legendary stories of the
Patriarchs and colourful details such as a description of the beauty
of Abraham's wife.[2]

6. The *War of the Sons of Light with the Sons of Darkness*. This is a
well preserved leather scroll some nine feet long and six inches
wide giving highly formalized directions for the conduct of a war
(clearly apocalyptic) between the tribes of Levi, Judah and Benjamin
(the Sons of Light) and the Edomites, Moabites, Ammonites,
Philistines, and Greeks (the Sons of Darkness).

7. The *Thanksgiving Psalms*. Twenty of these, largely in the
phraseology of the Old Testament, are contained in four scrolls.
While they are not on the same devotional or poetic level as the
Old Testament Psalms, they shed some light on the beliefs of the
sect and contain some moving passages, e.g.:

> But when I remembered the strength of thy hand,
> together with the abundance of thy mercy,
> I rose and stood up, and my spirit became strong,

[1] This was formerly known only in two incomplete medieval manuscripts found in a genizah in Old Cairo and published by Schechter in
1910. Fragments of eighteen different manuscripts have now been discovered in the Qumran caves. See H. H. Rowley, *The Zadokite Fragments
and the Dead Sea Scrolls* (1952).

[2] See " Last of the Dead Sea Scrolls Unrolled," in *The Biblical Archaeologist*,
Vol. xix, No. 1, February 1956.

standing firm before affliction;
for I leaned on thy steadfast love
and thy abundant mercy.

The initial discovery at Qumran was quickly followed by others in the surrounding district and soon manuscript material began to pour in, the richest yield coming from " Cave Four ". These later finds consist not of long texts like the major manuscripts discovered in the first cave but of fragments—some no larger than a fingernail— which have to be pieced together like a jigsaw puzzle. The work of sorting, cleaning and reconstructing this vast mass of material is in the hands of an international team of scholars working in the " Scrollery " of the Palestine Archaeological Museum at Jerusalem. The fragments are being published in a series entitled *Discoveries in the Judaean Desert*, edited by D. Barthélemy and J. T. Milik (Clarendon Press, Oxford), the first volume of which appeared in 1955. There is enough material, it has been said, to occupy scholars for fifty years. Altogether over four hundred texts have been identified, and among these about a hundred biblical manuscripts are represented. Indeed, parts of every book of the Old Testament, with the exception of Esther, have been found.

Among the later discoveries are two copper scrolls which together total about eight feet in length. Although completely oxidized and very brittle, they were opened at the Manchester College of Technology, one in the Autumn of 1955 and the other in January 1956, by being cut into strips. They have proved to be—as K. G. Kuhn had long since guessed—an account of the sect's buried treasure. Whether this is mythical, as de Vaux thinks, or actual, as H. H. Rowley believes, may never be known, since the places indicated would be extremely difficult to identify today.

The fierce controversy on the question of the date of the scrolls has now subsided. There are still divergent views, but, as H. H. Rowley observes, " it seems very improbable that anything will overturn the view that the Qumran material comes from a pre-Christian sect and was hidden in the caves early in the Christian era, and that it offers us evidence of the first importance on the development of Jewish sects and on the background of the New Testament."[1] The St. Mark's Isaiah scroll is thought by many scholars to belong to the second half of the second century B.C.

[1] *The Dead Sea Scrolls and their Significance* (1955), p. 24. Professor G. R. Driver has recently argued for dating the Qumran documents in the period of the Jewish War on the basis of an alleged identification, *inter alia*, of the Teacher of Righteousness with Menahem and the Wicked Priest with Eleazar ben Ananias.

If this is so, we now possess a Hebrew biblical manuscript a thousand years older than any previously known. More ancient still are fragments from a scroll of I Samuel which have been dated at the end of the third century B.C. and some Leviticus fragments in the archaic Phoenician script which may be even older.

The voluminous literature which has sprung up around the scrolls is some indication of their outstanding importance.[1] It is not possible here to do more than indicate the main spheres of this. In the first place, these manuscripts have provided invaluable material for textual criticism. We now possess, for the first time, examples of Hebrew and Aramaic texts that were in use in Palestine between the second century B.C. (perhaps even earlier) and the middle of the first century of the Christian era, and the measure of substantial agreement between many of them and the Masoretic text has shown the antiquity and general trustworthiness of the latter. The new evidence also enables us to place greater confidence in the Septuagint text, particularly in the historical books. Another and more specialized field in which the scrolls and fragments have provided new and exciting material is the study of the Hebrew language. It is now possible to trace with much greater accuracy the development of its script, spelling and grammatical forms. As more and more documents have emerged, however, and the excavations at Khirbet Qumran have shed light upon the community which owned them, their importance for the understanding of the background of the New Testament has been increasingly emphasized. In 1951 W. F. Albright stated that " the new evidence with regard to the beliefs and practices of Jewish sectarians of the last two centuries B.C. bids fair to revolutionize our approach to the beginnings of Christianity."[2] Perhaps " revolutionize " is too strong a

---

[1] Millar Burrows' selective bibliography given in *The Dead Sea Scrolls* (1955) includes over 400 books and articles. A very full bibliography up to 1952 is given in H. H. Rowley's *The Zadokite Fragments and the Dead Sea Scrolls* (1952), but Professor Rowley has said that in the following two years more than 350 further books and articles reached him; see his booklet *The Dead Sea Scrolls and their Significance* (1955), p. 14. For a selection of the more recent publications, see J. M. Allegro's Pelican book, *The Dead Sea Scrolls* (1956).

While the present work has been in the press, T. H. Gaster's, *The Scriptures of the Dead Sea Sect* (1957) has appeared. This fascinating book provides a complete and reliable translation of all the Qumran texts so far published (except the Isaiah scroll and the biblical fragments). Its Introduction and Notes make a valuable contribution to the discussion of the scrolls and it has two very useful indexes—an analytical index of major themes and concepts, and an index of biblical quotations and parallels.

[2] *Bulletin of the American Schools of Oriental Research*, Supplementary Studies, No. 10–12, 1951, p. 58.

word; at least we may say that New Testament study has been greatly enriched by these texts.

It is, therefore, in their bearing upon Christian origins that the chief value of the scrolls is to be found. But here a word of caution is necessary: we must beware of reading into these documents more than their evidence warrants. The plain fact, as F. F. Bruce has recently stated, is that " among the documents published to date, no unambiguous evidence has come to light which affords a direct contact with Christian origins."[1] This must be emphasized in view of assertions that anticipations of the distinctive features of Christianity are to be found in the scrolls. There are admittedly striking similarities between the organization, rites, ideals and discipline of the Qumran community and those of the Early Church; but there are even more conspicuous differences. The communal meal of the sect, for example, calls to mind the Church's observance of the Lord's Supper; but there is nothing in the table fellowship of the community corresponding to the communion of the body and blood of Christ through the symbols of bread and wine, which is the *distinctive* element in the Christian rite.[2] Again, the Pauline doctrines of the mystery of iniquity, the opposition of flesh and spirit, righteousness belonging only to God, predestination, salvation by faith have significant echoes in the Qumran documents; but the distinctively Pauline teaching of justification by faith *alone*—faith involving personal commitment to a crucified and risen Saviour, is noticeably absent. Similarly, we find in some of the scrolls the dualism of light and darkness, truth and error, good and evil so characteristic of the Fourth Gospel and the typically Johannine themes of faith, truth, judgment and love;[3] but St. John gives new content to these

[1] F. F. Bruce, *Second Thoughts on the Dead Sea Scrolls* (1956), p. 125. This admirable book examines in some detail the evidence of the scrolls in relation to Christian origins. See also Millar Burrows, *The Dead Sea Scrolls* (1955), pp. 326–45, T. H. Gaster, *The Scriptures of the Dead Sea Sect* (1957), pp. 21–30, and H. H. Rowley, *The Dead Sea Scrolls and the New Testament* (1957).

[2] A. Powell Davies, completely begs the question by suggesting that " the further words of Jesus, identifying the bread with his body and the wine with his blood, may well be a further duplication of the Essenic liturgy of which we do not have the written version." See *The Meaning of the Dead Sea Scrolls* (Signet Key book, 1956), p. 99. Cf. T. H. Gaster, *op. cit.*, pp. 29–30.

[3] For a comparison of the distinctive vocabulary of St. John's Gospel with that of some of the scrolls see Lucetta Mowry, " The Dead Sea Scrolls and the Gospel of John," in *The Biblical Archaeologist*, 17 (1954), pp. 78 ff. See also W. F. Albright, " Recent Discoveries in Palestine and the Gospel of St. John," in *The Background of the New Testament and its Eschatology* (C. H. Dodd Festschrift), ed. W. D. Davies and D. Daube (1956).

terms. " When he speaks of the true light, he is not thinking in abstractions; he is not primarily concerned with a body of teaching or a holy community; to him the true light is identical with Jesus Christ, the Word made flesh."[1] All that may be claimed from these verbal affinities is that " the Gospel and epistles of John and the Dead Sea Scrolls reflect the same general background of sectarian Judaism."[2] The importance of such striking parallels for Johannine study, as Millar Burrows points out, lies in the fact that " the scrolls thus show—and this has not always been recognized—that we do not have to look outside of Palestinian Judaism for the soil in which the Johannine theology grew."[3] And the same could be said, *mutatis mutandis*, regarding the affinities with the vocabulary of St. Paul.[4]

It is in the realm of Christology especially that claims have been made which far outrun the documentary evidence. Dupont-Sommer has maintained that " the Galilaean Teacher, as he is presented to us in the New Testament writings, appears in many respects as an astonishing reincarnation of the Teacher of Righteousness."[5] Similarly, J. M. Allegro, who infers on quite inadequate grounds that the Teacher of Righteousness was crucified,[6] asserts that the Early Church's expectations of the Second Coming of Christ " are extraordinarily like those of the sect about their own Teacher, persecuted and crucified, and expected to rise again as priestly Messiah."[7] Since we have among the scrolls documents

---

[1] F. F. Bruce, *op. cit.*, p. 134.

[2] Millar Burrows, *The Dead Sea Scrolls* (1955), p. 339.

[3] *Ibid.*, pp. 339–40.

[4] Such a conclusion is diametrically opposed to the views of A. Powell Davies who attempts, with more ingenuity than success, to enlist the evidence of the scrolls in support of the somewhat archaic thesis that " Christianity is largely composed of elements absorbed from pagan religion in the Mediterranean area during the early centuries of its development." See *The Meaning of the Dead Sea Scrolls* (Signet Key book, 1956). His misrepresentation of recent biblical scholarship is quite astonishing.

[5] *Aperçus préliminaires sur les Manuscrits de la Mer Morte* (1950), p. 121; English translation, *The Dead Sea Scrolls* (1952), p. 99.

[6] See Pelican book, *The Dead Sea Scrolls* (1956), pp. 98 ff.

[7] *The Radio Times*, January 13, 1956, p. 9. Quoted by F. F. Bruce, *op. cit.*, p. 126. A Jewish scholar, J. L. Teicher, who believes that the Qumran convenanters were Jewish-Christian Ebionites, actually identifies the Teacher of Righteousness with Jesus. For the influence of the Qumran community on Ebionite Christianity see Oscar Cullmann, " Die neuentdeckten Qumran-Texte und das Judenchristentum der Pseudoklementinen," *Neutestamentliche Studien* (1954), pp. 35 ff. and " The Significance of the Qumran Texts for Research into the Beginnings of Christianity " in the *Journal of Biblical Literature*, 74 (1955), pp. 213 ff. Cf. H. J. Schoeps, *Urgemeinde, Judenchristentum, Gnosis* (1956), pp. 69 ff.

belonging to the early part of the Christian era, it is natural that the founder of the Qumran community should be compared with the Founder of the Christian Church, but there is nothing in any of the texts so far published which warrants the conclusion that the distinctive features in the New Testament portrait of Jesus are anticipated in the references of the scrolls to the Teacher of Righteousness. Such theories—they are no more—rest upon a strained exegesis of obscure passages in the documents. There is no indication of how the Teacher met his death; much less is there any implication that he accomplished a redemptive work in any way comparable with that which the New Testament writers ascribe to Christ. Indeed, there is no evidence that the founder of the Qumran sect ever claimed to be the Messiah or that his followers ever believed him to be such.[1]

Parallels between the sayings of Jesus and the scrolls are no more surprising than are those which are to be found in Jewish rabbinic literature. The Old Testament revelation with its high moral teaching was accepted by the Qumran community as well as by Jesus and the rabbis, and it would be strange indeed if there were no affinities in the teachings of those who shared this common ground. It is certainly noteworthy that Jesus uses a characteristic

---

[1] The Qumran sect looked for two " Messiahs," a Priestly " Messiah " of the tribe of Levi and a Davidic " Messiah " of the tribe of Judah. It is laid down in the *Manual of Discipline* that the community shall live by its original rule " until there shall come a prophet and the Messiahs of Aaron and Israel." But the Teacher of Righteousness is not identified with either. Indeed the *Damascus Document* speaks of an interval between the " gathering in " (i.e. death) of the Teacher and the rise of " a Messiah from Aaron and from Israel." The Teacher is clearly not a " Messiah " but a forerunner, and even if his followers expected him to rise from the dead on the eve of the messianic age, which is doubtful, his role is still the same.

Since the above was written, T. H. Gaster has put forward the view that " the title ' Teacher of Righteousness ' (more correctly, ' true exponent of the Law ') designates an office, not a particular person." The Qumran community, he believes, had a series of inspired leaders (probably priests) each of whom was known as " the correct expositor " or " right-teacher." Hence, the various allusions to the " Teacher of Righteousness " in the Qumran texts are not in fact to one and the same person. Gaster maintains that the reference in the *Damascus Document*, cited above, is to a *future* teacher, " one who will arise to occupy the traditional office in advance of that forty-year period of ' Messianic woes ' of which we indeed read in Talmudic and later rabbinic literature." See *The Scriptures of the Dead Sea Sect* (1957), pp. 6, 15, 35–6. The term " Messiah," Gaster argues, has here no divine eschatological significance. The references to " the Messiahs of Aaron and Israel," therefore, mean nothing more than the installing, at the beginning of the Golden Age, of a duly anointed high priest and a duly anointed king. See *ibid.*, pp. 15, 29 and 36.

Qumran phrase like " the sons of light " (Luke xvi, 8), and there is a distinct parallel between the directions for dealing with an offending brother in Matthew xviii, 15–17, and the rule in the *Manual of Discipline* that " a man shall not bring against his neighbour a word before the masters (or the ' many ') without having rebuked him before witnesses." But before hasty inferences are drawn the significant contrasts should be noted. As Millar Burrows points out, the hatred which the *Manual of Discipline* demands for the sons of darkness is far removed from the love of enemies taught in the Sermon on the Mount; and " there is nothing in the Dead Sea Scrolls approaching the radical interpretation of the law given by Jesus, who made everything hang on Deuteronomy vi, 5, and Leviticus xix, 18."[1] Burrows, in fact, maintains that " in general the sayings of Jesus are related to the apocalyptic literature of Judaism more closely than to anything in the scrolls," and he concludes that " it may fairly be questioned, indeed, whether the teaching of Jesus and the beliefs of the Qumran community have anything in common which cannot be found in other Jewish sources also."[2]

To sum up: further study of the scrolls by some of the most distinguished scholars has made it increasingly clear that Dupont-Sommer spoke too strongly when he said in 1950 that " all the problems relative to primitive Christianity henceforth find themselves placed in a new light, which forces us to reconsider them completely."[3] The published documentary evidence to date does not warrant J. M. Allegro's recent categorical statement that " it now seems probable that the Church took over the sect's way of life, their discipline, much of their doctrine, and certainly a good deal of their phraseology, in which it is now seen that the New Testament abounds."[4] Unfortunately such generalizations, which are no more than theories, have been stated in unqualified terms and popularized as assured facts.[5] Allegro is on much firmer ground when he observes that the correspondences between the Qumran sect

---

[1] See *op. cit.*, p. 331. A startling contrast with not only the teaching of Jesus but also the teaching of the rabbis is found in the Sabbath regulations of the *Damascus Document*: " Let not a man help an animal to give birth on the Sabbath day; and if she lets her young fall into a cistern or a ditch, let him not raise it on the Sabbath." Cf. Luke xiv, 5.

[2] *Op. cit.*, p. 331.   [3] *Op. cit.*, Eng. trans., p. 100.

[4] *The Radio Times*, January 13, 1956, p. 9. Quoted by F. F. Bruce, *op. cit.*, p. 126.

[5] Cf. Edmund Wilson's statement that Khirbet Qumran " is perhaps, more than Bethlehem or Nazareth, the cradle of Christianity." *The Scrolls from the Dead Sea* (1955), p. 129.

sect and the Christian Church " must, at least, point to a common religious background."[1]

The Qumran community was one of many similar Jewish groups which flourished at the beginning of the Christian era. These, along with official Judaism, were the soil in which Christianity took root and grew. As H. H. Rowley observes, there are " innumerable links of idea and practice between the sect of the Scrolls and the early Church, and it is becoming clear that Christianity took up ideas and practices already current."[2] There is no reason why the Church may not have adopted some of the current phraseology and practices of the Qumran sect, just as it took over much of the worship and organization of the synagogue and later even appropriated certain elements from the pagan world. But whatever the Church took over, whether Jewish or pagan, was given a new content and invested with a new meaning in the fuller light of Christ. To recognize, however, the possible influence of the Qumran community, along with other aspects of contemporary Judaism, upon the Early Church is not the same thing as making Khirbet Qumran the cradle of Christianity. Millar Burrows, without in any way minimizing the importance of the Qumran parallels for New Testament studies, believes that " it is not necessary to suppose that any of the writers of the New Testament had ever heard of the particular sect that produced the Dead Sea Scrolls " and sees no definite evidence that they had. " For myself," he says, " I must go farther and confess that, after studying the Dead Sea Scrolls for seven years, I do not find my understanding of the New Testament substantially affected."[3] His carefully worded summary would seem to set the scrolls in their right perspective in relation to Christian origins:

Everything that is important for Judaism in the last two or three centuries before Christ and in the first century A.D. is important also for Christianity. By enriching our understanding of Judaism in the period in which Christianity arose, the Dead Sea Scrolls have given us material for a better understanding of the New Testament and early Christianity. . . . There is no danger, however, that our understanding of the New Testament will be so revolutionized by the Dead Sea Scrolls as to require a revision of any basic article of Christian faith. All scholars who have worked on the texts will agree that this has not happened and will not happen.[4]

[1] *The Dead Sea Scrolls*, Pelican book (1956), p. 148.
[2] *The Dead Sea Scrolls and their Significance* (1955), p. 22.
[3] *The Dead Sea Scrolls* (1955), pp. 342-3.
[4] *Ibid.*, p. 327. Cf. T. H. Gaster, *The Scriptures of the Dead Sea Sect* (1957), Introduction, VI-VIII, pp. 21-30.

SUBJECT INDEX

Abraham, call of, 4, 7, 9, 13, 79, 89, 140, 294; Church and, 208–9; covenant with, 199–200, 203; date of, 7–9; flood tradition and, 132; historicity of, 9–12; home of, 12–13, 130; no miracles ascribed to, 163–4; obedience of, 197–8; significance of, 9, 14; *zikkurat* of Ur and, 136.

Adultery, 268 ff., 279–82.

Aeschylus, 78 n.

Alexander the Great, 33, 137, 225.

Allegorism, 52–3, 54–6, 64 n., 251.

Amraphel, 7–8.

Antiochus Epiphanes, 34–5, 38.

Antitype, 55.

Apathetic fallacy, 112.

Apocalyptic, characteristics of, 2, 35–9; Jesus and, 221, 227; kingdom of God and, 217–18; symbolism of in New Testament, 146.

Apocrypha, 33, 261.

Apollinarianism, 191.

Aruru, Hymn to, 117.

Assyria, 29, 81, 134, 210.

Atonement, 196, 233–4, 250.

Atonement, Day of, 206.

Avaris, 15, 17.

Babel, Tower of, 127, 136–40, 197.

Babylon, 29, 30, 136–7, 210.

Bach, J. S., 308.

Barnardo, Dr., 297–8.

Basilides, 44 n.

Beethoven, L. van, 308.

Belshazzar, 38.

Borsippa, 136–7.

Bradlaugh, C., 305.

Brahmanism, 5.

Buddha, 261.

Buddhism, 5.

Cambridge Ancient History, 8 n.

Canon, 32, 33, 43, 44, 49, 57 n., 298–9.

Casuistry, 258–9, 276, 278.

Chalcedon, Council of, 191.

Christ, baptism of, 181, 212–13; cross of, 22, 139, 205, 214–15, 230, 256; miracles of, 167–71, 183–8, 191; Person of, 181–3; transfiguration of, 154, 159, 181, 213; significance of, 188–90. *See also* Death of Christ *and* Resurrection of Christ.

Church, Apostolic, 41, 49–51, 220, 249, 277; Bible and, 70, 89, 100, 107, 298–304, 307 and n.; Christ and, 5, 196, 199, 213 n.; continuity and uniqueness of, 40; Covenant and, 206–7, 298–9; faith of, 93, 298–301; Hebrew, 21; Jesus and, 288; medieval, 60, 126; miracle and, 171; as New Israel, 5, 14, 69–70, 154, 207–9, 215; New Testament and, 1, 39–44, 51–2, 194; Old Testament and, 5, 40, 49, 52; Resurrection and, 189; Suffering Servant and, 215; teaching of, 55; teaching of Jesus and, 255, 257–8.

Circumcision, 206.

Clement, Epistle of, 43.

Confucianism, 5.

Copernicus, 60.

Covenant, Abrahamic, 140, 200, 203; Bible and, 69, 199–200, 298–9; Book of, 31, 203; blood and, 199, 203, 205, 236–7; cultus

319

AUTHORS' INDEX

SCRIPTURE REFERENCES INDEX